Anthology of Contemporary Readings

SECOND EDITION

AN INTRODUCTION TO PHYSICAL EDUCATION

HOWARD S. SLUSHER
AILEENE S. LOCKHART

University of Southern California

WM. C. BROWN COMPANY PUBLISHERS
Dubuque, Iowa

Physical Education Series

Consulting Editor
Aileene Lockhart
University of Southern California
Los Angeles, California

Copyright © 1966, 1970 by
Wm. C. Brown Company Publishers

Library of Congress Catalog Card Number: 66-14912

ISBN 0–697–07150–2

Printed in the United States of America

John Flan and Ruth B. Glassow

Contents

Introduction

The task of merging the various forces and directions in physical education, through selected readings, presents both an intellectual and practical challenge. The intellectual challenge develops from the necessity of deciding upon an adequate conception of physical education and concomitantly allowing for the effective development of student insight. The practical challenge necessitates our questioning the outcome. We must ask what we want our students to be like? What do we believe they should know? And in what directions should they think and feel? In this volume, we have attempted to bring to the reader a collection of articles which we believe will conceptualize our theoretical and applicable concerns. The approach might be termed functional, that is to say, the articles are interpretive and often include applications to specific situations. The study of such material not only brings the profession into the "awareness" of the student, but should also assist the student in learning the specific subject matter of his profession.

The primary purpose of this work is to provide a stimulating and useful collection of articles which will afford the student of physical education the opportunity to explore various dimensions of the chosen profession. Originally conceived as a supplementary source for an "introductory course" in physical education, some instructors may wish to utilize this book as a basic source, in lieu of a traditional text book. Since the selected materials represent the thoughts of many leading contemporary physical educators and other educators who have been closely associated with physical education in recent years this publication might well also be a beneficial supplement in a more advanced course.

In selecting the contents for this book several important factors guided the editors. Among the primary concerns were: (1) usefulness in introducing the reader to the multi-dimensional aspects of physical education; (2) authoritative contributions written in language suitable for comprehension by the undergraduate student; (3) competent treatment of the subject matter; (4) significance; (5) style, form, and content thought appealing to the audience; and (6) representative authorship.

The organization and treatment of the book is such that any chapter, or specific article, might be utilized in any order desired by the instructor. The articles are grouped into areas. In this regard it should be realized that many sources might fit equally well in a different section of the work.

It is hard to know where to begin and at what point to end in acknowledging the contributions of those individuals who have made this book possible. Our most direct debt, of course, is to those colleagues whose work we have reprinted. Deep gratitude also is extended to the publishers of the copyrighted materials that appear in this book. Proper documentation as recommended by each publisher has been made in the text of this publication. We are also appreciative of the secretarial assistance given by Helen Harris, Suzan Hines, Dixie Shedwill and Dorothy Sparks.

Los Angeles, California   H.S.S.
January, 1966   A.L.

Introduction to the Second Edition

This work deals with "contemporary" physical education. It is our feeling that the thoughts and issues considered by selected authors, and not the dates of publication, are the determinants of what might or might not be judged as contemporary. Consistent with this thinking, included within this second edition are pieces published as many as forty years ago while other works were published as recently as 1969. Two other selections appear in print for the first time as part of this anthology.

Some of the included contributions have stood the test of time, and are recognized as classical contributions to our field, while others are too recent to warrant such claims. The second edition includes eleven articles not found in the first edition. It is not surprising that many of the "new" articles are written by individuals established as professional leaders; however, other selections presenting equally cogent insights are authored by persons whose ideas have not been as widely read. In all cases, the criteria of inclusion were focused on excellence of ideas as considered relevant to modern physical education.

We were struck by how much our literature has dramatically changed in the last five years; certainly a major focus of recent writings has been related to problems germane to the development of a discipline of physical education. In this context, the editors have felt it necessary to develop a chapter on the discipline of physical education—one which did not appear in the prior edition. It is hoped our choice of specific materials for this chapter, as well as throughout the book, will present challenging reading and will provide a foundation for enlightened class discussion.

At first glance one might think the materials included in this edition are too advanced for beginning students of physical education; however, it is our feeling that the freshman and sophomore years is not too early for one to begin a systematic orientation toward major concepts and issues in our field. It is hoped this work will facilitate such an attempt.

Obviously, this book is not limited to beginning students. We are pleased to note that the first edition was used widely on many levels—both horizontal and vertical. That is, it was employed in professional and non-professional classes and permeated both graduate and undergraduate courses. The materials for this edition were selected with the hope that they would provide levels of meaning applicable to students of varied interest and development.

The editors wish to thank the contributing authors and those holding copyrights to materials appearing in this edition for their cooperation in this venture. We are also indebted to all those individuals who were kind enough to make suggestions which were beneficial to this volume. Their comments and assistance were most valuable and greatly appreciated. Any errors, however, are our responsibility alone.

Los Angeles, California   H.S.S.
                                                                             A.L.

Chapter

Tradition of
American Physical Education

Education Through the Physical
JESSE FEIRING WILLIAMS*

No one can examine earnestly the implications of physical education without facing two questions. These are: Is physical education an education *of* the physical? Is physical education an education *through* the physical? It is clear that an education of the physical would have some concomitant learnings in addition and also that an education through the physical would produce some distinct physical gains. Nevertheless, there are in these two questions two points of view, two emphases, two ways of looking at physical education.

Education of the physical is a familiar view. Its supporters are those who regard strong muscles and firm ligaments as the main outcomes. Curiously enough this restricted view is not heeded alone by physical educators but also by those who talk about educational values, objectives, and procedures. In effect, such view is a physical culture and has the same validity that all narrow disciplines have had in the world. The cult of muscle is merely another view of the narrowness that fostered the cult of mind or the cult of spirit.

Modern physical education with its emphasis upon education through the physical is based upon the biologic unity of mind and body. This view sees life as a totality. Correct in their appraisement that the cult of muscle is ludicrous, those who worship at the altar of mental development too

---

*Jesse Feiring Williams, "Education Through The Physical," *The Journal of Higher Education.* Vol. 1, May, 1930.

frequently neglect the implications of unity. "Socrates with a headache" is always preferable to a brainless Hercules, but the modern spirit in physical education seeks the education of man through physical activities as one aspect of the social effort for human enlightenment. It is the plain truth of the matter that no individual, no community, no nation can depend upon one aspect of life for the whole of living. Deification of only the physical, or the mental, or the spiritual leads to disaster.

This recasting of the scene for physical education is no superficial move but a tendency toward deeper growth. It holds that we need to aim higher than health, than victorious teams, than strong muscles, than profuse perspiration. It sees physical education primarily as a way of living, and seeks to conduct its activities so as to set a standard that will surpass the average and the commonplace. There is in such a view something of the loftier virtues of courage, endurance, and strength, the natural attributes of play, imagination, joyousness, and pride, and through it all, the spirit of splendid living — honest, worthy, and competent — so much desired by each individual.

Physical education, however, stands not alone in the dilemma of special disciplines. Education has been, and still is, confronted with the problem. The old scholastic doctrine that separated mind from body, that held the body as essentially evil has emphasized the contrast today between an education for life and an education for death. A child born in sin, destined to do evil unless transformed by grace, made the chief business of education a salvation of man from the destiny of his own nature. In this view education is a reclamation project, a corrective endeavor. There are few today to espouse such a view openly, but it underlies the practice of many. On the contrary, educational theory today is dedicated to the proposal of education for life here and now. The child is viewed as a being of varying possibilities. The psychology of behaviorism has more forcibly established the fact of plasticity and unformed qualities of the young; the function of education as developed stands approved by science and common sense.

Education for life, or modern education, and education through the physical, or modern physical education, have mutual supports and confidences. On the one hand, education for life can hardly be conceived without generous allowance for this kind of physical education, and physical education pointed to its own culture, its own minor objectives, becomes not an education for life at all. The identity, then, of education for life (modern education) and education through the physical (modern physical education) requires understanding by educators of the aim, scope, and objectives of modern physical education and by physical educators of the objects and concerns of modern education.

From the view of living as it goes on among people, and not as the view of a specialist or expert in physical education, it would appear that education for life requires the development of those skills, attitudes, knowledges, and habits that make for fine living. The part to be played by physical education in the lives of boys and girls, men and women, in this enterprise of fine living must be studied increasingly. Perhaps its greatest value will be in the interests it arouses, in the values it emphasizes, in the attitudes it forms. Whereas at one time, its chief values were supposed to be posture, health, and strength, these may become obscure in the prominence given to motives, purposes, and incentives for life.

There is a drama of civilization enacted in every community. The play is still to be written and yet its *dramatis personae* are all trained for their parts. The drama, if written, would show the lives of people who lack the ability to use leisure wholesomely, either because of a great ignorance of serviceable skills or because of intense occupation with the industrial or business world — losing the ability to live wholesomely, and neglecting the very objects for which it is worth while to acquire riches in a feverish pre-occupation with the means by which riches are acquired.

We are unable to use for human happiness the magical liberation from the bond of labor undreamed of by our ancestors and striven for since the first log was used as material for a wheel and beasts domesticated for man's work.

We fail again and again to use this glorious thing, leisure, because of habits, preoccupation with small things, lack of education for leisure, and the mood of strenuosity that sits so heavily upon us.

Doubtless we will make little gain in the use of leisure until we overcome the notion that play must be profitable. In physical education we have been ready to recommend golf or tennis for their health values when they were of value in themselves — precisely as sitting in the sun, or fishing, or walking along the river bank. All of us have been indoctrinated by the school teacher not to let the golden hours slip by when it would have been the part of wisdom to understand that they are only golden when we let them slip.

Education through the physical will be judged, therefore, even as education for life will be judged — by the contribution it makes to fine living. The ability to punt 60 yards is on a par with some of the esoteric emphases in general education. It should therefore be declared that physical education seeks to further the purposes of modern education when it stands for the finest kind of living.

This declaration of allegiance of physical education to the legitimate purposes of general education demands rather than forbids a statement that

will need amplification or modification from time to time as new relationships appear.

Physical education in the university, first, is responsible for the organized physical activities of students. This responsibility is primarily an educational one in which the plans and purposes of physical education are to
be reviewed in the light of legitimate instructional purpose. It is obvious,
therefore, that varsity sports must come under the complete direction of
the university.

The university is, also, responsible for the interests, activities, and development of its students. No university today can cut itself off from the
large, vital, social aspects of the life of the students by insisting that the
purpose of the college is to train the mind. It is obvious, therefore, that a
rational program of physical education is required in every university to
the end that men and women may acquire not only mental, but also physical
skills with which to live an abundant life.

Physical education is responsible for the teaching of skill and the development of interests in types of activity that will serve the students in
the college and the graduates after collegiate days are over. Thus a physical
education characterized by neglect of minor sports through undue attention
to major ones, or with a chief reliance upon gymnastic drills should be
recognized for its limitations. It is precisely this principle of thorough going
function in young people's lives that tests the quality of physical education.

The university is responsible for providing adequate space, equipment,
time and facilities so that the capacities of young people for leisure-time
skills may be developed. A state university making plans for a stadium has
at present only four tennis courts for all the students. In the past, in many
universities, play facilities for all the students have been provided largely
out of surpluses of varsity athletics. The partnership of modern education
and education through the physical requires recognition of the need for
space, equipment, and facilities. Education for life means vigorous life.

Physical education is responsible as well for leadership in combating
all purely professional and educationally poor activities in the field. Therefore athletics, games, sports, dancing, gymnastics, et cetera, must be viewed
and organized with reference to significant functions in life. The whole
program must be examined to determine major emphases and to eliminate
undesirable practices.

Again, the university is responsible for the establishment of standards
of fine living. Those engaged in teaching sports and games especially should
be selected with reference to their ability to influence the daily preferences
of young men and young women. A university conscious of the need to
promote the physical education of all its students in types of activity that

may serve in living more completely will not appoint as director one who is interested only in the teams or gymnastic uniformity.

Jointly with the university, physical education is responsible for leadership in setting up among boys and girls those standards of behavior that represent the best social tradition of the day. The responsibility rests heavily on this special department because its activities present so many situations where the individual is impelled to act selfishly or anti-socially. The leadership is vital to favorable growth in desirable social and moral values, in wholesome attitudes toward play and generous reactions to opponents. While the reciprocal relationships have been indicated in the above items, the joint responsibility of the university and physical education is clear at this point.

How About Some Muscle?
CHARLES H. McCLOY*

For a profession that has glorified the physical side of man from before 500 B.C. until, shall we say, A.D. 1915, the physical education literature of today is strangely silent about the more purely body-building type of objectives. From the time of Homer to shortly after the time of Thorndike, the emphasis will be found to have been on the physical — education *through* the physical surely, but also education and pure training *of* the physical, for its own sake as well as in Education's sacred name. Then came the leavening influence of Thorndike's psychology and of Dewey's philosophy, enlarging our concepts of how to educate, and as a profession we made real progress. But this progress was made at the expense of the old model. We did not overhaul it, but, following the leadership of Mr. Henry Ford, we traded in all of the old equipment on the new. Twenty-five centuries of good experience — as all who read history discerningly must agree — abandoned over-night in favor of a new equipage whose worth to the ultimate consumer, the child, was yet to be appraised!

And why? Your guess is as good as mine. I think it was possibly a combination of three things. First, many physical educators had an inferiority complex. A few sensitive souls still have. We didn't quite belong to the educational fraternity; we were just "physical directors." The new educational emphasis gave us "face," and, exulting in our new importance, we forgot most of the fundamentals; we didn't want to be "strong."

*Charles H. McCloy, "How About Some Muscle?," *Journal of Health and Physical Education*. Vol. 3, No. 4, May, 1936.

Second, it was so easy to "educate" with a game book and a whistle. It saved time, preparation, and the mastering of a lot of difficult skills and the techniques of progression.

The third possibility is that the leaders of the new educational movement, carried away by enthusiasm for this valuable addition to our armamentarium, overstressed the new — as Luther Gulick was wont to do in pioneering a movement — and gave the impression to their pupils and to the readers of their papers and books that the educational aspect of physical education was *all* that really mattered. Whatever the reason, the result has been that when physical education went to college and added psychology, character education, mental hygiene, tests and measurements, and the new organization of principles to the curriculum, it quietly dumped most of its body-building emphasis into the educational garbage can and set it out on the curb.

Has this been justified? Let us examine the evidence. Ignoring the varsity teams who, we shall grant, get enough muscle building, let us consider the average pupil. I doubt if more than one-fifth of our physical education classes in the schools of today get enough exercise to contribute materially to any significant organic stimulation. Widespread strength testing has shown that in whole cities there are scarcely 20 per cent of the pupils who have a normal amount of strength, measuring strength by Roger's Physical Fitness Index; and Roger's norms for strength are quite moderate in their demands.

But is more muscle desirable? Let us marshal a few of the arguments.

1. In 1907 J. M. Tyler published *Growth and Education,* a book which was and is a milestone in physical education. In the first few chapters were assembled a galaxy of biological facts which have never been seriously disputed. Tyler showed that vigorous exercise of the great fundamental trunk and limb muscles is utterly essential during youth and young adulthood for the purpose of stimulating the normal growth and development, not only of the fundamental organ systems of the body, but of the brain and mind as well. And this exercise need — an inheritance from the remote past — is a need for more than pretty movements. What is needed is a great deal of oxidation within the body tissues. Tyler made clear the fact that an organism whose evolutionary development was dependent upon vast amounts of exercise could not function adequately on a semi-sedentary ration of activities.

2. The psychological literature of late years has spoken much of the fact of body-mind unity, but this same literature has usually gone on thinking and writing as though the school child was all mind. We in physical education, with our growing over-emphasis upon the educational aspect of physical education, are apt to fall into the same error. *Our organism is more body*

than mind, and it is only through the adequate functioning of all of it that the most desirable functioning of even the brain occurs.

3. From the standpoint of mental hygiene, a number of studies in our own field, some of them unpublished, have shown that the physically un-developed child and adult tend to develop inferiority feelings which grossly affect their social responses and their character and personality develop-ment. We need adequate bodies as well as play and recreation. While this is only a part of our mental hygiene problem, the physical educator should not forget that it is an important part and one which can be corrected funda-mentally only by developing an adequate body. It cannot be eradicated simply by *understanding* the problem. "Facing reality" in this case means development of the muscles, attaining a better carriage, and in general de-veloping and educating the physical self.

4. In considering the significance of physical strength, let us develop an imaginary situation. Let us suppose that someone were to request you to wear, day and night, a well-fitting canvas jacket lined with lead shot which increased your weight 25 per cent. Your response would undoubtedly be something like the following: "Don't be absurd! Why, to burden my-self with a load like that would result in my being utterly fatigued by early afternoon. I should have no energy for constructive work, and at night I should be too tired even for recreation. The added strain upon my heart would be harmful, and I would be so constantly fatigued, particularly during the latter part of the day, as to render myself more susceptible to minor infections, such as colds." And you would be right. However, the man who is 25 per cent overweight is constantly subject to just this strain. The same difficulty is encountered by an individual of a given normal weight who has only four-fifths of the normal amount of muscle. From the standpoint of fatigue, of inefficiency of movement, of susceptibility to minor infections, he finds himself in the same situation as the individual who is 25 per cent overweight; and this individual, be he school child or adult, does suffer some of the following handicaps:

(a) *Fatigue, both acute and chronic.* The under-muscled person tires easily. (Rogers has well shown that a certain type of endurance is almost perfectly correlated with strength relative to weight.) But this person is not only susceptible to occasional acute fatigue; this fatigue piles up in a normal life of activity. At the end of each week he finds himself almost sick — intoxicated with the accumulated poisons of a fatigued organism.

(b) *Muscular inefficiency.* Studies in the physiology of muscular work demonstrate that the efficiency of muscular contraction depends upon there being an optimum load on the muscle. Thus a muscle that is over-loaded has a smaller work efficiency than one which is not loaded too heavily.

The person of less than normal strength, in addition to his constant fatigue, is working always at a relatively lower level of efficiency than would have been the case had his strength been up to normal for his weight.

(c) *Susceptibility to infections.* It is the common experience of many people that their susceptibility to cold and like minor infections is greatest when they are most fatigued. This, for some reason, seems to be more true of continuous chronic fatigue than of moderate acute fatigue. Possibly it is because in almost all acute fatigue the person has recovered before the process of infection has proceeded far enough to be dangerous. It is a common observation that more colds result from mingling in crowds at the end of a week than under similar circumstances at the beginning of the week, when an individual is more rested. The under-muscled person is much more constantly in a condition in which he is susceptible to such infections than is the stronger person. This, of course, has nothing to do with specific immunities which seem to be dependent upon a chemical condition within the body.

(d) *Functioning of organic systems.* Tyler also established the fact that an abundance of muscular exercise strengthens the day-by-day functioning of *all* of the organic systems. This is perhaps most easily understood in the relationships to the functioning of the heart. This organ, which is itself a muscle, is exercised and developed by being forced to exercise more strenuously in response to the vigorous exercise of the voluntary musculature. The individual whose muscular experience is constantly at a subnormal level has a heart that is as flabby as his arms and legs. In times of emergency, not so much the running for a street car as the fighting of pneumonia, the weaker heart is more apt to be unequal to the task than is the well developed heart. Adequate strength is good life insurance.

All of these facts seem to me to afford convincing evidence that we need better-developed muscular systems than the current literature in our profession is demanding. The argument frequently proposed by non-physical-education educators that since we are not all going to be truck drivers we do not need to be well developed is not, it seems to me, even intelligent. A young adult having to toss his body, weighing from 100 to 200 pounds, around an office, up and down stairs, or around a golf course, needs a normal musculature. Therefore, I should like to propose that as a profession we re-think the whole problem of our more purely *physical* objectives, and that we emphasize them more. I yield to no one in our profession in my belief in the educational importance of physical education when adequately organized and taught; the health education procedures are also of great importance. But the basis of all physical education — developmental, educational, corrective, or any other aspect of our field — *is the adequate train-*

ing and development of the body itself — that should be thought of as a fundamental prerequisite.

In recent years there has been a swing towards an emphasis upon adult education. The physical educator, on the whole, has not kept up with this movement. Anyone who takes the trouble to visit city *turnveriens,* or some of the businessmen's classes of Y.M.C.A.'s, and sees young sixty-year-old men playing fast volleyball or doing stunts on the apparatus with the ease and grace and enjoyment — stunts that the majority of physical education teachers of today cannot do — or who sees fifty and sixty-year-old Englishmen playing soccer or cricket or rowing, almost with the vigor and finish of youth, must realize that most middle and old age deterioration is a function of inactivity. Adults who forget to maintain that muscular development which is the prerequisite to a youthful old age pay the penalty by losing that youth; it is hard to lose one's youth and gain it back again, but it is relatively easy to keep it.

It seems to me that the time has come when we may be expected to retain more than one major objective at a time in our intellects — to keep hold on the good of the past while we add from the worthwhile contributions of today. May we suggest that the best defense is a strong offense; and for the physical educator who feels inferior to someone who scorns the physical as he glorifies the Great American Intellect, it is suggested that he espouse the cause of body-mind integrated unity, fortify himself with the facts, and merrily conduct a major offensive that will place the feeling of inferiority back where it belongs, upon the physically feeble mental advocate who is simply compensating with much talk for his own feeling of physical inadequacy.

How about some muscle?

Moto Ergo Sum
PETER V. KARPOVICH, M.D.*

An ancient philosopher who strongly believed that motion is the most essential characteristic of life coined a phrase: "Moto ergo sum" or "I move, therefore I exist." He must have been a somewhat odd if dedicated man. When he became hoarse and could not talk, he would raise his hand and move his index finger as a symbol of his existence.

---

*Peter Karpovich, "Moto Ergo Sum," *Journal of Sports Medicine and Physical Fitness.* Vol. 1, No. 2, September, 1961.

I heard this story from my high school teacher of history, and I have forgotten the name of the philosopher, but I think he was a Greek. My library searchings for his identity invariably have lead me to a French philosopher, Descartes, who paraphrased this motto as "Cogito ergo sum" or "I think, therefore I exist."

I have no quarrel with Descartes' motto. As a matter of fact, these two mottos should be combined into "Cogito et moto, ergo sum" meaning "I think and I act, therefore I live." Today I will limit my remarks only to movements and actions.

You all have read about the poor Gulliver made motionless by the tiny Liliputians; and you probably have sympathized with him. Some of you probably also have read books by Lagrange, a French father of the physiology of exercise. Lagrange mentioned a prisoner who, upon being captured, was hogtied so that he could not move any limb. This, according to the prisoner, was the worst torture he had ever had.

However, besides Liliputians, illness and accidents, there is another and even more powerful factor which enforces muscular inactivity. It is our progressing civilization with its concomitant substitution of machines for muscles.

Since the progress of mechanization is inevitable and we can neither run away nor stop the clock, the outcome should be considered inevitable. Thus it follows that, in the near future, it will be normal for man to have flabby weak muscles since he will not need strong muscles anymore. If now-a-days automobiles are blamed for weak legs, what will happen when we have moving sidewalks in business centers?

There is, however, a certain fallacy in accepting weak muscles as normal. Braus, in his *Anatomy*, gives a very interesting illustration showing certain changes of the human foot. He compared the relative position of the heel bone in a chimpanzee, Neanderthal man and in our normal contemporary man. The human foot shows the unmistakable evidence of evolution. The vertex of the angle formed by the tibia and calcaneus in man points inward instead of outward. On this basis, then, we should accept the flat feet of a floor walker or of a policeman as normal feet, since eventually all men will have seemingly flat feet.

We would hardly agree with this. Firstly, because there is no reason to believe that the foot of the future will be flat; secondly, because if it becomes flat, it will take many thousands of years, and during that period some additional anatomical adjustment may develop which will strengthen the foot. Jumping, as it were overnight, into the future constitutes a pathological phenomenon, and therefore such an untimely "foot of the future" should be treated and its further appearance should be prevented.

The same attitude should be maintained toward muscles. There is one point which frequently is forgotten. We may deplore the ever progressing muscular weakness, and we may look back to the cave man as a symbol of superman; but what about the muscles of men who live now outside of civilization? One may find enough of them even now. Some of them still live at the Stone Age level. Are they supermen? A series of illustrations carried recently in Life magazine showed that Australian aborigines do not have excessively developed musculature. Most of them would not be a match for civilization tainted American varsity wrestlers. The life of these aborigines does not depend so much on excessive strength as on good muscular endurance which makes them fit for their environment. A student of Anthropology cannot find any evidence that the salvation of our weakening generation lies in hefting heavy bar bells and developing huge muscles. Common sense also would indicate that salvation will not be found in endless running, or swimming or in eating miracle foods. Then what should be done? Where should salvation be looked for?

This brings us to the responsibility of the American College of Sports Medicine and other similar organizations. Our primary task is the pursuit of physical fitness. This is such an important function that it should have been included in the Constitution of the United States, although it probably is implied in the "pursuit of happiness."

The pursuit of physical fitness means achieving and maintaining a desired level of fitness. We know how to develop and how to maintain physical fitness, but we do not know how much of fitness we need.

Our duty is to find the answer. The search will not be limited to just testing the muscles. It will involve a diversified research in physiology and medicine. One should only read the titles of contemporary studies pertaining to physical fitness to see that an investigator of physical fitness has to delve into both physiology and medicine. The laboratories carrying research in physical fitness look more and more like "physiology" laboratories, and there is no clear cut borderline indicating where physiological research ends and medical research begins.

We should develop tables showing relationship between the functions of various organs at various levels of muscular exertion.

We should establish how these relationships are affected by ambient temperature, atmospheric pressure, humidity and diet.

We should find the optimum and the limits of a desirable fitness in relation to sex, age, body size and type.

We should campaign for less lip service and more actual help in research in physical fitness. Funds should be provided for research, and a

National Institute for Research in Physical Fitness should be established. This Institute should have all the modern facilities and a well trained staff.

All this will take some time. What should we do in the meantime? Meantime and afterwards we should work. Work more and harder. The fellows of the American College of Sports Medicine should be more active in research pertaining to physical fitness.

Now what else can we do? We should co-operate and assist in the promotion of physical fitness by either governmental or private organizations. We may prevent an overemphasis of just one activity for growing boys and girls. It is true that playing basketball, riding a bicycle or even playing baseball does contribute to fitness and sometimes one of these activities is all that an individual needs; but it cannot be considered as the only activity needed by all. Especially by growing children.

However, no matter in what physical activity an adult participates, we should encourage this, instead of forcing him into an activity which he dislikes and in which he would not participate whole heartedly. Something is better than nothing, especially when we are not sure how much a man needs. Many people seem to derive all their needed exercise just from walking.

We may deplore an overemphasis on interscholastic varsity teams because they benefit a few at the expense of many. If we want to remedy this situation, we have to deal not so much with the school administration as with the alumni, and this often means with ourselves. And when it comes to the defense of athletics in the alma mater, we, the alumni, become dragons with many heads. And where is that modern St. George who can slay the dragon? Probably it is not slaying that is needed, because the alumnus mysteriously can turn into a goose who lays golden eggs, and who wants to destroy this biological mint?

I don't want to complete my notes in the spirit of Jeremiah. I want to assure you that I am very optimistic. When I think about physical education forty-five years ago and make a comparison with present conditions, I feel elated. Men and women engaged in physical education now are often considered to be educators. We are doing research, and we have strong organizations backing us. And what is forty-five years in the life of a nation or race? We should pave the way for the succeeding generation. Remember, physical education is a profession for tomorrow; and tomorrow is just one day ahead.

REFERENCES

1. Lagrange, Fernand. *L'hygiene de l'exercise chez les enfants et les jeunes gens.* 9me Ed., p. 1, Felix Alcan, Paris, 1910.

2. Braus H. *Anatomie des Menschen.* Vol. 1, p. 604, Julius Springer, Berlin, 1921.
3. Anonymous. Man at His Most Primitive. *Life Magazine,* p. 52, May 19, 1958.

The Greek Tradition and Today's Physical Education
ROBERT H. BECK*

The recent upsurge of national interest in physical fitness, in maintenance of good health, and in the recreation of men whose leisure will steadily be increased by automation, prompts a historian of education to remember that education for good health, for physical and mental well-being, and for the worthy use of leisure have been important educational objectives in the West since Homeric times some thirty-two or three-hundred years ago.

The history of education in the West runs back beyond the Hellenic Bronze Age of 1400 to 1200 B.C. But the older tradition, that of ancient Egypt and of the Mesopotamian civilizations of Sumer, Babylon, and Assyria, had no place for education and training leading to sound health, physical fitness, and prowess, or for recreation. The older civilizations were preoccupied either with training scribes who could write and keep accounts, or preparing priests and rulers. There appeared to be no call in Egypt or Mesopotamia, in those centuries, for such warriors as Homer's Achilles, "fleet of foot," Achilles of "giant might." Whereas the Greeks, *our* intellectual ancestors, memorized the tales of strength and courage that made up Homer's *Iliad,* the ancient Egyptians turned their back on life and showed their preoccupation with life after death by taking as their text the *Book of the Dead.* As for Mesopotamia, its great epic told of the wanderings of Gilgamesh and his friend, Enkindu. Whereas Achilles sought *arete* — that is, the honor that comes to a brave, powerful soldier — Gilgamesh wandered in search of the secret of immortal life.

To understand the Homeric view of education, in contrast to the Egyptian and Mesopotamian desire to learn to write, compute, and divine, one needs only read of the contests and games underwritten by Achilles in honor of the memory of his dear friend and comrade in arms, Petroculos, slain by Hector. The whole twenty-third chapter of the *Iliad* is a recital of recreation based on physical fitness. In that chapter we read of the "fleet chariot-racers," of the boxers, wrestlers, runners, archers, and others. I think no contest ever has been described that out paces in excitement the account of the chariot race between the competing Achaean tribes.

*Robert H. Beck, "The Greek Tradition and Today's Physical Education," *Journal of Health, Physical Education and Recreation.* Vol. 34, No. 6, June, 1963.

Homer wrote in the ninth century B.C. The times described in the *Iliad* had passed half a millenium earlier. But for five hundred years after Homer every Greek schoolboy recited the *Iliad*. In the *Iliad* were the examples of manhood Greek youth was to adopt.

By the seventh century B.C., the physical training that Homer describes as given noble, aristocratic youth was available to all free men. The vitality that we find missing in Egypt and in ancient Mesopotamia filled the life of Hellas. Every Greek city of the seventh, sixth, and fifth centuries — and for centuries later — had its gymnasium or palaestra, as well as its teachers of dance for boys and for girls. Many of the odes of Pindar were written for those who triumphed at the games at Olympus. Unhappily the time came when city-states so coveted the honor that came with Olympic prizes that professional athletes were hired. All historians of ancient Greece record that sports, games, and physical education all were corrupted by the zeal for prizes and the professionalization of the Olympic and other competition. We would have done well to have remembered the fate that overtook physical education and recreation in Greek times.

We only dimly remember how seriously the ancient Greeks took physical education. Plato has been incorrectly thought more or less contemptuous of anything but rigorous intellectual discipline. Granted that dialectic — what we would term logic and the analysis of philosophic issues — was the study Plato esteemed for the very few who continued their education until suited to be philosopher-kings. Plato was equally concerned that the education of the ordinary citizen, especially those who would guard the state, be sound. To glimpse Plato's views on the education of the guardians of the state, it is only necessary to read the short Platonic dialogue named *Laches*. In that dialogue, Lysimachus and Melasias discussed with two renowned generals, Nicias and Laches, the education of their sons. The subject of the dialogue reduces to opinion of the value of gymnastics practiced in the palaestra. Nicias was very much in favor of gymnastics; Laches opposed it.

The dialogue, *Laches*, becomes an arena in which Socrates, or Plato, lay out alternative views of the meaning of courage. Plato was anxious to convince his audience that courage is a matter of intelligence and moral strength as much as it is of endurance. Nevertheless, it is clear that Socrates and Plato sided with Nicias, who recommended gymnastic training not only for its advantages as preparation for war. "There is an advantage," said Nicias, "in their (the young men) being employed during their leisure hours in a way that tends to improve their bodily constitution, and not in the way in which young men are too apt to be employed." Moreover, Nicias went on to explain, training in gymnastics "inclines a man to other noble lessons."

It is said that Rome went to school in Greece. Surely a portion of what Rome took from the Hellenic philosophy of education was a belief in the importance of physical education, whether for sports and games to be played in one's leisure time, or for the cultivation of a handsome and healthy physique, or for the development of strength and courage needed in battle.

And when Europe emerged from the Medieval world into the Renaissance of the fourteenth, fifteenth, and sixteenth centuries, Greek and Roman confidence in the importance of physical education in the education of the young also was reborn. True, for centuries, really until the late eighteenth century, physical education, as secular education generally, was thought primarily for those who either would constitute the aristocracy or would serve the aristocracy as scribes and accountants. That was so simply because the scholars of the Renaissance knew Homer but did not know that physical training, sports, and games had become popular, and for all freemen, not only for the aristocracy.

Although nothing new was added by the Renaissance to Greek thought on physical education, the Renaissance did not downgrade the role of physical education. The famed intellectual humanists, notably John Milton, found a place in general education for physical education, and in typically Hellenic terms.

Moving to early modern times, to the eve of the French revolution, physical education received a tremendous boost in the educational writings of Rousseau. Looking into Rousseau's treatise on the education of boys, the *Emile,* the reader is left in no doubt that Rousseau believed in physical fitness for youth. The development of the body, after all, fitted Rousseau's conviction that education could not be reduced simply to the three R's. Development of all the physical potentialities of men, including their abilities to invent and use tools, commanded Rousseau's philosophy of education and became his principal dowry for succeeding generations of educational thinkers.

Educators in the area of health, physical education, and recreation should reserve a place of honor for the German educator, Basedow, much influenced by Rousseau. Basedow, who founded a boarding school in Dessau in 1774, included any number of sports and physical activities beyond gymnastics. His reputation was such that other schoolmen accepted Basedow's philosophy of education. Among these was Guts Muths, who wrote *Gymnastik fur die Jugend,* the first educational treatise on gymnastics.

It was just at this point in time that European monarchs awakened to the national importance of physical fitness programs. As in our own day, that Greek-like thought that a nation's sinews are in part those of its men and women boosted the reputation of physical education for physical fitness. The preparation of special teachers of physical education dates from 1799 when Franz Nachtegall of Denmark, opened an institute for training teachers of physical education.

The first attempts at scientific research in physical education appeared at about the same time. In no other field of education was the special preparation of teachers of a subject so rapidly associated with research. It was one of Nachtegall's own students, a Swedish student by the name of Pehr Henrik Ling who disciplined himself to make an extensive study of the anatomical and physiological bases of gymnastics. Ling's Royal Central Institute of Gymnastics, located in Stockholm, developed a most enviable reputation.

By the middle of the nineteenth century it seemed as though the future of physical education, and its twin collaborators, health education and education for recreation was fully accepted and on the way to becoming one of the most thoroughly studied, carefully developed studies in the schools.

Research by staff in physical education, in school health programs, and in the field of recreation could be remarked at formidable length. The fact is that despite the thoughtful manner in which the curriculum in health, physical education, and recreation has been built, schooling on this continent, in Latin America, and in most of Europe has permitted the appearance of a gulf between academic studies and those in physical education, in recreation, and in health.

Inquiry into the origin of the barrier between academic studies and all that is lumped into the non-academic — be it vocational training, driver training, extracurricular activities of all types, or physical education, recreation, and health programs — points to the mischief that was done in ancient Greece when the city-states exaggerated the importance of winning in the Olympic games and invested in professional athletes. The poor repute in which they have been held might have been distinguished from the excellent results being achieved by men and women teaching and coaching in physical education, in programs preparing leaders and participants in recreation and health programs.

The effect of the cold war plus the accelerating transformation of knowledge produced by modern science and technology has unbalanced American education. Our nation's leaders grant the importance of physical fitness but there is danger that all of health, physical education, and recreation will be reduced to attain strength needed in the days of cold war. Surely physical fitness is not to be undersold. Grant that and a very great deal remains to be admitted about the potentiality of health programs, as well as those in physical education and recreation.

Think first of recreation. Everyone knows that the work-week will be reduced, that automation will cause a good deal of physical work to disappear, and there will be more leisure. One hopes that this leisure will permit many more to read, to become caught up in the arts, in learning of all forms. But there will be time to learn to enjoy the out-of-doors. Is there a more effective alternative to complete urbanization and life lived in the rhythm of the machine than outdoor recreation in our parks far and near, in camping, in boating, fishing, and all that recreational programs touch upon?

And what of education for healthful living? There is no need to spell out the portions of a full-blown curriculum in health education. The very most tentative contact with the field quickens us to its values. But I think that those professionally concerned with health programs in our schools should help their colleagues in biology and in chemistry understand that the topic of physical, and indeed, mental health, affords excellent opportunities for units of study in the biological sciences and in chemistry.

In physical education of men and women there are just as many bridges that can be built with academic departments. Think only of the history of physical education. Any student of that history becomes a student of general history. One could not adequately study the social and cultural history of the West without becoming acquainted with the history of physical education.

Physical education instruction that looks forward to enhanced health and recreation can win recognition today equal to that accorded by the Hellenes. But the laurel will not be awarded without ambition and effort. If leaders in these fields accept the status of second-class educators, we will have turned our back on our Greek progenitors. There is no necessity of unseemly modesty. The better stance is one that shows leaders in physical education, in health education and in programs of recreation reflecting on their fields and clearly intending that these contribute to education of undeniable worth.

Chapter

Function of
Physical Education

Physical Education and the Tasks of the Body
ROBERT J. HAVIGHURST

Even before the human embryo is as large as a finger-nail, a tube has formed within it, enlarged at a certain point, and begun to pulsate. Thus the human heart has its beginning. It develops into a four-chambered organ which circulates the life blood for 80 years, without a stop in the pulsations which commenced in that tiny tube.

This is one of the tasks of the body — to develop and maintain an organ which is necessary to life. The body does this all unconsciously, and in the right timing and placing with respect to the other body organs.

In addition to the internal and unconscious tasks, the body also accomplishes a series of visible tasks of which a person is more conscious and which affect his feelings about himself as well as the attitudes of others toward him. These visible tasks of the body constitute the process, in part, of growing up and growing through the life cycle.

Consider, for example, the task of learning to walk. Sometime between the ages of nine and fifteen months the bones, muscles and nerves of the legs and trunk have developed to the point where they are equal to the task of walking. Then the infant learns to walk with varying amounts of help and stimulation from other people. This task is followed by those of running, jumping and skipping.

Presented as the R. Tait McKenzie *Memorial* Lecture. Reprinted from *American Academy of Physical Education, Professional Contributions*, No. 5, November, 1956.

The child learns to walk almost unconsciously. But even at this early level he gives evidence of being pleased with himself at this accomplishment, and he certainly experiences the approval of others as he masters this task. From this time on, the tasks of the body are accomplished with a growing awareness and interest in them by the individual. Although the body continues in its silent and organic way to accomplish the tasks of growth, such as readying the eyes for the task of reading, and preparing the gonads for the task of reproduction, the result is visible to the individual and to the people around him and they pay a great deal of attention to it.

The child soon learns that he will be judged by what his body accomplishes, and so he tries to make it do well, and he makes the best of whatever it does. This is one of the lessons of life — that we are judged by our bodies and can improve them.

This is true all through life. It is true of the events which constitute puberty, and of the events which take place in men and women around the age of fifty. It is true of the bodily reading apparatus at the age of 6, as well as at the age of 45. It is true of sweet sixteen and of bitter sixty-six.

The human body is never left alone to achieve its visible tasks uncriticized, as presumably is the case among oysters, ants, and butterflies. Among these organisms it seems unlikely that there is any social expectation about how one's body should develop, and therefore the individual oyster, ant, or butterfly is not likely to feel either social stigma or social approval for the way he looks. But with humans there is always a social judgment. A person is always judged by the way he looks, and he knows and feels this judgment. The extent to which a society judges people by their appearance varies from one society to another. The ancient Greeks were more conscious of their bodies perhaps than many others; but probably no society exceeds the present-day American in the emphasis it places on looks.

Therefore there are two aspects of physical development, both of which are important for the happiness of people. One, which we have been considering, is the development of the body as it is perceived and valued by other people. Society judges people, and gives them approval or disapproval, partly by the way they look.

The other aspect is that of health and performance. For obvious reasons it is desirable to have good health and for the body to perform acceptably the physical tasks expected of it.

One might easily say that good physical health and bodily performance are more important than having a physical appearance which pleases people, and in a sense this is true; but a person who is out of fashion because he has a big nose, or a receding chin, or is very tall or very short or very fat may feel this as keenly as someone else who has chronic ill health. Both aspects are important to the happiness of people, and physical education may well be concerned with both aspects.

Education can do three things for a person in relation to the tasks of the body:

1. Help a person to achieve these tasks through physical training, proper diet, cosmetics, and grooming.
2. Help a person to understand and accept inevitable bodily disadvantages, and to correct them as far as possible through instruments to aid the body, such as braces for teeth, and glasses for eyes.
3. Help a person to prepare for bodily changes in the course of physical growth.

We shall illustrate these three functions of education in relation to the physical changes of adolescence, which is the period when the body is of greatest concern to people.

Body Tasks of Adolescence

The human body grows from childhood to adulthood with such dramatic changes that everyone is aware of them, both the adolescents experiencing the changes and the remainder of the society witnessing them. Those who observe the changes expect adolescents to behave in accordance with their physical appearance, even though this may belie their chronological age. An early maturing 14-year-old girl will be treated by older girls and boys as their equal, and they will often say and do things to her which are beyond her understanding and experience. A 15-year-old, slow-maturing boy will be treated as a child by his own age-mates and those slightly older.

Most people remember their own adolescence with pleasure or discomfort depending on how well their own bodies met the expectations of the social group. Counsellors and medical practitioners report the concerns of boys and girls with their physical maturation and their physical appearance.

Some years ago C. Ward Crampton maintained a column of advice for adolescent boys in a boys' magazine, and he also offered to answer personal letters written to him. He has reported on the problems of these boys.[1] A few examples from their letters follow:

> A. "Here is my story. I want to be a *he-man* and to work hard. I want to broaden my shoulders, to increase my chest, to gain weight, to be a real husky, and put weight on my bones. Above all I want to be proud of myself and not ashamed as I am now. I have seen how much you have done for other boys, *please* do this for me."

---

[1]C. Ward Crampton and E. Dealton Partridge, "Social Adjustments Association with Individual Differences among Adolescent Boys," *Journal of Educational Sociology.* 12: 67ff., 1938.

B. "I am fourteen years old and weigh ninety-five pounds and measure five feet four inches. A few years ago my pals were the same weight and height as I was but now they are much taller and heavier than I. I eat lots of good food but I don't seem to gain weight or grow much. It would be swell if you could tell me how to catch up with my friends."

C. "I am fifteen and a half years old, weigh ninety-six pounds, and am only five feet in height. I still talk in a high pitched, girlish voice. I am several inches shorter than any one in my class, third-year high school. I have been told that it is just a case of delayed development, but just the same, I am beginning to worry as I show no signs of 'sprouting.'"

D. "I have what is termed a 'pigeon breast.' I am very sensitive about it, and it has spoiled many good times I might have had. I always have feared to bare my chest when I am with others, and the present popularity of swimming trunks makes me fear the time when I shall have to wear them. I have determined that I will get rid of it before long, and am seeking your advice on how to do this."

E. "I wish you would answer these questions with full frankness. I wish that you would recommend some good frank book on sex which I could ask my folks to get for me. There are many questions regarding sex which I would like to ask them, but they just emphasize the dark side of such matters as if it were a thing to be feared."

The fear that boys have of physical inadequacy is attested by many studies of adolescent personality difficulties. For instance, Schonfeld reported on the developmental and psychiatric evaluation of 256 boys aged 9 to 16 who presented personality difficulties and emotional conflicts associated with fears of physical inadequacy.[2] He says that during the early part of the second decade of life personality conflicts and psychosomatic complaints may result from an apparent or actual delay in the age of onset of sexual maturation, or inadequacy of masculine development.

In general it appears that adolescent boys get along best in American life if they are early-maturing or average-maturing. This is concluded from the University of California Adolescent Growth Study in which comparison was made of two groups of boys in the same school grade who fell at opposite ends of the scale in skeletal age or bone development. The two groups showed the greatest contrast in physical characteristics between the ages of 13 and 15. During this period the early maturing boys were tall, strong, well-muscled and "masculine" in build, while the late maturing ones were small, slender, poorly-muscled and "childish" in build. Physically accelerated

---

[2]William A. Schonfeld, "Inadequate Masculine Physique as a Factor in Personality Development of Adolescent Boys," *Psychosomatic Medicine,* 12: 49-54, 1950.

boys were considered by adults and classmates to be more mature and attractive in appearance. They were accorded more prestige without particularly striving for it. From their ranks came the outstanding student leaders.
The physically retarded boys exhibited relatively immature behavior, and re-
acted to their temporary physical disadvantage either by greater activity and
striving for attention, or by withdrawing from social activity.

A recent questionnaire study of high school students in Phoenix, Arizona,
confirms the prevalence of adolescent concerns with physique,[3] both with
the timing of maturation and with specific physical blemishes. Boys were
concerned over being short, girls over being tall. Girls were concerned over
having to wear glasses, with freckles and size of their noses, while both sexes
were concerned over acne.

Girls have somewhat different problems of physical development than
boys. Some of these problems are illustrated in the following excerpts from
anonymous essays written by women in one of the writer's graduate classes.
The class members were asked to recall their feelings about their physical
development during adolescence. While many of them had felt pride or at
least no discomfort at these changes, others had definite feelings of discomfort. In contrast with boys, girls appear to suffer from early physical maturation as well as from late. One person writes:

> I was unusually concerned about my physical development mainly be-
> cause I began to develop so early. At eleven, I was the tallest girl in all
> my classes and at twelve I began to menstruate. This all disillusioned me
> as I was under the impression that one usually began at sixteen. Being sub-
> jected to all this I reclined to the sidelines and was quite unhappy about
> the whole situation. It wasn't till I was a junior in high school that I came
> "out of my shell" and had a renewed interest in life.

On the other hand, a late-maturing girl had this experience.

> During grade school I was considered somewhat above the average
> scholastically, and graduated when twelve years old and was small for my
> age. When I graduated from high school I was probably in the tallest tenth
> of the class, but had not yet begun to menstruate — and did not until I was
> almost eighteen. That meant most of my classmates were a year or two
> older than I, and when over a period of some six years I was the only
> member of the group not physically mature and that alone might have had
> a psychological effect. However, something was probably really wrong
> physically, for beginning with about my sophomore year in high school I
> found I was not able to cope with the strenuous sports my friends and I
> loved. That meant I had to transfer to classes we all recognized as inferior;

---

[3]Alexander Frazier and Lorenzo K. Lisonbee, "Adolescent Concerns with Physique,"
School Review, 58: 397-405, 1950.

and my friends went forward while I went backward in achievement. Finally, my mother, instead of taking me to a doctor for reassurance that the condition would right itself naturally, ridiculed me in front of others for even speaking of it to her. Her idea was to make my worry seem as absurd as possible; but all she accomplished was to set up a barrier between herself and me that I don't believe was ever fully broken down.

Another girl who was just slightly advanced in physical maturation found it an advantage.

I was one of these 'young lady at fifteen' persons, having fully developed physically at a time when my female counterparts were awkward, unproportioned, childish, and my male peers were small, pimply-faced and gawkish."

This complete maturity (subsequent growth in height and width has been inconsequential) was a source of much comment among adults, who forever exclaimed, "Only fifteen, why, she looks much older!"

The consequences of looking older than one's years, provided one is young enough — as I was — to regard this as a blessing instead of a scourge, are many. I found myself quite popular with older boys and this esteem, in turn, enabled me to acquire wiles and little tricks that proved very intriguing to the younger ones. I was left a clear field for operations until the girls of my age also bridged the gap between childhood and adulthood. I also 'chummed' with other girls and had an opportunity to share their confidences and experiences. I always patterned my actions after those older by two or three years. This sophistication was not solely confined to the social realm. I early found a taste for 'heavy' literature, and read many of the classics as well as best sellers, so that I could compete with my friends. These interests caused my parents to extend to me liberties and concessions that I would otherwise not have obtained and in all, I feel unreservedly that this early growth was a source of pride.

Physical appearance was a source of embarrassment to two girls, for different reasons.

During my junior high and high school days I was extremely sensitive about my physical appearance. I was short and stocky and awkward. I wore glasses, had acne, and wore braces on my teeth. I was particularly self-conscious about my rather prominent nose. Two of the boys in junior high school indulged in teasing me about my nose and as a result I was very miserable during that period. I withdrew from my companions and had only a few friends. I spent a great deal of time in the library reading books which were usually of an adult level. I compensated, also, by studying hard and standing at the top of my class scholastically. My feelings of inferiority in so far as my physical appearance was concerned never quite left me, although I developed into a person who was average physically, and I realize that I no longer stand out as different from most people.

The physical changes accompanying adolescence were a source of constantly painful embarrassment to me. I was much fatter than anyone else in my group. I was mortified by the development of my breasts, which were very large. Menarche, while accompanied by no physical discomfort, seemed so disgusting to me that I tried desperately to conceal the fact of menstruation from everyone, even my mother. I was as ashamed of it as if it had been syphilis. My coming of age was a period of intense unhappiness.

A person whose attitude changed when she studied ballet dancing describes her experiences as follows:

> When I first noticed that I was acquiring pubic hair I was dramatically sorry for myself. I felt that it was a symbol of the complications of growing up, and I remember weeping because I did not want to cope with adult life. I was self-conscious about developing breasts and wanted to wear a tight brassiere so that they would be as inconspicuous as possible. While I was still growing I began to study dancing in a school that was training some of its pupils to be professionals. The attitude there was, of course, that it was a fine thing to have a good, mature figure. I soon felt the way they did about it and craved to be more advanced and developed than I was. The displeasure I had seemed to disappear and leave no scars.

As one becomes aware of the difficulties that some boys and girls have in adolescence of accepting their bodies and making the most of them, one sees how physical education might help them, through preparing them for the bodily changes of puberty, through helping them to understand and accept certain inevitable disadvantages, and through helping them to achieve the physical skills that are valued in adolescence and to make the most of their physical appearance through grooming and cosmetics. Specifically, there are three things which every high school department of physical education might do.

Use criteria of skill and physical development in grouping students for physical education. This is being done increasingly. The less skillful ones, and those whose growth is slow, are given a chance to compete among themselves in games, without suffering the recurrent disgrace of being chosen last and scoffed at for ineptness whenever a game is played.

In biology or hygiene, teach about the physical changes of adolescence, stressing the normality of variability. This has not yet been done to any appreciable extent. Yet this kind of knowledge would set at rest the worries about their normality of all boys and girls except the few who have serious emotional disturbances.

Make it easy for a student to ask for information and assurance with respect to his own physical development. Every school and college should have someone who is easily approached and who is prepared by personality and by training to discuss with students their concerns about their physical development. This person will usually be a doctor, a nurse, a teacher of biology or physical education.

The State of the Body is Only One of the Important Factors

The foregoing discussion might be interpreted by the unwary reader to support the proposition that the body takes priority; that the way it accomplishes its growth tasks determines the social and emotional functioning of the adolescent. There is no question that a tendency in this direction does exist — a tendency expressed by a correlation coefficient that is reliably positive, but not very high. But there are many individual exceptions to such a general proposition, as was pointed out by More in his study of the relations of the physical to other aspects of development in adolescence.[4] He found a number of early-maturing boys and girls who were not particularly early in their social development, even though the general rule was for early maturity to be associated with early social and emotional maturity. This tendency he found more pronounced in girls than in boys. The reason for the low order of relationship between physical, social and emotional aspects of maturity in adolescence is probably partly that the social and emotional qualities of a person are established by middle childhood and tend to carry over through adolescence, so that a child with an easy social personality and a stable emotionality moves through adolescence with these qualities regardless of how his body matures unless it is drastically deviant. Partly, also, the reason for the relatively low relationship of the physical to the social and emotional aspects of living in adolescence is that teachers and counsellors and parents have been relatively successful in helping boys and girls to accept their bodies and thus to adjust to physical deviations within the fairly wide range that can be called normal.

This discussion raises the question of maturation versus learning, or heredity versus environment. Physical education theory must be continually responding to our knowledge and our biases on the topic of the relative significance of heredity or environment in shaping a person's life. Heredity held sway until the early years of the 20th century, and then gave way to environmentalism which must have required a major reorientation of physical education theory. Now there appears to be something of a swing of the pendulum away from environmentalism though it does not approach the hereditarianism of 50 years ago. Physical educators are in a good situation to draw usefully and impartially from the growing knowledge and genetic and constitutional factors in human development as well as from the growing

---

[4]D. M. More, *Developmental Concordance and Discordance During Puberty and Early Adolescence.* Monographs of the Society for Research in Child Development. 18: No. 56, 1953.

knowledge of the effects of the family and the peer group and the educational environment on the person.

Body Tasks at Other Age Levels

The tasks of the body have their special forms at the several age periods, and consequently the functions of health and physical education should be carried out differently in the different age periods. There is something important to be done through education, however, in relation to the body tasks at all ages from 6 to the last years of life.

MIDDLE CHILDHOOD, 6-12

During middle childhood our society sets two major tasks for children which involve their bodies.

One is the task of learning the physical skills that are necessary for the games and physical activities of childhood — such skills as throwing and catching, kicking, tumbling, swimming and handling simple tools. The body prepares to accomplish these tasks through growth of bone and muscle, but they have to be learned, and they are learned partly from the peer group and partly through school. Boys are expected to do a better job of learning these skills than girls.

The other task is to learn wholesome attitudes and habits concerning the care of the body, which give a sense of physical normality and adequacy, the ability to enjoy using the body, and a wholesome attitude toward sex.

EARLY ADULTHOOD, 20-40

In early adulthood the sexes differ most widely in their bodily tasks, because at this time the female task of child-bearing takes priority over the other feminine tasks for most women. To perform this task well, both mentally and physically, a woman needs a variety of kinds of preparation, some of which can only come through health and physical education. It is not claimed here that preparation for the physical act of motherhood should be a part of high school or college education, though some interesting educational experiments have been made in this direction. Rather, this preparation is most likely to come in early adulthood through the informal means of coaching by one's mother and doctor and by reading, or through the more formal means of classes for expectant mothers maintained by adult education agencies. The preparation takes the form of exercises before and after childbirth, of diet, and of learning the pros and cons of nursing a child.

For both sexes there is the everyday but all-important task of learning to use the body wisely and effectively — to conserve one's energy and maintain one's health during the physical prime of life. This is the time when women and men can look their best, and when their success and satisfaction in life is dependent in a major way on their making the best of their bodies.

MIDDLE AGE, 40-60

In middle age there is a fundamental task of accepting and adjusting to the physiological changes that characterize this period. Aging of the body tissues has been going on, mostly unnoticed, since early adulthood. Muscular strength has been diminishing, neuromuscular skills have been fading, and the body has been slowing down. Some of the physical symptoms of aging are:

> Growth of stiff hair in the nose, ears, and eyelashes of men.
> Growth of hair on the upper lip of women.
> Drying and wrinkling of the skin.
> Deposition of fat around the middle.

Presbyopia — loss of accommodative power of the lens of the eye. The elasticity of the lens decreases steadily from childhood to old age, and by the age of seventy-five the lens is ordinarily completely inelastic, making it impossible for the eye to adjust itself unaided to the task of focusing on objects at varying distances.

The menopause, or climacterium, occurs in women over a period of several years, usually between forty-five and fifty-five. Menstruation gradually ceases and the ovaries become mere masses of connective tissue. With the cessation of ovarian activity, the delicate balance of the endocrine sytem is disturbed. Physical symptoms may take the form of hot and cold flashes, dizziness, sweating, insomnia, and excitability.

Thus the body accomplishes its natural task of growing older, but this tends to create real problems of adjustment as great or greater than those of adolescence. The exercise habits of men sometimes have to be changed. There are profound effects on the sexual activities and interests of men and women. A minority of people suffer from more or less severe psychological depression associated with physiological changes.

Women and men can make this period of life much more comfortable for themselves by understanding what is taking place in their bodies, by using various devices to keep their physical abilities up to earlier levels and to defend themselves against the attacks of physical middle-aging. For instance, it is a definite fact that a great many people at about age 50 cease to read more than a few minutes a day because "their eyes hurt," when a suitable adjustment of reading glasses or bifocals would clear up the trouble.

A most valuable kind of adult education is given through books, lectures, and classes on the conservation of personal physical resources in middle age.

LATER MATURITY, 60+

The slow downward trend of physical vigor and physical beauty which starts in middle age continues in the years of later maturity, sometimes just as slowly, and sometimes more swiftly. Most people maintain very good health and vigor well past the age of 70. Still, the body is aging, but the rate of aging varies enormously among individuals, and it seems likely that medical science will soon find ways to control and decrease the rate of aging in those people who now age most rapidly. The characteristic illnesses of later maturity — cancer, heart disease, and arthritis — are coming gradually under some degree of medical control.

No doubt people can aid their bodies to perform more effectively in later maturity by paying attention to their diet, to exercise, to grooming, and to the doctor's advice. An important part of any program of counselling or group study in preparation for retirement should be some lessons on the maintenance of health.

Conclusion

Thus we see that throughout the life cycle the body has its tasks to perform, appropriate tasks to each stage of life. The body has its own wisdom, but it can be aided by the kind of wisdom which we get from medical science.

The person has a great stake in how well his body performs its tasks, and he can help his body do better, given the kind of information and training which modern health and physical education provide. However, all people will have to accept the fact that their bodies are not performing as well as they would like, or that their physical appearance is not as good as they would like it to be. To some this comes early in life — to all it comes eventually. They can be helped by physical education to accept these unfavorable facts, and to do their best in the face of these facts.

The tasks of the body are especially important to personal well-being in the present-day American society, because our society sets such great store on the physical appearance of people. Possibly there will be less emphasis on sheer looks as time goes on, and as the proportion of older people in the society increases. But there is not likely to be any decrease in the social emphasis on health, and people will be expected more and more to make the most of their bodies. Perhaps there will develop a public opinion which blames people for their own ill health, as Samuel Butler suggested in *Erewhon*. In his Utopia Butler said that people might be severely censured if they became ill, because they were expected to know how to keep healthy, and illness could only come through gross negligence.

In any case it appears that the tasks of the body will be better performed at all ages if people accept the help of health and physical education, and if this profession does what appears to be its manifest duty.

Contributions and Relationships of Health, Physical Education and Recreation to Fitness

JAY B. NASH*

The name, American Association for Health, Physical Education and Recreation, involves a number of varied, intricate and sometimes vague relationships. To the title physical education in our association's name, the word health was added, but no one stopped to ask what it included. An individual possesses health; associations are concerned with health education. More recently, the word recreation was added; and here again definitions became varied, ranging from concepts of sports and games to a wide gamut of creative activities, or to some it means recreation education.

We are involved in the meaning of terms and confusion reigns. A word means one thing to one and another to his neighbor, another to his professional associate, and still another to an administrator or to the public. This paper is an attempt to clarify this situation. As we move through the discussion, words and phrases will be defined and relationships established, from the viewpoint of the speaker.

Phases of Development

Man may be thought of in terms of four phases of development: *organic; neuromuscular; interpretive;* and *emotional.* It is evident that all developments are bound into an integrated whole but the word fitness should be reserved for a quality of organic power. Yet, when fitness is discussed someone inevitably raises the question, "What about mental fitness?" Does it involve native intelligence, the I.Q., educational advancement, emotional balance, or just what is it? Then someone raises the question of moral and spiritual fitness. Unfortunately, I have no clear cut meaning for these words, though apparently many people have. Is there a standard definition for these terms which has eluded me or are they qualities differing for each man?

The word fitness should be reserved for organic development-optimum health. "Fit as a fiddle" is understood. When an athlete is "in the pink," we know what this means.

Total fitness is too vague a term. Such broad terms as "total" or "well-rounded" can be applied to all education, to life itself; but as the whole is the sum of its parts, can we not discuss the relationship of parts? If so, we must isolate physical fitness as the primary objective of physical education.

---

*A talk given at the Governor's Pennsylvania Conference on Fitness, 1960.

The physical education, health and recreation aspects of our education have been criticized for attempting to be all things to all men. Physical education and its associated areas cannot be all things to all men, but there are some things which they must be to all men.

Total fitness is the responsibility of all society — home, church, school and community. It seems to me that physical education should concern itself largely with the physical organism — optimum health. I know voices will be raised to defend fringe contributions of physical education and I shall agree, but in the breakdown of responsibilities, our major task is the development of an organism capable of performing sustained effort.

Various phases of education are assigned specific points of emphasis. One stresses history and literature; another, the sciences; another languages; another citizenship and still another the arts of vocational training. All are, or should be, interested in the health and physical fitness of an individual and, likewise, physical education should be interested in and contribute to all educational objectives. The physical educator's primary responsibility, however, should remain focused. One group of educators can select only a small portion of the total problem. Our attempt to do everything reminds me of the young suitor who sought the hand of a young lady in a large family. The father said to him, "Young man, do you think you can support a family?" The young man answered, "I'll do my best, sir, but I only want Sarah."

It would be better to talk about a man skilled in a specific activity rather than skill-fitness; the thinking, problem solving man rather than mental-fitness; the man who lives on an emotionally high level rather than moral-fitness. Health is only one phase of total man, and our responsibilities must be confined to this one phase though we, like every other discipline, contribute to the whole.

Men, throughout the ages, have been high on one or two of the four phases of development but seldom high on all four. Let us consider some examples. Ghandi was low on the organic level to the point of frailty. He wanted to weave but said, "My fingers are all thumbs." Intellectually, he was fairly high though he failed as a lawyer. Emotionally, however, he was a mountain peak. He helped to free 150 million untouchables in India; he preached tolerance for which his enemies took his life. Although Lincoln was not frail, his life fairly well paralleled Ghandi's.

Leopold and Loeb were high organically. They were skillful, they were intellectual but they were very low on the emotional level. Edgar Allen Poe was skillful only as a writer; though intellectually he was fairly high, he was emotionally unstable. Goebbels was insignificant in physique but he was a skillful maneuverer with a fantastic intellect. Emotionally, however, he was extremely low. Van Gogh, Milton and Toulouse Lautrec were not

physically fit. Each had his tremendous skill and doubtless would rank high intellectually; each though emotionally unstable was nevertheless courageous.

In a like manner, mountain climbers and athletes while high on the organic and neuromuscular levels may be at the same time either very low or very high on the intellectual and emotional levels. Examples of uneven development multiply with the names of Robert Louis Stevenson, Theodore Roosevelt and Elizabeth Barrett Browning all of whom were frail but maintained peaks of achievement on other levels. There are, on the other hand, classic examples of people high on all levels, such as Robert Frost, Carl Sandburg, Winston Churchill, Jean Sibelius and Justice William O. Douglas. One could also cite many who are low on all the four levels of development. It is obvious that one can be skillful and intellectual yet not be high in other phases of development. It is obvious too that one can be high or low in all. The point is that superiority in one phase of development does not guarantee the same pre-eminence in another.

Let us look more carefully at these four levels.

ORGANIC DEVELOPMENT

This is the ability of the human organism to resist fatigue and to sustain effort. We need people, for war and peace, high on this level. With the high standard set by the armed forces, rejections will never be much lower than in World War II because of hereditary backgrounds, accidents, or specific handicaps such as in eyes and ears and nerves.

We might think of health or physical fitness on a thermometer with the mercury moving up and down. Health is a condition of the organism. May I hasten to say that health is not the primary objective of life. What you do *with* health must always take precedence. There are numerous factors which help to raise the mercury in this thermometer. Some are: protection from infections; good medical and dental advice and care; high hereditary background; good habits of nutrition, rest and sleep; adapted exercise; etc.

When the individual functions in an atmosphere of joy, happiness and challenge, he is training for fitness or optimum health — the mercury reading is high—, but when he operates without these requisites, he causes the mercury on his health scale to lower. A high reading on this thermometer is to be desired.

Health or fitness, then, should be considered as a condition of the organism and not in terms of total life outcomes or objectives.

In a similar manner we might think of skills, the ability to think, and emotional status as thermometers with many elements tending to raise the mercury while others lower it. Illness and handicaps, hereditary or acquired, may readily lower or raise the skill-level or the thinking-level and may produce either bitterness or great faith. Elizabeth Barrett Browning, when urged by her friends to stop working because of her ill health said, "If work means headaches, perforce I prefer headaches."

NEUROMUSCULAR DEVELOPMENT

One may be highly or poorly skilled in any one of many areas — athletics, crafts, mechanics, science, painting, sculptoring, written or spoken language, picking pockets, or dozens more. The doers may be skillful and may be healthy but may not necessarily be ideal citizens. Skill ranges all the way from the beginning of gross movement to the performance of the artist. Skillful performance in strenuous activities helps the body to conserve energy and, hence, is closely related to organic development.

INTERPRETIVE DEVELOPMENT

This is the ability to think in one or more areas, to see relationships, to solve problems, to associate and remember, and to make sound judgements. A high rating on an intelligence test is not the sole criterion for this development. There are many kinds of intelligences, not just one. We think in terms of past experiences so we are largely a product of where we have been and what we have done. Skills give meaning to words and relationships. The hands are the "eyes of the brain." Thinking in one area, however, seldom assures competency in another.

EMOTIONAL DEVELOPMENT

This involves the problem of attitudes and feelings. On the highest level, it may assume a religious concept involving the mountain peaks of brotherhood and respect for all men. On the lower level it may be expressed in prejudice, hatred and intolerance.

These four developments are all related and the ideal is to be high on each of them but this attainment for all would be a utopia beyond the dream of the science fictionist.

Definitions

The next step is to discuss the meaning of several words which too often are taken for granted.

PHYSICAL EDUCATION must be defined in terms of certain objectives. It can be illustrated, and desirable outcomes may be cited. It involves the total body: nerves, organs, muscles, the master brain and the emotions. Activities, other than physical education, are also dependent on these same physical sources. The farmer, the dock worker, and the bank president utilize similar body-brain-nerve and emotional connections, but

> *Physical education involves activities whose primary outcome is in terms of organic and skill development. It is the training a man undergoes for the purpose of developing his body, with all its related processes to function so that he may live to his fullest capacity.*

Emotional development is and should be a by-product of physical education. Exercise involved in games and sports, swimming and gymnastics, camping and outdoor education have specific objectives in terms of body power, endurance and behavior. The objective here is exercise for health and organic development, while with the farmer, the carpenter and the dock worker the exercise involved in the pursuit of each and its outcomes is not the primary objective. The results in the finished product becomes the desired outcome.

Re-physical education has been used as a substitute for the term rehabilitation. Here again the object of the exercise is re-educating the body, not sandpapering a board.

RECREATION must never be thought of synonymously with leisure time. Leisure time activities may be high on the scale or they may be low. Recreation should involve creativity, a development of the ego, the "I made it, I did it" concept. Such values are widespread and always involve personal satisfaction; let's call it fun. As a definition of recreation I like the following:

> *When work, because of its routinization, mechanization and drudgery, ceases to be an outlet for satisfactions, recreation is the name we give to those activities which provide man with the spiritual outlook of creativity.*

RECREATION EDUCATION, one of the primary responsibilities of teacher training, refers to the process of exposing young and old to satisfying recreational pursuits, of helping them become skillful in leisure and of providing good facilities for them.

HEALTH is the ability to sustain effort and recover from fatigue quickly. It should be thought of, ideally, in terms of optimum organic functioning.

HEALTH EDUCATION on the other hand, involves a total educational process and is the result of the efforts of many people who try to raise the health status of man on the mercury scale.

Relationships

There are three relationships which must be considered: the relationship of Health to Physical Education; the relationship of Physical Education to Recreation; and the relationship of Recreation to Health.

HEALTH AND PHYSICAL EDUCATION.

This is primarily a relationship of exercise to optimum health within the individual's capacity. If you prefer, call it fitness. Many facets which promote optimum health and longevity are outside the physical education domain. Optimum health is promoted by the doctor, dentist, nurse, sanitation and public health officials, nutritionists and others who provide a wholesome atmosphere in which a person lives.

Exercise contributes to health in at least five areas. When many variables affect the health of man it is always difficult to prove this-did-that or if-he-had-done-this, the-results-would-have-been-that. It is very difficult to draw always or never conclusions. Man must take the advice of experts for they, by training and experience, are in the best position to know the truth. The expert source from which the following was drawn is *Exercise and Health,* published by the American Medical Association.

1. *Exercise and Fitness*: Paul Dudley White, M.D., heart specialist, hiker, wood-chopper and bicyclist, says:

> Regular exercise produces organic changes in the lungs and circulatory system which improve the function for normal living — exercise also helps to prevent clotting (thrombosis) in the veins — it improves the tone of the diaphragm — small blood vessels are made more active — digestion and nutrition are improved. There is a beneficial effect of exercise on the nervous system and the psyche.

Harold Diehl, Dean of Medical Sciences at the University of Minnesota, says:

> The most obvious effect of regular exercise on the body is an increase in muscular development. Soft, flabby muscles become hard and firm. This improves personal appearance, increases strength and endurance, and enables one to enjoy physical activities.

2. *Exercise and the Aging Process*: There is ample evidence that good exercise habits can delay the aging process and certainly can preserve physical capacity to enjoy life.

Henry Montoye, head of the Sports Physiology Laboratory at Michigan State University, has this to say about exercise as a means of postponing the aging process:

> . . . . . regular exercise of the proper intensities and duration can do much to postpone the deterioration which commonly occurs as individuals get older . . . . such regular exercise affects not only their physical capacity but their interest in other people and the world about them, their energy for doing mental work and, in general, their vim and vigor for carrying out everyday activities.

Walter McClellan, physiologist in the medical school at the University of North Carolina, says:

A regular plan of physical exercise properly followed through young adulthood and middle-age, I believe, will provide the older person with a better physical machine.

3. *Exercise and the Heart*: It is generally agreed that the normal heart cannot be injured through exercise, and that exercise strengthens the heart.

Charles H. Best, M.D., and Norman B. Taylor, M.D., a famed team of medical physiologists, say:

It is now generally admitted that the well-conditioned heart of the young adult is not damaged by even strenuous exercise. The skeletal muscles fatigue before a healthy heart. In other words the heart free from disease can perform the greatest task which is ever demanded of it . . . In persons after middle age, the state of the heart is always an unknown quantity, and for this reason excessive muscular effort should be avoided.

4. *Exercise and Rehabilitation*: It is an accepted practice that exercise must accompany any rehabilitation procedure. Muscles must be gotten into action, the individual must be "gotten on his feet."

Howard A. Rusk, M.D., now a famous figure in the field of rehabilitation and during the war a pioneer leader in advocating physical activity for the convalescent, summarized as follows:

The results of our experience with the convalescent training program are most gratifying. Spot checks in various hospitals have shown hospital re-admissions reduced as much as 25% because the men are being sent back to duty in much better physical condition. The period of convalescence in certain acute, infectious and contagious diseases has been reduced 30 to 40%.

5. *Exercise and Weight*: The problem of obesity begins early in life and is as much due to under activity as to overeating. At least 25% of the people in America are dangerously overweight.

L. B. Pett, M.D., Chief, Nutrition Division, Department of National Health and Welfare of Canada, says:

Keeping up physical activity, perhaps of a different kind but still enough to flex muscles and improve the circulation, is just as important as the diet in avoiding some aspects of senescence. It will help muscle tone and stimulate appetite and interest in life. . . .

A general conclusion of the relationships of the physical education type of exercise and health is provided in a joint statement made by the American

Medical Association and the American Association for Health, Physical Education, and Recreation:

1. Exercise is one of the most important factors contributing to total fitness.

2. The contributions of exercise to fitness include the development and maintenance of strength, speed, agility, endurance, and skill in persons who are physiologically sound. Active games, sports, swimming, rhythmic activities, prescribed exercises, and vigorous hobbies, such as gardening and other work around the home, all can make distinctive as well as worthwhile general contributions to fitness.

3. Individuals differ in their capacity to enjoy and benefit from participation in exercise because of constitutional variations in body size, strength, and structure as well as differences in previous experience and present condition.

4. Exercise should be graded according to age, individual reaction to activity, and the state of the person's fitness. After age 40, more frequent medical evaluation of the individual's capacity for exercise is imperative.

5. Activities for girls and women should be selected with regard for their psychological as well as physiological characteristics. Those which involve a minimum of body contact and do not stress heavy lifting should be favored. Regularity of exercise should be stressed, with activity continued, if it is well tolerated, during the menstrual period.

6. The training involved in preparation for athletic competition contributes as much to fitness as participation in the contests themselves. Systematic training for any activity contributes effectively to fitness.

7. Time and care taken to condition the body for sports and athletics through appropriate activities will improve enjoyment, upgrade performance, and increase the ability to continue participation over a period of years.

8. Certain types of exercises are appropriate to certain conditions of weather and climate. Common sense suggests that a person should not set excessive performance goals under unfavorable conditions.

9. The proper use of protective equipment is essential to safe and effective participation in certain sports. Careful maintenance and proper control of facilities for athletics and other types of participation will help to prevent accidents and reduce injuries.

10. The rules of the game or specifications for play in an activity are made to protect participants and to enhance enjoyment. They should be properly interpreted, scrupulously observed, and vigorously enforced.

11. The vigor with which an individual participates in an activity will have more to do with outcomes for fitness than the activities or events in which he elects to participate.

PHYSICAL EDUCATION AND RECREATION

There is a vital relationship between physical education and certain phases of recreation but always keep in mind that recreation is a much broader term than is implied in sports and games. For activity to have any value there must be sustained effort. In order to sustain effort there must be drive, interest and fun. Recreation, therefore, which takes one camping and in the out-of-doors, which gives a person enjoyment in a game of tennis, badminton or swimming, form a real point of articulation with physical education.

Even at retirement, slowing up a little should not mean coming to a complete stop. Life has a quick way of disposing of non-workers and inactive persons. Retirement should never be the lazy man's dream of doing nothing. Explosive types of exercises or exercise too long sustained or engaged in at high altitudes should be avoided but other exercises should be carried on not just to the age of forty but to seventy-five and eighty-five. Recreation-fun is the catalyst which sets off desirable fitness outcomes.

RECREATION AND HEALTH

There is a physiological rule called the "law of attention" — namely, when the organism gives its attention to an activity (to grasp a fishing rod, or a golf club, or a lathe or a violin), worries and tensions disappear. The 20th century killers are fears, insecurities and tensions. We are living in a coronary-stomach ulcer-decade and excessive tensions are the cause. Relaxing recreation, hobbies in the best sense, is needed.

We need some tensions, of course, as in the uncertainty of the game, the thrill of a new struggle, the hope of success. Boredom has many of the characteristics of fatigue. The answer to many a health problem is to get into action, do something in which you are interested, find a hobby, get going! The other end of the scale from boredom is undue tension. Surgeon Sir Heneage Ogilivie of London, England, notes:

> If we cannot relieve stress, we must break it somewhere in the chain. . .
> Only leisure can rehabilitate the overstressed mechanism of the mind. . .
> But mere idleness is not the answer. The kind of leisure men need in a machine-age civilization is rather some spare-time task or occupation that makes some call on their intelligence and restores their self-respect, transforming them once more from cogs in a machine to men among men.

Man has a quality of oneness. Happiness, just old-fashioned joy, which means the absence of stress, supports buoyant health in a positive way and helps to keep the body resistance high. Happiness is associated with challenge, accomplishment and mastery. Happiness involves hope and faith. Hope, faith and joy are medicinal. They are therapeutic. They represent the difference between living and existing and often, between life and death. Happiness, however, is more than entertainment and amusement, money or "eat, drink and be merry." The basic need is to have a goal in work and recreation, a feeling of being wanted, of belonging, of sacrificing for a worthwhile cause.

This recreation thesis is supported by some outstanding medical research scientists. Dr. Hans Selye, in his book *Stress of Life*, says:

> We hurry constantly and worry incessantly. The businessman drives himself at his office all day, then worries most of the night. The housewife tries to run her home, maintain a social life, and participate in community activities—and at bedtime is so jangled that she needs a sleeping pill. Glands attempt to adjust to the constant demands of stress. They pour out excess hormones to keep the body going. For a while they succeed. But in the end the defense mechanism itself breaks down. Arteries harden, blood pressure rises, heart disease develops, arthritis strikes.

These and other diseases, according to Selye, are all part of the stress picture which can be at least partially offset by recreation. The Journal of the American Medical Association says this may be one of the most significant medical statements of the century.

Also significant is the statement by Harold G. Wolff, professor of medicine at Cornell University, editor-in-chief of "Archives of Neurology and Psychiatry." In making a plea for hope and faith and for a man to keep challenges, Dr. Wolff, in his book *What Hope Does For Man*, points out the negative side showing what happens when these are not present.

> When a person sees his prestige endangered, the glands of internal secretion may respond as though his very existence were in jeopardy, as by starvation, or by the sudden unusual demands of violent action or of very low temperature.

> Contraction of the muscles of the extremities and back, inappropriately responding to threatening circumstances by preparing the individual for prompt action that never takes place, may cause cramps and aches.

> Even the master organ, the brain, shares in such evil effects. Thus, infants and children in a hostile atmosphere may not mature, and indeed may act as idiots. Men exposed to the prolonged abuse and hatred of their fellows, as in prison, behave as though their theretofore actively functioning brains were severely damaged. Complete isolation, lack of opportunity to talk, repeated failure and frustration, revilement by his fellows, makes a man confabulate, become more suggestible, and rationalize his own unacceptable behavior. He may abandon a value system for one utterly incompatible with his former principles. In short, the effects of prolonged adversity on brain function may be difficult to distinguish from the results of actual destruction of brain.

Though we lack definitive support for this early impression, we do have precise information from our own records of the war concerning the effect on life span and health of prolonged adverse life experience. Thus, of approximately 6,000 United States prisoners of war captured by the North Koreans, about one third died. Medical observers reported that the cause of death in many instances was ill defined, and was referred to by them as "give-up-itis." Occurring as it did in a setting of serious demoralization, humiliation, despair and deprivation of human support and affection, the prisoner became apathetic, listless, neither ate nor drank, helped himself in no way, stared in space and finally died.

In short, prolonged circumstances which are perceived as dangerous, as lonely, as hopeless, may drain a man of hope and of his health; but he is capable of enduring incredible burdens and taking cruel punishment when he has self-esteem, hope, purpose, and belief in his fellows.

Challenge

We now have ample support from scientists that health has a relationship to the religious, spiritual, work and recreational phases of life. One must see meaning in life. One must have a goal and travel hopefully to live and be healthy.

It is recognized that there are many other relationships between physical education and various life outcomes, following philosophical and physiological principles of living, but still the main objective of physical education remains organic development — health.

It must be apparent that desirable outcomes of education and of life and the outcomes of physical education cannot be adequately tested by any quantitative measurements. We can test speed, strength, agility, and to some extent, endurance, but we cannot test the will to live, the will to do and the will to conquer.

We have heard a great deal about the necessity of health and fitness, particularly since 1918; but so far as the schools are concerned, it has been mostly talk. As Russia increased the pressure of studies in the school-room, it correspondingly increased the time devoted to physical education. Rear Admiral H. G. Rickover commented wisely, "While you are developing the minds of children develop also their bodies through physical education. These, too, are paramount."

I am not too discouraged about the health of children of America. I will not admit that society has completely failed them. Today's children are taller, heavier and more mature. They are living longer and they are living fuller. We have successfully carried the initiative and physical endurance in two world wars. We will defend again, if need be, the principles of freedom, respect for personality and fullness of life for all men.

We still need today, however, some things to help young people. In the modern school program we must have a longer day. This extended time should lay the basis for a health-fitness-exercise program; it should also give children some leisure time opportunities in the performing arts. We could have a longer school week. Most European schools carry on for six days. In this time our children could master one or two foreign languages, improve their English and arouse curiosity through science.

There could even be a longer school year. Summers could be utilized for work experience in factory, shop and farm, or in well organized private and school camps. Boys and girls could get experience in conservation, in preserving and replanting national and state forests and in working on public lands. These areas of education could be as valuable as those in the class rooms.

For total development, education must recognize the many talents of young and old — the many phases of development: organic, neuromuscular, interpretive and emotional. There would be no drop-outs if the school curriculum were broad enough to meet the interests and abilities of all children. We need redirection of outcomes. Thus optimum health — fitness —, citizenship and joy in living would be encouraged.

The boys and girls of this country deserve administrative backing from our state and local boards of education and from all school administrative officials. Our young people have the will and all life is reborn with every child. We must not falter now.

Significant Experiences — A Challenge to Physical Education
ARTHUR H. STEINHAUS*

The word "significant" comes from two root words "signum," which means sign or mark, and "facere," to make, therefore an experience that makes a mark is a significant experience. Everybody wants to make a mark in the world. The kind of mark seems to vary with age. A boy wants to be a circus clown. Then he wants to be like his dad — that doesn't last very long I discovered! Then he wants to be a fireman, then he wants to make All-State, then he wants to get rich; later on he wants to make both ends meet, and finally he hopes to get his old age pension. So really these marks vary.

*Adapted from an address to the Midwest Association for Physical Education of College Women, April 24, 1959, at McCormick's Creek State Park, Indiana. Reprinted from *The Physical Educator*. Vol. 19, No. 1, March, 1962.

Another way to think about this is to inquire what experiences are re-membered. There is a school of psychology that places great emphasis on what you remember from your early childhood. I stuck my neck out once to tell a person that I remembered a fight at age 5 with my brother in which each of us got hold of the same rocking chair and ended by pulling it apart. Of course, the fellow analyzed it to show aggressiveness because the incident remembered was a fight. But since the recollection is that we came apart each with his share, like breaking up a wishbone, maybe we were interested in sharing.

I thought further to remember feeling badly after hurting the feelings of a little girlfriend. We were both eight or nine. Then I remembered seeing my father walking through the apartment. He died when I was four and a half so you can place that. My mother had baked some coffee cake. Father came by and broke a piece off the end, ate it, and walked on. He got away without being scolded! Another incident that haunts my memory occurred about 30 years ago when I asked a student to leave my class for reading a newspaper. Certainly these things don't hang together as a sign of psychological bent. But all of these experiences are in some way con-nected with emotion. That is the one thing they have in common. But whether emotion was aroused because of my aggressive nature, or whether perhaps because it was so different from my nature, is why it stands out, your guess is as good as mine. Perhaps it only indicates that experiences which were associated with strong emotion are the ones that stand out.

Every significant experience is in some way connected with strong feeling tone and this feeling tone makes it significant. Let us say the "heat" of the feeling burns the mark into our memory.

Neurology of a Significant Experience

In a model brain one sees the parts of the brain that react in what is called a significant experience. It would have taken more than this brain to answer this question in Old Testament days when, you remember, God searched the reins and the heart of man. The reins — that is the kidneys — were the seat of the mind and the heart the location of the soul. In New Testament times, we would have needed to bring along also the "bowels of tender mercy." Saint Paul speaks of the emotions being in the abdomen. But today we have it all localized up here in the head. Gall and Spurz-heim in 1829 stood before the Society of Biology in Paris to enunciate the principles of phrenology. These gentlemen had felt bumps on peoples' heads and were quite sure that by feeling around up there they could tell what was wrong or what was right with a person. Thus, they located the liberty axis up on top and to one side of it religion and the other side love. What could be nicer to encircle liberty. In high school my physiology teacher told us that bumps behind the ears meant that you were destructive. So all of us Lane Tech Indians felt behind our ears and found we were destructive. Today we know these bumps are mastoid cells; but Mr. Swem didn't know this.

The significant fact of phrenology is its attempt to connect parts of the brain with character traits — loyalty, honesty, purity, observing power, etc. This is the older viewpoint which now is found only where somebody sells rattlesnake oil with a picture of the brain as a backdrop.

In 1871 Fritsch and Hitzig, working on soldiers injured in the Franco-Prussian War and also on dogs, laid the foundation for our present day notion regarding mind and the brain. They found certain spots on the surface of the dog's brain which, when stimulated, caused movement of skeletal muscles on the opposite side. They found the same in soldiers whose skulls had been shot and the brain exposed. This discovery of the motor cortex was only the beginning. Then came many other findings to give us more and more information concerning the connection of the brain, not with character traits, but with parts of the body. This is the new principle of localization.

Today we know the motor cortex, where stimulation causes movement in muscles of the other side. We know the sensory cortex where stimulation gives rise to sensations of touch in various parts of the body. Back of this is an area which is necessary for sight and just in front of it is one for the interpretation of sight. On the anterior mesial surface there is something for smell and taste, and here on the temporal lobe is something for hearing. Other areas are less well understood.

Penfield working on conscious patients whose skulls were exposed in preparation for surgery for epilepsy stimulated parts of the temporal lobe, and the person would say, "I hear music. I hear a song that I knew in childhood. I hear a lullaby or I hear an orchestra playing." When stimulated the orchestra starts playing, stop stimulating, it stops. Stimulate again, and it starts again to play the same strains.

This is fairly good evidence that memories are stored in the cortex, and that these memories can be brought out by electrical stimulation. They are also brought out by the stimulation accompanying epileptic attacks and account for the aura that precedes the attack. To know where to operate, the surgeon now stimulates until he finds a spot that produces an experience similar to the aura that regularly precedes an attack. Removal of this area often brings relief from epileptic seizures.

But that is only part of the story. Simultaneously with these advances regarding the cortex some astonishing discoveries were made in the basal part of the brain. It goes back to the 30's when Professor Hess of Zurich found some 4,000 spots in the cat's brain stem which when stimulated gave rise to different actions in the cat, such as blinking, purring, falling asleep, and combinations of some activities. Here was uncovered a rudimentary brain that must have existed millions of years ago before this top cortex business arrived to make us human. This rudimentary brain still works in us.

Near the front end of the brain stem are centers for anger, rage, and pain, in the diencephalon. Just above these are pleasure centers. An electrode placed into this part of the brain can be wired so that when a cat touches a certain button it apparently feels a sensation of pleasure. Now this cat might, in the course of an hour, accidentally touch the button 15 to 20 times but when a circuit is connected so that it stimulates itself, it will do it 5000 times an hour to get this sensation of pleasure. So we know "pleasure" is located in the brain stem. We know pain is in there, too. We know other reactions of the body connected with the viscera are located here. This is the great new discovery — the reticular formation as it is called. We know that this part is connected with the cortex for two way communication. So every idea, if we could think of it that way, is connected with feelings down in this part and the feeling centers in turn communicate with the cortex. There is thus continuous inter-relationship between ideas and the centers for feeling tone, and we begin to see what must happen if we want feelings connected with experiences, so that when either is activated the other, also, reacts.

Then, also, there is a rather peculiar bump up front called the prefrontal lobe which is one of the most recent developments of the brain not found in the China man, (Sinanthropus pekinensis), at least not as far as we can reconstruct from his skull. This prefrontal lobe has a few interesting stories connected with it.

In 1848 Phineas Gage, a very sedate, Puritan-like man living in New England, while tamping gun powder into a blasting hole had the powder explode and drive the tamping rod into his prefrontal lobe. This has become the famous crowbar case of Harvard Medical School. This caused Phineas to change his nature completely. Previously a very honest, home-loving, well-disciplined, conscientious man, now with the piece of metal in his prefrontal lobe he was an entirely different person — no more a good Puritan as you would picture such a person. He lost interest in his family and became in a sense a loose liver.

Sometime later a woman became much depressed. So she put a gun to the side of her head and shot. She didn't die. When the hemorrhage cleared out of her eyes she recovered to appear rather normal. Instead of being completely depressed, she was now outgoing. She had shot off her worry bump.

I don't know whether she was depuritanized as was good old Phineas, but there have been many operations like that since. It is called psychosurgery. The prefrontal lobe of the brain is in a very special way connected with the diencephalon where nerve centers controlling emotional tone are lodged. Too much connection with these centers results in overloading our experiences with affective states, sometimes resulting in withdrawal. Consequently, an operation to sever this connection may bring relief. This was first done on man by the Portuguese neurologist, Moniz, in 1936.

Through the prefrontal lobes there are nerve paths that connect the cortex where ideas are stored with the centers of feeling. Incidentally, removal of the prefrontal lobes doesn't change your IQ by the ordinary tests; but you are not as wise as you were before. Knowing facts and being able to answer an examination is knowledge. Wisdom is knowing how to use these facts and this is in some way connected with feeling. When you begin to connect feelings with ideas then you may sense that one is better than the other. When you connect pain with one kind of action and pleasure with another, you have the beginning of conscience. Dr. Dandy, one of the early surgeons on this part of the brain, had removed the prefrontal lobe from a patient whom he retained at the hospital as a handyman. One day Dr. Dandy assigned this handyman without a prefrontal lobe to show some noted visiting neuro-surgeons around the hospital grounds before bringing them to his office. These surgeons noted nothing unusual in the handyman.

People who lack prefrontal lobes often do a lot of bragging and punning, but who doesn't, sometimes! Maybe they just lack structurally what some of us lack *functionally*. Thus far we have seen that in man's brain there are opportunities for all connections necessary to make a significant experience, i.e., to tie ideas up with feeling tone and to inject feeling tone back into the ideas. This is the neurologic basis of significant experiences.

Significant Experience and Age Levels

Let us go beyond neurology to think in terms of significant experiences at various ages in life, particularly those experiences about which physical education can do something and which therefore are a challenge to physical education. Let us think of the child that is just beginning to crawl in its crib. It raises its head and moves around, it pulls up one arm and finally it stands up very proudly. Of course it doesn't say, "I'm proud"; but look at it and you can tell that it feels proud of what it can do.

Then pretty soon it starts to climb. A little later it climbs up and jumps down. Then it climbs a little higher and a little higher before jumping.

Imagine what is happening in the brain of this child. We know that the cortex is very poorly developed. The child cannot write a letter to its Senator, it cannot debate with its parents. All it can do, at least all that can be mentioned in public, is jump, struggle, spit, and cry. These are all muscular activities. Now imagine that this child has climbed up on a rock. Now look at it. The child is excited, leaning forward. You can see expressions of pleasure, of excitement, and a little fear all in that same face. Here it faces a challenge. It calls, "Mama, look." "No! No! No! Let me help you down!" That's one kind of mother. Another mother controls herself and says, "Okay, jump."

At this age it is very important what kind of physical education a child gets; and the mother is the physical educator. The girls who are now in your college classes are the physical educators of tomorrow's pre-school child. What does this jump mean to the child? Obviously, the only way it can express itself is by doing something within its ability. Modern psychology has taught us that very early in life we develop our feelings of self-worth, our feelings of acceptance or non-acceptance of self. It is important to that child to jump, to feel it is somebody. Long before it can say, "I am somebody," it feels that way. If it is constantly told, "No, no, no, let me help you down; you can't do that; you will hurt yourself," what kind of a child are we raising? Here is the great remaining "gold mine" for physical education to exploit in its effort to influence the character, the personality, the traits of courage, or whatever you want to call them — of the adult to come. As the twig is bent, so grows the tree. It is also true that one who has never learned to accept himself, cannot accept others, because he will project on others the feelings he has about himself.

To illustrate my opinion of the far reaching effect of such childhood experiences let me outline an investigation I would like to undertake. I would go to the Red Cross, the National Foundation, the YMCA, the YWCA, the Boy Scouts, the Girl Scouts, and other organizations that are constantly enlisting volunteers and ask what kind of reactions they get from the men and women whom they seek to be chairmen of their committees, boards, etc. They would report those who say, "Oh, no, I can't do that, no, no, get somebody else. It's impossible!" And then there would be others who say, "I don't know, but let's try." In the second phase of this research, with these persons in two piles, I would investigate their early childhood home life as far as possible. I would put my money, that the fellow who says, "No, I can't" is one whose mother said, "No, no, don't; let me help you down." He was denied the feeling of trying something and being successful early in life. The child that jumps and gets a feeling of success is having a significant experience.

We must help to bring such experiences into the lives of more children long before they come to school. Watch kids in the first and second grade when their classmates urge them to attempt a daring feat. Some come running and then turn back; others go to it with abandon. They may trip but what's the difference, they go on. Similarly some adults are constantly holding back while others are trying. We must touch the lives of these young children, through our present high school and college girls, the mothers of tomorrow. This is physical education for the pre-school child.

Let's look at the child the first time it is in a game where it must await its turn. Recently I observed some fourth grade boys playing a modified form of handball. Each boy in turn batted the ball against the wall to see how many times he could return it on the first bounce. When he missed the next fellow came up. The boys were lined up carefully, each waiting his turn. If one got out of turn he would undoubtedly have been forcibly corrected long before the teacher said anything. This standing in line awaiting one's turn is a significant experience. In this sense the play life of our city and rural schools is a crucible of democracy that has been denied the children of many lands where life is too earnest for play.

Then there is the first time a child played in a game with official rules where one might have gotten away with something when the official wasn't looking or when the teacher was not very observant. That was a significant experience. Was there then a coach who said, "This does not go; you've got to play the right way or you don't play." Was there someone back there who gave that boy the first real feeling of respect for rules, perhaps connecting it with diencephalic pain connected through the prefrontal lobes to the ideas in the cortical part of the brain when he said, "This thing doesn't go! If you don't play right, you're out! You're a disgrace!" For this reason there is no such thing as "just a kid's basketball game that doesn't count." The first game is perhaps the most important one.

These significant experiences in the lives of youngsters that may start them in one direction or another, are a challenge to us in physical education. They make it important that even in elementary schools there be somebody in charge who knows the rules and sportsmanship, and who is both capable and alert to make sure that the right thing happens.

Moving up a bit, let us look in on a high school. Visualize a boy sitting in a literature class where Shakespeare must be read. What is he doing? His lips are moving a bit. Especially when the teacher is looking, he goes through motions of being interested; but somewhere in his subconscious he is thinking of something else. He has a bit of athlete's itch on one foot; so one foot is scratching the other. The bell rings and *Henry VIII* goes out the mental window. This is no pretty picture of integrated activity. But watch this same boy in the closing minutes of a basketball game with the score tied and you will see the whole boy playing, completely integrated with but one purpose.

We've said a lot about the whole child going to school; but what do we do with the whole child? In the lower grades we can perhaps occupy him. Here they read a story and then act it out. But in that high school literature class, the boy's eyes and lips may be there, but the rest of him is most likely some other place. There is little that demands he give himself, totally. This leads me to say that an integrated activity is a significant experience. Unfortunately, we have less and less of that as we go up the academic ladder in our schools. The only place where the average fellow still gets a totally integrating experience, one in which the whole individual acts, thinks, and feels together — eyes, ears, muscles, brain, glands — everything, is in the gymnasium or on the athletic field. Maybe this is why play is so important to people; this is why youngsters like it so much.

Too much of modern day life depends on the use of the eyes and ears only. But we know that the ideas in our minds, concepts, if you wish to call them that, are composed of everything that comes into the cortex from the sense organs — from eyes and ears, yes, but these are not enough. What comes in from the muscles may often be just the feeling of sitting on one's seat. This does not ensure formation of a true-to-life concept because a related, true-to-reality proprioceptive component is lacking. The child that cannot distinguish between the moon, a cookie, and a ball that are held before it may grab for each but soon learns to distinguish between the moon on the one hand, and the cookie and the ball on the other when he can or cannot reach them or get his hands on or around them. Until he gets his hands around a ball he does not really know what a ball is and even though he can't get them around the moon, his appreciation of the roundness of the moon depends on the fact that he has had a ball in his hands. The third dimension experience, the depth dimension of our concepts comes to us from muscle and joint senses, i.e., the proprioceptive system. Too much of modern life is limited by two dimensions. Too much is just seeing pictures and reading the printed page. It is short on muscle and joint experiences.

Elementary education is better in this important respect than is secondary and higher education except for laboratory work. Acting out stories brings much more meaning to Macbeth or to Robin Hood than just reading the words. Could you imagine a nation going wild over a world's series game reported by radio if its people had never actually played some kind of ball game? Recently, I talked with an artist, who paints in oils. To my question, "What is your hobby?" he answered, "It's funny, I get very tired of painting because that's confined to a flat surface. Frequently I feel a need to get my hands around something. I make mailed armour for my hobby." Have you ever wondered why the "fix-it-yourself" business is so popular? You get your hands on something! The man who writes letters all day, or dictates them, or engages in wordy conversation wants something that will use more of his muscles and mind together. Denied such experiences some people develop a deep-seated hunger for them, others have so often ignored the feeling that they have lost the craving. Many people cannot express their feelings as did the artist. People find these concept-fulfilling experiences, not only in physical education activities, but also in gardening, in handicrafts, and in many other physical activities. This is terrifically important, lest we come to live in a completely unrealistic, flat world; and has far reaching significance.

Let me illustrate this another way. Visualize two individuals. One has done a great deal of work in the gymnasium lifting weights or tugging at this or that. He has felt tension in his muscles. He has felt tension in his entire body and with it he has felt success in pushing objects and overcoming big obstacles. Here is another man who has a little trouble with his back. Virtually, the only muscle tension he experiences is when he straightens out his lumbago back. What are the experiences and meanings that these two men associate with the word "tension," even "international tension?" The concept "tension" gets its full dimension, its feeling tone, partly from the muscle sense associated with it. In this way muscular experiences contribute meaning to ideas and supply them with a most important, real, and down-to-earth kind of feeling.

Let's try another illustration. Visualize two men who each day go to work. One must run for his streetcar, then run for a ferryboat, and then take a bus to get to his office. The other fellow is cadillacked to his front door and pushes a button to be taken upstairs. Which of these men really feels the seriousness of what it means to "miss the boat" let us say, in an important conference where because he had not carefully prepared the facts, "he missed the boat." I'll bet on the man who has on occasion missed the ferryboat and had to wait for the next one. To him the concept has a deep sense of reality.

A carpenter and contractor friend whom I've known since we were kids never made the grade in college and I'm still going to school. I've learned to admire that fellow in a special sort of way because somehow he goes right to the heart of a problem. He senses when a politician is crooked, when a politician is selling us short. What does the word "short" mean to him, and what does it mean to me. When Jack saws a board and it is one inch short he has to saw another or something may slip and let him down. To him the word "short" is possessed of real meaning from real life. What does the word "short" mean to me? I cut a lecture or a conversation short or hang up the telephone receiver a little too soon. Much of civilized life takes us too far away from physical experiences with "short." Jack is more level-headed than many of us who don't have the down-to-earth experiences of cutting boards and working with our hands. Maybe you call this common sense. Whatever you call it, it is something born of association with physical reality. It happens systematically in physical education, in the laboratory, in shop classes. For these reasons I have come to value my training in a technical high school, where daily we worked with our hands on real things.

Too often, instead of doing the thing with our hands, we just write a check and somebody else gets the real experience. Thus deprived of bodily experiences with reality our concept forming mind suffers a kind of malnutrition due to a deficiency in the proprioceptive component of the diet of sensory experiences — the muscle and joint component. The resulting sickly formed concepts may account for some cock-eyed thinking and failure to cope decisively with problems even in high places. In times of national and international crisis, a farmer, a foot soldier, a miner, or even a paper hanger may rise to replace the talkers. Probably combinations such as railsplitter-lawyer or carpenter-teacher dedicated to high values would be even better. In a time when such experiences are disappearing from urbanized American life our concepts may well become correspondingly "anemic" and unrealistic. But this is no propaganda for a "back-to-the farm movement." The farm is also becoming push-button. It does argue for supplementing the unbalanced sensory diet of civilized life with consciously selected dosages of muscular experience.

There are other ways in which modern life destroys integration. If you get mad at somebody, you don't dare show it, lest you get into trouble, especially if he's your boss. But let's go to the zoo and stand in front of the monkey cage. Do something to make the monkey mad. There'll be no question about it, he'll display his anger so everybody knows it. We call this honesty. Let us call it integrity or "oneness." When I was a youngster a Jewish friend told me, "There's something about you I like. You are what we call 'one'." It took me years to grasp the real meaning of what he said. He meant that I said what I felt and felt what I said. In this sense the monkey is also one. Obviously, this does not happen regularly in modern life. You have had people call you wonderful and yet you were afraid to leave the room for fear of what they would say when you were gone. It's good that people don't always tell me what they think about me. I couldn't take it. This kind of behavior is found only on one tiny twig of the animal tree. It's the schizic branch where man sits at the top where behavior is split — where we say one thing when we feel another. It is civilization. One can have only a few friends to whom one can talk as he feels. How awkward it would be otherwise.

A young woman who in the summer of 1937 sat in my class at the University of California gave me a good idea. It was in the days when some of us swore at modern dance and others swore by it. She was all for it. "Tell me," I said, "why are you so crazy about this modern dance?" She gave this very significant answer. "Well, since I'm a woman, I'm supposed to act like a lady; I must take short steps and I have to be dainty whether I want to or not. But in modern dance I feel big, I can make a big movement and if I want to stamp, I can stamp. It's okay." Dance gave her the opportunity to do and feel as one. Dance gave her the wonderful feel of integration. Could we say that modern dance brings to man the healing balm of monkey wholeness?

But you don't have to do modern dance to get the feel of such an experience. You can get it with a minimum of activity. Will all of you please say, "flat." Now say "point" and move your lips back. Say "flat" and point your lips. It's true also in other languages. Always if you speak simple words like "up," "down," "flat," and "point," the face moves with it. I've discovered another interesting and related fact. If you ask a person to repeat the word "spitz" for instance, and he imitates the sound without knowing what he is saying he will very likely do it poorly. But if you tell him "spitz means point" he'll do a much better job. This reminds me of what I've been taught by my modern dance friends. They say, "If you imitate, it isn't modern dance. But if you feel it first and then do it, it's modern dance." This is the way I learned the meaning of modern dance and how to understand the ladies who do it so well.

We men may get the same feeling in other ways. I can recall playing football in a snow storm, over forty years ago. As offensive tackle it was my job to block the opposing line men. Hitting the line again and again with almost bone crushing force with body, mind, and emotion all together hell-bent with others on going in one direction, provided such an experience that one never forgets. Similarly when a piece of wood connects squarely with horsehide and the ball goes places, the whole individual operating with split second perfection gets this feeling of togetherness. All of us have such experiences once in a while. Many of us don't have them often enough. One explanation for satisfaction gained from swatting a ball involves imagining it's your mother-in-law to get all the aggressions out of you. To me that is an unnecessarily complicated explanation. One can get something very direct from hitting the ball just right, without anthropomorphizing the little sphere. It may help some people but not me. Perhaps this is a tribute to my mother-in-law.

We don't yet fully understand the implications to mental health of thus constantly splitting ourselves rather than acting as one. It has not been proven, but I fear that such continual splitting must weaken the force of one's personality. Continuous ambivalence or something approaching that must put a strain on the structure of mind. I've tried to coin a companion term of "monivalence" or "univalence" but the nearest I can get to it is "integration" or "wholeness" as the contrasting condition that builds inner strength. When we center attention on feelings we sometimes speak of mixed feelings. That is the feeling you are supposed to have when your mother-in-law drives your brand new Cadillac over a cliff. If we insist on taking mother-in-law for a ride in our analogies, then think of mother-in-law driving your old, decrepit Chevrolet on which you have plenty of insurance over the cliff. That would be all feelings going in the same direction.

If a given object or experience makes us feel two ways, for example, if I have to feel nice toward you and at the same time I do feel another way, this is disintegrating. The boy who wants to win so badly that he's willing to do anything to win, even though his own code of ethics says it's wrong is having a disintegrating experience. It's like a woman falling in love with a married man. That's an awfully disintegrating experience because the object, the man, calls out two feelings in her — one which says "go" and the other which says "no." This tears things apart. But this need not be in sports. In good sports, properly coached, we learn to play hard and fair, to win — but not at any cost; if winning has not been pitched too high. Obviously it is most important that the right kind of leadership is given to the youngsters at the time when feelings are tied up with what is right and wrong in sports. Then all goes together in the right direction.

The theme song for what I've been saying may well be that song from Oklahoma, "Oh, What A Beautiful Morning, Oh what a wonderful day, I have a wonderful feeling everything's going my way." The weather is right. The girls are right, everything is right. These are significant experiences. They can happen in play life; they should also happen in our work life. But too often our work life does not permit this because we must be nice even though everything within us is justifiably angry. So here again our play life provides relief. It makes for sanity.

There is still another significant experience that should enter the life of every person. One of my freshmen students put it this way. "The greatest thrill to me was when one day my gym teacher told me, 'You can be a teacher.'" This happened when he was eleven or twelve years old. An almost identical story was reported by a coed. In her case it was her leader in a boys' club who told her she could become a gym teacher if she put her mind to it. When someone places faith in you and gives you a feeling of worth you have a significant experience. This comes in many ways. It comes to the young lady who is entrusted with responsibility in her girls' athletic association; it comes to the boy or girl who is selected to play on a team.

Why are boys so crazy about playing ball or playing on a team? It isn't because they like to run around. It isn't only because they enjoy the game. There is something else about it. It is this feeling of being needed, this feeling of being a part of something that is greater than one's self and feeling important to it. These are significant experiences. These are the experiences that often keep a boy in high school when he otherwise would drop out. No doubt there are comparable experiences in the lives of girls, experiences that provide a genuine feeling of worth not for personal aggrandisement with arrogance, but in service to a group or to the school. We can provide many opportunities for such significant experiences to our young people. We must learn to make each such experience provide 100% significance in the finest sense possible. This happens best when somebody in position of leadership understands what should happen and helps it to go that way.

Athletes as a whole do their best work at about age 25. That's roughly when most of the athletic records are made. Skilled laborers reach their peak at age 35. Brain workers at age 45. Inventions come most commonly between the ages of 31 and 35. Poets and dramatists ripen between 44 and 50. Of course there are always exceptions, but these are the averages. And after 50 there is nothing left for us but to become philosophers. That explains why you asked me to speak, which, by the way, has also shown me another time when one can have a significant experience. That is when some big idea takes hold of one.

I recall talking to Bernard Baruch the night before he announced the American proposal of policing atomic installations on both sides of the Iron Curtain. He presented it, you recall, before the United Nations. He didn't tell me what he was going to present but he said, "I think I've got it now." And then he told me how his mind seems to work. He said he listens to all kinds of ideas from all kinds of people, for a long time. For a time it is all somewhat confusing. "Then," he said, "sometimes at night something happens in the back of my head and everything becomes clear." It probably happens in another part of Mr. Baruch's brain but this was his way of putting it. It happens when little pieces suddenly fit together into larger pieces, when the many facts that we have picked up begin to make sense in the larger setting of the whole, as when many pieces of a jigsaw puzzle suddenly take form and we see the picture. This happens at all ages, starting in a small way in the young mind.

The older we get the more pieces should come to fit together to ensure for us a satisfying philosophy for our profession, for our life. The philosophy is the picture, the facts are the parts. The mind sits in front of the pieces, unhappy, until they begin to fit together. The mind wants to see the picture, it is confused by the disjointed parts. The bringing together of more and more facts into an ever enlarging consistent and satisfying philosophy of our task, of our profession, of our place in the larger scheme of things, is the most difficult and never ending task for the human mind. Progress in its accomplishment brings feelings of satisfaction commensurate with the significance of the experience.

Research Implication — Then and Now
RUTH B. GLASSOW*

A discussion of the topic, Research — Then and Now, should begin with a clarification of terms. For "Then," two periods, in which research had a definite characteristic, have been selected. It is logical on this the seventy-fifth anniversary of our national association (AAHPER) to begin the first "Then" in 1885 and, as will be seen later, to mark its close in the first decade of the twentieth century. There followed a period of transition from the one type of research to another which began in the 20's and extended to the 40's. This again was followed by a period of readjustment in research and it is interesting to note that during both transitional stages this country was engaged in war. "Now" will be considered as beginning in the 50's.

Was there research in each of these three periods and if so, what was its chief characteristic? What were the influences which shaped the investigations? It has been said, "Science owes many of its spectacular advances to improvement in methodology and the introduction of new techniques." (Weiss, *Simposia of the Society for Experimental Biology*, No. IV, 1950.) As each period is summarized, these two factors, methodology and techniques, will be seen as important in research in our field.

It will be well, as the three areas are surveyed, to have in mind the meaning and the nature of research. Briefly, research is a search for truth. Note that the word is a combination of search and the prefix re-. Current truth is scrutinized and re-examined to determine whether it is still true or whether a new statement should replace or expand the old. Steinhaus, in describing research to physical educators, said, "The methods of research, though endlessly different in their specific application, are fundamentally simple. Essentially they comprise four steps: (1) observation; (2) recording and treating the observed data; (3) generalization to the formulation of a theory; (4) testing the new formulation with further observations." (*Re-*

---

*A paper presented to the Southern Association for Physical Education of College Women, April, 1960.

search Methods Applied to Health, Physical Education and Recreation,
AAHPER, 1949.)

Looking now at the first Then, were physical educators searching for
truth in the late 1800's? Certainly they were making observations, were recording these, and to some degree treating the data. No well-trained physical
educator in that day would begin classes until students had been measured
and tested. In many an institution physical education classes did not begin
until two or three weeks after the opening of school. This did not mean that
the physical educator was idle; on the contrary, she was perhaps the busiest
person on campus. From the time of the opening bell until the dinner hour,
she was measuring heights, weights, sitting heights, girth of forearm, upper
arm, necks, thighs, calves, length of arms and legs, strength of backs, legs,
chests, and volumes of lung capacity. And if there was a right and left, both
measures were taken.

The interest of the profession in this type of measure is shown in the
appointment of committees on Statistics and Measurement, the first in 1885,
the last in 1903. The final report of this committee was made at the national convention in 1905, thus providing a closing date for this Anthropometric Age. (Clarke, *Research Quarterly,* October, 1938). These successive
committees, during their quarter century of existence, suggested and approved
items which were to be tested or measured; at one time the list included 50
items. Thus, making observations, the first step in research as listed by
Steinhaus, was a large scale, almost universal, operation.

Did the physical educator carry out the second step, recording and treating the observed data? With the limited statistical techniques which were
available, scores were recorded and treated. Based on hundreds and even
thousands of measures, charts showing averages and percentile ranges were
published for men by Hitchcock, Sargent and Seaver, and, for women, at
Wellesley, Oberlin and the University of Nebraska. (Bovard and Cozens,
Tests and Measurements in Physical Education, 1938.) Each student was
given a chart of these group measures and on it were plotted his own scores,
thus showing individual standing in comparison to his peers. Using these
charts, the instructor planned a program of gymnastic exercises for each
student. This profile of individual status and needs is today considered sound
and desirable. Our profession can take pride in these pioneer procedures and
would do well to continue them. The items measured will differ; the general
procedures are sound.

The data were also used to present evidence of the values derived from
participation in physical education. At Wisconsin as late as 1912, the department reported that 220 freshmen women had been examined in the
Fall of 1911. Fifty-one left school during the year, but the remaining 169
were measured again in the Spring. At this time, there was an average gain

in weight of two pounds (121 to 123); no change in height (63.1); chest girth decreased .2 inches (31.1 to 30.9); lung capacity increased five cubic inches (169 to 174); five strength measures increased — right forearm 7.6 pounds (53.9 to 61.5); left forearm 5.6 (49.9 to 55.5); chest, 18.9 pounds (106.6 to 125.5); back, 20.4 pounds (123.9 to 142.3); legs, 21.3 pounds (162.1 to 183.4). The total measured strength in the Fall was 496.4 pounds and in the Spring, 568.2 pounds, a gain of 71.8 pounds.

Reports on gains made as a result of participation in physical education would be as commendable and as desirable in 1960 as it was in the beginning of the century. Each of us would like to present such figures, but we can be assured that whatever the gain, questions would be asked. Are the gains significant and can they be attributed to physical education classes? Did the Wisconsin student of 1912 gain in leg strength because she exercised in the gymnasium or because each day she climbed the hill on the Madison campus?

From the treatment of the data, it can be assumed that the physical educator implied that gymnastic exercises increased strength and lung capacity. This was an accepted theory before the observations were made; the theory was not tested. Research of this first Then was limited to the first two of the four steps in research.

In research, facilities are important. There must be personnel capable of conducting investigations; there must be time for observation, for organizing data, time for thinking and theorizing; there must be space and there must be equipment for making the desired observations. This list does not name funds specifically, but it is obvious that if time, space and equipment are not adequate, often these lacks can be attributed to insufficient funds. Even adequate personnel may depend on the budget.

Was the personnel of the first Then capable of conducting investigation? It was comprised of graduates of one, two, and eventually three years of courses of study at normal schools of physical education. Most of these schools were supported by private rather than public funds. The founders were often medical men, attempting to meet the demand for teachers through condensed courses and curricula. Students were trained in what to teach and how to teach; they were not stimulated to question the What nor the How. The authority of the physician was accepted. The physical educators of the day could well have been adept in using calipers, dynamometers and spirometers, but they were not trained in experimental procedures.

Equipment was not costly. The most expensive were the dynamometers, but these were long-lived. Many purchased before 1900 are usable today. Neither space nor time were problems. The entire department staff and the entire department space were available for the measurement period. Perhaps some staff member sat up all night to calculate averages without the aid of a calculator; yet college enrollments were small, as were those in secondary schools and wholesale measurements in elementary schools were not common.

The last report of a national committee on Anthropometry marks a significant date in the Measurement of Man. It was in 1905 that a French psychologist, Alfred Binet, published his first series of tests to measure human intelligence. Binet made revisions of his tests up to the time of his death in 1911. Educators in this country were interested in the new device and during the first World War, with the availability of the service men, the first large scale measurement of intelligence was conducted with the administration of the Army Alpha Test. Binet's tests were revised for use in American schools, courses in measurement were added to psychology and education departments, and became a necessary part of teacher training.

By the 20's, some colleges and universities offered an undergraduate major in physical education leading to a Bachelor's degree. In 1925, a national committee recommended that all directors and supervisors of physical education should have a bachelor's degree, and that all college teachers, with the exception of specialists, such as coaches and teachers of dance and swimming, should have equal preparation. With professional training in the colleges and universities, the student in physical education came in contact with the rapidly developing tests for mental ability. One of the early statisticians, McCall of Teachers College, Columbia University, enthusiastically proclaimed that anything which exists can be measured. Physical educators are not likely to ignore a challenge. If mental capacity and ability could be measured, why not motor ability, native and acquired? And so began the Motor Measurement Millennium.

Physical educators following the pattern set by psychologists and educators undertook the task of devising tests to measure human ability. Preliminary observations had already been made. It was and is common knowledge that individuals have motor abilities and that the degree of ability differs. Even a child in choosing players for his team makes his selection on a judgment of skill.

However, such judgments are not scored numerically and experts may disagree on ratings. Investigators undertook to find test situations in which numerical scores could be obtained and in which differences of judgment would be minimized.

Their methods of procedures in devising tests followed a general pattern; analysis of the elements of the skill, selecting and devising situations in which performance could be objectively scored and then subjecting the scores to statistical analysis. Young and Moser's presentation of the process of obtaining a battery of tests to measure basketball ability illustrates these steps. The elements contributing to successful performance are according to their analysis, (1) ability to handle the ball, throwing and catching; (2) ability to handle the body in relation to the ball, to move quickly, to change direction, to jump; (3) ability to make baskets. As a result of the ingenuity of the investigators and search through basketball literature, 36 situations were listed as possible measurement devices. These were administered to classes and on the basis of subjective evaluation and statistical treatment, seventeen tests were studied more intensively. Finally, on the basis of statistical evidence of reliability and validity, five tests were recommended as a battery which would measure the ability to play basketball.

Investigators of motor ability have generalized from their observations and treatment of data, step three in methods of research. Many such batteries to measure ability in various sports were presented in this period, as were measures of more general abilities. The fourth step in research, testing the new formulation with further testing, was not common. Most of the batteries were the outcomes of Master's theses and Doctoral dissertations.

During the 20's and 30's, there had been a rapid increase in the number of colleges offering graduate majors in physical education. In the first decade of the century, three schools offered courses leading to an advanced degree — Columbia, Oberlin and Springfield College. During the 20's, eleven more schools offered such courses and by 1942 the number had increased to fifty-six. (Hewett, *Research Quarterly*, May, 1942.) Had it not been for the need of presenting a thesis for these degrees, perhaps such batteries as Brace's Motor Ability Test, Humiston's and Scott's Tests of Motor Ability, Dyer's Test for Tennis, and the French and Cooper's Volleyball tests and many others would not have been developed. Once a battery had been proposed and the thesis completed, there was no demand for the fourth step of further testing and evaluation of the hypothesis.

Not only was there no demand for this step, there was often active opposition. Survivors of the Anthropometric Age were still members of the teaching staff; for many of them such terms as reliability and validity, standard deviation and correlation had little meaning. Development of test batteries took precious time from teaching. The measures of this period never were used as universally as were the anthropometric and strength measures. For the staff members reluctant to use the new devices, these years were anything but a millennium.

With disagreement within the profession, there was no longer time allotted to research projects. Time was available only for the graduate student because it was a part of the study load. There was little demand for special research equipment. The batteries were devised for use in classes, and equipment for testing was limited to that which was needed for the game itself.

Some insight into the facilities which would stimulate research was obtained in 1937 from a questionnaire which Dr. Frances Hellebrandt and I sent to all member institutions of the National Association of the Directors of Physical Education for College Women. Replies were received from 91 schools and of this number 10 indicated that faculty members had a definite time on their schedules for research. In two cases the amount was not defined; in one college, it ranged from 1 to 4 per cent; in seven colleges, from 10 to 30 per cent. Only two schools indicated that space was set aside for research; in 6, there was special research equipment; 7 had research funds in the budget — these were $10, $25, and $75; others were $300 and $650. Only two schools reported research assistants. There was one each on half-time in these schools and the salaries were $500 and $600 for 10 months.

The investigators who developed the test batteries were exploring a new field. They were usually experienced teachers, but not experienced in research. They learned techniques as they developed their problem. These advisors had little more experience than did the students; few had a doctoral degree. Perhaps the most valuable outcome of the period was not the research, but the training which it gave to students and faculty. These individuals were to become the investigators of the present period, the Now of this discussion. They are among the chief influences which make Now a Period of Promise.

The present is promising because research facilities are better than they have been at any time in our history. Facilities, as stated earlier, include personnel, time, space, and equipment. No nationwide survey of these is available and I shall therefore compare the department with which I am most familiar with its facilities in the 30's and those which it has today. This one situation will illustrate the status of departments offering advanced degrees. Some will be better equipped than is the example, some not as well.

First, the personnel. In 1930, there were on the staff one doctor of medicine, four women with Master's degrees, and the remainder of the staff had bachelor's degrees. Today, there is one doctor of medicine, four staff members have Doctor of Philosophy degrees, and, in general, only those women who have Master's degrees are taken on as full-time staff members. The qualifications for scientific investigation of the staff are now vastly superior to those of the 1930's, not only because there have been longer periods of preparation, but because the training in research procedures through which the staff members achieved their degrees is superior to that which the 1930 staff had experienced.

Second, the time for research. In the 30's, whatever research was done by staff members was done in addition to a full teaching load. Many a midnight hour and many a Sunday was spent in the laboratory and office attempting to follow some line of investigation intriguing at the time. Today, the department is attempting to develop a schedule which will include time for research as a part of the teaching load. Each staff member of professorial rank, and there are ten of these — three full professors and three associate and four assistant — will have such time for a given period. If at the end of the period she has demonstrated no drive for investigation, research time will not be allowed.

Frequently, a research grant makes possible additional time. At present, such arrangement has made a 40 per cent reduction in one staff member's teaching load.

Research assistants can also be considered as adding to the staff member's research time, for these assistants do the routine work and take over many details of projects, thus enabling the staff member to accomplish more in the investigations. In the 30's, there was one half-time assistant in the department; today there are eight. Three of these are supported by university funds, not considered a part of the department's budget, and five are supported by grants from off-campus organizations. Thus, it might be said that the research time is equivalent to the total load of at least six people.

Third, the space. In 1930, there was no space which the investigator could consider his own. Today, there are two large laboratories assigned to research projects. In addition, when the study demands, the entire staff is cooperative in making available space which is ordinarily used for other purposes. In a recent study which involved volume measures of the human body, a tank was set up in one of the gang showers because a ready supply of water and a drain to carry off the water was needed. Another study required the use of the gymnasium for a two day period. Not only did the instructors of classes give up the space allocated to them, but they acted as assistants in that two day project, as members of their classes were measured in the overarm and underarm throws and in the standing broad jump.

Fourth, equipment. One laboratory has a calculator and the School of Education has a laboratory where calculators are available at all times. In addition, the university maintains a Numerical Analysis Laboratory where electric computers are available without cost for all staff projects and to students working on theses and doctoral dissertations. One set of scores which was analyzed presented the investigator with over 3,000 correlations and 18 means and standard deviations. Had these been calculated in our own laboratory, it would have required months; with the electric computers, the work was done in less than two days. Educators and physical educators are today applying Henry Ford's guiding principle, "Never do for yourself what a machine can do for you better, faster, in greater quantity, and at lower cost." (B. L. Bruckburger, *Image of America,* 1959.)

The projects of one of the staff is concerned with strength studies. The dynamometers purchased in the early part of the century are still available, but the investigator prefers the tensiometer. That was purchased some ten years ago, and for the past six years that investigator has moved the testing table and the tensiometer to a neighboring elementary school where 8 muscle groups have been measured on the same group of children during that period. At other times the equipment is used for studies with college students.

There are also ergographs for measuring the amount of work which can be accomplished if a muscle group is exercised until fatigued. The distance a load is lifted and the time for lifting are recorded on another piece of equipment. These provide means of studying and comparing methods of improving strength.

For measurement of energy expenditure in exercise, there are Douglas bags to collect expired air. There are recorders to measure the intake of oxygen. These have long been used by physiologists.

In one of the laboratories, a small space has been insulated to permit electromyographic studies. It has long been recognized that a logical analysis of muscle action is not a valid picture of functioning muscles. Except for studies of walking (University of California, Prosthetic Devices Research Project, Vol. I), there have been no sound reports of muscle action in the skills which comprise physical education curricula. A recent electromyographical study reports an observation which is of interest to those attempting to develop motor skill. It was found that when the free foot was plantar flexed, the initial activity appeared in the peroneus longus if the performer thought of pushing the forefoot downward. On the other hand, if the performer thought of bringing the heel upward, the resulting plantar flexion was initiated by contraction of the soleus. (A. L. O'Connell, *American Journal of Physical Medicine,* Dec., 1958). This suggests that the idea which is in the mind of the performer may be important in bringing into action the desired muscles and could be important to all teachers of motor skill.

And last in this list is the photographic equipment. Pictures of motion taken at high speeds are essential for the physical educator as is the microscope for the biologist. Most descriptions of sports skills and locomotor skills are based on what the eye can see or on what the performer thinks he does. Both have been shown to be erroneous. Our equipment includes a 16 mm. camera, which can expose 4,000 frames per minute and which is equipped with a wide one inch lens and a three inch lens. For studying film, there is a time-motion study projector, by which one frame can be projected for unlimited time without danger of burning the film and which can be turned by hand. It can also be run at various speeds, forward or backward. More satisfactory for tracing film is the Recordak. Six of these are in our laboratory, three of which expose three frames at a time; the others, one frame. The projection is at table height convenient for tracing, and the film can be turned forward or backward by a handle within easy reach.

These photographic aids have enabled us to study lever action in various skills. For example, one of our graduate students recently analyzed her own overarm throw. She found that the contributing joint actions were rotation at the left hip, spinal rotation, medial rotation in the right shoulder, elbow extension, and wrist flexion. The elbow extension, since it is not moving in the direction which the ball is to be projected, did not contribute directly to the ball's velocity. The contribution of the others were:

hip rotation	15 ft. per second or	14.7 percent
spinal rotation	1 ft. per second or	.98 percent
shoulder rotation	69 ft. per second or	67.6 percent
wrist flexion	17 ft. per second or	16.6 percent
Total	102 ft. per second	

The ball velocity was measured from the film also and was 98.5 feet per second. The slight difference of 3.5 feet per second could be due to error in measurement or to failure to include some contributing factor.

Analysis of the joint action in the standing broad jump has shown that the action cannot be understood if the explanation is vigorous extension of hip, knee and ankle. Film study shows that the knee extensors and gravitational force are the main contributors to projection of the body. Ankle and hip extension maintain the direction of projection. To see that the downward force of gravity can pull the foot upward is to gain in appreciation of the Wisdom of the Body in motor performance, as Cannon saw that wisdom in physiological functioning in the early part of this century (Cannon, W.B., *Bodily Changes in Pain, Hunger, Fear and Rage,* 1929.)

Film study shows that the performer uses joint actions of which he is not aware. If these actions are not voluntarily controlled, how is the movement brought about? A possible explanation is that the human nervous system is equipped with inherent motor patterns, that the voluntary part of the skill is only the decision to perform and that the details of the act are taken over by that part of the nervous system which is below the level of consciousness. Inherent patterns have been recently studied in forms of life other than Man. Lorenz has indicated that patterns are inherited as surely as are physical features (*Scientific American,* 199, 6, December, 1958) and Sperry has suggested that an affinity between specific muscles and specific neurones determine possible coordinations. Broer has shown pictorially the similarity of pattern in underarm throw, the volleyball and the badminton serve; in the overarm throw, the badminton clear, and the tennis serve; in the sidearm throw, the tennis drive and batting. (*Efficiency of Human Movement,* 1960.) If such patterns are inherent in Man, how early do they appear?

In observation of boys of pre-school age, we have found in a three year old the sidearm, overarm, and the underarm pattern in well established coordination. Teaching may well begin with the basic pattern, rather than with a description of detail.

These many avenues of study make possible a pooling of the findings of each in an attempt to look at motor development and skill from many angles. It is attack on the Unknown from many aspects rather than effort along one line only as was characteristic of the Anthropometric Age and the Motor Measurement Millennium. For example, when our photographic studies indicated that the principle projecting force in the standing broad jump was that due to contraction of the knee extensors, the staff member who was studying strength in the same subjects reported that the correlation between the distance of the jump and the strength of knee extensors was greater than it was with either ankle or hip muscles.

Each line of investigation now requires special apparatus, which in many cases is designed for the project. Each investigator will develop technical methods which will result from long experience. Those who study by means of photography will have skills and information which differ from those of the student of strength. The department which was used as an illustration is only one of many. In each, there will be other special lines of investigation. Each investigator, confident in his ability to conduct research, will follow the leads suggested by his findings. Results from all parts of the country will attack the Unknown from many more aspects than will any one department. Research in physical education has reached maturity and the years ahead are indeed a Period of Promise.

Chapter

Meaning in
Physical Education

The Excellence of Patroclus
ELEANOR METHENY*

In this Olympic year, when virtually everyone is talking about the virtues and vices of sport, it may be timely to ask: What is sport all about? Who originated the idea of throwing sticks and stones at the nothingness of empty space? What motivated him to devise rules for the performance of this absurd action? What emotions were generated by his attempts to perform this empty action in accordance with the rules he had devised for himself? And why were those emotions so complex? And why were they so often ambivalent?

In all truth, no one knows how it all began. But certainly the custom of holding stick-throwing contests at funerals was well established by the time of the Trojan Wars—which were fought some three thousand years ago; and fortunately Homer repeated the legendary story of one of these funeral contests in the *Iliad*—so we may start our speculations about man's involvement in sport-type competitions with that early chapter in the long and always controversial history of sport.

As you probably remember, Patroclus was a nobleman, a warrior, and a hero, who fought and died on the bloody plains of ancient Troy. In his brief lifetime, he did well and gloriously all that the gods and other men might expect such a man to do; and so, at his funeral, his companions thought it fitting to remind the gods of "the excellence of Patroclus" by calling attention to some of his most glorious deeds.

---

*Paper presented at Luncheon Meeting of Faculty Club of the University of Southern California, November, 1968.

Thus, his companions threw javelins, hurled stones, drove horse-drawn chariots at full speed, ran as fast as a man could run, and wrestled with each other in hand-to-hand combat. But they did not perform these glorious deeds in the same way that Patroclus had performed them in the heat of battle.

On the battlefield Patroclus had seldom had an opportunity to demonstrate how far he could throw a spear. On the battlefield he had to throw on the run, and he had to throw at other men who were running toward him with their own spears at the ready; so he had to adjust his aim and force to the requirements of the moment, always keeping his own guard up to ward off the enemy spears and arrows. As he threw, other warriors often jostled him, or his feet slipped in the muck, or his throw was hampered or hindered by any one of the countless circumstances and necessities of war.

In the funeral competitions, the companions of Patroclus tried to rule out all of those hampering and hindering circumstances; and they tried to give each warrior a fair chance to demonstrate his own maximum spear-throwing ability. They did this by converting the deadly act of spear-throwing into the harmless act of throwing a stick at empty space, and they identified this non-consequential act as a wholly voluntary action which a man might choose to perform for his own reasons. Then they set aside a time and a place for the performance of this action, and announced a set of rules which would impose the same conditions on all competitors; and they appointed an official judge, giving him the power to impose those same conditions on all men who entered into the competition.

Thus, as each warrior stepped up to the starting line, he knew precisely what he was going to try to do; he knew he would have a fair chance to perform that action as well as he could perform it; and he knew how the outcomes of his efforts were to be evaluated—and by whom.

Freed of all the hampering circumstances of war, he was free to go all out, holding nothing back; he was free to focus all the energies of his mortal being on one supreme attempt to hurl his own javelin at the nothingness of empty space. He was free to throw his own stick as far as he could throw it; or he was free to run as fast as he could run, to hit as hard as he could hit, to leap, to jump as high, as far, as he could leap and jump. In short, he was free to use his own human powers in open contest with the powers of other men; he was free to bring all the forces of his own being to bear on the performance of one self-chosen human action.

The Greek warriors created this moment of freedom for themselves—and for all men—by devising the paradoxical rules of sport competition. These rules impose restrictions on human behavior by defining one set of actions and by specifying how those actions may be performed; but within those restrictions they offer every competitor an opportunity to know the feeling of being wholly free to go all out—free to do his own utmost—free to use himself fully in the performance of one act of his own choosing.

These paradoxical rules created this man-made moment of freedom by ruling out the conditions that cloud the realities of man's earthly existence. They created this moment of freedom by ruling in the pattern of an idealized world in which every man might have an opportunity to make full use of himself—an ideal world in which every man might make full use of all the energies of his mortal being, unhampered and unhindered by the necessities of his life.

And so we must note that the Greek warriors did not show the gods how well Patroclus had actually performed the glorious actions of his life in the heat of battle. Rather, they showed the gods—and other men—how well each warrior could perform the empty action of throwing a javelin at the nothingness of empty space under ideal conditions which offered him a fair chance to do his own utmost as a man among men.

What values did the Greek warriors find in the performance of these idealized and non-consequential actions? Here we may turn to the experiences of their modern counterparts, letting three college students speak for all devotees of sport competition.

In one of the conversations that have been going on in my office for many years, Jim, a 250 pound lineman, put it this way. He told me about the "explosion of joy" which pervades every shred of his being when he does succeed in getting every ounce of himself into action. He said: "It's beautiful. . . . " Naively, I asked if it didn't hurt to hit and be hit; and he said: "No, not really . . . because the explosion of joy is all I feel." But then he added: "That's only when I really make it . . . when all of me is really there; but if I miss . . . if I goof off . . . if I don't get all of me into the action . . .then it hurts like hell."

Bob is a gymnast, and he said it this way: "There's a feeling of wholeness in doing a routine on the parallels. When I start a routine, I'm not thinking about any part of myself . . . or what . . . or why. I know what I'm going to do; and there are no questions, no indecisions, no holding back, no rationalizing, no self-deception. From start to finish, all of me is involved in that action, and nothing is left out, nothing left over. It's like you say . . . every shred of my being is involved in that routine . . . and in that action I am a fully-integrated, fully-functioning, fully-involved human being. It's beautiful . . . it's beautiful to experience your own wholeness . . ."

Ann isn't much of an athlete, really. She is a very reserved young woman who comes to the physical eduaction building to play table tennis during the noon hour. She put it this way: "Maybe this sounds silly . . . but battling that absurd little ball back and forth across the net sort of makes me whole again. Most of the time I'm such a scaredy-cat . . . fussing, worrying . . .

afraid, pulled in a dozen directions . . . so I can never really go all out about anything. But somehow, when I pick up that paddle, I know what I'm doing . . . and even though I don't do it very well, for a few minutes all of me is there . . . and somehow I seem to come into focus. Maybe it's silly to care so much about a silly game that I'm not very good at . . . but for me it's the most . . . the greatest . . . just to go all out without holding back . . . it's beautiful!"

A man-made moment of freedom. A feeling of wholeness. The excellence of Patroclus. Truly it may be said that these are beautiful ideas. But what about the realities of sport competition? Does every sport contest reflect the beautiful ideals of human freedom, human wholeness, and human excellence?

Alas, no. Homer's description of the funeral contests does not support any such exalted theory; and neither does any newspaper account of the events now occuring in Mexico City—or any recollection of my own experiences on the golf course.

So let it be said to the glory of the Greek warriors—and to the glory of sport from that day to this—that most of the competitors did honor their own paradoxical man-made rules, and many did demonstrate their own human excellence within the idealized rules of sport competition. But they also argued with the officials and with each other. They boasted and bragged; they belittled the powers of other men; they devised strategies that gave them advantage over other competitors; they lost their tempers; they were often vindictive and vengeful; and many of them cheated their own rules when the officials were not looking—even as you and I have done in our own self-revealing moments of human wholeness—even as you and I have done in our own moments of commitment to the values we find in our own human actions.

Or, as the competitors in the early Olympic contests put it, every man who would submit his own excellence to the test of sport competition must "stand naked before his gods" and reveal himself as he is in the fullness of his own human powers. Stripped of all self-justifying excuses by the rules of sport, he must demonstrate his own ability to perform one human action of his own choosing; and naked of all pretense, he must use himself as he is, in all the wholeness of his being as a man.

In that self-revealing moment, every competitor must experience himself as he is—in all the complexity and ambivalence of his own feelings about himself, his gods, and other men who claim the right to share the universe of his existence. If he is a proud man, he will experience his own pride. If he is a domineering man, he will experience his own need to dominate the lives of other men. So, too, a fearful man will know his own fears; a resentful man his resentments; and an anxious man his anxieties. An idealistic man must recognize the reality of his own ideals—and the conflicts he experiences as he tries to live up to them. A chauvinistic man must come to terms with his own chauvinism; a loving man must reveal the limits of his love; and a hating man will experience his own fearful hate.

In the self-revealing moments of sport competition, every man who would know himself at his best must also know himself at his worst; and he can not escape the implications of either image—because this is what he is, this is how he feels, and this is what he does when he has a fair chance to use himself fully in the all-out performance of one self-chosen human action.

Or, as Wallace Stevens has put it:

> I measure myself
> Against a tall tree.
> I find that I am much taller,
> For I reach right up to the sun
> With my eye . . .

> Nevertheless, I dislike
> The way the ants crawl
> In and out of my shadow.

And so it was with the Greek warriors who celebrated the excellence of Patroclus by throwing their own javelins at the nothingness of empty space on the bloody plains of Troy some three thousand years ago. And so it is with the excellent young men and women who are now throwing their own modern sticks at the thin air of Mexico City—or on the campus of modern Troy. And so, too, it is with many learned professors who bat tennis balls back and forth across holey nets or knock golf balls into empty holes.

Or perhaps I should say—this is how it seems to me . . .

Sport and Modes of Meaning

JAN FELSHEIN*

It might seem semantic playfulness to ask whether meaning gives structure to individual existence, or if it is structure that lends meaning to life. But if culture is seen as a prearranged, imposed, and somewhat restrictive design for man's potential actualization, then the meaningfulness of his activities is inseparable from this structure. Whether culture is, in fact, acting to free man, in the sense that he does not have to replicate countless

---

*Jan Felshein, *Journal of Health, Physical Education and Recreation*, 40:5:43, May, 1969.

formulations and decisions, or to restrain him within its social order, it is the notion of pre-designed structure which is compelling.

Experience itself cannot be said to be wholly culturally formed. But insofar as man's confrontation with reality is symbolic, experience does have a dimension of cultural content. Since human experience is essentially an outgrowth of the capacity for abstraction, it is both formulated and interpreted within a pervasive system of symbols which is culturally structured. As man both creates and is created by culture, there is an ongoing process by which the individual internalizes culture and absorbs both its content and modes of thinking, feeling, and acting.

Although we may speak of such generalized human motivations as drives or needs, or even instincts, and somehow conceive of these as sources of meaning, it is only the culturally shaped modes of expressing, fulfilling, or gratifying them that may be explored or understood. Our concepts of human selfhood and its expression depend on the same capacities for abstraction that have given rise to culture. The individual experiences his own motivations, but he has come to seek their fulfillment and expression in ways that are learned as generally appropriate. And, ultimately, meaning must be viewed as modal; that is, related to the unconscious, perhaps, but absorbed dispositions formed by cultural experience.

Generically and specifically we may refer to sports as subcultures, and in doing so imply the existence of another structured and abstracted reality. In fact, the symbolic reality of sport is generally recognized more easily than that of culture as a whole. The only point that may need to be reaffirmed is that abstraction does not imply bloodlessness, and the symbolic reality of sport, though organized in an action or "effective" domain, is structured for most in relation to affective factors.

Sport is a personal-social phenomenon and to examine modes of meaning in the sport experience as either *only* personal or *only* social may be inadequate. In some sports, of course, there is no actual social interaction involved in performance, but there are socializing agents and models, social roles and statuses, and a pervasive social context.

On one obvious level, social values and norms simply become a mode of meaning for the individual in sport. There is little doubt that people pursue sport for the satisfaction of many social motives and achieve gratification of many related drives and needs through sport participation and success.

Similarly, success in sport can be used as a certain kind of self-adequacy affirmation. Either because of personal achievement-need or because of its relationship to such things as popularity and prestige, sport simply is a potential proving-ground for the self.

There are, however, many areas of human endeavor other than sport in which modes of meaning based on concepts of socialization and self-validation can function. Despite the fact that we can talk about a generalized kind of culturally imposed appropriateness of meaning-expression, experience is modified and created and, more importantly, *chosen* by the individual.

In order to understand modes of meaning particularly or singularly related to the sport experience, perhaps we need to examine the structure that gives meaning to sport. One way to view structure is to conceive of it as freeing the individual rather than restraining him. The fewer the variables or alternatives which are *not* prescribed, the greater the freedom the individual has within those alternatives. Where a great deal of the activity in a situation is prescribed, or governed by pre-existing rules, performance becomes focused on those aspects which are not so ordered. The individual may be said to have been "freed" by the restraints within which he must operate. In sport, the individual is "free" from having to deal with (that is to think about or make decisions about) a host of situations and variables. These are "covered by the rules," and, furthermore, usually enforced and affirmed by "overseers" who do deal with them. The player is thus free from many kinds of responsibilities. In both our sport and our society, this kind of freedom is lately symbolized as being free to "do your own thing." But the question must be raised about the difference in modes of meaning of choosing to "do your own thing" as a hippy, with as few restraints as is culturally possible, and as an athlete within a context of defined and enforced restraints. Obviously, if the feeling of freedom is the source of meaning, the mode of meaning is defined by the choice.

The structure of sport exemplified in pre-designed and replicated experiences also provides the means for continual refining of responses. If the sport experience was, indeed, the same each time, we can only assume that eventually it would become "boring" rather than "interesting"; that is, it would not have continual meaning. This element of challenge, either because there are no upper limits established or because there are pervasive "better ways to do things," becomes another potential source of meaning within the structure of sport. "Response to challenge" and "mastery" are related concepts of meaningfulness to most people. Although both of these may be seen in their relation to self-validation, the repetitive and continual challenge of sport experience suggests that this is not the only mode of meaning involved. In sport, challenge is defined and perceivable. It is related to the areas of freedom; that is, whereas many variables are held constant, both freedom and challenge exist in relation to those variables which are not held constant. Certainly, some notion of mastery is a more likely source of meaning when the challenge is at the level of successful participation in general, rather than when it is more sophisticated and related to freedom. In the sense that the freedom *becomes* the challenge, or at least its focal point, the mode of meaning is defined in the structure.

One of the most important aspects of meaning in sport is the involvement that relates to the complexity and kind of structural demands. "Sport" may even be defined as involvement; to choose to enter and re-enter the structured reality of sport is to be involved in it—to "care" about it. If the sport choices of individuals or societies are expressive of some kind of cultural life interpretations, then the mode of meaning is that which is demanded by involvement in the sport. These demands are related to the structure of specific sports as well as to the general affective dimensions of all sports; that is, to the importance of "winning and losing," "scoring or not scoring," "improving one's mark or performance," and the whole perceptual frame of self as a sportsman or competitor. The notion of involvement is not restricted to sport. Many activities are engrossing and compelling enough in their challenge, complexity, and mystique so that they endure as areas of human significance. It is true that sport involvement is not only individual but is manifest in cultural and social ways, and perhaps there is another characteristic of sport that further clarifies its compelling modes of meaning.

It is the effective realm that truly characterizes sport, and movement is *real*, not symbolic; the body is a source of sensation, and in human experience it is sensation which has the least cultural content. The sensations produced in movement in sport are related to the feelings of power to affect the environment; to act. In the sense of its use of movement, sport is the effect of man's biological technology on the environment. And on that level, sport is inherently meaningful. The question of whether meaning yields structure or structure lends meaning is, finally, *ad hoc*. Why would man develop and impose structure, except that something was initially and inherently meaningful? Structure and meaning are, thus, interactive, and sport, based on man's inherent power to act, embodies his modes of meaning in its structure.

Physical Education and the Good Life
H. Gordon Hullfish*

The previous speaker has done, appropriately and sensitively, what it would be presumptuous for me to undertake.[1] An appreciative evaluation of the contributions to your field of R. Tait McKenzie could be made only by one who had labored long and thoughtfully in the same vineyard. I am sure you need no further reminder of why it is that your American Academy of Physical Education pauses annually, in his memory, to assess your present

---

*Presented as the R. Tait McKenzie Memorial Lecture. Reprinted from the *American Academy of Physical Education, Professional Contribution* No. 8, 1962.

[1]This is a reference to the introductory remarks of Delbert Oberteuffer who commented briefly on "R. Tait McKenzie — The Great Teacher."

state of being. I am honored to have been accorded the privilege of sharing this platform with your Academy this morning.

It has always been proper for an educational group to ask itself what ends it should serve. Often, however, the query is made perfunctorily; habit having so established the answer that further investigation, while recognized as part of the ritual, is unnecessary. But the meaningless habit will no longer prove adequate. Education is under attack on every hand. Critics (I was tempted to say "experts") are emerging from every nook and cranny of the culture. Some of them, because they speak from a background of professional concern and insight, must be taken more seriously than others; yet none should be ignored, whether speaking from a background of insight or of ignorance, since all speak as members of a public which, properly, has a stake in the schools of the nation. Their right to speak makes the educational situation somewhat messy and does the legitimate educational expert less honor than he deserves; it represents, nevertheless, the burden the educator has to bear in a free world. And this burden is now considerable. What is at issue is nothing less than the continuity of the free world itself.

We are confronted today by a brute fact. A determined and, by our standards, a ruthless nation is on the march. Its intention is nothing less than world supremacy and it rightly sees that this country alone, of all of the countries that prize freedom, has the strength to stay its hand. Moreover, its leaders, unhampered by a need to please an electorate, are able to move toward their goals with a directness that would be the envy of the heads of government within the free world — did not the latter know that, were they able to act with comparable ease, they would no longer be representatives of freedom.

Turmoil and anxiety have characterized the years since the end of World War II. The peace we thought we had secured at war's end yet eludes us. We have had the comfort of knowing, however, that we were an advanced nation and it has been disconcerting to discover, as we recently have, that the Russian people, thought by many to lack either the knowledge or the incentives to catch up with our scientific and technological know-how, have made clear in fact what too many of us have heretofore treated only as theory — namely, that no nation has a monopoly on intelligence. Sputnik I and Sputnik II shattered our complacency and brought us down to earth abruptly, if I may phrase it so, there to watch these instruments, seen always as potential agencies of destruction, move in their orbits around us. Our own Explorer and Vanguard have given us a measure of reassurance but Russia's invasion of outer space, catching us not only grounded, but also bickering about how best to take off economically, made it evident that we are involved in a contest of brains.

This is the latest cause for criticism of our public schools. We are hastily comparing our curricula with those of the Russian schools. We are

demanding that more scientists be trained. We are insisting that the frills
and froth in education be eliminated. We are pleading that education become
an intellectual endeavor and that the merely social and physical emphases
be eliminated. We are told all this without sufficient recognition of the fact
that the Russian pattern of education would be inappropriate in the free
world. The excited critics seem not to know that more than curriculum content is at issue. We cannot assign students to the niche we want them to
occupy. We cannot move them from the classroom to, say, a collective farm
if they lag behind in their studies. We will not (at least, no scholarship program has yet been this visionary) support fully all students of promise,
whether their educational interests are in science or in the Russian language,
and then place them in government service upon graduation. Nor are we prepared to pay the salaries teachers are said to get in Russia. And, despite
the occasional cry that we appoint a czar of this or of that, we cannot channel
intellectual and economic life to carry out the will of our leaders; there
being no czars, in fact, and hence no single will. We face, in short, no mere
problem of *schooling,* a term much narrower than *education,* yet one which
the critic constantly confuses with the latter. *A way of coming at life* — a
conception of the good life — is at stake.

The terms of the good life, of course, have been set forth in many patterns, including, in our culture, a pattern that permits men to conceive
the appropriate terms differently. It has been said that Aristotle, in his
relationship to his teacher, Plato, while a student in the Academy, "was
completely free to go another way if he chose, leave his master and follow
his own path. There were no fixed dogmas in the Academy; everything was
open to discussion, to attack and defense. No one claimed to be teaching the
truth; all were seeking it." (8) Here is the root idea of our culture, the freedom
of individual man to follow the challenges to, and the leads of, his thought.
We have held as worthy the aspiration that man should rise above a servile
state. We have found life good when men were free to follow their own paths,
no longer compelled to tread paths others approved as proper and right. We
have seen no reason to quarrel with Aristotle's conclusion that the essence
of being a slave is to be without either the opportunity or need for thought.

We need seek no further to discover why our forebears took education so
seriously that they created a system of public education to serve all of the
children of all of the people. There is no freedom to think when men so lack
knowledge they are compelled to accept as true that which the informed
claim to be true. There is no freedom to think when men have no habits of
questioning, when they have been conditioned by their culture to accept custom uncritically. The right to think freely comes into being only as men,
collectively, prize the goods that flow from this ability sufficiently to work
to create and to maintain the conditions that make such learning possible

on the part of all. The free man, to remain free, has to work continuously to share his achievement with others who, should they find the good life somehow reflected in their ability to suppress thought, may deny him what he has come to look upon as right. The price of liberty is, indeed, eternal vigilance. Thus, our interest is at one and the same time in the individual, since it is his development which is paramount; and in society, since, apart from nourishing social conditions, the individual's growth as a reflective being will not be valued. At bottom, then, for free men, the individual and the social interests are identical and, if this were but better grasped, we would quarrel less at the political level about which interest is being represented and would be less critical, as we examine education, about the social emphases it currently expresses.

As men have lived with the idea of freedom they have realized that its acceptance has consequences for more than what is often called "man's inner life." Men can, as the courageous lives of prisoners of war attest, create a world of thought which helps them survive when all that surrounds them is calculated to degrade them, if not to destroy them. But their selfhood will flower, as they well know, when, released from restraining conditions, they are free to move about as they wish; to work at that which tests the adequacy of their aspirations, to give expression to ideas and thus test them against the ideas of others, to associate with those in whose company they find fulfillment, to remain quiet and refrain from speaking when they wish to do so. Further, as men have made the educative act a matter of study, they have learned that more is involved than the conditions of the classroom, if the end of education is to incorporate more and more of youth in the shared life of freedom. Irwin Edman summed up this point when he said: "It is no accident that in the United States, from Thomas Jefferson down, public education has been considered a primary business of democracy if democracy is to survive. But such education does not mean, obviously, the mere provision of free schooling for all. The habits essential to intellectual freedom must be the central business of education. Neither information nor indoctrination, even of democratic ideas, is enough. The temper of intelligent criticism is the essential not only of a liberal culture but even of a free society. And that temper can be cultivated only in those sufficiently well clothed, well housed, and well fed to be able to think with composure and alertness and to sense a share in the general welfare." (7, see p. 188-89.)

A further conditioning factor, one that has increasingly disturbed the public conscience since Edman wrote these words in 1941 is this: one must be sufficiently well integrated into the full life of citizenship "to be able to think with composure and to sense a share in the general welfare." And this means more than clothing, housing, and food, as the United States Supreme Court has recently recognized. Man is not educable, in the full sense of the good life as free men have conceived it, if he is arbitrarily cut off, by virtue of the conditions of his birth and of his growth, from free participation in the affairs of his culture. Nor, on the other hand, are those who insist upon restricting the development of others as free as their sense of power leads them to believe. We are caught up in an associated life; and this, without any planning on our part. If we are to make it a good life, we shall need to engage in a creative, shared effort. Any restriction placed upon any individual, or any opportunity to achieve freedom granted him, means, in fact, restriction or opportunity for all.

Freedom, as I have been arguing, is an achievement — a social achievement — as well as an individual one. It is not a gift. Yet the achievements of prior generations make the problems of freedom easier for later generations. Most of our citizens, for instance, gain the right to vote today simply by living long enough to meet the requirements of the states in which they live. Were they called upon to fight for this right, generation by generation, the right to vote would be a limited right, indeed. This is a fact that the women of this country should readily recall; it is a fact that some citizens of this country are painfully aware of today. The achievements of past generations (we need only recall the accepted right of the working man of today to organize in the interest of improving the conditions of his labor, if a further illustration is needed) to provide a cultural inheritance that extends the opportunities of later generations to participate more fully in the co-operative task of building a free world. But, unfortunately, as the rise of the authoritarian state in its new form in this century has shown, any generation may create social conditions that will deny freedom to the unborn for generations to come. It is small wonder, whatever mistakes modern education may have made and however harsh the voices of the critics, that our schools have been concerned to create educative conditions that exemplify the essential qualities of free and democratic men. Information alone, no matter what the quantity transmitted, will not promote the good life for free men. Again, to turn to Edman, we find him saying correctly that it is "only on the basis of institutions nourishing the ancient ideals of freedom, justice, and equality that men will be liberated to come to their full stature, to live richly in themselves and in mutually stimulating and understanding peace with one another." (7, see p. 192.) And one of these institutions, of course, is education, as the school men of this country have rightly seen.

A word of caution is in order here. We are not the sole inheritors of that vision of the good life which has been created as men over the ages have struggled to attain these conditions of decency and humaneness upon which the gaining of freedom depends. Nor are we alone today as the struggle continues. The specific character of our inheritance has made it possible for us to maintain and extend the conditions of freedom for ourselves, but it has challenged others to a comparable achievement, men whose initial opportunity for development was not as favorable as ours. The challenge has been accepted and, from one quarter or another, there will be tension and struggle until the ends of freedom and independence are gained, or until a contrary approach to life prevails. We too often forget that what we have achieved, by a combination of fortunate circumstances and determination, has become for others a vision of a life good to live and that, therefore, the leadership expected of us is a leadership so devoted to freedom that it works ceaselessly to help all men experience it.

Arnold Toynbee, attempting to forecast what the historian will say of this century 300 years hence, has said this age will be remembered chiefly for having been "the first age since the dawn of civilization . . . in which people dared to think it practicable to make the benefits of civilization available for the whole human race." (10) In the development of this idea, Toynbee contends that this "vision of a good life for all is a new one, and — whatever our success or our failure may be in the attempt to translate this vision into reality — this new social objective has probably come to stay. That the ideal of welfare for all is new is surely true; for, as far as I can see, it is no older than the seventeenth century West European settlements on the East Coast of North America that have grown into the United States. And it has surely come to stay with us as long, at any rate, as our new invention of applying mechanical power to technology, for this sudden vast enhancement of man's ability to make nonhuman nature produce what man requires from her has, for the first time in history, made the ideal of welfare for all a practical objective instead of a mere utopian dream." Finally, he notes the moral obligation which this vision of the good life imposes upon those who have thus far been its beneficiaries, saying, "When once the odious inequality that has hitherto been a distinguishing mark of civilization has ceased to be taken for granted as something inevitable, it becomes inhuman to go on putting up with it — and still more inhuman to try to perpetuate this inequality deliberately."

We identify this vision of the good life with democracy and, in so doing, run the danger, as is always true when a covering label is handy, of obscuring its essence, the continuing quest by all for a life that is good to live. We are not dealing with a completed vision, with a way of life so complete that, viewing it as finished, we may set out to teach it as we may teach an unquestioned body of fact. It was for this reason that earlier I used the expression *a way of coming at life* in referring to our conception of the good life. We know that we are dealing with an open world, not a closed one. We know that we get our directions from an active and probing intelligence, not from a recipe book. We know that concern for others, respect for ideas and for the individuals who express them, and readiness to consult and compromise as the differences we cherish conflict, are principles that help us keep on the right track as we find our way amidst the ever-new problems which arise. We know, even as we at times forget it, that callous action which excludes either appropriate persons or relevant ideas is always a denial of the spirit of democracy, whether this occurs on a playing field or at a summit conference of world leaders. We do, in short, have ways of testing ourselves as to how well we are living up to our commitments in the daily round of our lives.

Some years ago, John Dewey asked whether we could find supporting reason for our preference for democracy or whether, as many thoughtful people insist, we hold this preference simply because we were born where the concept was rooted historically, in much the same way that some people prefer strong seasoning in their food, to the distress of those whose tastes were differently developed. This is a basic question. If we are dealing with no more than a matter of taste, of unreasoned preference, it is sheer lunacy to claim that what we find good will be good for others (a point, parenthetically, that should be kept to the fore when some current plans for reconstructing education are under consideration). Dewey's answer moves us from the plane of taste, provides supporting reasons, and, in my view, sums up the principles that should guide us as we *come at life* for the purpose of securing more completely the conditions of freedom for all. "Can we find any reason," he asks, "that does not ultimately come down to the belief that the democratic social arrangements promote a better quality of human experience, one which is more widely accessible and enjoyed, than do nondemocratic and antidemocratic forms of social life? Does not the principle of regard for individual freedom and for decency and kindliness of human relations come back in the end to the conviction that these things are tributary to a higher quality of experience on the part of a greater number than are methods of repression and coercion or force? Is it not the reason for our preference that we believe that mutual consultation and convictions reached through persuasion, make possible a better quality of experience than can otherwise be provided on any wide scale?" (3)

If I have labored long over my point about the nature of the good life, I have as an excuse only my conviction that it was important to do. We have heard much of late about making education consistent with the nature of man, though those who press this point often write as if man in the study of man had learned nothing in the last two thousand years. Interest is centered on a strong mind, with the strength of the vehicle, the body, being left presumably to inheritance or, perhaps, to you. We hear much, also, of the need to provide an education that will be appropriate for all times and for all places, a position that considers the prevailing conceptions of the good life as these emerge within differing cultures to be irrelevant and which, to take a case in point, would give the United States and Russia identical educational patterns. Your place in this scheme of things is surely restricted, since it is doubtful that you have been provided for within the immutable and unchanging principles said to be directive of this pattern of thought. And, at another level, much is said, as I noted earlier, of clearing the schools of the debris left over from a once-held enthusiasm for progressive education in order that proper subject matter may again be emphasized. This case could be argued, if its adherents did not use the label "progressive" so loosely as to make it meaningless, and if they did not act as if subject matter had an inherent power to educate people on contact. Of course, subject matter is important but, in the classroom, it becomes important only as it enters the reflective experience of students and leads them to an understanding of their talents and to a grasp of its social significance. As the case is argued, however, the uncritical acceptance of organized knowledge as the focus of educational effort should give pause to those who know how this conception at an earlier time led to so much boredom in the classroom. As for your field under this view, I am afraid you will be benched, unless you are permitted to enter the game from time to time to serve as tranquilizers for overwrought students.

But perhaps I need not turn to the present-day critics of education to uncover the problem of your place in the scheme of things. A well-known professional book (6) that deals with the high school curriculum, the second edition of which was issued in 1956, contains almost 600 pages and is divided into 32 chapters. The 31st chapter (11) discusses the place of health education in the curriculum; the 32nd, (12) the place of physical education. I could assume that the editor placed these chapters at the end of the book to provide the capstone for this treatment of the high school curriculum. Yet I recall that, recently, I spoke to the high school teachers of the academic subjects in a large city school system while, at the same hour, meetings were being held for the elementary school teachers and for the teachers of special subjects, including health and physical education. Am I right in asking myself these questions: Are you part of the public school *show*, but not essential to the development of its basic educational program? Will the last two chapters of this book be dropped from the third edition?

Now, I am aware, of course, that you are concerned with more than muscles, that you do not ask students to put their mental life in their lockers during their hours with you. I know that such matters as health in general, or health specifically, sanitation, immunization, hygiene, special and corrective exercises, understanding of and respect for a self that is manifested through behavior, an appreciation of what it means to be of one sex and to grow in relationship to the other, skill in individual exercises or in competitive games, and the like, are all matters that concern you as teachers. I know, also, as Jesse Williams has stated, that your thinking is directed by such principles as these: "Physical education will be an education through the physical rather than an education of the physical;" "Recreation belongs in the good life;" and "The qualities included in the term 'sportsmanship' are primary objectives of certain physical activities." And I am aware that what you do is tested against carefully formulated criteria, and that you are sensitive about certain hazards in your field, such as the ease of slipping into regimented drills and of permitting sports to be exploited commercially. But I recall, also, that Williams has said of games, sports, and athletics that, "these are the heart of the program" and I am afraid the public generally and the critics specifically think of them as the total program. Moreover, the public and the critics tend to associate you with playing fields and physical activity, rather than with classrooms and mental activity.

If the public has been misled, your academic colleagues must share with you some of the blame for this. They have been only too happy to be looked upon as the guardians of intellectual halls, even as they have joined the public in increasing the hazard of exploiting those whose talents lead them to significant participation in games, sports, and athletics. They have found it good, on the one hand, to be identified with the essential intellectual center of education, and, on the other, to be associated with schools that gain enthusiastic public support because of their excellence in athletic events. But this only means that we are dealing with an area of human activity in which it is hard to keep an eye on the ball. No activity of a school is warranted that does not have educative consequences for those to whom it is directed or, to state it differently, in which the intellectual component is not central. This is as true in a science classroom as it is on a playing field, when either involves meaningless, repetitive acts, though its absence in the former may not be equally obvious. Classroom teachers may "call the signals" as readily as playing field teachers. They are, then, equally guilty of the exploitation of human material, of degrading the educative process. The fact is, of course — and this is the point of my argument throughout — that your field should either contribute to the good life we aspire to or have no place in the education of free men. But this conclusion applies to all fields of knowledge. All that we teach should liberate the individual from binding custom and uncriticized habit and move him into the larger life of shared insight and understanding. Whatever is thus liberated is, in the essential meaning of the term, liberal. And here is to be found the ground on which you stand equally with other fields of knowledge. However each field differs in specific concerns, all stand together in advancing the common quest for the good life.

We should expect the critics (I refer, of course, to those who speak from an educational background, not to those of the Zolliah era who spoke intemperately and from dubious motives) to see the problem more clearly than the public. And in many respects they do, especially when they consider educational aberrations of the following sort: First, a failure to understand that the doctrine of interest should neither exalt the passing whim of the student nor eliminate hard work from the program. Second, the false assumption that to emphasize adjustment means to emphasize conformity, or adjustment *to* things as they are, instead of, as John Dewey pointed out, to be concerned with an adjustment *of* conditions so that plans of action may be tested and the conditions that initiated them reconstructed. Third, a misinterpretation of the place of *doing* in learning, so that any activity (often miscalled "experience") is viewed as educative, when, in fact, (again to turn to Dewey), it is only as the method of intelligence is operative that "reaction is turned into response," into meaningful behavior. Fourth, the inability to maintain perspective, illustrated, on the one hand, when athletic programs overshadow educational endeavors; or, on the other, when sentiment so dominates the proper emphasis upon individual development that the freedom given young people denies the teacher, as Dewey once remarked, the freedom to direct this development. That these aberrations have occurred is a fact to reckon with, and it is proper that critical guns be turned upon them. Such guns were rolled into position, in fact, before the newly emerging critics started firing — as they should know.

My repeated reference to John Dewey in the above paragraph was deliberate. He is currently being held responsible for most of the ills of public education. None seem to realize, however, that John Dewey, commenting on the difficulty of changing either individual or institutional habits in 1952, noted the way in which the latter tend to assimilate and distort new ideas "into conformity with themselves" and concluded emphatically: "This drive or tendency in the educational institution is perhaps most glaringly evident in the way the ideas and principles of the educational philosophy I have had a share in developing are still for the most part taught, more than half a century after they began to find their way in various parts of the school. In teachers colleges and elsewhere the ideas and principles have been converted into a fixed subject matter of ready-made rules, to be taught and memorized according to certain standardized procedures and, when occasion arises, to be applied to educational problems externally, the way mustard plasters, for example, are applied" (1). The aberrations may be facts of the situation. They bear no necessary relationship to the ideas and principles of Dewey's thought, however; nor does their presence invalidate these ideas and principles. By ignoring this, it is convenient for the critics to sweep Mr. Dewey from the scene, an act which inadvertently illustrates his point that the habits of individuals and institutions change slowly.

The bearing of this upon your area is more direct than may at first seem apparent. Modern, or progressive, or current, education is said to be anti-intellectual; and, by implication, Dewey's philosophy is held to be the responsible agent. Oddly, it would be hard to find anyone whose writings were more concerned to bring a liberating intelligence into the daily affairs of man and who wrote more pointedly to reveal the function of education in advancing this end. He did not think of intelligence, however, as "a peculiar possession which a person owns" (2), with each individual having a given quantity at birth; nor did he think of it as the highest faculty of a mind that was given to all alike. He knew that each of these views had had its day in court, that each had been repudiated. Intelligence, as a term, meant to him "a shorthand designation for great and ever-growing methods of observation, experiment and reflective reasoning . . ." (5). He was concerned, therefore, with the process of inquiring. Within it, he found qualities of behavior that differentiated it as an act from acts of routine or of impulse. Hence, his interest was in the distinctive qualities of this way of behaving. He found it no longer necessary to refer to a separate entity that caused the behavior, that served in Gilbert Ryle's admittedly abusive term, as "the Ghost in the Machine" (9). He concluded, rather, that the "conception of behavior in its integrity, as including a history and environment, is the alternative to the theory which eliminates the mental because it considers only the behavior of the mechanism of action as well as the theory which thinks it ennobles the mental by placing it in an isolated realm" (4). He thus moved beyond the long-held dualistic conception of separate realms of mind and matter (a formulation Alfred N. Whitehead termed "unfortunate"), without succumbing either to the mechanisms of recent behaviorism or to the futility of a preceding mentalism.

Where present-day critics of education are concerned with the aberrations, the excesses, found in our schools, we should join hands to bring about their elimination. *We have no dogmas to protect.* If there has been an unreasonable emphasis upon mere activity, upon doing that which is without meaning, whether in a laboratory or shop, a classroom or gymnasium, upon a stage or a playground, this does not mean that education should swing to an extreme of mere contemplation. Where there is learning there will be doing but the doing will not itself be the learning, though one may learn, as William H. Kilpatrick has put it, what one does. Doing, in short, is not restricted to overt bodily activity; nor is learning restricted to the operation of an inner mind. If there has been an over emphasis upon social adjustment, leading either to the false view that the purpose of education is to conform to things as they are or that its end is exclusively to help the individual be a jolly, good fellow, this does not mean that we should suddenly lose interest either in the social ideal that has given significance to the lives of free men or in the social significance of that which the student learns. It it has seemed to some that there is not sufficient respect for knowledge in education as it is presently conducted, this does not mean that classrooms should become places where information and inert ideas should be paraded before young people endlessly. Information becomes knowledge for the student, when it does, as it bears upon what he is trying to do and helps him do it with an enlarged understanding and extended control. When this happens, students respect knowledge, without benefit of preachment. If schools have seemed to be so concerned with health that responsibility has been taken away from the family, the alternative is surely not to ignore health, since at this point in many instances may be found the critical factor that has led teachers to look upon a student as uneducable. If education has been too practical, the contrast we seek is not an impractical education. The issue here is to teach whatever is taught so that meaning is progressively added to the life of the student. It is in this sense that theory may be more practical than activity. But this is true only when the theory illuminates activity in which the individual engages. Both the merely practical and the merely theoretical, untouched by meaning, will seem abstruse to the student.

The danger is that we shall permit our present anxieties to throw us off balance. The critics have found weak spots in our practices. But we had better watch their proposed remedies, especially when they emphasize intellectual activities as if they were cut off from the stream of physical life. The "tempter of intelligent criticism," as Edman has noted, is dependent upon many factors. It will not be cultivated simply by the study of a certain body of subjects, nor will it be cultivated when what we know about man and his learning is ignored because we are intrigued by a noble and historic, though wrong, conception. *The physical is in the educational picture to stay.* It is one aspect of the total individual with whom we deal. Our problem is to differentiate inquiring, reflective, purposeful behavior, behavior that is illuminated by the consequences it forecasts and that is checked against what in fact occurs, from behavior that is irrational, irresponsible, capricious, or blind. We cannot lift ourselves above behavior into a realm of "pure" experience, since there is no experience worthy of the name where there is no meaning; and meaning, finally, is grounded in the individual's ability to do what his ideas assure him that he can do.

Intellectual development is central in an educational program that is designed to create men who may, in turn, create the conditions that enhance freedom for all. But this is not to suggest, as I am afraid many critics do, that only an assumed intellect is the object of educational interest. Far from it. What is of interest are active individuals whose present level of interests, concerns, and knowledge make it possible to arouse them to engage in further activity within which what they presently know will be reconstructed as new information, ideas, insights are encountered.

In these terms, physical education may make a major contribution to the achievement of the good life on the part of free men. Indeed, the basic potential of your area is distinctively a *human* potential. Many of our activities bring individuals together intimately, both competitively and co-operatively, and place them under the discipline of living up to established standards and rules. Moreover, the failure of many, even at the teaching levels, to live up to the rules brings to the fore something more than an interest in skills. Questions then arise from experienced problems, not from manufactured ones, questions that cannot be answered by a rote application of rules. Choices, and hence moral decisions, have to be made; since rules cannot substitute for intelligence. Rules do carry over into the present, however, what men in the past have found good, and thus serve as the means to help individuals become intelligent and sensitive in dealing with new problems. They make possible the games to which they apply and, also, make it possible to judge both the claim of validity of those who want to change the rules and the integrity of those who claim to live under their direction.

The physical education teacher, without announcing it, may help young people continuously, if his eyes are lifted above the level of skills and performances, shape up a conception of the good life. Problems that confront the student with the need to make choices will arise, also, when rules of health are under discussion. In fact, whenever the function and appropriateness of a rule is considered, differing conceptions of life are then weighed one against the other. The intellectual and moral components of your field are potentially high. They will not be realized, however, without insight and understanding and effort on your part. They will not be realized at all, if the notion prevails that intelligence may arise only in classrooms that claim to be turned into the realm of mind, a realm that will be disturbed if the body is too much with us.

You have a further opportunity, to the degree that games, sports, and athletics are "the heart" of your program, that is given to few teachers. You deal with individuals who want to learn. You engage them in activities where their learning makes an immediate difference, a difference they can grasp and understand immediately. You do not have to keep assuring your students, as other teachers must, that some day they will be glad you made them study. The game is the thing and they can play at once. But even more is involved. The necessity of co-operation (I am disturbed to hear your area justified so often as one that nourishes the competitive spirit) brings together into joined effort all of the diversities among our people. The individual is judged by what he does, by what he contributes to the common effort. He is not asked to show credentials of birth, of economic status, of religion, or of race. On this score, indeed, you have helped the average citizen, often without intending to do so, to gain an appreciation of others, whatever their background.

You have provided, where your work has been properly conceived, an opportunity for the individual to be a person, a person gaining respect for himself as he understands what he can do and what he represents, as well as a person who contributes freely to the gains of others. Difference of backgrounds and diversity of talents are joined in the exciting effort to achieve together what none could achieve alone. And yet the sad fact is that men may compete or co-operate under the guidance of degrading ends. You cannot rest your case, therefore, on these abstractions. You must bring them to life as they serve an appropriate educational end. This end, it should be clear, is to help students rise to an appreciation of how their growth is ultimately related to their ability and willingness to create and maintain the conditions within which the spirit of freedom for all will be forever nurtured.

BIBLIOGRAPHY

1. Clapp, Elsie R. *The Use of Resources in Education.* Introduction, "John Dewey." New York: Harper and Brothers, 1952, p. X.
2. Dewey, John. *Democracy and Education.* New York: The Macmillan Co., 1916. p. 155.
3. Dewey, John. *Experience and Education.* New York: The Macmillan Co., 1938. p. 25-26.
4. Dewey, John. *Philosophy and Civilization.* New York: Minton, Balch & Co., 1931. p. 314-15.
5. Dewey, John. *Reconstruction in Philosophy.* Enlarged ed. Boston: The Beacon Press, 1948. p. viii-ix.
6. Douglas, Harl R., editor. *The High School Curriculum.* 2nd ed. New York: Ronald Press, 1956.
7. Edman, Irwin. *Fountainheads of Freedom.* New York: Reynal & Hitchcock, Inc., 1941.
8. Hamilton, Edith. *The Echo of Greece.* New York: W. W. Norton & Co., Inc., 1957. p. 95.
9. Ryle, Gilbert. *The Concept of Mind.* New York: Barnes & Noble, Inc., 1949.
10. Toynbee, Arnold J. "Not the Age of Atoms But of Welfare for All." *New York Times Magazine,* Oct. 21, 1951. p. 15.
11. Williams, Jesse F. "Health Education in the Curriculum." *The High School Curriculum.* 2nd ed. New York: Ronald Press, 1956.
12. Williams, Jesse F. "Physical Education in the Curriculum." *The High School Curriculum.* 2nd ed. New York: Ronald Press, 1956.

Holism in Training for Sports

J. KENNETH DOHERTY*

Holism as used in this paper is a method of understanding and finding solutions to the many problems of sports training and competitions. It begins

*Prepared for the First International Conference on the Psycholoy of Sports, Rome, 1965.

by looking at these problems as a whole, upon the athlete-in-his-physical-and-social environment as one all-inclusive problem. It progresses by focusing sharply upon each aspect of this problem, but uses whatever methods and devices of thought, feeling and action, especially those of semantics, that may help avoid the illusion that these aspects are separate entities.

Holism does not deny individuality, nor the uniqueness of each individual's structure or motivations or freedom to choose this or go there. Rather it assumes this uniqueness emerges out of the ever-new inter-relationships of "wholes," much as a blue rose, uniquely individual as it would be, could arises only out of "blueness"- "roseness"-and-the-surrounding-environment.

In its relations to the individual, holism emphasizes the unity of mind-body in which body can be abstracted from the whole for purposes of understanding and communication, but not as an entity separate from mind or from the person. For example, holism is wary of speaking of a muscle injury. For an injury is always to the person as a whole; it has a muscle or physical aspect to be sure, but it also has a mental-emotional aspect whose healing is just as crucial and often more difficult than the physical. As one more illustration, fatigue is often dealt with in purely physical terms, as work decrement, or as the accumulation of waste chemicals from activity; holism considers it a psychophysical complex out of which we can abstract certain mental-emotional aspects or certain physical aspects. But holism does its utmost to be clear that the abstraction is not "the" thing.

Traditional Systems

In contrast, our language, our science, our entire Western culture are geared toward separateness. We name a concept such as muscle injury, or strength, or fatigue, or interval training and very soon thereafter act as though we had created it as a separate entity. Similarly, traditional systems of sports training tend to divide, analyze, classify. A friend of mine describes these proponents as being impaired by hardening of the categories. They view the athlete as being strongly influenced by many factors in his environment, both physical and social, but as inherently isolated from them, and often opposed to them. They speak of conquering Nature in both its environmental and personal sense. They fight to overcome fatigue as the Englishman Hilary fought to conquer Everest.

In similar fashion, traditional systems function as though the athlete were divided into separate and often opposed parts. Workouts are planned and their effects measured primarily in terms of physical effects. It was not coincidental that the creators of the widely used system of interval training were physiologists, and that its values are measured primarily in terms of the heart and the blood capillary systems. It hardly needs to be added that the measuring instruments of how far and how fast were the steel tape and the stop-watch. After all, what instruments do we have for measuring gains in confidence or in commitment to running as an avocational way of life?

Traditional sports training systems have tended to view such traits as competitive spirit, or the will to train, as outside their direct responsibilities. A man either had or did not have such traits. That such traits, or better, such powers can be developed within the potential range of each individual by sound planning and every-day practice, just as can such powers as strength, relaxation, or coming to terms with fatigue, is· a new concept that is only beginning to gain acceptance.

Fortunately, the work of many great coaches has been broader and more sound than what they have considered to be their training system. Coaches of running like Sweden's Gosta Olander (Gunder Haegg), Australia's Percy Cerutty (Herb Elliott), or New Zealand's Arthur Lydiard (Peter Snell), have had an intuitive sense of the whole man. Cerutty wrote, "First I train the man, then his legs and heart." But in general, their efforts were intuitive, not the outgrowth of specific and deliberate planning.

The Holistic Approach

In summary, a holistic approach to sports training requires five assumptions:

(1) That there is a basic unity of the individual-situation. The individual-within-his-physical-and-social-environment is a more valid expression than to name the individual, his physical environment, and his social environment as three separate entities.

(2) That there is a basic unity of the individual. Mind-body is a more valid expression than mind and body as separate entities.

(3) That all aspects of the individual-situation which affect performance, either positively or negatively, are essential concerns of a sound system of training and *must be included in its regular planning.*

(4) That, though all are essential to maximum performance, some of these related aspects are more basic than others in influencing performance; their demands must be met first. In a country where starvation is a serious concern, or in an individual whose economic or prestige safety is threatened, sports energies are likely to be low.

(5) That, coordinate with these first four assumptions, a temporary or expedient concentration upon the "separate" individual, or upon the "separate" body, or upon the "isolated" action of an arm or leg, or upon an "isolated" will-to-achieve, as might occur in whole-part-whole learning, is both valid and essential to a sound system of training and to maximum development. To act for a time *as though* these were separate is absolutely necessary.

Unity of the Individual-Situation

A most effective example of the unity of the individual-situation can be found in the sport of swimming. Looked at casually, there seem to be at least two separate factors: the swimmer and the water in which he swims. A non-swimmer or beginner is keenly aware of this separateness. For him the water is a separate entity, a dangerous enemy which he must fight against and conquer if he is to survive at all, and he must work against its resistance if he is to progress in his swimming. In contrast, a champion swimmer comes to terms with the water, comes to accept its resistance but also its buoyancy, learns to relax physically-mentally-emotionally within an element in which he is "at home" in some ways even more than when he is within the atmosphere. In a true sense, he is "at one" with the water and uses it; he does not fight against it or attempt to conquer it.

Mind-Body Unity

The second assumption of a holistic approach to sports training is that it is a man (woman) that is active, not just a body; a man with a body-aspect to be sure, but equally a man with a mind-aspect and a motivational aspect. The ordinary coach believes that practice which is mechanically correct makes perfect. The holistic coach assumes that in addition to being mechanically correct, practice should be mentally-emotionally correct also. Brutus Hamilton, of California and head coach of the 1952 United States Olympic team, used to tell his high jumpers, "First throw your hearts over the bar, and you'll be amazed at how easily your body will follow after." When you're in for a thing "heart and soul," or "wholeheartedly" so to speak, the muscles act with much greater precision and power than when they act in isolation.

But the holistic coach also knows that the mind also has to clear the high jump bar if the body is to reach greatest heights. The mind has to look at the bar as a bar-that-can-be-cleared. But it does this subconsciously; its attention is on the jumping. If its attention is vague and diffused, the details of technique are not likely to be improved. If attention isolates an action, is too greatly concentrated (on the high throw of the lead leg, for example) then the jumper will have difficulty in even getting off the ground. A holistic approach then, would suggest the following:

(1) Assume mentally and feel in your muscles that there is a bar-higher-than-your-head-which-is-to-be-cleared;

(2) Before jumping, think and feel through, in a mind-muscle sense, the jump as a whole, including the run and all;

(3) Now feel through that special phase of the jump which you are trying to perfect;

(4) Jump in terms of this part-in-whole awareness;

(5) Immediately after landing, think-feel through the right and the wrong of what was just done.

The Need for Total Planning

It could be argued that all training systems are holistic, in that they do make provision for such life-essentials as food, rest, social relations, vocation, finances, etc. But such systems do so with little understanding of their relative importance and therefore with only occasional planning for them. Problems that should be met at their weakest point, before they arise, become exaggerated by neglect and may become crucial.

To do his best, an athlete must lose himself in the related activities of sports training and competition. There can be no reservations, no inhibitions, no hindering doubts or fears, no counter-demands of unsatisfied basic needs. This is true for sports as for all great human enterprises.

A holistic approach to training is aware of the relative potency of various human needs. When hunger is present, neither safety, nor love, nor social recognition, nor self-realization such as occurs in sports are operative. But when hunger is satisfied, the next level of need becomes dominant. These levels are not fixed nor inflexible. To judge personal safety as being invariably more potent than love or social recognition would be a conclusion hard to substantiate. But consensus probably would be that the needs satisfied by participation in sports would usually be at least secondary on such a list. Until the more basic needs are satisfied, we cannot assume that the requirements of sports training and competition will be given satisfactory consideration.

Every successful coach operates in terms of such hierarchies of human needs. They undoubtedly lie behind the American college systems of scholarships, training tables, and academic tutoring which have been so much maligned throughout the world. But the holistic-minded coach is clearer about the ways in which they are effective, and makes them an essential part of his continuous planning.

The Necessity for "Separateness"

In our society, "separateness" is absolutely essential. To deny this is to deny the values of science; in fact, to deny the values of words and thought itself. We must at times consider the "body" as though it were the entity-body; and the "mind" as though it were the entity-mind. We must perform isometric training as though it developed muscle fibers only, and interval training as though it developed the heart and capillaries directly and alone.

In so doing, however, we must maintain our awareness of the quotation marks which help to unmask the illusion and underline the "as though." As Kurt Goldstein stated so succinctly in his 1963 Preface to *The Organism*, "Biological knowledge is a form of biological being." I would add: "and must be stated in ways that are consistent with it."

BIBLIOGRAPHY

John Dewey, "The Unity of the Human Being," in *Intelligence in the Modern World*, edited by Joseph Ratner, New York: The Modern Library, 1939, pp 817-836.
Kurt Goldstein, *The Organism*, Boston: The Beacon Press, Paperback edition, 1964, 339 pages.
Kurt Goldstein, *Human Nature in the Light of Psychopathology*, New York: Schocken, Paperback edition, 1963, 251 pages.
Eugen Herrigel, *Zen in the Art of Archery*, New York: Pantheon Books, 1953, 109 pages.
Karen Horney, *The Neurotic Personality of Our Times*, New York: Norton & Company, 1937.
Wendell, Johnson, *People in Quandaries*, New York; Harper and Brothers, 1946, 532 pages.
Kurt Lewin, *Field Theory in Social Science*, edited by Dorwin Cartwright, New York: Harper & Row, Publishers, Paperback edition, 1964, 339 pages.
Abraham H. Maslow, *Motivation and Personality*, New York: Harper & Row, Publishers, 1954, 411 pages.
Gardner, Murphy, *Human Potentialities*, London: George Allen & Enwin, Ltd., 1960, 340 pages.
Alan W. Watts, *The Way of Zen*, New York: Pantheon Books, Inc., Paperback edition, 1959, 224 pages.
Roger J. Williams, *Biochemical Individuality*, New York: John Wiley & Sons, Inc., 1956, 214 pages.

The Dedication of a Building

EARL V. PULLIAS[*]

I am deeply pleased to be a part of this great occasion. This dedication is simply another step in your long effort to provide the youth of this state with the best in education. Your achievements in education are a signficant

---

[*]Based upon an address given at the dedication of the new Physical Education Building, Western Washington State College, Bellingham, Washington, March 30, 1962.

part of the great American dream for humanity — a dream which as it becomes reality may yet point the way to a much better life for all mankind.

As I have viewed this beautiful and useful building today, my mind has been moved in fancy to see the generations of young people, many yet unborn, who will work, play, and learn here. They will go into every part of the life of this commonwealth, and wherever they go, because of their experiences here they will be better prepared for their responsibilities: in homes, public service, teaching, business or elsewhere.

We are here tonight to dedicate this building — a beautiful building, but still a physical object. It is good that we should do this, but I am sure that all of us gathered here sense deeply that in reality we do something much greater than merely dedicate a building. It is the nature of all things material to grow old and decay. Fifty or at most a hundred years from now, people will walk by this spot and they will say, "What old building is that? I understand it was dedicated in the early 60's of the last century." Here I am reminded of a great poem by Shelley, which expresses vividly the passing nature of man's material achievements.

> I met a traveller from an antique land
> Who said: Two vast and trunkless legs of stone
> Stand in the desert . . . Near them, on the sand,
> Half sunk, a shattered visage lies, whose frown,
> And wrinkled lip, and sneer of cold command,
> Tell that its sculptor well those passions read
> Which yet survive, stamped on these lifeless things,
>
> The hand that mocked them, and the heart that fed:
> And on the pedestal these words appear:
> "My name is Ozymandias, king of kings:
> Look on my works, ye Mighty, and despair!"
> Nothing beside remains. Round the decay
> Of that colossal wreck, boundless and bare
> The lone and level sands stretch far away.

Certainly we do not dedicate this building in such vanity as that expressed by the ancient, prideful king. In truth, our pride in this structure rests upon our awareness that it symbolizes a noble spiritual ideal which time and usage will enrich rather than destroy.

What then is the deep, the genuine, the eternal meaning of this dedication? To answer this question, in such measure as our time and sensitivity will allow, let us do three things: (1) Sketch very briefly the central nature of our times. (2) Suggest a few of the qualities of mind and body and spirit which such times demand of us. (3) Indicate something of what Physical Education can and should do to meet these demands. In each case you will understand we must on this occasion be very brief. A sketch will suffice, for your minds inspired by this occasion will fill in the details.

1. What can we say of our times? Only three big things can be mentioned:
   a. We are in a period of deep and broad transition in every phase of human life. Some argue that the crisis of this time is little different from any other. I believe the transition through which we now pass is of the nature of three or four large transitional periods in the history of man. For example, like that when man moved from the stage of being a hunter to that of being a farmer. The changes of our times involve our concept of values and morals, of the nature of the universe, of the relations between peoples, of the necessity of work, of government. All of these concepts and others are in an unstable state and are demanding reconsideration. As Prime Minister Smuts said: "Modern man has pulled up his tent stakes and is on the march."
   b. This is a time of great and increasing tension at every level of life. Modern man seems determined to let no one rest from urgent demand. Our cities are a maelstrom of speed and pressure. Through our means of communication this spirit of urgency has spread to almost every part of man's life. From the kindergarten through the university, the steady cry is to demand more and do more. Nearly every family strives to better its condition. It often seems that the conclusion is that life is not worth living unless one is above average. Spreading over all of this urgent activity is worldwide fear and suspicion of real and imagined danger. One need not continue the picture, for it is known to all who observe. The point here is that ours is a time of tension that constantly threatens the basic health of man: the health of his body, the health of his mind, the health of his spirit.
   c. We live in a time of religious and philosophical confusion when the meaning of life is unsure; when a thousand contradictory voices scream to all of us, and especially to our young people, proclaiming the way we should go; when the temptation is great — sometimes overwhelming — to allow doubt and fear to replace faith; to permit fretful frustration and despair to grow where hope has been; to allow ugly hatred and violence to choke out the healing plant of love. Prolonged, unrelieved confusion is a poison at the very root of man's confidence in himself, in man, and in the light of God.

2. What then are the character needs of such times? What basically must we be like to make them into a new birth rather than a death for mankind? Again I select three great requirements:

   a. Faith in oneself, in mankind, and in the Infinite. Without this faith, man rapidly becomes cynical, fearful, violent, petty — a mere distorted fraction of what he can be at best. With such faith, poverty or prosperity, triumph or failure, suffering or well-being can be grist for the mill of growth — a means to the complete realization of man's full potential.

b. Health of body, mind, and spirit. These are the instruments with which we perform in life. The health of these three aspects of our natures are intricately interrelated. With health, our capabilities are almost limitless; without health, we are easy prey to evils, small or great.

c. Integrity in all phases of life. This great old term, integrity, means in essence wholeness, oneness, genuineness. The man of integrity eschews that which is false, phony, cheap, irresponsible, mean. He stands firmly and steadfastly for what his best knowledge causes him to believe is the true, the beautiful and the good. He is enlightened by continuous, humble inquiry.

In summary, my suggestion is that our times characterized by (1) rapid, far-reaching transition; (2) almost unbearable tension; and (3) unnerving confusion require (1) a steady faith in oneself, in mankind, and in God; (2) resilient vibrant health of body, mind, and spirit; and (3) integrity of character centered in the best mankind has learned about himself and the world.

Perhaps you will remember that only one point remains; then our thought together at this dedication must cease.

3. What can the activities which are related to this building do to help us become the kind of people we need for these times? It is my sincere belief that no phase of education can do more for modern man than physical education. I know this is a strong statement, but my experience of more than thirty years of studying all phases of man's nature and his education leads me to believe it to be so. Proper support of this thesis would require a volume, but again I limit myself to three or perhaps four significant contributions of physical education to the optimum education of modern man.

a. It places proper emphasis upon the whole person: upon the magnificent unity of man — indeed the unity of all of life; it teaches us to remain in close touch with nature and with the spirit of nature; it emphasizes our kinship with all men.

b. Physical education at its best keeps us in touch with reality, including ourselves: its potential, its limits, its basic laws. Its study and practice protect us from overabstraction, unreality, and pretense. It promotes the fresh directness of experience that keeps learning alive.

c. Physical education contributes to the establishment and maintenance of the basic health of man. This point cannot be further developed here, but it is fundamental to all that can be said about education.

For really mankind in genuine health can be trusted as being fully capable of the work, imagination, wisdom, and love needed for whatever problems face him. Think for a moment of what happens to life when men are sick in body, in mind, in spirit: then they befoul and destroy all they touch. Surely in our shortsightedness we will not withdraw support from these people who strive to give our youth the vision and practice of health, without which all of life becomes distorted; without which we have no chance to meet our problems creatively.

d. Physical education can give us practice in struggle, of which life is so largely made, at the level of play. Thus it perhaps can teach us to engage in that struggle as behooves wise, courageous, and good men: giving our best to every endeavor, yet with abandon and relaxation; learning to win and to lose with equal poise and grace; remembering always that the thing that counts is not whether we won or lost but how we played the game; learning a deep respect for the human body, mind, and spirit in unified action.

Therefore, we dare hope that every thought and activity carried on in this building and its related facilities will contribute (1) to our young people becoming whole men and women balanced in action and thought; (2) to their remaining in close touch with the nature, limits, and laws of reality; (3) to their conception and practice of health to the end that their bodies may be strong, their minds free and clear, and their hearts love-guided and genuine; and (4) to their playing the intricate game of life with zest, skill, and compassion.

Thus the dedication we observe is much more than the dedication of a physical building. Time will make this building, and all things physical, old and out-of-date. In truth, we dedicate ourselves anew to the highest ideals and conduct which man can envision. These things are eternal and do not perish with time.

Chapter

Foundations of
Physical Education

Philosophical Profiles for Physical Educators
D. B. Van Dalen[*]

To many physical educators, philosophy is a province for professional speculation, and is of little practical value to a teacher. When dealing with the urgencies of daily life in the classroom, they contend that one must apply good common sense, for there is no time to mull over abstract theories. But what is the nature of their "common sense?" Not uncommonly it is a haphazard collection of concepts that they have unconsciously or uncritically acquired from varied cultural contacts. Many of their practices may be surprisingly sound, but some of them may be directed toward the achievement of objectives that are philosophically incompatible. All too frequently when common sense is the criterion for determining what to do in the classroom, it boils down to doing that which requires the least effort, or that which is professionally chic at the moment, or that which current pressures for conformity demand.

Rare is the physical educator who does not long for a better sense of direction, who does not ask: "What is my purpose here? What should I be doing with and for these students?" To answer these and other related questions, he must first critically examine his basic beliefs. Not until after asking what is life all about, what is the real nature of the world, and what is of greatest significance in life, can he make discriminating decisions about what and how to teach. All of us hold certain beliefs about life, of course, but many of us may not be able to state them explicitly and may never have

[*]D. B. Van Dalen, *The Physical Educator*. Vol. 21, No. 3, October, 1964.

submitted them to sharp scrutiny. A physical educator who wishes to burst out of this cocoon of complacency can profit from examining philosophical explanations that endeavor to make our existence intelligible and meaningful and to give direction and purpose to our activities.

Philosophers are concerned with three basic problems: What is reality? What is truth? What is of value? The problem of reality (ontology) forces them to decide what is fundamental, real — what is the ultimate nature of being or existence. The problem of truth or knowledge (epistemology) makes them probe into how man arrives at knowledge and how he can be certain that it is true. The problem of value (axiology) causes them to consider the worth of things. They may, for example, give attention to ethical, aesthetic, religious, social, educational, recreational, or health values. Their basic concern is to ascertain what is good in human conduct, in social organization, and in art.

Adherents of various philosophical schools have come to somewhat different conclusions about the nature of reality, truth, and value. The *idealist* believes that ultimate reality lies in a "thinking being" — a self, mind, spirit — rather than in "physical things" — matter. Men live in a world of ideas; what they know of the physical world is what their minds have created. In contrast, the *realist* believes that reality is independent of human experience; it exists in the laws and order of nature which are neither subject to the human will nor dependent upon a human mind for their existence. The *pragmatist* contends that the only reality we know is that which we actually experience each day. He does not believe in an all-inclusive reality, an unchanging order. Reality is not something that is static or everlasting — it is an ever-changing flow of experience. The *existentialist* contends that ultimate reality resides within the individual human person. Reality is a man's own experience of being: the awareness of his moral self and his irrevocable responsibility for making choices that will fashion his essence.

How do the various philosophies differ in regard to the nature of truth or knowledge? The *idealist* believes that true knowledge consists of universals or ideals that are eternal and purposeful. Man discovers them through mental activity, insight, and intuition. The *realist* believes that true knowledge consists of the real things in the physical world — the laws and order of nature. These laws exist by themselves; they are independent of the mind and self. Man discovers them through sense perception, through scientific reasoning, through objective means that are free of any personal, emotional, or subjective approach. The *pragmatist* believes that knowledge is discovered through experience, and he questions the possible absoluteness of truth. To him, truth is a matter of consequences. If a suggested solution to a problem works in a given set of circumstances, it can be considered as truth for the time being. But, to the pragmatist, truth may change as circumstances change; what is true today may not necessarily be true tomorrow. As men gain greater insight into the world through experience, they will continue to revise and correct their knowledge. The *existentialist* does not believe that truth is forced upon him by an external or objective reality, but rather that the individual is the final court of truth. He contends that all knowledge, all intuiting, all experiencing, arise within the heart and mind of the individual and receive certification by him. Knowledge — truth — is what exists in man's consciousness and feelings as a result of his experiences and the meaning he has given to them.

How do the various philosophies differ in regard to the nature of value? To the *idealist,* the essential values of life are eternal, fixed, and man discovers them through his intellect. Sometimes man imperfectly interprets or perceives what is good or bad, beautiful or ugly, right or wrong, but the values themselves do not change. The *realist* believes that a thing is good, right, or beautiful if it conforms to the laws and order of nature, that it is evil, wrong, or ugly if it does not, and that these values are not variable. The *pragmatist* is skeptical of fixed and immutable values. He contends that value is based on human judgment. Man creates his own values through purposeful action and the interpretation of his experience. Good is that which the group discovers, works out satisfactorily in practice — not in a selfish sense, but in a social sense. To the *existentialist,* the final arbiter of what is good or beautiful is the individual. He rejects the uncritical acceptance of value systems that have been established by social, political, scientific, or theological groups, because he does not want to forfeit his essential existence — his freedom to choose. The *existentialist* looks within himself for an understanding of what is good and beautiful, and establishes his own value system. He assumes full responsibility for contributing to the moral and aesthetic essence of man, through personally deliberating about and practicing what he decides is best for himself and mankind.

The *idealist, realist, pragmatist,* and *existentialist* look upon education in light of their particular beliefs concerning reality, knowledge, and value. Consequently, they develop different, but not mutually exclusive philosophies of education. It is rather difficult to generalize concerning their beliefs because adherents of each philosophy express various shades of opinion, and members of different schools embrace similar as well as different views. In bold outline, however, eliciting answers to the following questions will tend to set these philosophies apart.[1]

First, let us ask: What is the objective of education?

---

[1]For a more detailed discussion of the relations of these philosophies to physical education, see E. C. Davis, *Philosophies Fashion Physical Education,* Dubuque, Iowa: William C. Brown Company Publishers, 1963.

The *idealist* encourages a vigorous, full development of the individual's creative powers in a manner that will bring him into harmony with the highest ideals. Seeking ever greater individual perfectability includes the development of the body and good health. This objective is placed at the bottom of the hierarchy of values, but it is considered basic for the realization of the social, moral and spiritual aims.

The *realist* does not emphasize the "self" — the individual — for he believes that reality exists in the laws and order of nature. Hence, the objective of education is to acquire verified knowledge of these laws and to mold youths so that they will live in conformity with them. The educator is to build competencies in youths that will enable them to understand and make an adequate adjustment to the real, external world.

The *pragmatist* is not interested in "absolute ideals and inexorable laws," but in the obvious realities of life — the here and now. His objective is to have students solve successfully the problems of life as they arise. He strives to stimulate a desire for continuous growth and helps students become functional members of society by providing opportunities for ever-changing experiences. In brief, he seeks many sided social efficiency.

The *existentialist* elevates the individual to a position of central prominence, for he contends that self-determination is the ultimate objective of pedagogical attention. Education is to awaken the student to a knowledge of his moral self. It is to make him understand that the responsibility for choosing what he will become and for living with what happens as a result of his decisions rests with him alone.

Secondly, let us ask: What is the nature of the student?

To the *idealist,* the student is not merely a biological organism that is shaped by the physical environment; he is a "mind, personality, soul" — a "self" whose body is responsive to his will. As Horne explains, "It is not so much the stimulus shaping the individual, as the individual responding to the stimulus."

To the *realist,* the student is a biological organism with a highly developed nervous system that interacts with the physical environment. The physical stimuli within and without the student determine his behavior — not his personal whim, his will, or blind chance.

To the *pragmatist,* the student is an active, doing organism who grows through effective interaction with the ever-changing, social-physical environment. Upon meeting problems in life situations, he proposes hypotheses and tests them to find workable solutions.

To the *existentialist,* the learner is a unique, autonomous individual who independently makes the commitments and takes the action that determines what he will be.

Third, let us ask: What is the nature of the curriculum?

The *idealist* is primarily concerned with content that consist of ideas — the humanities, but he includes physical education in the curriculum as a means of providing for the full development of the individual and the realization of an ideal society. To him, any content or activity is acceptable that acquaints students with the accumulated wisdom of the race and permits them to recreate truth, goodness, and beauty in their own thoughts, feelings, and actions.

The *realist* believes in a rigorous, systematically organized curriculum that places emphasis on the transmission and mastery of content — particularly scientific facts and principles. The contents and sequence of the curriculum are scientifically determined. The realist is primarily interested in quantitative subject matter, and the idealist is interested in qualitative subject matter.

The *pragmatist* utilizes any activity that gives students experience in applying the scientific method of solving problems. The curriculum is not a systematic structure consisting of rigid work units that are presented in a particular sequence. It may consist of related or disparate units of work and may utilize any content that will help the problem at hand. The curriculum is closely related to pupils' interests and to community and current problems; new activities are added whenever there is a need for them. Emphasis is placed on "group activities," "cooperation," "doing," "problem solving;" hence, sports and games provide an excellent medium for instruction.

The *existentialist* believes that the curriculum cannot be prefabricated for the child. Rather the child is made aware of his moral self and of a wide variety of alternatives, activities, and tools. He is absolutely free to appropriate those that will help him fulfill his unique purposes. In the existentialist curriculum, individualized activities would probably predominate. Group activities would be self-chosen. A deep conviction of the need to act with others to become the person that the individual wants to be would cause him to join or organize group activities. The objective of the group would not be to impose the will of the majority on members, but rather to help one another bring about a realization of their individual essence and develop a genuine relationship with society. The curriculum would not shield the child from the wholeness of life — it would make him aware of evil and good, the ugly and the beautiful, joy and tragedy, pain and pleasure, so that he could prepare himself to meet them squarely as a part of life.

Fourth, let us ask: What is the nature of the teacher and his methods?

To the *idealist,* the teacher is more important than facilities, equipment, or any physical "thing." He is a firm, friendly individual who thoroughly understands his subject and pupils. His personal example of wholesome, vigorous living and the attention he focuses on personalities and works of inspiring greatness stimulate students to develop their full creative powers. His pupils are surrounded with positive influences and are shielded from deleterious ones. They are provided with inviting opportunities for creative effort; challenged to put all of their powers into their performance; and given ample opportunity for discussion, self-initiative, and self-direction. Students learn — fashion their character — through making decisions, judgments, and analyses. Whenever possible interest is utilized to evoke effort, but external discipline may be employed to stimulate enough effort to cultivate interest and establish the habit of self-discipline. When evaluating pupils, the idealist is not especially concerned with quantitative assessments of the mechanics of an activity and the reproduction of specific knowledge, but rather in the changes in "self."

The *realist* rejects the idealist's subjective, personal approach to teaching. In his classes, pupils are brought into contact with the real world through demonstration, experiments, field trips, and audio-visual aids. They are exposed to clear, distinct facts in an objective and logically ordered manner and are drilled in the mastery and application of scientific principles. External discipline is utilized, if necessary. Learning proceeds inductively; it starts with elements and details and builds toward a systematic whole. When selecting equipment, grouping students, choosing teaching and administrative techniques, the realist makes decisions upon the basis of scientifically demonstrated facts. When evaluating students, he employs objective rather than subjective tests and seeks quantitative measures of achievement.

The *pragmatist* guides students so that they can find successful solutions to problems as they arise. The emphasis is placed on "how" to think rather than on "what" to think. The teacher serves as a "co-worker and co-learner" who helps students identify problems and apply the scientific method of solving them. In this socialized approach to learning, group decision making is stressed. Ample opportunity is given for the free interchange of ideas and continuous evaluation of progress. Little emphasis is placed on systematic lectures, terminal tests, and traditional coverage and organization of subject matter. The learning environment is often extended beyond the walls of the classroom. The pragmatist believes that if students tackle problems that intensely interest them, they will spontaneously put forth the effort required to seek solutions. Consequently, the teacher will neither have to lure them with external rewards or have to serve as a drill master or moralizer.

The *existential* teacher is not a transmitter of information, nor a director of projects, nor a model to imitate. He is a provocateur of thought who awakens the child to the moral dimensions of life. Through posing moral and intellectual questions, he causes a student to think seriously about who he is, what he is in the world for, and what he should make of his life. The existential teacher establishes an intimate, exploratory communion with the student in which an atmosphere of free association prevails. After getting the student authentically concerned about moral issues and encouraging him to search for facts, to examine alternatives, and to consider probable consequences, he strictly refrains from prescribing a course of action. The student is required to make his own choices in light of what he thinks man ought to be and is held strictly accountable for what happens as a result of his decisions. The existentialist sees little value in traditional testing procedures that are based on group norms and that measure prescribed subject matter.

This brief summary of selected philosophical concepts and their relationship to education suggests how some of the most profound and productive minds of the past two thousand years have grappled with the problem of helping man understand the awesome cosmos. By delving more deeply into this invaluable intellectual heritage, a physical educator can start on a long, rigorous, and rewarding pilgrimage of thought and criticism. As he re-examines his beliefs and teaching practices and strives to clarify his philosophy of life and education, many questions will arise: "How did he come to accept a belief? Is it ambiguous? Is it defensible? Does it conflict with other of his beliefs? Are some of his basic beliefs and teaching practices inconsistent? How can he eliminate contradictions and conflicts?" By applying philosophical methods, the physical educator can remove some of the perplexities that arise when he attempts to say systematically and clearly what he is doing in education and why.

Inquiring into the nature of his beliefs, appraising his teaching practices in light of what they imply about his beliefs, weighing whether his beliefs and practices are worth retaining or need to be revised will be a disturbing but an exhilarating experience. The physical educator may decide that one school of philosophical thought is most compatible with his beliefs and provides the most meaningful insights for clarifying his educational problems and directing his professional life. On the other hand, he may find that his beliefs do not fit into the straight jacket fashioned by any of the existing philosophical approaches. Becoming familiar with views of the world and concepts of the purpose of education that others have developed in detail and have submitted to rigorous examination should sharpen his critical consciousness, but blindly accepting beliefs, standards, and practices that others impose upon him cannot be condoned. A physical educator must engage in a never ending personal quest to clarify and to coordinate the concepts that constitute his personal act of commitments. Building, broadening, and deepening his own philosophy of physical education, eliminating inconsistencies, and developing the capacity to articulate his ideas to others is a professional responsibility of the highest order.

The Contributions of Physical Activity to Social Development
Charles C. Cowell*

We socialize our pupils or contribute to their social learnings when they learn the ways of the group, become functioning members of it, act according to its standards, accept its rules, and in turn become accepted by the group. We socialize youth by helping them acquire social experiences, social habits, and social relationships. Our interest is in the development of the social phases of personality, attitudes, and values by means of games, sports, and related activities.

Thoughtful people agree that emotional and social learnings are important, for real education is an emotional and social as well as an intellectual experience, and that there must be an effective curriculum for personal-social education that parallels and often intertwines the academic curriculum. The direction for improving social education demands the utilization of insights and studies from many disciplines from which health education, physical education, and recreation draw their basic principles. We must, therefore, look not only to the research and thoughtful study of specialists in the areas of biology, psychology, and medicine, but also to the social sciences of sociology, cultural anthropology, and social psychology.

We can be scientific in our respective fields to the extent that we employ intelligent and persistent endeavors to revise current beliefs, weed out error, improve upon the accuracy of our beliefs, and search for the significant relationships between facts drawn from the several disciplines previously mentioned. The *method,* not the content, defines the body of knowledge as a science. Physical education, health education, and recreation become scientific to the extent to which we apply the scientific method to the phenomena that are their subject matter.

There must be some cause and effect laws in the way human beings behave just as there are cause and effect laws in the way steel, rubber, or the atom behaves. Where do we look for these principles? The behavioral sciences provide possibilities by honest, exhaustive, intelligent, interdisciplinary searching for facts and their meaning or implications with reference to any given problem in our field.

In the area of psychosocial development it is exceedingly difficult to establish functional relationships between numerous variables involved. This makes the task of validating causative explanations of individual behavior a terrifically challenging and difficult one.

*Charles C. Cowell, "The Contributions of Physical Activity to Social Development," *Research Quarterly*. Vol. 31, No. 2, Part II, May, 1960.

It is hoped that the numerous studies drawn from the several disciplines attempting to show the effects of physical activity upon the personal and social adjustment of people will be examined with careful scrutiny and realization of the paucity of significant definitive research which bears on this important problem of the social dividends of education.

Social Development in a Culture

Culture consists of the things that we have learned to do, to make, to believe, to value, and to enjoy in our lifetime. Our culture expresses the basic values of our society. The forces which interact on the playing fields, in the gymnasium, and elsewhere provide for children a steady flow of motivations and feelings which gradually shape the personality. In the sense that we as teachers have a part in controlling or influencing to some extent these factors in our culture, we become guardians and developers of personality by influencing the dominant attitudes and goals of that part of our culture related to games, sports, and recreation in general.

Four investigators related interest and participation in sports to social values and learning in children.

Thrasher (97), in the study of city boys' gangs, indicated that physical prowess is an important factor in group leadership, but not essential. Boys physically deficient received positions of leadership by traits of "daring, decisiveness, and brains."

Hawkes (46), using an inventory entitled "making choices," found that boys (grades 4-6) placed friendship, excitement and recreation, and family life at the top of the rank order and valued least privacy, power and control, and recognition. Girls (same grades) valued friendship, family life and excitement, and recreation in descending order. At the base of the rank order they placed physical freedom, recognition, and power and control.

Dennis (28), comparing American, Armenian, Arab, and Jewish children in Lebanon, found that American children were rewarded with praise for performing in sports and games three times more frequently than were the Arab and Jewish groups. He pointed out that the kinds of behavior being rewarded played a role in the socialization of the child.

Broer and Holland (16) found that college women recognized the social values of physical education. Of some 1115 freshmen and sophomore women who responded to an interests and needs questionnaire, 83.5 percent checked "to have fun," 56 percent "to make new friends," 42.3 percent "to learn to control myself and be a good sport," 40 percent "to get along with and understand other people," 22.2 percent "to feel that I belong to a group." Co-educational class activities which had a strong social and dating element headed the list.

Social Psychology

It is well known that participants of a culture or in a group take on the existing values or norms of the group. A democratic "climate" produces democratic values, and a sportsmanlike "climate" produces attitudes of sportsmanship. We perceive these situations in terms of the norms we bring from the group situation. We deal here with the role of suggestion in the formation of attitudes.

Using parent rating and child behavior rating scales, Baldwin (4) found that democratically raised children were more active, were more extroverted (friendly and hostile), and were favored in their group. They rated high in intellectual curiosity, originality, and constructiveness. The variable "indulgence" seemed to produce the opposite effects of democracy.

Sherif (84) found that individual subjects tended to be strongly influenced by others in the group, the degree of influence being effected by the prestige and leadership qualities of certain group members. His findings have implications for values stressed in games and sports, for major attitudes are derived from groups to which we relate ourselves or of which we regard ourselves as members.

Dunker (30) found it feasible to influence nursery school children's food preferences through social suggestion. After determining the children's preferences and their tendency to imitate others, stories were told to present certain foods in an attractive light and other foods in an unattractive light. Sixty-seven percent of the children in the experimental group chose the food presented as attractive against only 13 percent of the children in the control group. Implications may be drawn for seeking character education outcomes through play situations.

Symonds (94), studying normal adolescent boys and girls, concluded that the greatest need of these adolescents was opportunity for social participation and that the greatest personality handicap was social isolation. Physical education and recreation activities were indicated.

Kight (52), Stone (91), and Lifshitz and Sakoda (62) have drawn conclusions concerning camping experiences in the changing of social attitudes and in meeting social and emotional needs of children and adolescents.

School and Teacher as Social Forces

The school represents a social structure and system of its own — of students, teachers, administrators, and service personnel. In the various social sub-groups which are constantly forming and reforming, pupils get to fill social roles in many different groups, such as classes, clubs, athletic teams, orchestras, student councils, and a host of others. The experiences in these various groups provide the social and psychological settings and conditions for the development of many aspects of social learning — knowledges, attitudes, skills, and values. The teacher and administrator must find ways in which all participants relate themselves to one another so that new social learnings result not only in greater social integration and efficiency but also in individual satisfaction of needs.

Several studies highlight the influence of the classroom climate. Lewin and his associates (60) found that autocratic situations produced tension, individual hostility, and less stability in the group structure whereas in the democratic situation there was greater constructiveness and a stronger feeling of group property and group goals.

Pressey and Hanna (75) compared two classes, one operated in the traditional manner, the other in a more or less permissive manner which encouraged social interaction. Students in the social interaction class knew the names of more of their classmates than in the traditional class. Obviously, proper social atmosphere is essential for social contracts.

Nedelsky (70) indicated that the child's first social world is his family; he then shifts to a world in which his orientation grows out of being a part of a group of other children whom he accepts as equals. The school then becomes the social system which is an important setting in which children relate to one another.

Swensen and Rhulman (93), in analyzing questionnaire responses from 1217 university sophomore men and women concerning many aspects of their extracurricular activities, found that the four chief reasons for participating were (in rank order) relaxation, working with people, professional reasons, and opportunities for service. The highest percentage of participation in campus activities was in social living groups (dormitories, fraternities, etc.). Athletic events were the most popular spectator-type activities.

Todd (99), in a sociometric study on the senior high school level, demonstrated the value of the democratic method of physical education class management by objective data showing greatly increased acquaintanceship and significant decrease in the number of unpopular and unwanted girls during a one-semester experimental period. Anonymous questionnaires revealed that the pupils found the sociometrically selected squads more enjoyable and efficient than any other grouping method they had ever experienced.

McGuire and Clark (65) reported upon two alternative indexes of peer status that have been recently developed. The two forms seem to approximate essential aspects of the level of acceptance of subjects in classroom groupings and in age-mate societies. It appears that level of acceptance could be a variable for distinguishing and identifying individuals and sub-groups in a population for further study.

Two studies report the social influence of the teacher. Leeds (59) found that the personality characteristics of the teacher affect the social and emotional development and adjustment of children. Comments as to why pupils liked or did not like certain teachers indicated that affective, personal, and human factors provided the basis for differentiating between well-liked and disliked teachers. Witty (113) analyzed 12,000 letters from children and adolescents describing "the teacher who helped me most." All teacher personality attributes which tended to bolster the security and self-esteem of the pupils were valued highly. Praise and recognition, kindliness, fairness, sense of humor, interest in pupil's problems, and similar qualities were prominent, and these attributes markedly affected the personality development of pupils.

Social Development

Much social interaction centers around physical skill. The child lacking motor skills is often barred or not accepted in social participation. Human personality cannot be developed apart from the social group and since our children are destined to live in a highly organized social order, the physical activities of children and youth should be used progressively from kindergarten through high school to develop social learnings and a gradual intensification of social consciousness.

The social implications of play and sports are revealed in several studies. Foehrenbach (35), when inquiring into the social motives operating to make high school girls participate in after-school sports, found that "going with the crowd" and "imitation of older girls" were prominent in the thinking of junior high school girls, while "making new friends" was a stronger motive for senior high school girls. "Fear of failure to do well" kept about one-sitxh of the junior high girls from participating, and the fact that they had no friends who were participating restrained one in ten.

Bunker (17) studied 50 male college students active in physical education and sports and 50 who tended to be inactive in these activities. Histories indicated that participation in team games by the "actives" was consistently greater through the upper grades than for the "inactives." While 64 percent of the actives reported that the greater part of their daily play as children was in neighborhood groups, only 36 percent of the inactives so reported. Bunker concluded that the bases for active participation must be laid in the elementary grades.

Shugart (85), while a psychiatric case worker in the receiving ward of a large neuropsychiatric service in a naval hospital, invariably found histories of meager play experiences in men being referred to the hospital. Patients experienced lack of interest in play as children, and deficiencies therein were evident in both quantity and quality. Further study, elsewhere, of the play histories of 60 psychotic children showed that these children had suffered serious deficiencies which assumed characteristic forms of expression.

Studies of the holding power of secondary schools have revealed that extracurricular activities are important means of keeping students in school. Thomas (96) studied high school drop-outs and discovered "that not one person who dropped out before completing the third year had engaged in even one activity, and that 89 percent of those who finished, had." Since intramural and interscholastic athletics are administered as student activities in practically all high schools, it can be seen that few drop-outs participated in sports activities.

Gough (38) used four high school senior classes in his study. Students who had a high number of extracurricular activities seemed to be characterized as: (a) frank, unpretentious; (b) self-disciplined, but tolerant of others; (c) broader cultural and intellectual interests; (d) identification with and acceptance by the group; (e) possessed effective social skills; and (f) optimistic, with higher levels of drive and energy.

Wells (110) administered a 38-item battery of physical fitness tests and Cattell's 16 Personality Factor Inventory to 80 male college students. Dynamic strength related negatively to personality traits described as emotional, tense, and withdrawn; and positively with traits described as being less anxious, less emotional, more poised, and less unsure. Various body measurement variables were found to relate significantly to many personality traits.

Comparing academically successful and unsuccessful children, Volberding (105) found that the child considered most likely to succeed is more intelligent, better adjusted socially and personally, more interested in active play, prefers play in competitive groups, attends movies less often, and listens to radio more frequently.

Latham (57) classified 837 junior high school boys according to level of sexual maturity. They were classified by their teachers, also, into three leadership categories — elective, appointive, and athletic. Athletic leaders were found to be sexually more mature than their contemporaries who led in nonathletic activities. None of the other categories of leaders showed clear discrimination of the mature from immature boys.

Jones and Bayley (50, 51) reported that late maturing boys ranked relatively well until the middle of junior high school in social behavior and related personal attributes. Then they tended to drop to a lower level. Early maturing boys became student leaders in high school. Boys maturing late were mostly below average in Espenschade's test of motor ability; early maturers were unusually large and superior in strength and skill.

Duffy (29) studied 16 nursery school children, age 2 years, 11 months to 3 years, 10 months. His observations suggested a possible correlation between muscle tension and various aspects of behavior, such as number of physical contacts in free play, number of words used, degree of restlessness, and degree of inattention.

Resnick (79) studied the relation of high school grades to satisfactory adjustment as judged by scores on several standardized inventories and found that pupils earning the higher grades also secured the highest mean satisfactory adjustment scores. In general, categories related to adjustment in relation to other pupils, to social competency, social participation, satisfying work, recreation and interpersonal skills were significantly in favor of the student with higher honor point ratios.

Reaney (78) tested more than 600 boys and girls on their ability to play certain games (they were also found to be leaders of these games). It was found that the children who were best at playing games were also superior in intelligence and general ability.

From a larger group of normal children, Rarick and McKee (77) selected for investigation 20 third graders. Ten had a high level of motor achievement and the other 10 a low of motor achievement. Though a small number of cases were observed, those children who attained a high level of motor proficiency tended to be more frequently well adjusted in school and personal relationships. Also they appeared to have fewer irregularities and difficulties in infancy and early childhood.

Partridge (73) studied factors of leadership in six different Boy Scout troops totaling 226 boys by using a "five-man-to-man" plan of rating. He found that outstanding leaders excelled others in age, intelligence, athletic ability, scout rank, scout tenure, and physique.

Betz (7) found low but significant relationships between several physical fitness test variables of adult men participating in an afternoon adult physical fitness class and certain personality traits as determined by Catell's 16 Personality Factor Inventory items.

Antisocial Behavior

Children's insecurities and frustrations show up directly or symbolically in their free play. The aggressive, destructive, unsocial, or antisocial attitudes are acted out in play. As professionally mature physical educators, health educators, and recreation specialists we must try to decipher the real meaning of these activities as sensitive indicators of personality development. We must try to structure play situations that will facilitate release and expression of impulses, feelings, and fantasies. Games and sports often become substitute responses which redirect behavior and satisfactorily reduce the original instigation by satisfying emotional and social needs.

Frank (36) states:

Sometimes a child who is outwardly apathetic or seemingly withdrawn may, in a congenial and encouraging play situation, emerge with increasingly spontaneous participation, as if waiting for such a favorable opportunity to escape from his own self-imposed restriction. Similarly, an aggressive, destructive child in a play situation offering little opportunity or provocation may discover new ways of relating himself to others through more cooperative play. Children, and especially those "withdrawn" and those over-aggressive, may need to translate their private world and feelings into play situations, to make these more or less "objective" outside themselves, so they can deal with them, and begin to alter and revise them toward the patterns of the consensual world.

Hambridge (42) illustrates how structured play therapy enables child and therapist to bring energy to bear where it will count. The therapist acts to focus attention, to stimulate further activity, to give approval, to gain information, to interpret, or to set limits. The structured play situation is used as a stimulus to facilitate the independent, creative free play of the child in treatment.

In tracing the evolution of play therapy, Lebo (58) concludes that if play therapy had developed solely from the theoretical explanations of play it would be used to educate children to play properly.

Bernstein (6) asserts that play is a natural means of expression for the child and can be clinically useful in diagnosis, therapy, and research. Play may diminish anxiety in children and be helpful in evaluating the need for psychiatric help.

Cox (27), in studying sociometric status and individual adjustment before and after play therapy, found that sociometric status was shown to be an effective index of adjustment for a group of 52 orphans, aged 5 to 13 years. The findings supported the theory that the sociometric status is a sensitive and valid index of behavioral change.

Chittenden (21) used play situations as a means of helping children get a better understanding of their own problems and as a means of finding whether they gained in understanding. Play was used also as a means of direct teaching of manners and techniques that would help children to avoid quarrels.

Shaw (83) found that an inconsistent or conflicting environment retards the development of socially sanctioned behavior. He showed quite dramatically the influence of the group, or small segment of society and its mores, upon the attitude and behavior of individuals.

Wattenberg (108) noted that in any group of full-fledged delinquents, the first signs of behavior difficulties appear in later childhood, often before the age of ten. For eleven year olds, poor school performance and gang activities are strongly related. Frustrations met in school may have led to hostile feelings which were vented in destruction of property or fighting. The author suggests that for those who failed in efforts to earn social recognition in sports or scholarship, daring deeds of theft and bravado may have been a compensation.

Thomas (95) described the experimental use of the summer camp as part of a remedial program for juvenile delinquents.

Personal-Social Adjustment

Adjustment is the dynamic process by which organisms meet their needs. Physical education and related activities satisfy many of these needs by siphoning off dammed-up tensions in wholesome and socially acceptable ways. If satisfied in opposite ways, neurotic or delinquent behavior may be the result. Studies reveal that socially well-adjusted persons tend to be more successful in athletics, physical fitness, and physical education activities than are persons who are less well adjusted socially.

Jones (49), Hardy (44), and Wenger (111) found some relationship between muscular function and social adjustment. In Jones' study, subjects with high strength scores were rated high in popularity and social prestige and were well adjusted, whereas subjects with low strength scores had social difficulties, inferiority feelings, and personality maladjustment. Hardy found substantial positive correlations between being esteemed by one's classmates and leadership, health, cooperation, I.Q., and E.Q., and between general behavior traits and school attitudes, muscular strength, and physical achievement. Wenger found positive correlations which confirmed the hypothesis that individual differences in characteristic level of muscular tension in skeletal musculature are positively related to differences in (a) frequency of overt muscular activity, (b) speed of movement, (c) emotional behavior and instability of response, (d) aggressiveness, and (e) irritability.

Reynolds (80) found an r of .414 (significant at the 1% level) between scores on the Cowell Personal Distance Ballot and performance on the Purdue Motor Fitness Test, using preadolescent boys as subjects.

Several investigators related social adjustment to physical education performance. Cowell (26) found that social adjustment ratings by teachers and by classmates were positively and significantly related to physical education grades. Breck (14) found correlations ranging from .27 to .90 between choice of friends and skill ratings in activity classes at the University of California, Los Angeles, with those selected as desirable friends having the higher skill ratings.

Using a rating scale for measuring character and personality of persons in physical education classes, Blanchard (9) found that desirable character and personality traits are stimulated by participation in physical education activities. Walsh (106) reported that girls whom others seek as teammates and playing companions seem to be the ones who can perform well in physical activities. Edwards (31) found that performance in the Cowell Athletic Aptitude Test correlated .389 with the Partridge Leadership Ballot, and .371 with the Cowell Personal Distance (Acceptance) Ballot. These correlations, obtained with preadolescent faculty sons, were significant at the 1 percent level of confidence. Also using the Cowell Personal Distance Ballot, Stover (92) found a correlation of .661 between this measure of social acceptance and a 12-item battery of physical achievement.

Another group of studies revealed a relationship between athletic achievement and social adjustment. McKinney (66) found that well-adjusted college students tended to be more athletic, to be more interested in the opposite sex, to participate more in extracurricular activities, and to be of a social nature. Brace (13) found a marked relationship between athletic ability and social status among pupils in grades 6 through 9.

Henry (47) obtained a positive correlation between general athletic ability and favorable attitudes about physical education. The correlation was highest in performances demanding extreme sustained physical exertion and lowest with agility and coordination. Similarly, Biddulph (8) found that students ranking high in athletic achievement showed a significantly greater degree of personal and social adjustment than students ranking low in athletic achievements.

Sperling (88) and Signorella (86) found differences in adjustment between athletes and nonathletes. Sperling found athletes to be more extroverted and ascendant. Signorella found that differences in amount of athletic participation were moderately related to scores on the Cowell Social Adjustment Index.

Zeleny (114) indicated that researchers on leadership are in practically unanimous agreement that leaders are superior to nonleaders in intelligence, scholarship or knowledge, vitality, social adaptability, and athletic ability. Stogdill's (90) summary of leadership research to 1947 found height, weight, energy and health, and especially athletic prowess all associated with leadership.

Reputation of youngsters among their peers has been related to social adjustment by three investigators. Scandrette (81) compared classroom choice status of eighth graders with scores on the California Test of Personality and found that the four components which significantly differentiated the two groups were sense of personal worth, sense of personal freedom, feeling of belonging, and freedom from withdrawing tendencies — all more characteristic of the higher status group. Bonney (10) found, at the sixth-grade level, that among children frequently chosen as playmates there was more "in-group" feeling whereas among children infrequently chosen as playmates there was little acceptance of each other. The rejected children were those considered to be poor playmates.

Tuddenham (104) pointed out that the Reputation Test can be used to reveal problems for social maladjustments much earlier than they are ordinarily detected by adult observers. The test diagnoses a child's social adjustment to his peers.

Comparing "fringers" with "active" junior high school boys, Cowell (22) found that fringers were less acceptable, socially, to other boys and girls as compared with actives and were deemed less able to fill school positions.

Studying students' objectives in physical education, Schurr (82) found that 450 freshman high school girls most want to learn to get along with and understand others, to learn to control emotions and be a good sport, and to learn to lose graciously.

Sociometrics

Sociometrics is the study of the patterned relationships between members of groups. Data from such studies enable us to try to understand and adjust those currents of influence that unite or separate the individual members of any group. Health, strength, and physique determine to a great extent what, and especially how well, a child plays. Play skills, in turn, are of major importance in companionship and friendship in the social relationship of children. The physically excellent child has opportunity to lead in games and to learn thereby the very important techniques of leadership and co-operation.

Many studies demonstrate that athletic prowess contributes to social status. Tuddenham (103) applied the Reputation Test to boys and girls in grades 1, 3, and 5. He found that athletic competence, daring, and leadership were sources of prestige for boys, while attractiveness and demure friendliness were important for girls. Tryon (102) found that in middle adolescence social excitement is directed toward the athletic leader or one whose physical, dramatic, social, or intellectual skills give status. McGraw and Tolbert (63) reported a moderately high relationship between sociometric status and athletic ability in almost all groups of junior high school boys in a school in Texas. Kuhlen and Lee (55) studied 700 children in grades 6, 9, and 12. They found that those most acceptable were judged more frequently to be popular, cheerful, happy, enthusiastic, friendly, and those who would enjoy jokes and initiate games and activities.

Todd (100) states that squads chosen on the basis of sociometric information are likely to produce happy, cooperative work and play. Furfey (37) showed that when boys selected chums, physical development had a larger correlation with companionship than did intelligence.

Flowtow (34) and Ondrus (72) both found that members of athletic teams had higher social status than others not able to make the team. Along somewhat the same lines, Marks (67) pointed out that boys with higher sports scores were more sociable than those with lower sports scores. This indicates the social stimulus value of strength and physical ability among adolescent boys. However, at the sixth grade level, Austin and Thompson (3) found that being "skillful in games" was sixteenth on the list of reasons for choosing someone as a friend. In another study of reasons for choosing friends, Williams (112) found that among adolescents such items as "full of fun," "fair and square," "good sport," "athlete," and the like were prominent.

Bretsch (15) further verified that sports participation is related to social skills and activities of adolescents which distinguish socially accepted from unaccepted adolescents.

Wellman (109) found that differences in size, strength, and health seemed to be more important factors in social adjustment than are moderate differences in intelligence. With quite similar findings, Bower (12) pointed out that popularity was unrelated to intelligence, height, home ratings, or school achievement but was significantly related to strength and to physical ability.

Lieb (61) in pre-Nazi Germany found that both boys and girls mentioned physical superiority most frequently as a basis for leadership.

Success in the classroom and social status were investigated in three studies. Gronlund and Whitney (40) showed that sociometric status in the classroom is a fairly reliable index of a pupil's general social acceptability among his peers. Buswell (18) concluded from her study of a classroom of boys and girls in the early and upper grades that in general those who are succeeding in their school work will also be succeeding in their social relationships with their peers. Bonney and Powell (11), studying first graders, found that the highly acceptable differed from those sociometrically low by smiling more frequently; engaging in some form of cooperative, voluntary group participation; and making more voluntary contributions to their groups. They were also less likely to be alone during free play or activity periods.

Two investigators studied drop-outs and social status. Kuhlen and Collester (54) found that drop-out was related to such factors as health, unhappiness, and a sense of lack of status. Kuhlen and Bretsch (53) found that those who dropped out of school were less acceptable socially to their classmates and were judged by their classmates to possess traits of personal and social maladjustment.

Activity Preference, Physique, and Personality Characteristics

Studies of personality and somatotyping suggest that there are fundamental types which influence choice of physical activities. These findings have implications for planning physical education on an individual basis.

Thune (98) conducted a study to discover some of the differences in attitudes and personality traits which may exist between weight lifters and other active team sport athletes. He found that training with weights appeals to a certain personality group. Weight lifters tended to be strong and dominant individuals who received more satisfaction in winning an individual championship than being a member of a winning team. They definitely disliked traditional sports.

Hanley (43) reported on the relationship between body type and reputation as measured by a reputation test of the "who's who" type among two groups of boys, ages 16-20. Boys of mesomorphic (athletic) build were described as "good at games," "real boy," "takes chances," and "leadership." Ectomorphic boys were "bashful," "untidy," "not quarrelsome," "admissive."

Personality was found to be a factor in selecting physical activities by Flanagan (33). Results indicated that fencers seemed to be more dominant, more feminine, and more extroverted than those engaged in badminton, basketball, volleyball, boxing, and swimming. Volleyball players seemed to be more submissive, more introverted, and less emotionally stable.

Nelson (71) studied the personality and attitude differences of those who chose ROTC in preference to the physical education program. The military students were less in favor of physical activity and competition, and displayed a withdrawing disposition in social situations. They preferred organized uniformed groups and had a more favorable attitude toward authority and position.

Cabot (19), in studying the relationships between characteristics of personality and physique in adolescents, found that a good physique disposes boys to develop traits of self-expression, social acceptability, and physical vitality.

An analysis of data covering ten years at the United States Military Academy by Appleton (2), revealed significant positive relationships between physical ability of cadets at the time of entrance and the criterion of success or failure to graduate from the Military Academy.

Ragsdale (76) compared 45 women physical education majors and 45 non-majors in the ratings given by high school principals. The two groups were equal in appearance, manners, and purposeful use of time. The physical education group was superior in leadership and initiative, and more of this group displayed a high degree of emotional control.

Bayer and Reichard (5) reported that somatic androgyny indicates a relationship between physique and certain psychological reaction patterns.

Social Mobility

The social mechanism called social mobility involves many factors which become social sifting devices for selecting, promoting, or demoting individuals and distributing them in terms of social class. Athletic sports and games, as common denominators, bring youth from various socioeconomic levels together on a common basis. The athlete in school tends to become more socially mobile than the nonathlete and, other things being equal, has greater opportunity to achieve upward social mobility.

Annarino (1) found a critical ratio of 9.0 favoring greater campus social mobility for Purdue athletes as reflected by their dating girls in socioeconomic levels superior to their own.

La Place (56) studied personality traits in relation to success in professional baseball. Results indicated that major league players were better able than minor league players to apply their strong drive toward a definite objective, to adjust to occupations requiring social contact or the ability to get along with others, and to exercise initiative.

Popp (74) had five administrators and teachers select ten boys "most nearly like sons they would like to have" and ten boys "least like sons they would like to have." Of the boys who fell into the desirable category, 69 percent had high PFI's; of the boys in the undesirable category, 75 percent had low PFI's.

Cowell (25), in a study of 1400 boys and girls in grades 7 to 12, indicated that the purposes students try to satisfy in physical education change with the process of maturation but "mastery of game skills," "to have fun," and to "learn to control myself and be a good sport," are strong in both sexes. Muscular development is strong for boys at all levels but is a fairly strong purpose with girls only at ages 12 and 13. Social purposes related to submerging one's ego for the good of the team, "to be with my friends," and "to get along with and understand others" are well up in the upper half in the ranking of student purposes by both sexes.

Cowell, Daniels, and Kenney (24) studied the purposes that 500 male first-year college students endeavored to fulfill by means of physical education activities. The students considered that purposes such as "to learn to control myself and be a good sport," "to make new friends," "to feel that I belong to a group," and "to get along and understand other people," had the same index of strength as the purpose "to develop strong muscles."

Social Integration

An integrated social group is one in which there is a great deal of social interaction within the group and people are bound together by such organizational bonds as common goals and purposes. A good team and a good school as miniature societies illustrate integrated social groups. The quantity and quality of friendships developed by students in a physical education class or on an athletic squad should be a concern of a good teacher. They are also personal concerns of students. In a well-integrated social group each individual would tend to accept every other individual in the group at a close personal distance.

Trapp (101) revealed in his study the evidence of social integration possible in a college football squad. The process of social integration in the team, as a whole, was positive and continuous throughout the season. There was an increase of social acceptance of the freshman by the seniors. There was a positive and continuous process of social integration between the members of the freshman class. The only subgroups showing an increase in social distance between them were the fraternity members and the independents within the squad. As the season progressed, a decrease in social distance between the linemen was apparent. The backfield men were drawn closer to the lineman in personal distance as the process of social integration proceeded. Skubic (87) used 326 freshmen and sophomore women in physical education classes in her study. She reported that by placing emphasis on students becoming acquainted with each other as soon as possible, the volume of social interaction over a period of six weeks almost doubled in all cases, regardless of the type of activity.

Gustad (41), in summarizing the research literature dealing with factors associated with social adjustment and maladjustment, noted that those participating in social activities tended to have fewer significant scores on adjustment inventories and to exhibit less maladjustment. They were generally more extroverted, stable, and dominant than nonparticipants. Participation in extracurricular activities was associated, also, with above average academic achievement. This was complicated by the fact that social leaders tended also to be brighter than the average student. There was no evidence that a reasonable amount of extracurricular activity affected grades.

Erwee (32) found a positive statistical relationship between employee participation in the sports activities of a large industrial plant and the merit ratings of supervisors. The merit ratings were based on aspects of dependability, accuracy, efficiency, safety, and social adjustment.

Cowell (23) found that some of the outstanding social traits which homeroom teachers, physical-education teachers, and special observers ascribed to actives and which differentiated between junior high school boys who participated wholeheartedly in the activities of the physical education program and those who did not were "unembarrassed and at home in a crowd," "talkative and active," "gave considerable leadership to the group," "a good mixer," "seems to like and seek social contacts," and other social behaviors indicative of satisfactory adjustment.

Cavanaugh (20) concluded that students who were well adjusted as measured by the Neurotic Tendency Scale of the Bernreuter Personality Inventory tended to participate in more recreational sports activities and had more hobbies than their fellow students who indicated neurotic tendencies. These relationships were somewhat closer for men than for women.

Walters (107) presented an analysis of the change in social adjustment of motivated and nonmotivated groups in a seven-week bowling class. The results seem to indicate that though both groups became more socially adjusted as a result of group participation and acquaintance, the motivated group became better adjusted than the nonmotivated. The good bowlers seemed to be better accepted socially.

Aggression and Competition

A cooperative school social situation is one in which the goal will be possible of attainment by individual pupils only if all individuals can also attain the goal. Conversely, a competitive school situation exists when the goal is reached by an individual or a limited number of individuals and the rest of the pupils will be unable to attain it. Uniquely, sports and games involve *both* competition and cooperation based on a system of values or rules of conduct which guide the behavior of players.

May and Doob (68) related cooperation and competition to personality and culture. By the use of experimental problems, they came to certain theories or propositions. American children work more effectively in competitive than in cooperative situations. The individual will compete or cooperate if he feels he can achieve his level of aspiration. In a cooperative situation, the presence of an outside competing group changes the social form of the behavior and the performance of the cooperators.

Greenburg (39) studied the growth of the competitive impulse in the use of building stones. A well-defined and orderly course seemed to be apparent. Children two to three years old showed no competition. The child discovered himself in relation to the material and was interested in functioning with that material. The age group three to four years showed some competition and a little better idea of excelling: the child discovered the other child and was more interested in the social relationship than in the competitive situation. At four to six years of age, the child showed a desire to excel and thus compete. Competition was greatest with the group six to seven years of age. There was increased critical judgment along with the competitive spirit.

Stendler and his associates (89) studied cooperation and competition of second graders through the painting of a mural. In cooperation, every child was to get a prize if the mural was done well. Under competition, they were told that only the best painter would receive a prize. Painting sessions and subsequent play session were observed. Results showed that positive inter-actions were below negative interactions under individual reward conditions. Subsequent play of the children did not appear to be affected by the experi-mental conditions.

Johnson and Hutton (48) tested eight college wrestlers with a personality test under three conditions. The first was before a wrestling season, the second four to five hours before the first intercollegiate match of the season, and the third the morning after the competition. Several group tendencies re-vealed were decrement of functioning intelligence, increased aggressive feel-ings, and increased neurotic signs in the before-match condition.

Problems of Future Research

The problem of selecting, evaluating, and interpreting current research in social learning and social development resulting from physical education and related areas has been solved with considerable arbitrariness and there are many gaps. Many existing sources are omitted due to lack of space and the fact that they lie hidden away in many related disciplines such as child development, social psychology, sociology, cultural anthropology, and similar behavior sciences. We need an interdisciplinary approach — cooperative research.

Too much meaning has been read into test scores and behavior profiles without enough attention being given to finding out what such scores and ratings actually mean. We need more quantitative rather than descriptive research to assist more intelligently in the personality, character, and social development of children and youth and enable us to identify more clearly the important factors contributing to socialization.

A few problem areas and needs are here identified.

1. More definitive diagnosis of play behavior and a deeper understand-ing of the psychology of play.

2. Quantification of projective psychological tests involving play tech-niques.

3. A realistic approach to the casual factors of delinquency.

4. Social and psychological diagnosis of our present culture patterns related to games and sports in order to see what happens when children are pushed into excessive competition before they are emotionally and physically ready for it.

5. More research in the relationships of play, physical education, and recreation experiences to the psychosocial development of people.

6. Simplification of sociometric techniques and a wider use of these in physical education.

7. The study and use of play histories in understanding personality de-velopment and the etiology of mental illness.

REFERENCES

1. Annarino, Anthony A. *The Contribution of Athletics to Social Mobility.* Master's thesis. Lafayette, Indiana: Purdue University, 1951.
2. Appleton, Lloyd O. "The Depth Dimension of Physical Fitness." *Sixty-Second Annual Proceedings.* Washington, D. C.: College Physical Education Association, 1958.
3. Austin, Mary C., and Thompson, G. G. "Children's Friendship Study of the Bases on Which Children Select and Reject Their Best Friends." *Journal of Educational Psychology* 3:101-16; February, 1948.
4. Baldwin, Alfred Lee. "The Effect of Home Environment in Nursery School Behavior." *Child Development* 20:49-61; June, 1949.
5. Bayer, Leona M., and Reichard, Suzanne. "Androgyny, Weight, and Personality." *Psychosomatic Medicine* 13:358-74; November-December, 1951.
6. Bernstein, Isidor. "Uses of Play in the Treatment of Children." *Journal of Pediatrics* 39:503-508; October, 1951.
7. Betz, Robert L. *A Comparison Between Personality Traits and Physical Fitness Tests of Males* 26-60. Master's thesis. Urbana: University of Illinois, 1956.
8. Biddulph, Lowell G. "Athletic Achievement and the Personal and Social Adjustment of High School Boys." *Research Quarterly* 25:1-7; March, 1954.
9. Blanchard, B. Everand. "A Comparative Analysis of Secondary-School Boys' and Girls' Character and Personality Traits in Physical Education Classes." *Research Quarterly* 17:33-39; March, 1946.
10. Bonney, Merl E. "Personality Traits of Successful and Unsuccessful Children." *Journal of Educational Psychology* 34:449-72; November, 1943.
11. Bonney, Merl E., and Powell, Johnny. "Differences in Social Behavior Between Sociometrically High and Sociometrically Low Children." *Journal of Educational Research* 46:281-95; March, 1953.
12. Bower, Philip A. *The Relation of Physical, Mental, and Personality Factors to Popularity in Adolescent Boys.* Doctoral dissertation. Berkeley: University of California, 1941.
13. Brace, David Kingsley. "Sociometric Evidence of the Relationship Between Social Status and Athletic Ability Among Junior High School Boys." *Professional Contributions Number 3.* Washington, D. C.: American Academy of Physical Education, 1954.
14. Breck, Sabina J. "A Sociometric Measurement of Status in Physical Education Classes." *Research Quarterly* 21:75-82; May, 1950.
15. Bretsch, Howard S. "Social Skills and Activities of Socially Accepted and Unaccepted Adolescents." *Journal of Educational Psychology* 43:449-58; December, 1952.
16. Broer, Marion R., and Holland, Dolly A. J. "Physical Education Interests and Needs of University of Washington Women in Service Classes." *Research Quarterly* 25:387-97; December, 1954.
17. Bunker, Herbert. "The Selective Character of the Active and Non-active Student in Physical Education." *Journal of American Association of College Registrars* 20:350-66; April, 1945.
18. Buswell, Margaret M. "The Relationship Between the Social Structure of the Classroom and the Academic Success of the Pupil." *Journal of Experimental Education* 22:37-52; September, 1953.
19. Cabot, P. S. "The Relation Between Characteristics of Personality and Physique in Adolescents." *Genetic Psychology Monographs* 20:3-120; February, 1938.
20. Cavagnaugh, Jean O. "The Relation of Recreation to Personality in Adjustment." *Journal of Social Psychology* 15:63-74; February, 1942.
21. Chittenden, G. E. "An Experimental Study in Measuring and Modifying Assertive Behavior in Young Children." *Monographs of Society for Research in Child Development* 2; 1942.

22. Cowell, Charles C. "An Abstract of a Study of Differentials in Junior High School Boys Based on the Observation of Physical Education Activity." *Research Quarterly,* 6:129-36; December, 1935.

23. Cowell, Charles C. "Physical Education as Applied Social Science." *Educational Research Bulletin* (Ohio State University) 1:147-55; September, 1937.

24. Cowell, Charles C.; Daniels, Arthur S.; and Kenney, Harold E. "Purposes in Physical Education as Evaluated by Participants, Physical Education Supervisors, and Educational Administrators." *Research Quarterly* 22:286-97; October, 1951.

25. Cowell, Charles C. "Student Purposes in High School Physical Education." *Educational Research Bulletin* (Ohio State University) 18:89 92; April, 1939.

26. Cowell, Charles C. "Validating an Index of Social Adjustment for High School Use." *Research Quarterly* 29:7-18; March, 1958.

27. Cox, F. N. "Sociometric Status and Individual Adjustment Before and After Play Therapy." *The Journal of Abnormal and Social Psychology* 48:354-56; July, 1953.

28. Dennis, Wayne. "A Cross-Cultural Study of the Reinforcement of Child Behavior." *Child Development* 28:431-38; December, 1957.

29. Duffy, E. "Muscular Tension as Related to Physique and Behavior." *Child Development* 3:200-06; September, 1932.

30. Dunker, K. "Experimental Modification of Children's Food Preferences Through Social Suggestion." *Journal of Abnormal and Social Psychology* 33:489-507; October, 1938.

31 Edwards, Joseph F. *The Relationship Between the Cowell Athletic Aptitude Test and Some Selected Social Measures.* Minor research project. Lafayette, Indiana: Purdue University, 1959.

32. Erwee, J. J. *The Relation of Industrial Recreation to Certain Evidences of Personnel Morale.* Master's thesis. Lafayette, Indiana: Purdue University, 1948.

33. Flanagan, Lance. "A Study of Some Personality Traits of Different Physical Activity Groups." *Research Quarterly* 22:3; October, 1951.

34. Flowtow, Ernest A. "Charting Social Relationships of School Children." *The Elementary School Journal* 46:498-504; May, 1946.

35. Foehrenbach, Lenore M. "Why Girls Choose After-School Sports." *Journal of the American Association for Health, Physical Education, Recreation* 24:34-38; June, 1953.

36. Frank, Lawrence K. "Play in Personality Development." *American Journal of Orthopsychiatry* 25:576-90; October, 1955.

37. Furfey, Paul H. "Some Factors Influencing the Selection of Boys' Chums." *Journal of Applied Psychology* 11:47-61; January, 1943.

38. Gough, Harrison G. "Predicting Social Participation." *Journal of Social Psychology* 35:227-33; May, 1952.

39. Greenburg, P. J. "Competition in Children: An Experimental Study." *American Journal of Psychology* 44:221-48; April, 1932.

40. Gronlund, Norman E., and Whitney, Algard P. "Relation Between Pupils' Social Acceptability in the Classroom, in the School, and in the Neighborhood." *The School Review* 64:267-71; September, 1956.

41. Gustad, John W. "Factors Associated with Social Behavior and Adjustment — A Review of the Literature." *Educational and Psychological Measurements* 12:3-19; spring, 1952.

42. Hambridge, Gove, Jr. "Structured Play Therapy." *American Journal of Orthopsychiatry* 25:601-17; October, 1955.

43. Hanley, Charles. "Physique and Reputation of Junior High School Boys." *Child Development* 22:247-60; December, 1951.

44. Hardy, Martha Crumpton. "Social Recognition at the Elementary School Age." *Journal of Social Psychology* 8:365-84; August, 1937.

45. Harlow, Robert G. "Masculine Inadequacy and Compensatory Development of Physique." *Journal of Personality* 19:3; March, 1951.

46. Hawkes, Glenn R. "A Study of the Personal Values of Elementary School Children." *Educational and Psychological Measurement* 12:645-63; winter, 1952.

47. Henry, Franklin M. "The Relation Between Motor Performance and Certain Psychological Measures in College Men." *A.A.H.P.E.R.* Convention Report, Seattle, Washington, April, 1947.

48. Johnson, Warren R., and Hutton, Daniel C. "Effects of a Combative Sport Upon Personality Dynamics as Measured by a Projective Test." *Research Quarterly* 26;49-53; March, 1955.

49. Jones, H. E. "Physical Ability as a Factor in Social Adjustment in Adolescence." *Journal of Educational Research* 40:287-301; December, 1946.

50. Jones, Mary C.; Bayley, Nancy; and Jones, Harold E. "Physical Maturing Among Boys as Related to Behavior." *American Psychologist* 3:264; July, 1948.

51. Jones, Mary C., and Bayley, Nancy. "Physical Maturing Among Boys as Related to Behavior." *Journal of Educational Psychology* 41:129-48; March, 1950.

52. Kight, Stanford S. "How Camping Can Change Social Attitudes." *Camping Magazine* 25:11-12; January, 1953.

53. Kuhlen, Raymond G., and Bretsch, Howard. "Sociometric Status and Personal Problems of Adolescents." *Sociometry* 10:122-23; May, 1947.

54. Kuhlen, Raymond G., and Collester, E. G. "Sociometric Status of Sixth and Ninth Graders Who Fail To Finish High School." *Educational and Psychological Measurements* 12:632-37; Fall, 1952.

55. Kuhlen, Raymond G., and Lees, Beatrice J. "Personality Characteristics and Social Acceptability in Adolescence." *Journal of Educational Psychology* 34:32; September, 1943.

56. LaPlace, John P. "Personality and Its Relationship To Success in Professional Baseball." *Research Quarterly* 25:313-19; October, 1954.

57. Latham, A. J. "The Relationship Between Pubertal Status and Leadership in High School Boys." *Journal of Genetic Psychology* 78;185-94; June, 1951.

58. Lebo, Dell. "The Development of Play as a Form of Therapy: From Rousseau to Rogers." *American Journal of Psychiatry* 112:418-22; October, 1955.

59. Leeds, Carrol H. "Teacher Behavior Liked and Disliked by Pupils." *Education* 75:29-36; September, 1954.

60. Lewin, Kurt. "Experiments on Autocratic and Democratic Atmospheres." *Social Frontiers* 4:316-19; July, 1938.

61. Lieb, A. "Vorstellungen und Urteile von Schuelern Ueber Fuehrer in der Schulklasse." *Zeitschrift für Angewante Psychologie* 20:341-46; 1928.

62. Lifshitz, Adele B., and Sakoda, James. "Effect of Summer Camp on Adolescents." *Journal of Child Psychology* 2:257-65; 1952.

63. McGraw, L. W., and Tolbert, J. W. "Sociometric Status and Athletic Ability of Junior High School Boys." *Research Quarterly* 24:72-78; March, 1953.

64. McGuire, Carson. "Social Effects and Correlates of Education." *Review of Educational Research* 22;25-31; February, 1952.

65. McGuire, Carson, and Clark, Rodney A. "Age-Mate Acceptance and Indices of Peer Status." *Child Development* 23:141-54; June, 1952.

66. McKinney, F. M. "Concomitants of Adjustment and Maladjustment Among College Students." *Journal of Abnormal and Social Psychology* 31:435-57; January-March, 1937.

67. Marks, J. B. "Interests, Leadership, and Sociometric Status Among Adolescents." *Sociometry* 17:340-39; November, 1954.

68. May, Mark A., and Doob, Leonard. "Competition and Cooperation." Washington, D. C.: National Social Science Research Council, *Bulletin No. 25*; April, 1937.

69. Moore, Joseph E., and Sturm, Norman H. "Relation of Hand Strength to Personality Measures." *American Journal of Psychology* 65:1; January, 1952.

70. Nedelsky, Ruth. "The Teacher's Role in the Peer Group During Middle Childhood." *Elementary School Journal* 52:325-34; February, 1951.

71. Nelson, G. A. "Personality and Attitude Differences Associated with the Elective Substitution of R.O.T.C. for the Physical Education Requirement in High School." *Research Quarterly* 19:2-17; March, 1948.

72. Ondrus, Joseph. *A Sociometric Analysis of Group Structure and the Effect of Football Activities on Inter-personal Relationships.* Doctoral dissertation. New York: New York University, 1953.
73. Partridge, E. DeAlton. *Leadership Among Adolescent Boys.* New, York: Bureau of Publications, Teachers College, Columbia University. Contributions to Education, No. 608, 1934.
74. Popp, James. *Case Studies of Sophomore High School Boys with High and Low Fitness Indices.* Master's thesis. Eugene: University of Oregon, 1959.
75. Pressey, S. L., and Hanna, David C. "The Class as a Socio-Psychological Unit." *Journal of Psychology* 16:13-19; 1943.
76. Ragsdale, Clarence E. "Personality Traits of College Majors in Physical Education." *Research Quarterly* 3:243; May, 1932.
77. Rarick, Lawrence, and McKee, Robert. "A Study of Twenty Third-Grade Children Exhibiting Extreme Levels of Achievement on Tests of Motor Proficiency." *Research Quarterly* 20:142-52; May, 1949.
78. Reaney, M. Jane. "The Correlation Between General Intelligence and Play Ability as Shown in Organized Group Games." *British Journal of Psychology* 7:226-52; 1914.
79. Resnick, Joseph. "A Study of Some Relationships Between High School Grades and Certain Aspects of Adjustment." *Journal of Educational Research* 44:321-40; January, 1951.
80. Reynolds, Thomas F. *The Relationship Between the Cowell Personal Distance Scale and the Purdue Motor Fitness Test.* Minor research project. Lafayette, Indiana: Purdue University, 1959.
81. Scandrette, Onas C. "Classroom Choice Status Relates to Scores on Components of the California Test of Personality." *Journal of Educational Research* 47:291-96; December, 1953.
82. Schurr, Evelyn L. *A Study of Student Purposes of Freshmen Girls in the High Schools of Hammond, Indiana.* Minor research project. Lafayette, Indiana: Purdue University, 1954.
83. Shaw, C. *Delinquency Areas.* Chicago: University of Chicago Press, 1929.
84. Sherif, M. "A Study of Some Social Factors in Perception."*Archives of Psychology,* No. 187, 1935.
85. Shugart, George. "The Play History: Its Application and Significance." *Journal of Psychiatric Social Work* 24:204-209; September, 1955.
86. Signorella, Michael. "Social Adjustment and Athletic Participation." Minor research project. Lafayette, Indiana: Purdue University, 1953.
87. Skubic, Elvera. "A Study in Acquaintanceship and Social Status in Physical Education Classes." *Research Quarterly* 20:80-87; March, 1949.
88. Sperling, A. P. "The Relationship Between Personality Adjustment and Achievement in Physical Education Activities." *Research Quarterly* 13:351-63. October, 1942.
89. Stendler, C. B., and others. "Studies in Cooperation and Competition: The Effect of Working for Groups and Individual Rewards on the Social Climate of Children's Groups." *Journal of Genetic Psychology* 79:173-97; 1951.
90. Stogdill, Ralph M. "Personal Factors Associated with Leadership: A Survey of the Literature." *Journal of Psychology* 25:35-71; 1948.
91. Stone, Walter L. "Meeting the Needs of Children Through Camping." *Camping Magazine* 25:18; January, 1954.
92. Stover, William M. *The Relationship Between Physical Achievement and Social Acceptance in Junior High School Boys.* Master's thesis. Columbus: Ohio State University, 1936.
93. Swensen, Jean, and Rhulman, Jessie. "Leisure Activities of University Sophomore Class." *Educational and Psychological Measurement* 12:453-66; autumn, 1952.
94. Symonds, Percival M. "Education for the Development of Personality." *Teachers College Record* 50:163-69; December, 1948.

95. Thomas, John W. "Experimental Use of the Summer Camp as Part of a Remedial Program for Juvenile Delinquents." *Religious Education* 42:211-16; July, 1947.
96. Thomas, R. J. "An Empirical Study of High School Drop-Outs in Regard to Ten Possibly Related Factors." *Journal of Educational Sociology* 28:11-18; September, 1954.
97. Thrasher, F. M. *The Gang.* Chicago: University of Chicago Press, 1936.
98. Thune, John B. "Personality of Weightlifters." *Research Quarterly* 20:296-306; October, 1949.
99. Todd, Frances E. *Democratic Methodology in Physical Education.* Doctoral dissertation. Stanford University, 1951.
100. Todd, Frances E. "Sociometry in Physical Education," *Journal of the American Association for Health, Physical Education, Recreation* 24:23-24; May, 1953.
101. Trapp, William G. "A Study of Social Integration in a College Football Squad." *56th Annual Proceeding.* Washington, D. C.: College Physical Education Association, 1953.
102. Tryon, Caroline M. *Evaluation of Adolescent Personality by Adolescents.* Monograph of the Society for Research in Child Development, 4:4 (Serial No. 23); 1939.
103. Tuddenham, Read D. "Studies in Reputation: III. Correlates of Popularity Among Elementary School Curriculum." *Journal of Educational Psychology* 42:257-76; May, 1951.
104. Tuddenham, Read D. "Studies in Reputation: I. Sex and Grade Differences in School Children's Evaluations of Their Peers: II. The Diagnosis of Social Adjustment." *Psychological Monographs* 66: No. 333; 1952.
105. Volberding, Eleanor. "Characteristics of Successful and Unsuccessful Eleven Year Old Pupils." *Elementary School Journal* 49:405-10; March, 1949.
106. Walsh, Eleanor A. *The Relationship Between Motor Proficiency and Social Status of Elementary School Girls.* Master's thesis. Madison: University of Wisconsin, 1955.
107. Walters, C. Etta. "A Sociometric Study of Motivated and Non-Motivated Bowling Groups." *Research Quarterly* 26:107-12; March, 1955.
108. Wattenberg, William W. "Factors Associated with Repeating Among Preadolescent Delinquents." *Journal of Genetic Psychology* 4:189-95; June, 1954.
109. Wellman, Beth. "The School Child's Choice of Companions." *Journal of Educational Research* 14:126-32; September, 1926.
110. Wells, Harold P. *Relationships Between Physical Fitness and Psychological Variables.* Doctoral dissertation. Urbana: University of Illinois, 1958.
111. Wenger, M. A. "Muscular Processes and Personality." *Child Development* 9:261-76; September, 1938.
112. Williams, P. E. "A Study of Adolescent Friendships." *Pedagogical Seminar* 30:242-46; December, 1923.
113. Witty, Paul. "An Analysis of the Personality Traits of the Effective Teacher." *Journal of Educational Psychology* 40:663; April, 1947.
114. Zeleny, Leslie Day. "Leadership." *Encyclopedia of Educational Research.* New York: The Macmillan Company, 1950.

Towards a Sociology of Physical Education and Sport, Some Theoretical Considerations
Cyril M. White*

Introduction

Physical education as a maturing discipline has now reached the stage where new dimensions are being continually presented as areas for investigation. This is as it should be for the study of human physical activity, of which physical education is a part, is vast in scope as well as far reaching in its potential for developing our body of knowledge. Two characteristics are immediately outstanding; first, our subject is enormous; second, it derives background material from a large number of other subjects. A few examples of the sources of our developing dimensions are anatomy, physiology, physical medicine, psychology, neurology, philosophy, history, administration theory, and sociology. The present interest in the sociology of physical education and sport is one such dimension, and the aim of this paper is to examine some of the social aspects of physical education and sport, develop some sociological theories from the studies already in existence and suggest, hopefully, some areas for sociological research in this our most common and least understood social institution.

Significance of the Problem

Considering the problem as significant from the sociological point of view, it is a fact that the first man to run a mile within four minutes was called upon to broadcast as the spokesman of his generation; that in the British Commonwealth mountain climbers, cricketers, footballers and a jockey receive knighthoods; that college football is big business in America and that the Olympic Games have their diplomatic as well as their athletic importance. Today sport is a social institution permeating education, economics, art, politics, law, mass communications, big business and international diplomacy and relations. In fact, in some areas of the modern world, sport is now being used as an ideological weapon of the first magnitude for at the present time nearly everyone has become involved in sport in some way, however vicariously. It has been reported that more than 80 million people in Europe as well as America watched "live" on television the recent boxing contest between Cassius Clay and Sonny Liston, and more than 200 million in many parts of the globe the XVIII Olympiad of the Modern Era in Tokyo.

---

*A paper read at the National Convention of the American Association for Health, Physical Education, and Recreation, Conrad Hilton Hotel, Chicago, Illinois, March 18, 1966, *Gymnasium, International Council on Health, Physical Eductaion and Recreation*, Vol. IV, 1967.

As an economic enterprise alone sport represents an annual expenditure by the American public of more than $20 billion[1]. It has now become so potent a social force that it has an economic capacity to create needs ranging from $18,000 per annum pent houses in the Houston Astrodome to stretch pants in pastel shades from the haute coutures of the fashion world. Yet despite the magnitude of modern man's commitment to sport as a social phenomenon, it has received little serious study.

The presence everywhere of sports has been taken so much for granted that a clear description, let alone an explanation of this social force, is practically non-existent. Both social scientists and physical educators have contributed to this situation by taking sports so much for granted as if they did not exist. Yet the basic characteristics of sports are well-known. Well-known in the sense that nearly everyone has some familiarity with them, but they are far from well-known in another and far more important sense. They have not been stated in such a way that a body of scientific knowledge can be built on them, thereby giving as a concomitant, insight into fundamentals.

It is interesting to speculate why social scientists and in particular, sociologists, have so far neglected investigating the tremendous influence of sport on society. It may well be that the sociology of sport has the same unattractive characteristics that Gross[2] believes retarded the sociology of education until recently. These characteristics were, first, the quality of the existent literature and the large body of published material that had little or no sociological relevance largely consisting of hortative essays. Second, the low academic prestige of education and the understandable reluctance of sociologists to risk further loss of prestige for members of a discipline (sociology) that itself had not yet received full acceptance by many members of more entrenched departments. And finally, the "applied" emphases in education generally. All these combined to make the sociology of education "unfashionable" for sociologists until at least 1955. This of course has now changed markedly, but we in physical education and sport just can't wait until sociologists find our field "attractive" or "fashionable" enough for investigation. Time is short so we have got to do the job ourselves. It will be necessary, as Zeigler points out, for researchers and scholars in our field to set up tentative hypotheses based on the findings of scientists in related fields and our own, and to apply all known methods and accompanying techniques of research carefully and painstakingly to problems which appear to belong uniquely to physical education and sport. This task belongs to us alone and we must

---

[1]Gerald S. Kenyon and John W. Loy, "Toward a Sociology of Sport," *Journal of Health, Physical Education and Recreation*, Vol. 36, No. 5, May, 1965, 4 pp.

[2]N. Gross, "The Sociology of Eductaion," *Sociology Today*, Ed. R. K. Merton, et al., New York. Basic Books Inc., 1959.

accomplish this goal primarily through our own efforts. No other discipline will do this for us, except in a secondary way and belatedly.[3]

Theory Building

The question is now posed; how are sociological theories formulated and further, how can these theories be applied to the sociology of sport? To make some attempt at answering the first part of this question let us consider the views of Robert K. Merton of Columbia on the apparent conflicts in regard to sociological theory development in general. Merton writes:

The recent history of sociological theory can in large measure be written in terms of an alternation between two contrasting emphases. On the one hand, we observe those sociologists who seek above all to generalize, to find their way as rapidly as possible to the formulation of sociological laws. Tending to assess the significance of sociological work in terms of scope rather than the demonstrability of generalizations, they eschew the 'triviality' of detailed small-scale observation and seek the grandeur of global summaries. At the other extreme stands a hardy band who do not hunt too closely the implications of their research, but who remain confident and assured that what they report is so. To be sure, their reports of facts are verifiable and often verified, but they are somewhat at a loss to relate these facts to one another or even to explain why these, rather than other, observations have been made. For the first group the identifying motto would at times seem to be: 'We do not know whether what we say is true, but it is at least significant.' And for the radical empiricist the motto may read: 'This is demonstrably so, but we cannot indicate its significance.' Whatever the bases of adherence to the one or the other of these camps—different but not necessarily contradictory accountings would be provided by psychologists, sociologists of knowlege, and historians of science—it is abundantly clear that there is no logical basis for their being ranged against each other. Generalizations can be tempered, if not with mercy, at least with disciplined observation; close, detailed observations need not be rendered trivial by avoidance of their theoretical pertinence and implications.[4]

However, Merton himself does have an orientation in the way sociological theory should be developed. In his address to the Biennial Conference of the British Sociological Association in London in 1957 on the general theme "Sociology in Retrospect and Prospect," Merton makes his ideas quite clear when he says:

[3]Earle F. Zeigler, "A Point of View—The Need for Consensus and Research," A paper presented to The Design Conference, Chicago, Illinois, October, 1965.

[4]Robert K. Merton, *Social Theory and Social Structure*, Glencoe, Illinois: The Free Press, 1964.

The principal bases of advancing sociological theory today consists, I believe, in much the same modest and limited development of ideas which occurred in the early modern period of other sciences, from natural history to chemistry and physics. Such theories of the middle range consist of sets of relatively simple ideas, which link together a limited number of facts about the structure and functions of social formations and suggest further observations. They are theories intermediate to comprehensive analytical schemes and detailed workaday hypotheses. In emphasizing what seems to me the distinctive importance of theories of the middle range, I would prefer not to be misunderstood. There is of course no contradiction between such theories and more comprehensive theory, such as that advanced by Talcott Parsons. Nor am I suggesting that only theories of the middle range merit our attention. There is no substitute for such efforts as Parsons' to develop a wide ranging and comprehensive theory of the social system as a whole, which will incorporate, with successive modifications, more highly delimited theories. But by the same token, there is room also for another kind of theorizing which is at the outset, and for some time to come, limited to more restricted ranges of phenomena than those encompassed by a system of thought like that of Parsons. The two kinds of inquiry can usefully follow their own course, with periodic reconnaissances to see to what extent specific theories of a limited range of phenomena are found to be consistent with the theory of larger scope. On this view, the consolidation of delimited theories in sociology largely come about through successive convergence of initially disparate ideas.[5]

Line of Development for Sports Sociology

The question can now be put as to how we, who are interested in sport, can work toward developing a sociology of sport that is in accordance with contemporary sociological thinking? An analysis of Talcott Parsons' concepts reveals that for the physical educator they are rather vague, complicated and too far removed from the basic material with which physical educators work. The groups that the physical educator is involved in are small, personal, relatively permanent and face-to-face, or, as Cooley named them, "primary groups," groups in which the members are *directly* related as opposed to secondary groups whose members are but indirectly related. The prevailing characteristic of a primary group is one in which "we" is the natural expression for describing the group's sympathy and mutual identification.

---

[5]Robert K. Merton, "The Role-Set: Problems in Sociological Theory," *The British Journal of Sociology*, Vol. VIII, No. 2, June, 1957.

Merton's suggestions then would appear more pertinent to physical educators when considering a theoretical framework for the development of a sociology of physical education or sport. This framework is necessary in order to view the significance of creative thinking, to test ideas, and enable efficient interpretation of results and their integration into existing knowledge. In addition it should provide the basis for inspiration, be a source of new ideas and further enable problems which need answering to be perceived. Finally, it should be in accordance with contemporary sociological thinking and be in the traditions of the social sciences.

But it needs to be emphasized at this stage in the proposed development of a sociology of physical education and sport, that the framework should have a scientific orientation. This is another way of saying that we should use the scientific method in our development of theory. A scientific frame of reference is quite discriminating for it will only admit those facts on which scientific knowledge can be built. If we have an adequate theoretical approach or frame of reference, significant advances on the sociology of physical education and sport will come rapidly, without it we will fail to bring sociological order out of the riot of experiences that confront us daily as physical educators or sports mentors.

The German sports sociologist, Günther Lüschen, has recognized these prerequisites and suggests a theoretical approach which merits serious consideration and is also in accordance with Merton's orientation. Lüschen suggests that we work from the basic premise that modern sociology is primarily an inductive science in which reasoning and/or problem-solving proceeds from the specific to the general. From this premise Lüschen proposes a line of development for sports sociology which starts with scientifically descriptive studies giving rise to *ad hoc* theories which in turn can be investigated as *ad hoc* theory studies of special cases. These studies could suggest further observations which, in turn, may produce studies out of which could be developed sport sociological theories of the middle range, theories consisting of sets of relatively simple ideas which link together a limited number of facts about the structure and functions of sports formations and suggest further observations.

Existing Studies

From the literature, various research studies can be utilized to illustrate this suggested development.

The first is a descriptive study of the occupational culture of the professional boxer.[6] Within any society, particularly if it is specialized and

    [6]S. K. Weinberg and H. Arond. "The Occupational Culture of the Boxer," *The American Journal of Sociology*, Vol. LVII, No. 5, March, 1952.

urbanindustrial, will be found groups or categories of people who share sub-cultures. Such groups or categories will participate in the total culture, for example, they will share the behaviors which most members of their society have learned but, *in addition,* they will have learned a set of behaviors peculiar to their group. These behaviors are termed a subculture. In "The Occupational Culture of the Boxer," Weinberg and Arond describe the value system and behaviors of the prize fighter. Through a combination of personal experience, the reading of firsthand literature and by interviews with sixty-eight boxers and former boxers, seven trainers, and five managers, the authors investigated and described the subculture of the professional boxer up to 1952. The aspects covered are recruitment, practices and beliefs and the social structure of the boxing world.

This study clearly illustrates the impact of ethnic minority status and of low socio-economic status, in shaping the boxers occupational subculture.

The second study goes beyond description and proposes the hypothesis that group interaction in a class of first year physical education majors has a significant bearing upon the subsequent performance in the university examinations. Start[7] used sociometry to analyze the social structure of the class group and illustrated that the social interaction, so identified, was related to the subsequent educational performance of the group.

The final study is the bowling group in William F. Whyte's "Street Corner Society."[8] This study, in association with others (illustrating similar sociological elements) has been built by George Homans[9] into a theory of the middle range, a theory, it will be remembered, Merton defines as being analytical and systematic, of limited scope, involving sets of ideas or abstractions and not too far removed from the data of sociological observation. From the data acquired in these studies Homans has developed a framework of hypotheses intended to coordinate the phenomena of group activity, this framework he calls the "external and internal system." The core of Homan's findings is that the forces which affect behavior are in a constant state of mutual dependence, the group therefore being in a state of dynamic social equilibrium.

In conclusion it needs to be emphasized that a sociology of sport and/or physical education will of necessity have to deal with the phenomena associated with collectivities of people interacting in small groups of say between five to forty and on up to aggregates of many tens of thousand and even millions. Large social aggregates illustrating collective behavior of a

---

[7]K. B. Start. "Group Interaction and Examination Results," *Physical Education* (London), Vol. 55, No. 166, November, 1963.

[8]W. F. Whyte, *Street Corner Society*, University of Chicago Press, 1943.

[9]George C. Homans, *The Human Group*, New York: Harcourt, Brace and World, Inc., 1950.

sports nature can now be studied by using the methods suggested by Neil Smelser.[10] The riot resulting from the Washington, D.C. high school football championship on Thanksgiving Day, 1962, is one example of collective behavior that could well be studied Sociologically using Smelser's concepts as a theoretical framework.

Discussion

We have seen from our investigation into some of the aspects of the sociology of physical education and sport that a wealth of socially significant information lies in these areas, areas one might add, that each year grow increasingly in importance in our modern world. Up to the present much of the writing on these subjects has varied widely in scope and depth.

What we need for a start is a readily available bibliography of studies, articles or references of a sports nature that have sociological relevance. Lüschen in Europe has set himself the task of compiling such a bibliography. To date he has located nearly 500 references, but the vast majority are not in English and, furthermore, most of them are speculative rather than descriptive. We can see from all this that we need many more empirical studies of a descriptive nature. From these, using modern techniques of data analysis, we would be in a position to classify and thus give a basis upon which to start developing *ad hoc* theories leading, hopefully, to theories of the middle range.

Sociometry would appear to be a very profitable technique in investigating teams or physical education classes. By this method we could identify and describe the structure, the norms and the leaders of the group. As one of the central problems of sociology is the nature of the social bond (how people are held together in association not only because of their common activities, but also in spite of their diversified behavior) this kind of investigation would prove very valuable in a sociological as well as a sports context.

Another area for investigation is the loyalties that result from team participation. Stone[11] makes the point that the adolescent development of team loyalties among men is a lasting affair and may have positive consequences for their continued conception of self. In few groups are team loyalties greater than those developed in a college football team. It is suggested that much could be learned from an investigation of, say, the social and occupational culture of the college football player. It is because football has such social influence and its ramifications so far reaching in our present day culture that this topic is suggested as an area for sociological investigation.

[10]Neil J. Smelser. *Theory of Collective Behavior*, New York: Free Press of Glencoe, 1963.

[11]G. P. Stone. "Some Meanings of American Sport," C. P. E. A. 60th Annual *Proceedings*, Columbus, Ohio, 1957.

Conclusion

In this paper an attempt has been made to indicate a theoretical approach based upon empirical investigation to the study of sport in our culture. Some published studies have been briefly reported and commented upon and, finally, some areas for sociological investigation suggested.

When many more studies are completed, similar to those reported in this paper, we will then have made a start and some headway toward developing a sociology of sport and physical education.

The Contributions of Physical Activity to Psychological Development
M. GLADYS SCOTT[*]

The parents, educators, recreation leaders, clinicians, and therapists who advocate activity, play, or exercise have in mind some benefit to be derived. The parent may assume it is an inevitable part of the child's growth. The teacher sees it as a means of modifying behavior and improving the individual's capacity to live more fully. Those from the medical profession see some preventive or remedial goal. But everyone consciously or unconsciously sees more than a physiological organism going through motor gyrations or having fun. Each recognizes that play and exercise have some effect on the behavior patterns of the person.

When one deals with the concepts of motor movement and physiological derivatives and concomitants, one is led to an entity which man everywhere recognizes as "play." Huisinga says:

> This intensity of, and absorption in play finds no explanation in biological analysis. Yet in this intensity, this absorption, this power of maddening, lies the very essence, the primordial quality of play. Nature, so our reasoning mind tells us, could just as easily have given her children all those useful functions of discharging superabundant energy, of relaxing after exertion, of training for the demands of life, of compensating for unfulfilled longings, etc., in the form of purely mechanical exercises and reactions. But no, she gave us play, with its tensions, its mirth, and its fun.
>
> Now this last-named element, the fun of playing, resists all analysis, all logical interpretation. As a concept, it cannot be reduced to any other mental category. . . .It is precisely this fun-element that characterizes the essence of play. Here we have to do with an absolutely primary category of life, familiar to everybody at a glance right down to the animal

———————
[*]M. Gladys Scott, "The Contributions of Physical Activity to Psychological Development," *Research Quarterly*. Vol. 31, No. 2, Part II, May, 1960.

level. We may well call play a "totality" in the modern sense of the word, and it is as a totality that we must try to understand and evaluate it.

Since the reality of play extends beyond the sphere of human life it cannot have its foundations in any rational nexus, because this could limit it to mankind. . . . Play cannot be denied. . . . In culture we find play as a given magnitude existing before culture itself existed, accompanying it and pervading it from the earliest beginnings right up to the phase of civilization we are now living in. We find play present everywhere as a well-defined quality of action which is different from "ordinary" (17:24).

In this interpretation of play, the educator, the sociologist and the anthropologist more or less agree. Mead (44:44), speaking from the anthropologist's view, says that all the elements of a game are quite deeply human and that therefore games can be easily communicated or transmitted. It is the process of the game that is important to the players. According to a saying, sometimes attributed to the Dutch, "It is not the marbles that matter, but the game." And as Huisinga (17:49) points out, "Success gives the player a satisfaction that lasts a shorter or longer while as the case may be." Some of the fruits of that success are prestige, a sense of superiority, and satisfaction of that fundamental need to be honored and praised for one's excellence.

And so whether the physical educator is philosopher and anthropologist enough to visualize the human compulsion of the activities done freely, without work goals and objectives, he is nevertheless practical psychologist enough to observe the inherent elements which operate to mold the behavior of the individual and of the group. It is on this basis that we have stated our claims for psychological outcomes. And in these claims can be seen the close interrelationship of health, physical education, and recreation.

These claims may be summarized as follows:
1. Changing attitudes
2. Improving social efficiency
3. Improving sensory perception and responses
4. Developing sense of well-being — mental health
5. Promoting relaxation
6. Providing psychosomatic relief
7. Acquiring skill

For the past three or four decades the literature pertaining to play, to physical education, and to recreation has made assertions within the framework of the above points. Cowell, Daniels, and Kenney (11) give a report which more or less summarizes views. They include many of the above points in their study of values. The entire AAHPER yearbook, *Developing Demo-*

cratic Human Relations (3), is based on the premise that health, physical education, and recreation contribute to personal and interpersonal relations and to the individual's attitudes.

These assertions are perhaps more profoundly believed today than ever before. Let us examine the evidence accumulated through the work and publications of those doing research.

Attitudes Are Changed

Attitude is a feeling or mood relative to action. The professional concern is for attitudes which are relative to learning of motor skills, participation in physical education classes and in recreational use of the skills acquired, to physical activity as a way of recreation, to use of prescribed exercise for maintenance of fitness, or for therapeutic purposes, to development of appreciation of excellence in movement, and many others.

It is recognized that attitudes are frequently in flux. If they are not improving, they are apt to deteriorate before long. The factors considered to have a bearing on these attitudes include such diverse matters as appropriateness of the activity for the ability and maturation of the class, the method of instruction and class conduct, and the freedom of the individual to choose and determine his own activity and goals. It appears that this is an area in which comparatively little has been done to verify our observations and assumptions.

The tools for measuring attitudes are fairly numerous. Wear (63) constructed an effective attitude scale for the college man with respect to physical education classes, and Plummer (41) developed another for the college woman. McGee (31), Scott (50), and McCue (30) developed scales for attitudes of parents and teachers toward athletic competition. Bowman (8) constructed scales both for the elementary school child and for measuring parent attitude toward the child's active play experiences. All these show individual differences ranging from "highly favorable toward" to "indifference" and "highly antagonistic."

Attitudes toward health have also had some study. Kent and Prentice (24) stated increased interest from use of motion pictures in classes. Turner and others (58) studied health attitudes, knowledge, and practice with apparent high interest in obtaining facts on health topics.

In the area of recreation, attitudes have been studied primarily through inquiries about the individual's interests or desires, or "what he would like to do" or "knows he should do." However, the reports on what he actually does show a wide discrepancy. Examples of this may be found in Adams (1), Toogood (60), and Wylie (65). These leave the reader with the question as to whether attitudes are as effective in governing action as we are prone to think and also with the unanswered question of the effect of rapid change in attitudes.

There has been very little done in the study of modification of attitudes. If Smith's (57) "level of aspiration" can be considered as an expression of attitude, then we have evidence on effect of success and failure in an athletic situation. The level rose with success and dropped with failure. The failure group also tended by overt action to escape from the failure producing situation. This seems to be in accord with the observations of teachers, coaches, and recreation leaders and may largely account for the drop-outs in recreation programs.

Annett (2) hypothesized that skill determined level of interest and attitude toward participation. He found in the area of dance that the earlier the age at which dancing was started and the more frequent the experience the greater the skill and the interest. The most popular dance was the one best known.

Plummer (41) found several factors affecting attitudes of the college woman toward physical education. They were mostly personal problems such as competition of other interests, physical appearance, previous experience, finance, and response to the group, but also the facilities and general environment.

McAfee (28) reported on a test of sportsmanship attitudes for sixth, seventh, and eighth grade boys. Progressive deterioration of attitude seemed to call for some revision of teaching methods to alter this trend. This again emphasizes the assumption that attitudes can be modified and that changes can be a direct objective of teaching.

The evidence is far from adequate on questions such as relative importance of different factors in affecting attitudes; individual differences in response to these factors and in "fluidity" of attitudes; relationship of attitudes to actual overt response in the presence of group stimulation, and other motivating stimuli.

As to the value of attitudes, little doubt remains from educational research or experience that intent to learn, receptivity, and motivation toward learning and participation are conducive to accomplishment and lack thereof is inhibiting.

Social Efficiency Is Improved

This suggests a broad area of human functioning. Professional goals deal with the individual's capacity to be a part of a group and to accept and work with other individuals in the group. Likewise, the individual is expected to demonstrate characteristics of integrity and honesty, fair play, acceptance and understanding, generosity, reliability, and other characteristics considered to be indications of a mature and socially desirable personality. Allegations with respect to character and personality growth are broad, covering development through participation in learning situations, engaging in competition, and establishing patterns of recreation participation. This development is alleged to make the individual more mature and more socially acceptable in a moral and ethical sense. At the same time that he emerges as a strong personality he also becomes an asset in the social groups of which he is a part.

Research, of course, deals with fragments of this problem. Our answers to the total must be built on a summation of evidence.

Probably the greatest amount of research to date has been in the area of social interaction and the development of the sociometric tools and methods of analyzing them. These are products also of the last 15 to 20 years. Breck and Skubic were among the first to adapt the work of Mareno (32), Jennings (21), and others to physical education groups. Breck (9) developed scoring methods. Skubic (50) used the test on classes which were taught as usual with the additional objective of trying to promote acquaintanceship within the class. Fewer social isolates were found and more social leaders emerged during a six-week period. They agreed with Jennings that leadership and isolation are products of interpersonal interaction rather than attributes of persons. Perhaps one of the important findings here is that change did occur, a fact substantiated by Yukie (66).

Fulton and Prange (13) used this technique for comparing motor learning of the chosen and unchosen class members. They found no significant difference for the college women. On the other hand, McCraw and Tolbert (29) found a relationship between sociometric status and athletic ability of boys.

This problem is discussed in more detail in the article by Cowell in this supplement. However, it is essential to relate interpersonal patterns to individual behavior responses, and so it is presented briefly here.

Almost as much interest has been shown in personality changes in the individual. Because of the nature of the personality scales, these are apt to be interpreted as indicating good or poor social adjustment. Biddulph (6) found such a high relationship between athletic achievement and social adjustment that he emphasized the importance of athletic experience for all. Bentson and Summerskill's (5) study of the entering college man seems to indicate a relationship between social adjustment and success in athletics. This is a point often ignored in studies or observations of outcomes and may have led to erroneous conclusions. However, Biddulph was studying the younger boy and at that age adjustment may be more readily occurring. When considering the participant versus the nonparticipant in Little League baseball play, Seymour (51) found no significant difference in terms of needs and problems or in personality traits except "leadership." Here the participant started higher and gained more. Seymour by hypothesis, measurement design, and conclusions does recognize that with regard to personality the participant starts at a higher level and maintains it. It is failure to recognize this higher starting point that has led some authors to attribute more marked gains from competitive athletic programs than are actually demonstrated in their measurements.

Closely associated with this matter of adjustment is the effect of method. Todd (58) experimented with the "democratic" method and through sociometric analysis found improved acquaintanceship, upward mobility of most students, fewer isolates, better group cohesion, and group approval and satisfaction. Similarly Walters (62) found that group cohesion and unity improved as well as motor performance under motivation of team organization and recognition. The same was found for dance experiences. Page (38) said that when groups are working together, rhythmic cooperation has the ability to synchronize the efforts of the many who are concerned with the common task and to increase the pleasure and efficiency of the participants.

The other aspect of this problem which has been studied is the immediate and temporary effect of competition in athletics upon tensions and emotional control. Johnson and Hutton (22) believed they had demonstrated that the projective test is suitable to identify the altered pattern of precompetition anxiety, body consciousness, and aggression, and the postcompetition release whether or not subjects won their wrestling event. Husman (18) also used projective tests and differentiated athletes in boxing and in other sports and the changing characteristics before and after competitive seasons.

Ulrich (61) also found "prestress" effects which were greater for the inexperienced than the experienced group where sport competition was the stress variable. In the poststress period the experienced group showed greater effects if they had not been permitted to play and the inexperienced group showed highest stress evidence if they had participated. Ulrich used evidence of eosinophil in the blood. Skubic (52, 54) worked in a similar problem with boys in Little League by means of the galvanic skin response. Both agreed that competition in Little League play had no greater effect than competition in physical education classes.

All of this evidence seems a bit inconclusive as to meaningful changes. Seymour makes a conclusion which probably summarizes the situation in terms of present evidence.

> As a final conclusion of this comparison of behavior characteristics of participant and nonparticipant boys in Little League Baseball, it would seem prudent to exercise caution in ascribing with any degree of certainty behavioral changes, whether desirable or undesirable, to Little League Baseball or to any comparable program for youth (51:345).

It is by uncritical quotation of certain findings that the total issue is obscured. Such an example is found in that of Hale (14). He falls into the error sometmes made in statistical interpretation of talking about significant findings in the absence of statistical significance. On such erroneous interpretation he then goes on to say that competitive athletics are not detrimental but rather beneficial for pre-high school age children. He further quotes Skubic (53, 54) as confirming his case. But at another point he says that more studies need to be made before the final report can be prepared. Longitudinal studies are needed, as well as more study of emotional responses, on the effect of rejection from participation and on effect of athletic competition for girls.

> Skubic's statement on the present status of information is very clear. It should be remembered that this study was concerned with only one phase of the total problem of competition — the immediate effects of competition on emotionality. In order to completely solve the problem of highly organized competition, data must be gathered relative to the physical, sociological, psychological, and economic aspect of competition. Furthermore, to resolve the specific controversy concerning emotional effects of competition, it is necessary that additional data be secured particularly in regard to the influence of emotion on personality now and later in life (52:351).

Since psychiatrists attribute most of the psychological problems of youth and adults to earlier experiences and their emotional impact on later behavior, it would seem that actual "value interpretations" must wait for more objective evidence on long-term behavior patterns and personality characteristics.

Improved Sensory Perception and Responses

Claims in this area are less frequent, at least in written form. Yet it is from isolated instances and studies based on such hypotheses that recognition seems desirable in this review. These cases range through reaction time, depth perception, visual perception, speed, kinesthetic awareness, and empathy.

Olsen (37) attempted to determine if relationships exist between degree of athletic success and reaction time, depth perception, and visual span of apprehension — and whether differences exist between athletes in various sports. In general, relationships were found, but sports differences were not. In a still broader series of psychomotor tests fencers and nonfencers were nondifferentiated (40). Keller (23) studied athletic groups on "quickness of movement" and Slater-Hammel (55) studied balance in athletic groups of varying skill levels. Both found their groups differed but like Olsen refrained from attributing these increments to increased experience. In light of present knowledge, the hypothesis that possession of the trait contributes to athletic success is as plausible as the reverse, that is, that athletic experience produces a higher degree of the capacity.

The effect of activity on kinesthetic awareness is a debatable point, partly because of lack of evidence, but also because of lack of agreement on a precise definition of kinesthesis. Research to date does indicate a high degree of specificity in kinesthetic functioning (46, 48, 64). This is partly responsible for the lack of clarity in definition.

Those who propose the concept of an improved kinesthetic awareness from physical activity are doing so on the premise that learning takes place here in the same way that musical training may improve the individual's perception of quality or tone differences, or that experience can help the discriminative capacity of the person in the sensations of taste or smell. The other basic hypothesis is that higher kinesthetic acuity is associated with greater achievement. At least a few studies have been conducted on these hypotheses. Typical of these are Roloff (45), Honzik (15), Lafuze (25), Mumby (36), and Phillips (39).

Evidence in general does not support such hypotheses. However, the imperfections of measures on both learning and kinesthesis may be responsible for the apparent lack of evidence. It appears to this author that it is too early to draw conclusions.

Empathy is another of the human responses to what one sees going on. Physical educators have considered empathic capacity as the very basis of appreciation of quality in performance, of esthetics in movement in general or dance in particular; of ability to see detail in demonstrations or observations as one goes through the learning process. The difficulty here is similar to that in kinesthesis. The educator and the researcher are talking about an entity within another human being, an entity which has no check in the same way one can verify that the subject sees the same color as the investigator, or hears the same whistle another hears.

As to the values of these sensory capacities, we can conjecture that they may facilitate learning, provide capacity for better neuromuscular performance, and enrich living in general by making the person more sensitive and responsive to his environment. However, our research to date does not give us a basis for confidence in the outcomes or for building a premise of values.

Improved Sense of Well-Being

Good mental health is sometimes defined as being comfortable with one's self and with others. This has very broad implications if considered carefully. The health and physical education teacher and recreation worker claim mental health outcomes from physical activities and affirm the claims of their colleagues in the related health fields. The physical activities considered are particularly those labeled play, that is, having a fun or diversionary function, and those serving to redirect effort or to afford emotional release or creative outlets. The educator and recreation worker are most prone to base such assertions on case studies, that is, an individual carefully observed in his work, or on the clinical records and conclusions of the psychiatrists and physicians.

Jackson and Todd write comprehensively of the outcomes and values of play, based on extensive research on and therapeutic treatment of the very young child. Their interpretation of play and its meaning is revealed in the following quotation:

> It [play] has educative as well as enjoyment value, yet in a broader sense than either Gross or McDougall assigned to it. The child's learning through play is more subtle and more general than is implied in Gross's theory, and his acquisitions far less obvious. By playing the part of father, mother, engine-driver, or doctor, he acquires no knowledge of how to behave in these parts when he grows up. What he does achieve is the experience of imaginative identification and intuitive understanding; what he gains is not practical skills, but an inner balance on which depends his future emotional development and the success of his relationships with other human beings (19:12).

The goals of the physical educator and recreation leader are based on evidence and conclusions such as that cited in the quotation and source above. It is commonly conceded that these goals are logical for the school-age child and perhaps even for the younger ones of the teen-age level. There are many outside the professions of play leadership who doubt that there is any necessity or value other than a fun value for the adult in his play activities. Again the best evidence on mental health values comes from the psychiatrist. William Menninger writes from experience in the clinic and on research associated with patients in the clinic. The following quotations represent his conclusions from this evidence.

> Mentally healthy people participate in some form of volitional activity to supplement their required daily work. This is not merely because they wish something to do in their leisure time, for many persons with little leisure make time for play. Their satisfaction from these activities meet deep seated psychological demands, quite beyond the superficial rationalization of enjoyment.

> Too many people do not know how to play. Others limit their recreation to being merely passive observers of the activity of others. There is considerable scientific evidence that the healthy personality is one

who not only plays, but who takes his play seriously. Furthermore there
is also evidence that the inability and unwillingness to play reveals an
insecure or disordered aspect of personality (33:343).

Good mental health is directly related to the capacity and willingness
of an individual to play. Regardless of his objections, resistances, or
past practice, any individual will make a wise investment for himself
if he does plan time for his play and take it seriously (33:345).

I also wish to point out the fact that the most constructive and beneficial play is something that has to be learned and is not likely to be an
accidental ability or an inherited trait. For maximum satisfaction, one
requires not only encouragement but almost always some instruction.

An effective community recreation program is just as important to
mental health as sanitation is to physical health (33:346).

Surely these statements make it clear that every individual has need for
participation in some type of play activity and that instruction in these
play skills is very important.

The Josiah Macy, Jr., Foundation-sponsored Conference on Group
Processes made an analytical study of games and their effect upon children's behavior. Chairman of the conference was Fritz Redl, of the Child
Research Branch of the National Institute of Mental Health (44). He attempted to guide the conference through a "mental hygiene assessment" of
game ingredients. The record of the conference discussion represents a
philosophical weighing of game structures by a most competent interdisciplinary group of scientists; it should be read by all who deal with games
as a means of helping the individual and should be a basis of very careful selection of play activity. This is indicative of one kind of research
which we could promote within our own profession and in collaboration
with the psychiatrist and psychologist.

Better Relaxation Is Promoted

Relaxation is here referred to as the capacity to release muscular tension from whatever cause derived and the capacity to adjust effort in
amount and sequence for a smooth, efficient functioning of *all* aspects of
motor response.

Hypertension and relaxation have been among the harder aspects of
human behavior to study. One of the earliest comprehensive statements
is that of Rathbone (42), who also has a more recent volume (43). These
verify the possibility of modifying degrees of hypertensions and are in
agreement with medical clinicians, such as Jacobsen (20) and Zeiter and
Lufkin (67). All agree that education has a responsibility in this aspect of
health learnings.

Probably the greatest contribution of Bullen (10) is to emphasize the individual variations in response to stress and tension producing environments.

The effect of exercise directly on relaxation is open to some doubt, probably because it varies with types of exercise and conditions under which the exercising is done. Mitchem and Tuttle (35) found magnitude of hand tremor (indicating stress) to vary directly with intensity of arm exercise, leg exercise, and general fatigue from work on the ergometer. Slater-Hammel (55) failed to find the same results with respect to leg exercises. Scott and Matthews (49) also failed to find this relationship in strenuous exercise of various types, and unpublished research by this author failed to find this relationship. It appears probable that other stress factors are more important in exercise well below all-out effort.

It would appear more probable that exercise tends to relieve these other forms of stress. This would support a popular assertion of the health and physical educator. This seems to be supported by Michael (34), who theorizes on the basis of his findings that regular daily exercise improves the organism's ability to withstand emotional stress through hormonal effects on the nervous system.

The value of a tension-releasing medium could not be denied in the present state of society and world affairs. However, the objective evidence is far from complete. This is an area in which those in health, physical education, and recreation could join efforts with the physiologist and psychologist.

It also appears likely that variations in the activity and its outcome affect the degree of tension or relief therefrom. That is certainly indicated in Bullen's (10) investigation of work by adults. Likewise, Baldwin and Lewin (4), working with children in "success and failure" situations found emotional states resulting from exposure of ability. They also interpreted their results and others as indicating that test failure tends to produce increase in speed and decrease of accuracy in repetitive motor tasks.

Relief Provided on Psychosomatic Problems

It has been medically demonstrated that certain physical states are at times at least partially of psychogenic origin. These states vary from hysterical paralysis to chronic fatigue, psychological limits of work output, discomfort from bodily function, and the like. We are therefore dealing with a condition not unrelated to the one discussed above, hypertension versus relaxation.

The health, physical education, and recreation claims in this area are concerned more with chronic fatigue, fatigue postures, dysmenorrhea, phobias, and the like than with the clinical cases more often seen by the physician and psychiatrist. While the statements are common that exercise and recreation are diverting, are a means of releasing tension, and are a means of improving one's sense of well-being, there is little on specific conditions.

Posture therapy and prevention are substantiated more on the basis of physiological and mechanical improvements. Nothing is presented in evidence on the psychological ramifications of postural deviations.

There is probably more objective evidence on effects of exercise on dysmenorrhea than on any of the other aspects. Lundquist (27) found regular exercise over a period of several weeks relieved dysmenorrhea in its various symptoms, except for the women known to have structural defects. Cessation of exercise tended to revive the dysmenorrhea. Hubbell (16) went further in study of exercise effects by introducing a placebo exercise series. This group on nonspecific exercises had as much relief as the other two groups, leading her to hypothesize that there might be a psychic factor in the relief oriented presentation of the series. Billig (7) and Dick and others (12) give too little actual data on which to evaluate conclusions, but the high incidence of favorable modification of work habits would lead one to hypothesize in line with Hubbell.

Skills Are Acquired

The problem of skill learning and how it occurs is presented elsewhere. It is beyond the scope of this chapter but is mentioned here because it is believed important that we recognize the psychological implications of the learning process and not just the recognition of learning or its absence.

Physical education has suffered from the old adage "practice makes perfect." It has led to wasted time under the supposed tutelage of the educator and to frustration in those practicing both with and without the educator's supervision. We would do well to remember the importance of our instruction as cited by Menninger: "For maximum satisfaction one requires not only encouragement but almost always some instruction." This was a statement made to recreation leaders and should point to opportunities for instruction in recreation programs, not just a permissive program of participation and play. It would seem to be imperative to learn more about *how* learning takes place and all the conditions which affect learning.

Summary

There is perhaps no area of our professional background that offers more challenge to us than psychological development. The challenge is multiple. We need a better background in general psychology, personality development, social psychology, and cultural anthropology. We need to develop research competencies in these areas and to pursue our understandings of prophylactic and therapeutic contributions of experiences in motor skills. As teachers and administrators, we must be ready to modify our practice in line with new evidence.

The 1954 yearbook of the American Association for Health, Physical Education, and Recreation, *Children in Focus,* has a concluding chapter by Dorothy La Salle, entitled "Looking Ahead." Her words would seem to set the challenge for consideration not only of psychological development but of all areas represented in this 75th anniversary supplement.

> To look ahead with any degree of hope implies that we know where we want to go and where we now are. The profession of physical education is in substantial agreement regarding where it wants physical education to go. . . .Where are we now in relation to these goals? Are we realizing them for the boys and girls of the nation? Indications in many instances are that we are not. . . .The problems in school health today are essentially the same as they were a generation ago. . . . Do these things happen because we do not yet believe that education for leisure is important? Do they happen because the school is not yet assuming responsibility for improving cooperation between agencies which promote recreation?
>
> What then is the task? The job is difficult and has many facets: to study, to conduct research, to glean the facts from other disciplines which bear on health education, on physical education, and on recreation; to improve the education of teachers, to work unceasingly for improved facilities, instructional aids, and time allotment; to integrate our work in schools with community resources; to become expert in sound argumentation. These are the tasks for the next decade (26:276).

REFERENCES

1. Adams, L. Carroll. "Active Recreational Interests of Columbia College Alumni." *Research Quarterly* 19:43-47; March, 1948.
2. Annett, Thomas. "Study of Rhythmical Capacity and Performance in Motor Rhythm in Physical Education Majors." *Research Quarterly* 3:183-91; May, 1932.
3. American Association for Health, Physical Education, and Recreation. *Developing Democratic Human Relations.* Washington, D. C.: American Association for Health, Physical Education, and Recreation, 1951.
4. Baldwin, Alfred L., and Lewin, Harry. "Effects of Public and Private Success and Failure in Children's Repetitive Motor Behavior." *Child Development* 29:363-72; 1958.
5. Bentson, T. B., and Summerskill, John. "Relation of Personal Success in Intercollegiate Athletics to Certain Aspects of Personal Adjustment." *Research Quarterly* 26:8-14; March, 1955.
6. Biddulph, Lowell G. "Athletic Achievement vs. the Personal and Social Adjustment of High School Boys." *Research Quarterly* 25:1-7; March, 1954.
7. Billig, H. E., Jr. "Dysmenorrhea: The Result of a Postural Defect." *Archives of Surgery* 46:611-13; May, 1943.
8. Bowman, Mary O. *The Relationship Between Students and Parent Attitudes and Skills of Fifth Grade Children.* Doctoral dissertation. Iowa City: State University of Iowa, 1958.
9. Breck, Sabina June. "Measurement of Status in Physical Education Classes." *Research Quarterly* 21:75:82; May, 1950.

10. Bullen, Adelaide K. *New Answers to the Fatigue Problem.* Gainesville: University of Florida Press, 1956.
11. Cowell, Charles; Daniels, Arthur S.; and Kenney, Harold E. "Purposes in Physical Education as Evaluated by Participants, Physical Education Supervisors and Educational Administrators." *Research Quarterly* 22:286:97; October, 1951.
12. Dick, A. C.; Billig, Jr., H. E.; and Macy (Mrs.), H. N. "Menstrual Exercises, Absenteeism Decrease and Work Efficiency Increase." *Industrial Medicine* 12:588-90; September, 1943.
13. Fulton, Ruth E., and Prauge, Elizabeth M. "Motor Learning of Highly Chosen and Unchosen Teammates." *Research Quarterly* 21:126-31; May, 1960.
14. Hale, Creighton J. "What Research Says About Athletics for Pre-High School Age Children." *Journal of Health, Physical Education, Recreation* 30:19; December, 1959.
15. Honzik, C. H. "Role of Kinesthetics in Maze Learning." *Science* 84:373; October, 1936.
16. Hubbell, Josephine W. "Specific and Non-specific Exercises for Relief of Dysmenorrhea." *Research Quarterly* 20:378-86; December, 1949.
17. Huisinga, Johan. *Homo Ludens, A Study of the Play Element in Culture.* Boston: The Beacon Press, 1950.
18. Husman, Burris T. Aggression in Boxers and Wrestlers as Measured by Projective Techniques." *Research Quarterly* 26:421-25; December, 1955.
19. Jackson, Lydia, and Todd, Kathleen M. *Child Treatment and the Therapy of Play.* Second edition. New York, N. Y.: The Ronald Press, 1950.
20. Jacobsen, Edmund. *Progressive Relaxation.* Chicago: University of Chicago Press, 1948.
21. Jennings, Helen, *Leadership and Isolation.* New York: N. Y.: Longmans, Green and Company, Inc., 1943.
22. Johnson, Warren R., and Hutton, Daniel C. "Effects of a Combative Sport Upon Personality Dynamics as Measured by a Projective Test." *Research Quarterly* 26:49-53; March, 1955.
23. Keller, Louis F. "Relation of 'Quickness of Bodily Movement' to Success in Athletics." *Research Quarterly* 13:146-55; May, 1942.
24. Kent, F. S., and Prentice, H. A. "A Comparison of Two Methods of Teaching Hygiene to College Freshmen." *Research Quarterly* 10:133-36; May, 1939.
25. Lafuze, Marion. "Learning of Fundamental Skills by Women of Low Motor Ability." *Research Quarterly* 22:149-57; 1951.
26. LaSalle, Dorothy. "Looking Ahead." *Children in Focus,* Yearbook. Washington, D. C.: American Association for Health, Physical Education, and Recreation, 1954.
27. Lundquist, Cordelia. "Use of the Billig Exercise for Dysmenorrhea for College Women." *Research Quarterly* 18:44-53; March, 1947.
28. McAfee, Robert A. "Sportsmanship Attitudes of Sixth, Seventh and Eighth Grade Boys." *Research Quarterly* 26:120; March, 1955.
29. McCraw, L. W., and Tolbert, J. W. "Sociometric Status and Athletic Ability of Junior High School Boys." *Research Quarterly* 24:72-80; March, 1953.
30. McCue, Betty F. "Constructing an Instrument for Evaluating Attitudes Toward Intensive Competition in Team Games." *Research Quarterly* 24:205-209; May, 1953.
31. McGee, Rosemary. "Comparison of Attitudes Toward Intensive Competition for High School Girls." *Research Quarterly* 27:60-73; March, 1956.
32. Mareno, Jacob L. *Who Shall Survive?* Washington, D. C.: Nervous and Mental Disease Co., 1934.
33. Menninger, William C. "Recreation and Mental Health." *Recreation* 42:340-46; November, 1948.
34. Michael, Ernest D., Jr. "Stress Adaptation Through Exercise." *Research Quarterly* 28:50-54; March, 1957.
35. Mitchem, John C., and Tuttle, W. W. "Influence of Exercises, Emotional Stress and Age on Static Neuromuscular Tremor Magnitude." *Research Quarterly* 25:65-74; March, 1954.

36. Mumby, H. Hugh. "Kinesthetic Acuity and Balance Related to Wrestling Ability." *Research Quarterly* 24:327-34; October, 1953.
37. Olsen, Einar A. "Relationship Between Psychological Capacities and Success in College Athletics." *Research Quarterly* 27:79-89; March, 1956.
38. Page, Barbara. "The Philosophy of the Dance." *Research Quarterly* 4:5-49; May, 1933.
39. Phillips, Bernath E. "The Relationship Between Certain Phases of Kinesthesis and Performance during the Early Stages of Acquiring Two Perceptive Motor Skills." *Research Quarterly* 11:571-86; October, 1941.
40. Pierson, William R. "Comparison of Fencers and Non-Fencers by Psychomotor, Space Perception and Anthropometric Measures." *Research Quarterly* 27:90-96; March, 1956.
41. Plummer, Tomi C. *Factors Influencing the Attitudes and Interests of College Women in Physical Education.* Doctoral dissertation. Iowa City: State University of Iowa, 1952. Microcard PE 128.
42. Rathbone, Josephine L. *Residual Neuro-muscular Hypertension: Implications for Education.* New York, 1936.
43. Rathbone, Josephine L. *Teach Yourself to Relax.* Englewood Cliffs, New Jersey: Prentice-Hall, 1957.
44. Redl, Fritz. *The Impact of Game — Ingredients on Children's Play Behavior.* Fourth Conference on Group Processes, October, 1957. New York, N. Y.: Josiah Macy, Jr., Foundation, 1959.
45. Roloff, Louise L. "Kinesthesis in Relation to the Learning of Selected Motor Skills." *Research Quarterly* 24:210-17; May, 1953. Microcard PE 148.
46. Russell, Ruth I. *A Factor Analysis of the Components of Kinesthesis.* Doctoral dissertation. Iowa City: State University of Iowa, 1954. Microcard PH 36.
47. Schaffner, Bertram, editor. *Group Processes.* Transactions of the Fourth Conference. New York, N. Y.: Josiah Macy, Jr., Foundation, 1959.
48. Scott, M. Gladys, "Measurement of Kinesthesis." *Research Quarterly* 26:324-41; October, 1955.
49. Scott, M. Gladys, and Matthews, Helen. "A Study of Fatigue Effects Induced by an Efficiency Test for College Women." *Research Quarterly* 20:134-41; May, 1949.
50. Scott, Phebe M. "Comparative Study of Attitudes Toward Athletic Competition in the Elementary Schools." *Research Quarterly* 24:352-61; October, 1953.
51. Seymour, Emery W. "Comparative Study of Certain Behavior Characteristics of Participant and Non-Participant Boys in Little League Baseball." *Research Quarterly* 27:338-46; October, 1956.
52. Skubic, Elvera. "A Study in Acquaintanceship and Social Status in Physical Education Classes." *Research Quarterly* 20:80-87; March, 1949.
53. Skubic, Elvera. "Emotional Responses of Boys to Little League and Middle League Competitive Baseball." *Research Quarterly* 26:342-52; October, 1955.
54. Skubic, Elvera. "Studies in Little League and Middle League Baseball." *Research Quarterly* 27:97-110; March, 1956.
55. Slater-Hammel, A. T. "Influence of Order of Exercise Bouts Upon Neuromuscular Tremor." *Research Quarterly* 26:88-95; March, 1955.
56. Slater-Hammel, A. T. "Performance of Selected Groups of Male College Students on the Reynolds' Balance Test." *Research Quarterly* 27:347-51; October, 1956.
57. Smith, Carnie H. "Influence of Athletic Success and Failure on the Level of Aspiration." *Research Quarterly* 20:196-208; May, 1949.
58. Southward, Warren H.; Latimer, Jean V.; and Turner, Clair E. "Health Practices, Knowledge, Attitudes, and Interests of Senior High School Pupils." *Research Quarterly* 15:118-36; May, 1949.
59. Todd, Frances. "Democratic Methodology in Physical Education." *Research Quarterly* 23:106-10; March, 1952.

60. Toogood, Ruth. "A Survey of Recreational Interests and Pursuits of College Women." *Research Quarterly* 10:90-100; October, 1939.
61. Ulrich, Celeste. "Measurement of Stress Evidenced by College Situations Involving Competition." *Research Quarterly* 28:160-72; May, 1957.
62. Walters, C. Etta. "A Sociometric Study of Motivated and Non-motivated Bowling Groups." *Research Quarterly* 26:107-12; March, 1955.
63. Wear, Carl. "Construction of Equivalent Forms of an Attitude Scale." *Research Quarterly* 26:113-19; March, 1955. Microcard PE 59.
64. Witte, Fae. *A Factorial Analysis of Measures of Kinesthesis.* Doctoral Dissertation. Bloomington: Indiana University, 1953. Microcard PH 20.
65. Wylie, James A. "A Survey of 504 Families to Determine the Relationships between Certain Factors and the Nature of the Family Recreation Program." *Research Quarterly* 24:229-43; May, 1953.
66. Yukie, Eleanor C. "Group Movement and Growth in a Physical Education Class." *Research Quarterly* 26:222-33; May, 1955.
67. Zeiter, Walter J., and Lufkin, Bernardine. "Progressive Relaxation in Physical Therapy." *Archives of Physical Therapy* 24:211-14; April, 1943.

Contributions of Physical Education to Physical Fitness

H. HARRISON CLARKE[*]

At the outset, it should be stressed that man cannot be divided into separate components. In considering the concept expressed in the one unqualified term "fitness," therefore, the individual is regarded as an indivisible unit, acting and reacting as an integrated whole. The individual exists as an entity; each part acts upon and is affected by the others. Thus, each person, in order to satisfy his own own needs and, at the same time, to fulfill his obligation to society, must possess organic soundness, strength, and vitality; emotional stability; social consciousness; knowledge and insight to solve problems; values and skills; and spiritual and moral qualities.

While the fitness of the individual is a totality, in actuality, recognition of the separate components is the only realistic way to deal definitely and specifically with the fitness problem as it affects the lives of youth. The total aspect is so diffuse as to endanger losing sight of the parts in the whole, which is fully as serious as losing sight of the whole in the part. The purpose of this paper is to deal with the physical aspects of fitness, so permit me to do so with the understanding that what affects the physical affects other aspects of the individual as well.

[*]This address was delivered at the joint session of the American Academy of Physical Education and the Society of State Directors of Health, Physical Education, and Recreation, Cincinnati, Ohio, April 4, 1962.

Reprinted from the *American Academy of Physical Education, Professional Contributions* No. 8.

What Is Physical Fitness?

The physician traditionally and properly is concerned primarily with conditions likely to impair function and vital processes and to cause death; medical practitioners rightly devote themselves largely to protecting the organism from disease and to prolonging life. The physical educator, on the other hand, generally accepts the individual free from disease, organic drains, and handicapping defects and, through proper activities, develops a body that is physically strong and capable of prolonged effort. The physically fit person should be able to carry out the activities of the day, whatever they may be, and should still have ample energy to enjoy his leisure and to meet life's unforeseen emergencies.

Thus the basic physical fitness considerations are the organic soundness and nutritional adequacy of the body itself. Once assured of these qualities, the appropriate activities and methods of physical education take over to maintain and improve the alertness and vigor of the body. Through the proper selection and presentation of physical activities, physical education can improve three fundamental fitness components: muscular strength, muscular endurance, and circulatory endurance. These are the plus qualities which constitute physical education's primary contribution to physical fitness.

To this point, physical fitness has been related to pragmatic considerations of doing daily work, enjoying leisure, and meeting emergencies. This is too narrow a view. Researches from several disciplines have demonstrated that physical fitness through exercise brings other benefits at every age — from improved peer status and increased mental alertness in youth to a decreased incidence of degenerative diseases in later life. Bortz (1) expressed this thought in writing on exercise and aging: "It begins to appear that exercise is the master conditioner for the healthy and the major therapy for the ill. Fitness implies a dynamic homeostasis, the ability to respond to life's physical, emotional, and social ongoing demands." Thus, other things being equal, the individual when physically fit will be more effective in his many applications than when physically unfit.

The physical educator's role in physical fitness is a historic one. In this country, physical education was initially patterned after European systems, especially those devised in Germany and Sweden to develop a strong citizenry for national defense. By 1860, just a century ago, activity programs were being designed to meet the physical fitness needs of individuals after those needs had been detected by examinations and tests. With few exceptions, the physical education leaders between the Civil War and World War I were trained in medicine. These physicians recognized more clearly than is generally true today that the primary function of physical education should be the care and development of the body and that such care and development contributed to the individual's mental, emotional, and social effectiveness. Thus, although starting from a physical base, they recognized the totality of man; this is now an inevitable result obtained by physical educators when analyzing the physical fitness deficiencies of boys and girls.

Following World War I, physical education in practice generally abandoned its biological heritage. Too frequently, the improvement of physical fitness became a concomitant of an activity program designed to realize other educational objectives. Hope has been expressed by Charles B. Wilkinson that the leaders in the field will join with the President's Council on Physical Fitness in an effort to correct this situation. (2)

Today's Emphasis on Physical Fitness

Oberteuffer (3) has pointed out that we are now in the fourth discernible period in the twentieth century of intensified interest in the role of physical education in physical fitness. As identified by him, these periods are: (1) Theodore Roosevelt's advocacy of the vigorous life to make our nation strong; (2) draft statistics following World War I, which shocked many legislators into passing state laws requiring physical education in the schools; (3) the all-out effort during World War II to prepare our populace to wage total war, initiated by action of Franklin D. Roosevelt; and (4) since 1955, when Dwight D. Eisenhower and, later, John F. Kennedy, took executive actions to establish and continue a President's Council on Physical Fitness.

Interestingly or tragically, depending on your point of view, three of these periods were inaugurated by presidents of the United States, and four presidents were actually involved. Initially, in each instance, the physical education profession and its leaders were completely ignored; nonprofessional administrators, promoters, and politicians were placed in charge. For example, there was not a single physical educator invited to President Eisenhower's White House Luncheon to consider the fitness of American youth and what to do about it. Each time, however, the physical education profession subsequently got busy and gave active support to these movements. This constitutes a serious indictment of the major profession in the United States closely allied to the nonmedical aspects of physical fitness, the aspects emphasized by the presidents.

The latest period of intensified interest in physical fitness was triggered by the results of a very simple and minimal test of muscular fitness with which a non-physical educator compared United States children with children from Austria, Italy, and Switzerland, much to the discredit of American youth. A rash of similar surveys with the same test followed: our boys and girls were compared with boys and girls in Pakistan, Japan, New Zealand,

and Canada; Eastern Seaboard children were compared with children from Iowa, Indiana, or Oregon. Now we have another test and the comparisons mount in crescendo: England, Denmark, Japan again. And it still goes on. What are we trying to prove? Is it that we did not know before the 1955 "expose" that great numbers of our youth were not fit? Ridiculous! Some physical educators have used physical fitness tests for more than a quarter century; *they knew*. There were the dramatic results of such testing in the Armed Forces during World War II; the deplorable condition of many of these men was well known. But the profession as a whole did not act until President Eisenhower "lowered the boom."

May I inject parenthetically that there are definite dangers in these fitness surveys. We have used these extremely negative (from our point of view) results to pressure the American public in general and educators in particular into increasing their support of physical education — and this has certainly been effective. But, there are basic questions in this situation which an intelligent and responsible professsion should answer. Certain of these questions are: (1) How adequate are the tests used by the surveys in evaluating the basic components of physical fitness? (2) How representative of our youth population are the norms? (3) Were the samples drawn in an identical manner? (4) Were the testing techniques precisely the same? (5) Did testing of foreign samples provide or permit motivation by competition with American children, while the opposite was not true when the American sample was tested? We definitely need sponsored research which will permit an adequate answer to these questions, as well as others related to the fitness status of our boys and girls.

We know that events occurred which have, for the moment at least, profoundly affected our profession. At first there was presidential intervention, nationwide publicity, conferences, and speeches. The expressed purpose of the first President's Council on Youth Fitness was "to act as a catalyst," to cause fitness activity throughout the nation without entering into it. The second President's Council on Physical Fitness (4), issued a publication (5) containing "suggested elements of a school-centered program," in which some most encouraging operational features for a youth fitness program are recommended. The executive and legislative financial support for this Council, however, has been and still is shockingly inadequate.

As a profession, we have held conferences which have been so short and cumbersome that only limited results were possible. Reams of publicity have been issued and innumerable speeches (such as this one) have been made. The American Association for Health, Physical Education, and Recreation has (1) provided printed materials, suggestions for program development, a steady program of mailings to leaders in the 50 states, and a clearing house for ideas, and (2) provided operational projects which can be adapted for local utilization, such as the AAHPER Youth Fitness Test program, the Track and Field Project, and the Lady Be Fit proposals. (6) Under the stimulus of publicity and a national award system, over 25 million youth fitness tests have been given in this country and the test has been adopted in 17 countries. These figures are truly exceptional, but before assuming them to represent progress, or how much progress, we need to know what is done with the test results; to test just because testing is fashionable has little value.

Without doubt, benefits have accrued from these diverse efforts. In fact, they probably saved the profession in many places. "Sputnik," instead of blasting education into orbit with it, sent educators into a tailspin to remake our educational system into one dominantly "scientific" — the cult of the brain sprang up throughout America. We were headed for trouble (and may still get plenty of it) as educators proposed suppression of the physical in education. Then, the "blast off" for physical fitness started, and the indispensable need for physical education became manifest. The exploits of those men chosen to be our astronauts have not only made abundantly clear the necessity for developing the superior minds of our young men and women, but have also shown that those minds must be emotionally stable and must be accompanied by a body developed far beyond the normal to withstand the rigors associated with those scientific exploits.

Convincing evidence is available to show that lack of physical education leads inevitably to the physical deterioration of boys and girls in schools and colleges. As a recent example, all University of Oregon and Oregon State University entering freshman men and women were tested in the fall of 1961 with standard physical or motor fitness tests. For students graduating from Oregon high schools the preceding June, contrasts were made between those who participated and those who did not participate in physical education in the eleventh and twelfth grades. The tests given were as follows: Physical Fitness Index for University of Oregon men; a local motor fitness test for Oregon State University men; and the Oregon Motor Fitness Test for women at both institutions. For all comparisons, the means of the non-physical education groups were much lower than the means of the physical education participant groups.(7)

How successful have we been, in the eyes of others than our unbiased selves? Just before taking office, John F. Kennedy, President of the United States, wrote: "Over the past five years, the physical fitness of American youth has been discussed in forums, by committees and in leading publications. A 10-point program for physical fitness has been publicized and promoted. Our schools have been urged to give increased attention to the physical well-being of their students. Yet, there has been no noticeable improvement." (8) The basis for the President's assessment is not clear: did he have facts to support it or was this judgment an expression of his general negativism during that pre-presidential period when he viewed with a jaundiced eye anything the Republicans had done during the preceding eight years?

Undoubtedly, the above evaluation notwithstanding, there have been physical fitness improvements in many places, although, perhaps, not sufficient to provide an observable increase in the fitness level of the nation as a whole. Certainly, an increased recognition of physical fitness as a prime objective of physical education and a greater awareness that physical educators should do something about it is progress of a sort. However, we still have a crazy-quilt program pattern without a hard central core identified as basic physical fitness process. We must be willing to denounce that just any physical participation will suffice, that the administration of tests only has value, that publicity implies progress, and that viewing sports is a substitute for playing them. So, in the next section, this observer has the temerity to present his basic views relative to the nature of a proper and effective physical fitness program.

Basic Views for a Physical Fitness Program

Three features considered fundamental and recommended for achieving improvement of physical fitness by the President's Council on Physical Fitness are enthusiastically endorsed in principle. (1) "Pupils who have a low level of muscular strength, agility, and flexibility should be identified by a screening test. . . .Pupils so identified should be required to participate in a program of developmental exercises and activities designed to raise their physical performance to desired levels." (2) "Objective valid tests of physical achievement should be used to determine pupil status, measure progress, and motivate pupils to achieve increasingly higher levels of physical fitness." (3) While giving priority to these recommendations, "the school should strive to provide a comprehensive program of health education and physical education for all pupils." (9) As a matter of fact, these have been basic views of the speaker for many years and expression of them will be found herein.

1. *Activities should be selected to develop strength and stamina as basic for the development of physical fitness.* The view is fallacious that adequate physical fitness will result if all should exercise in any manner whatsoever. It can be demonstrated that fitness values from participation in some physical activities are definitely limited, that, depending upon one's exercise tolerance, unrestricted participation in vigorous activity may be most distressful, and that participation solely in any one physical activity, such as basketball or weight lifting, will not serve all aspects of fitness. Similarly, the proposal of a "daily dozen" or a set conditioning drill for all is a totally

inadequate approach to physical fitness. Effective exercise for fitness involves the proper selection of activities to develop specific components of physical fitness and participation in them in accordance with sound principles of exercise.(10)

Stress has been placed upon the acceptance of muscular strength, muscular endurance, and circulatory endurance as the basic nonmedical aspects of physical fitness. Exercise programs should be balanced effectively with activities selected and presented to achieve the improvement of these components. Within this basic framework, provisions can be made for the development of other traits associated with motor fitness, such as agility, power, flexibility, speed, and body balance.

For the development of muscular strength and muscular endurance, activities utilized must offer considerable resistance to the muscles. Such resistance may be applied in various ways: (1) by parts of the body, as in conditioning drills, football grass drills, guerilla exercises, etc.; (2) by inanimate objects, as in training with weights; (3) by the entire body, as in exercises on the parallel bars, horse, horizontal bar, climbing rope, and trampoline; (4) by another individual, as in wrestling, contact football, and a great variety of individual-to-individual resistance combatives.

Circulatory endurance is developed by participation in activities which require major adjustments of the circulatory and respiratory systems. Particularly desirable forms are hiking, running, and swimming, since the exercise dosage can be reasonably well controlled. Many sports have a high stamina element; among these are basketball, soccer, handball, lacrosse, water sports, and other sports and games requiring sustained running. In general, these sports also develop fast reactions, quick responses to constantly changing situations, agility, and flexibility. Further, when the sports are properly conducted, a host of personality and character traits may be affected favorably.

2. *Scientific principles of exercise should be applied in the conduct of activities for the improvement of physical fitness.* The physical fitness value of any activity has no meaning except as associated with the way it is applied. A potentially valuable activity for the improvement of a physical fitness component can be rendered largely ineffective if conducted in a lackadaisical manner. A set conditioning drill or a common run applied indiscriminately to all is just right for some but wrong for most. Thus, the application of scientific principles of exercise is essential for best results.

While there are others, the following five principles are proposed: (1) Exercise should be adapted to each individual's exercise tolerance. Exercise tolerance refers to the ability of the individual to execute a given exercise, or series of exercises, or activities involving exercise, in accordance with a specified dosage without undue discomfort or fatigue. (2) Overloading should be applied to induce a higher level of performance. In overloading, the individual's exercise is of greater intensity or for longer duration than normally; thus, overload is a relative term, extending from slight to severe. (3) The exercise plan should provide for progression. Progression may be accomplished by increasing either the intensity or the duration of exercise. (4) The individual's psychological limits of exercise should be advanced. (5) Motivation should be provided to increase the individual's desire to be physically fit.

3. *Allowances should be made for individual differences of boys and girls in providing physical fitness programs for them.* This principle may seem an obvious one, but nevertheless, it is largely disregarded in practice. Just how great these individual differences are among boys has recently been brought forcefully to the attention of the speaker as a consequence of the Medford, Oregon, Boys' Growth Study for which he is responsible. Examples of the nature and extent of differences found among 40 boys at each age 9 to 15 years, each boy being tested within two months of his birthday, are the following: At each age, the standard deviation for skeletal age was approximately one year; the ranges for the different ages were between four and five years. The following somatotype percentages were found: 7%, endomorphs; 21%, mesomorphs; 24%, ectomorphs; 10%, endomesomorphs; and 38%, midtypes. For single ages, the standard deviations for weight ranged from 10 pounds at 10 years to 24 pounds at 14 years. The standard deviations for the Strength Index ranged from 154 at 9 years to 466 at 14 years; the ranges at these same ages were 688 and 1928 respectively. Physical Fitness Indexes for the various ages ranged approximately between 50 and 175, a difference of 250%.

The significance of these individual differences has been studied. In all instances of significant differences between the means of advanced, normal, and retarded maturity (skeletal age) for boys at given ages, the boys in the more mature group were larger, stronger, and had greater explosive power. In studying somatotype categories, the endormorphs and endomesomorphs had greater body-bulk measures, but were seriously handicapped in performing pull-ups and push-ups; the mesomorphs showed superiority in both gross and relative (to age and weight) strength. The fact that structure affects function is borne out by the following high correlations between lung capacity and strength tests at the junior high school level: .86 with mean of 12 cable-tension strength tests, .84 with McCloy's Athletic Strength Index, .81 with elbow flexion strength, and .80 with Strength Index.

Certainly, the motor performance expectations of each boy and girl should be judged, in part at least, from a realization of his or her maturity, physique, and structural characteristics, as these factors impose limitations upon physical performance.

4. *Proper tests should be used to evaluate physical fitness components in order to identify boys and girls with deficiencies, measure progress, and motivate pupils.* Tests should be selected and given for a clearly defined purpose, and the test results should be used in the effort to improve the physical fitness of our youth. The follow-up program — the use of test results for program modification in order to serve the pupil better than would otherwise be possible — is the real justification for the administration of tests.

Comment on the use of norms may be appropriate at this time. As generally utilized, norms have a statistical connotation, providing a basis of reference for all sorts of performances, including those related to basic physical fitness components. However, the use of the word "normal" as referring to norms for a test can be most unfortunate. The test norm is usually an average and may not be a desirable level at all; it could well be too low, so by tying ourselves to it we would perpetuate weakness. As expressed by Gertrude Shaffer (11): "There is a vast difference between what is *normal* and what is *average* when we discuss the physical fitness of the American children. The *normal* youngster is extremely active, but the *average* American youngster, extremely inactive, lacks body control and has a poor physique. The connotation of *normal*, healthy children implies more than freedom from disease or disability; it implies that they have *normal* physical *development* as well. It is not *normal* for any child who is free from mental and physical disorders to fail the highly controversial Kraus-Weber test, which is a clinical test for minimum muscular fitness to maintain *normal* health."

This discussion is especially appropriate in view of the wide use of AAHPER Youth Fitness Test. Evidence is mounting to indicate that these standards are much too low for communities where children have regularly participated in physical education. As one illustration, Burke (12) reported that all boys and girls in grades 6 through 10 and those electing physical education in grades 11 and 12 of the Eugene, Oregon, public schools were tested with this test. In only one instance was the mean of these pupils below the national 50th percentile; this was a percentile mean of 47 for pull-ups by sixth grade boys. The lowest mean for the girls was 56 for the eighth grade softball throw. The highest means were 96 for ninth grade boys' sit-ups and 90 for twelfth grade girls' sit-ups. The means of all groups exceeded the 75th percentile in sit-ups, except the sixth grade boys (72). In light of such evidence, therefore, the norms for the AAHPER test may be recognized as the *average*, but most certainly should not be accepted as being *normal.*

5. *A major and essential process in raising the physical fitness level of our youth is to improve the status of those boys and girls who are subpar*

in basic physical fitness components. Activities and other procedures should be utilized specifically to improve the muscular strength, muscular endurance, and circulatory endurance of subpar boys and girls. For this group, physical activity and methodology should be directed toward meeting individual needs; ten identifiable steps have been developed for this purpose. Briefly, this process consists of the application of valid tests to identify the physically unfit; the use of case studies, living habit surveys, and other tests to determine the cause or causes of unfitness (and there are many); adaptation of activities and methods to alleviate the causes of unfitness; referral to other specialists as found desirable; and retesting periodically to assess treatment efforts and restudying those who fail significantly to improve.

This process for improving the physical fitness of boys and girls who are below acceptable standards is not just theory; it has evolved through trial over many years in school and college physical education. An example of an approach for instituting such a program is contained in the Oregon pilot physical fitness project of 1955-56, conducted under the auspices of the Oregon Association for Health, Physical Education, and Recreation. (13) In this project, physical education faculty and students at the University of Oregon, with cooperation from Southern Oregon College, Portland State College, Oregon State University, Lewis and Clark College, and Willamette University, were utilized as testers. In addition to administering the Physical Fitness Index test to at least 100 boys and 100 girls in each of 11 Oregon schools, a testing clinic was held for physical educators from the area near each school, a seminar was conducted on procedures to be followed in meeting the needs of unfit pupils, the local test results were interpreted to school personnel, and a process of public relations related to the local program was inaugurated. Retest results three months later showed very positive improvement in the fitness of participating boys and girls. With adequate continuing support from professional leaders in the state, this project could have placed Oregon in the forefront of the national drive for physical fitness. However, the lethargy so frequently encountered in difficult, prolonged, and unglamorous efforts doomed it to near extinction.

Many local school and college physical education programs have utilized procedures similar to those put into motion in Oregon. There has been some pronounced success in meeting the individual needs of unfit students.

6. *The entire scope of physical education in meeting the individual needs of boys and girls should be recognized and steps taken to realize its full potentialities.* In addition to programs of general developmental and conditioning activities for the physically unfit, the following functions may be included: (1) body mechanics training for individuals with nonpathological conditions, (2) adaptation of physical education and recreation activities for the handicapped, (3) psychological and social adjustments of "normal"

individuals with atypical tendencies, (4) relaxation activities for individuals suffering from chronic fatigue and neuromuscular hypertension, and (5) counseling, guidance, and assistance with physical fitness, personal adjustment, and social problems. (14)

7. *The physical fitness level of our youth in general should be raised.* While the plight of the unfit has been stressed as a major concern of any adequate physical fitness program, this does not mean that the fitness status of those who achieve minimum standards should not also be improved; they definitely should. Minimum physical fitness levels, unless those levels are so high that only a relatively small number can attain them, should never suffice. A practical solution would be to establish a sliding scale over a period of several years. Using the Physical Index test as an example, the initial level could be 85 and then gradually increased by 5 or 10 point increments until it reached 115. Within the general physical education pattern, it should be a simple matter regularly to include vigorous activities for the improvement of basic physical fitness components.

8. *Exercise should be presented to all as a way of life.* In our push-button society, people frequently question the need for much strength and stamina; this feeling is apt to be especially prevalent among those whose jobs are essentially sedentary. Many researches in such fields as medicine, physiology, nutrition, psychology, growth and development, geriatrics, and physical education, however, attest to the fact that exercise, with attendant fitness benefits, has far-reaching effects upon vital processes and upon the functional realization of one's maximum capabilities. (15) A synthesis of these scientific findings leads inevitably to the recognition of the totality of man, by which the organism acts and reacts as an integrated whole rather than as a trichotomy of body, mind, and spirit. As a consequence, exercise should be continuous throughout life.

9. *The present push on physical fitness should not be allowed to become just another swing of the pendulum.* In the past, our profession generally has had a propensity to go to extremes. At different times, we have gone all-out for leisure time skills, for sports programs, for character development, for group dynamics, and the like; seldom has balance been achieved among all of physical education's potentialities. With present presidential pressure applied to physical fitness, the temptation to go all-out for this one objective of physical education, to the neglect of all others, is great. So, now you witness one who has advocated a positive, planned approach to physical fitness throughout his professional career pleading for balance with social, moral, and democratic values.

A positive effort should be made to develop socially efficient individuals, who function harmoniously within themselves, in their relations with others, and as members of the society of which they are a part. Provisions should be made for the enrichment of human experiences through activities that lead to the better understanding of the environment in which the boys and girls find themselves. Attention should be given to activities contributing to recreational competency for leisure. Let the profession be mature, imaginative, ingenious, and stable enough to achieve coordination among multiple objectives.

A Conclusion and a Recommendation

The time is long past when physical education should solve its professional problems by expediency. We should not wait until an emergency confronts us, or we have been threatened, or we have been pressured by the President of the United States of America. We must get out from under the umbrella we invariably erect to cover all things for all people — physical fitness at the moment. It should not be just another name for the same old program, dressed up with ballyhoo and special incentives. We are too eager to please all interests, too anxious to bathe in the spotlight of publicity, too loathe to come to grips with fundamental issues, too reluctant to tackle processes that are tough, slow, and lacking in glamour. If this be a harsh evaluation, so be it. But, let's have positive, considered, and fully effective action.

What should we as a profession do? Unwieldy conferences lasting a few days or yearbooks written piecemeal are not adequate means of providing proper direction for establishing physical fitness processes within the framework of the over-all physical education program. What is essential is a concentrated effort, for as long a period as necessary, of a limited number of professional workers who have a solid record of achievement in conducting physical fitness programs, who are realistically comprehensive in their approach to professional problems, who are vitally mature in their national perspective, and who have a strong background in the research of this field. When ready, the "first-draft plan" of this group should be presented to various professional conferences and organizations for review and suggestions before final formulation. A continuing commission of some sort should be established for purposes of constant study and revision of the fitness plan in the light of new thought, new experiences, and new research. The best brains and experience of our profession should be brought to bear on this issue.

REFERENCES

1. Edward L. Bortz, "Exercise, Fitness and Aging," *Exercise and Fitness* (University of Illinois, College of Physical Education Colloquium Report). Chicago: Athletic Institute, 1960, p. 1.
2. Personal letter from Charles B. Wilkinson. The White House, Washington, D. C., February 26, 1962.

3. Delbert Oberteuffer, "The Role of Physical Education in Health and Fitness." Presented at the Joint Session of the Sections on Maternal and Child Health, School Health, and Nutrition of the American Public Health Association and the American School Health Association, November 14, 1961.
4. The name of the Council was officially changed, by Executive Order, from President's Council on Youth Fitness to President's Council on Physical Fitness in January, 1963.
5. President's Council on Youth Fitness, *Youth Physical Fitness: Suggested Elements of a School-Centered Program.* Washington: U. S. Government Printing Office, 1961.
6. Louis E. Means, "Three-Year Progress Report," *Journal of Health, Physical Education, Recreation* 33:73; February, 1962.
7. "Fitness Status of Oregon University Freshmen," *Physical Fitness News Letter,* University of Oregon, December, 1961.
8. John F. Kennedy, "The Soft American," *Sports Illustrated,* December 26, 1960.
9. *Youth Physical Fitness,* p. 14.
10. H. Harrison Clarke and David H. Clarke, *Developmental and Adapted Physical Education.* Englewood Cliffs, N. J.: Prentice-Hall, Inc., 1963, Chapter VII.
11. Gertrude Shaffer, "Why the American Children Are Physically Unfit," *The Physical Educator* 17:60; May, 1960.
12. "AAHPER Test Results, Eugene, Oregon," *Physical Fitness News Letter,* University of Oregon, February, 1962.
13. H. Harrison Clarke, "Report: Pilot Physical Fitness Project," University of Oregon, 1956 (mimeographed).
14. Clarke and Clarke, *op. cit.,* Chapter II.
15. H. Harrison Clarke, "Physical Fitness Benefits: A Summary of Research," *Education* 78:460; April, 1958.

Basic Body Mechanics: An Interpretation

MARTIN H. ROGERS[*]

Physical educators, teaching through the medium of games, sports, and big-muscle activities, evidence concern for the efficient mechanical and healthful function of the body. This interest has lead to the development of a number of concepts of function categorized as basic body mechanics. But physical educators, though they may share similar purposes and objectives, have failed to achieve general agreement concerning these concepts of body mechanics. As a result, body mechanics has been interpreted variously as a problem of posture and health, as a matter of kinesiological efficiency, or as aesthetic form and performance.

While it is unfortunate that there should be a lack of agreement concerning the meaning of basic body mechanics, this is nevertheless a situation quite normal in a growing and developing profession. Progress in any profession is characterized by changes in four directions — breadth, depth, convergence (specialization), and divergence (generalization). The profes-

[*]Martin H. Rogers, "Basic Body Mechanics: An Interpretation," *Journal of Health, Physical Education and Recreation.* Vol. 32, No. 9, December, 1961.

sional aspects of physical education are being influenced by these changes and by the varying orientations of thought implied by these changes.

As the profession has increased in breadth, interest has spread to encompass exercise for physical stature and symmetry, exercise for health and the correction of bodily defects, the adaptation of exercise for individual differences, programs for the development of fitness, and the development of physiological efficiency. Our interests span widely differing aspects such as health, recreation, therapy, physical development, aesthetics, and competition. In each of these areas the concept of body mechanics may take on a different meaning and imply a different set of values.

Exploration in depth in physical education has stimulated research related to competition in areas of physiology, the mechanics of superior skill, the development of fitness, and the psychology of competition. Anatomy and physics, as well as physiology, have been probed for their relations to exercise-therapy. Research in art and music has contributed to the development of concepts of the desirable human form and graceful function. Again, the meaning of body mechanics in these various areas varies with the interests of the researcher.

The phenomena of convergence and divergence may also be illustrated. The expert in sports skills, the coach, reduces his problems to the principles of the mechanics of operation of the human body; the expert in therapeutic exercise reduces his problems to the principles of body mechanics; the expert in aesthetics in activity reduces his problems to body mechanics. All of these, specializing in different areas and interested in different outcomes, have converged at a common, basic, foundation. Moving in the opposite direction, the single concept of posture may be treated in different ways — as a static physical discipline, as a goal for healthful body development, as a factor in efficient body function, or with disregard, as a relatively minor problem, not particularly significant to the health or efficiency of an individual.

Let us examine these varying interpretations of body mechanics for the purpose of synthesizing a theory of basic body mechanics which might receive more universal acceptance. A clear cut statement should help to obviate the confusion created by the variety of meanings now existing for the term basic body mechanics.

The Traditional Concept

It has become traditional to relate basic body mechanics directly to various concepts of erect human posture. In our literature many books with "body mechanics" in their titles are devoted to a discussion of human posture; units in health education texts use the terms "body mechanics" and "posture" synonymously; reference sources list "posture" under the heading of "body mechanics"; and many school and college courses in body mechanics are, upon investigation, posture training. This juxtaposition of body mechanics and posture might seem to indicate universal acceptance of their inter-relatedness, but a critical view suggests that the idea is less than adequate. One reason for this is a lack of uniformity concerning the concept of posture itself. Another reason is a difference in meaning — the concept expressed by the term "posture" suggests status and position, while the concept expressed by the term "mechanics" implies movement and dynamism.

It has also been traditional to accept a concept of correct posture in which the body is held truly erect, with certain body landmarks falling along a straight and vertical line. Defined as normal posture, this erect position is described in health texts and is illustrated in an assortment of shadow pictures and silhouettes. Deviations from this vertical alignment are graded A, B, C, and D postures, depending upon the amount of departure from the vertical plumb line. In many physical education programs, posture correction is based upon this alignment, and exercises are performed to train muscles to hold the body in this position.

What is not often understood is that this body position was selected arbitrarily by Braune and Fischer in 1890 as a convenient, standardized position from which to measure normal deviations, since all reference points of the posture lie along a single line. Termed by them the "Normal-Stellung," it served merely as a statistical point of departure, a line of zero deviation; it had no relation to what might be the usual, desirable body position. Rather, they hoped to collect data on deviations from the vertical, to show how normal posture deviated from the vertical. Braune and Fischer, in setting up a measuring scale, had no intention of depicting that as the ideal posture, though their work has been widely misinterpreted in that direction for 70 years. Little wonder, then, that we have experienced difficulty in training people to maintain habitually this posture — a hypothetical norm at best, an artificial concept, and one which even an athletic and healthy individual can hold only momentarily.

Fortunately, a drift away from this misconception of posture is reflected in recent definitions of posture which are more functional and deserving of understanding and acceptance. Katherine F. Wells describes posture "in terms of efficient movement of the body as a whole and its adaptability in response to the various demands made upon it" (JOHPER, November, 1948, page 591).

The idea of posture as a static position is deposed in favor of posture as a movement, or a position for movement. In their textbook, *Kinesiology* (C. V. Mosby, 1950), Laurence Morehouse and John Cooper described posture in a similar vein. "Normal posture, then, is that posture which best suits the individual in accordance with his own condition and the condition of his environment." They describe an *attention* situation of erectness and readiness, a *fatigue* situation in which the body sags on its ligaments to conserve energy, and a *readiness* situation characterized by ease and efficiency of motion from one position to another. Eleanor Metheny has stated that correct posture is a solution of the gravity problem which allows free and efficient movement, and that it is the job in physical education to rework and rebuild movement patterns to achieve efficiency (JOHPER, March, 1954, page 27).

These views reconcile some otherwise uncomfortably contradictory facts. If we are thinking in terms of efficiency and readiness, it is not strange that the traditional posture of verticalness is difficult to maintain. We are comforted by the knowledge that, physiologically, a "relaxed" standing position requires 10 percent less energy than an "easy" standing position, and 30 percent less energy than a "military" standing position. On this basis, a requirement of a formal position of attention during certain phases of physical education seems quite untenable. Further, we need not be bothered by the elusive relationship between posture and health. Minor deviations from an arbitrary vertical line are only deviations from a *statistical* norm, not deviations from what is correct. It is hardly strange that we can observe many such deviations with no paralleling disturbance of health status. There is little or no evidence that postural deviations affect health. We may also be reassured that deviations from the "Normal-Stellung" in athletes is not contradictory. It may even be that the round-shoulderedness found in many high-class professional basketball players, for instance, is for them the posture of efficient movement.

The dynamic interpretation of posture involves mechanics and leads to a logical relationship between posture and body mechanics. Posture, dynamically conceived, involves movement of the body from some starting position to a new position or series of positions, and necessarily includes the machinery and process of movement. Physiologically, as well as mechanically, this concept is more palatable, for it involves movement. The primary characteristic of all living things is movement, a constant flow of motion as the organism adapts itself to its environment. Life is never static; only a dynamic concept of posture should be acceptable.

Now let us interpret body mechanics as it relates to posture. Webster defines "mechanics" as that part of physical science which treats of the action of forces on bodies. That part of mechanics which considers the action of forces in producing rest or equilibrium is called *statics;* that which relates to such action in producing motion is called *dynamics;* the practical application of the principles of physics, especially the laws of motion, and of the effect of forces upon the properties of bodies, to the construction, action, and work of machines or mechanical tools or devices." By projection, *body* mechanics is the practical application of the principles of physics, the laws of motion and the effects of forces, to the properties, action, and work of the human body. It is the process by which the tendency of the body to move, as well as its movements, are directed to desirably efficient ends. Basic body mechanics comprises the principles of mechanics fundamental to the execution of body movements — the most appropriate principles of motion applicable to the efficient function of the body.

Basic body mechanics, thus interpreted, implies that there is less interest in body positions per se and more concern for the effective integration of the body as it performs. The aesthetics of a standard static position are less important than the aesthetics of an efficient and graceful skill. Even our standards of grace may be modified, and beauty of performance may be judged more by results than by stylized patterns in space. A healthy distrust of traditional styles and form in performance will stimulate a constant search for still more effective performance techniques and physical skills.

Principles of Body Mechanics

Principles applicable to basic body mechanics are discussed by Wells, Morehouse and Cooper, and other authors of kinesiology texts. Among these are principles of equilibrium, including the position of the center of gravity, size of the base of support, and mass of the body; inertia and momentum; friction; segmentation, angular motion, and componential forces; and the summation of forces. Several of these principles have been applied to skills in selected sports. Research in electromyographic analysis of muscle action has contributed to improvements in golf and tennis styles and added to our understanding of summation of forces in human movement. Further study of the movements of unsupported bodies and rotary motion leads to new skills in diving and increased performance in the discus throw and jump-shots in basketball. Through the application of these principles, faults in body integration, posture, and equilibrium are eliminated, and desirable body mechanics are achieved. The primary aim is efficient function. Good posture — in the aesthetic sense — may be a desirable secondary result.

For purposes of application, many of the specific principles may be grouped in three operational principles of body mechanics: (a) the equilibrium of being off-balance, (b) diagonal and reciprocal arm-leg coordination, and (c) rotary motion, its relation to supported or nonsupported bodies, and the direction of a thrusting force upon the body's center of gravity. A few selected activities may illustrate the application of these principles.

The principle of the equilibrium of being off-balance utilizes the force of gravity and other forces to overcome inertia, maintain momentum, and assist in changes of direction. Human locomotion is often described as a process of falling forward and then walking or running to catch up to one's self. If locomotion is attempted from the "Normal-Stellung" the body is held erect and the legs reach forward for each step, but they are unable to extend strongly because of limited extension potential in the hip joint. The body is in balance as long as the feet are in contact with the ground and momentum is minimal. A slight change in technique exploits the force of gravity. From an easy standing position the trunk leans forward until the center of gravity is forward of the base. Gravity takes effect and the body moves in a forward direction. As the rear foot swings forward to catch the weight the forward leg is extending and the body base moves forward under the center of gravity. However, with the body lean, the center of gravity also moves forward. Constant propulsion is provided by the force of gravity and by the muscles of the legs. Abdominal muscles are well fixed to anchor the pelvis and provide a foundation for the swinging movements of the legs, but a slight pelvic tilt is essential to allow for sufficient hip extension to propel the body. This would be impossible otherwise, since the tension of the iliofemoral ligament normally prevents extension of the hip joint beyond 180 degrees.

Running, basically an exaggeration of the walking principle, involves greater forward lean of the trunk. A greater effect from gravity is encouraged. The body tends to move forward so fast that it is necessary for the legs to leap from point of support to point of support to keep up with the falling tendency of the trunk.

Another example of the equilibrium of being off-balance is the ordinary throw. By moving the front foot forward, or off the ground, the front corner of the body is unsupported and the center of gravity is suspended slightly in front of the base provided by the rear foot. The body tends to fall, thus giving impetus forward. To the force of gravity is then added a push from the rear foot and the motion of the throwing arm in a typical summation of forces. In the illustrations used, gravity is exploited to provide initial momentum for the hips and trunk, conserving muscle energy for additional force to the trunk, or for more effective movements from a moving foundation.

The second group of principles, concerned with the diagonal and reciprocal coordination of the arms and legs, is most obvious in simple walking movements. The coordination which swings diagonally opposite arms and legs forward or backward in the stride is a natural and inherent neurological structure in the human body. Efficient use of the body calls for the application of this principle in a variety of movements such as reaching, one-handed pulling or pushing, door opening, and lifting, where the arm action is accompanied by a stride position of the legs with the forward leg being that which is diagonally opposite to the working arm.

An interesting application of this principle is in ladder climbing. As an individual mounts the ladder, the diagonally opposite arm and leg support the weight on the rungs, while the other pair moves to the next higher rung. As these movements follow in sequence the center of gravity of the body (located at a point on an imaginary line connecting the diagonally opposite arm and leg) ascends in a straight line, with no lateral momentum, and the ladder does not swing. If another type of coordination is used, with the arm and leg on the same side alternately supporting or moving, the center of gravity ascends in a zig-zag motion which ultimately causes the ladder to sway and become unstable. The desirable coordination is nothing more than an extension of normal walking to a vertical plane.

Throwing is another activity in which the reciprocal coordination is extremely important. Leg action, rather than arm action, should be stressed, for if leg action is clear the arm action will follow almost automatically. Stepping forward with the foot opposite to the throwing arm, and leaning forward with the trunk, moves the center of gravity ahead of the base and puts the body weight into the throw. The throwing arm coordinates easily with the leg action. The naturalness of this coordination is demonstrated in teaching a right-handed person to throw with the left hand. While holding the ball left-handed, the individual steps out on the right foot, stressing the action in his mind. With the strong step, the arm is allowed to follow through naturally, and a reasonably good throw is achieved.

The third group of principles, concerned with rotary motion, has many applications. Fancy diving and rebound tumbling employ endless variations. If the thrust of the diving board or trampoline is along the long axis of the body and the center of gravity is also in that same line, curvilinear motion of the body will follow; if the trunk leans either forward or backward at the hips so the thrust is in back of, or in front of, the center of gravity, rotary motion in the form of a somersault will follow. Spinning in the air, or rotation around the long axis, is most frequently achieved by swinging one arm toward the trunk; the body then spins toward the arm in accordance with the principle of action (arm) and equal and opposite reaction (body). Other applications of this principle are made in the lifting and carrying of heavy objects, the shot-put, the sprint-start in running, the racing dive in swimming, and the use of body in football blocking and body checking.

In teaching, these basic mechanical principles should be accompanied by exercises designed to develop muscle groups employed in the basic coordinations. Such conditioning contributes to an individual's ability to execute proper mechanics; leads ultimately to the development of mechanically correct habit patterns in movement; and helps reach the goal of a well-developed, well-integrated body performing physical skills without strain, without waste, in the most efficient and graceful manner possible. These are the purposes of an understanding of basic body mechanics.

Child Development Research: Implications for Physical Education
Anna S. Espenschade[*]

Physical education is an integral part of the elementary school curriculum and makes important contributions to the objectives of education in a democratic society. Periodic re-examination of purposes and goals in the light of changing environment and new knowledge is essential for planning optimum programs.

Taller and Heavier

Research in physical growth has important implications for physical education since there is an intimate relationship between size and physical abilities. The longitudinal studies of the 1920's and '30's have presented a clear picture of the pattern of growth of various body segments. Standing height, probably the most easily obtained measure of all, has been found to be one of the most significant for interpreting individual growth. Body weight in relation to height is a rough predictor of nutritional status.

Systematic collection of height and weight data at six-month or even annual periods increases the value of the measures, especially when the results are plotted on a grid such as the Wetzel or those developed at the University of California at Berkeley and the State University of Iowa. The grid graphs indicate nutritive failure and the need for referral for medical examination. They also show rate of growth and this has implications for every aspect of development, mental, social, and emotional as well as physical.

Children in the United States today are growing taller and heavier faster than at any period in our history. A recent survey at an Oakland, California, junior high school showed that eighth-grade girls are on the average one inch taller and four pounds heavier than girls of the same age and grade in the same school were 24 years ago. For boys the increases were 1.8 inches and 10 pounds. Statistics do show that the average height and weight of American adults is gradually increasing, but the rate of change is far below that noted in this particular sample.

---

[*]Anna S. Espenschade, "Child Development Research: Implications For Physical Education," *The National Elementary Principal.* Vol. 39, No. 5, April, 1960.

The explanation for these extraordinary changes must be found in good nutrition, freedom from disease, and possibly climatic conditions. There is no evidence to indicate racial or socio-economic changes in the sampling. These children have grown up in a period of relative prosperity. An optimum combination of factors has evidently stimulated the rate of growth and a greater percentage of mature height and weight has been attained by these eighth graders than was true 24 years ago.

The important fact to recognize is the increasing rate of maturity which is occurring in some children in the elementary schools today. It is not uncommon to find girls of 8.5 years and boys of 9.5 years who have already entered the pre-adolescent period of accelerated growth. At the same time, there are wide individual differences. Some children will not reach this phase of development during the elementary school years. Quite probably, the most homogeneous groups from the standpoint of rate of physical growth will be found in the second and third grades.

Deficiencies in Strength

Although children in our country are taller and heavier and are in better health than ever before, there is a growing body of evidence to show that there has not been an accompanying increase in muscular strength and in physical abilities. Surveys of Kraus and associates on muscular fitness of various samples of U. S. and European children found the latter to be markedly superior at all ages from six to sixteen years. The Kraus tests are designed to measure what he calls the minimum strength necessary for health and well-being of abdominal and back muscles, plus back flexibility.

A number of independent investigators[1] in the United States have obtained results similar to, although in most cases somewhat better than, those reported by Kraus. Some improvement with age in performance in all strength tests has been observed by all investigators. This has not been true of the flexibility test. American boys are especially poor in this measure.

Although no comparable data for the United States as a whole have ever been collected, the present averages indicate very poor performance in tests of dynamic strength and endurance such as pull-up (chin), push-up, and sit-up.

These deficiencies in the physical development of youth in the United States were brought to the attention of President Eisenhower and, in 1956, the first American peacetime conference on "Fitness of American Youth" was convened. The President's Council on Youth Fitness was created and

---

[1]Phillips, Marjorie, and others. "Analysis of Results from the Kraus-Weber Test of Minimum Muscular Fitness in Children." *Research Quarterly* 26: 314-323; October, 1955.

has stimulated a great number of projects, including a national survey of physical abilities of children in grades five through twelve.[2]

The state of Connecticut has recently completed a survey on fitness of youth and used the national test battery as one of the measures.[3] The findings reveal marked weakness in arm and shoulder girdle strength. Preliminary results of a state-wide project in California indicate that these same strength measures show lower averages than those obtained in California in the 1920's.

In addition to tests of muscular strength and endurance, the national battery includes various events in running, jumping, and throwing. These are designed to measure power and coordination, agility and flexibility of arms, legs, and body. Many state and local programs include similar, if not identical, events. A number of studies are in progress at the present time and results are not yet available. Some data from earlier years will be useful for evaluative purposes but direct statistical comparisons will be possible in only a few instances.

The evident deficiencies found in children today in comparison with Europeans or earlier Americans in arm and shoulder girdle strength reflect the absence of lifting, climbing, pulling, pushing, and possibly tumbling and similar activities in which the weight of the body or of other objects is frequently carried by the hands and arms. These same activities make important contributions to development of abdominal muscles. Only a cursory examination of today's living with its high rate of urbanization and automation is needed to show the extent to which natural opportunities for muscular development have been taken away from our children. Walking to and from school is no longer a part of the life of thousands of rural or urban children. Even stair climbing is being eliminated as many houses and schools are built without stairs!

Fitness for What?

The word "fitness" has many connotations and inevitably raises the question, "Fitness for what?" The President's Conference recommended that we be alert to the facts that "in this age of automation the fitness of our youth cannot be taken for granted; indifference to the softness which comes from lack of participation in health-giving activities will bring erosion of our strength; and physical fitness goes hand in hand with moral, mental, and emotional fitness. Intensive, continual, and cooperative research must

---

[2]American Association for Health, Physical Education and Recreation. *Youth Fitness Test Manual.* Washington, D. C.: the Association, a department of the National Education Association, 1958.

[3] Connecticut Association for Health, Physical Education and Recreation. *Fitness of Connecticut Youth.* Danbury, Connecticut: the Association, 1959.

be conducted to supply the factual base for formulating fitness policies, plans, and programs."[4]

Since in the United States today the physical demands made on men, women, and children by the tasks of daily life tend to be minimal, the desirability or necessity of developing strength and gross motor abilities may be questioned. A substantial body of evidence points up the need for exercise, however. Biologically, man is made to be active and must be active for optimum mental and physical health.

The American Medical Association, in a pamphlet entitled *Exercise and Health,* has summarized medical observations and research findings in this area. Interaction between structure and function is important for development. Systematic muscular exercise is a factor in growth in height, weight, and vital capacity of children and youth. It has recently been found that regular physical activity will eventually increase the density of the bones of the body and elasticity of connective tissues. This increases their resistance to stress and strain, a resistance which is lost if exercise is not continued.

Regular physical activity also produces organic changes, particularly in the lungs and circulatory system, some of which improve function for normal living and also give protection against stress and strain. The heart is a muscle and develops through use. The healthy heart responds to exercise by increasing in size and functional capacity. The exercised heart is stronger, slower in rhythm, and steadier than the untrained one and is capable of more sustained effort. It must be recognized that there are certain age differences which are not eliminated by training. The heart of the young child, for instance, beats more rapidly than that of an older one and blood pressure is lower in childhood. Breathing is done by muscles, also, and both the chest muscles and the diaphragm are developed by exercise, especially by that of the more vigorous type.

Obesity is becoming a serious problem in children as well as in adults today. Although no single causative factor can account for this, underactivity as well as overeating is important in the total picture.

There are some obvious implications here for the physical education program in the elementary schools. Certainly the school can take only limited responsibility for meeting the activity needs of children. It has been estimated that children of elementary school age should have from four to five hours of activity every day and this includes week-ends and vacations. The school can, however, make a major contribution in providing space and

---

[4]President's Conference of American Fitness on Youth. *Fitness of American Youth.* A report to the President of the United States. Washington, D. C.: Superintendent of Documents, Government Printing Office. 1956. p. 3-4.

equipment for vigorous activity and in planning a program designed to give systematic and demanding exercise to all parts of the body. This is just as important for girls as boys.

Recent research substantiates a common observation that some individuals need more exercise than others. Body build is a factor here. Some children are quite literally built for exercise and enjoy large amounts of it. A unique pattern of endocrine factors, determined in large part by heredity, shapes the body and controls the rate of growth of each child. Almost certainly, these same factors regulate the characteristic energy level also. Energy level in any individual is related to basal metabolic rate. It may be momentarily influenced by time of day, state of health, amount of sleep, kind of breakfast, and a host of other things, but the overall pattern is a part of the individual and an essential part of personality. There is a sex difference in energy level in the direction of greater energy in boys than in girls, but the difference between sexes is less than that between individuals of the same sex.

Early Experiences Important

Activity and multiple stimulation, both intrinsic and extrinsic, are now recognized by psychologists as vital factors in both physical and psychological maturation. The vital necessity for mental development of the learning going on in infancy, the product of early experience, has been clearly demonstrated only rather recently. Even a very limited environment will provide much of the necessary stimulation.

Generalized experience is necessary to normal intellectual development.[5] The multiplicity of sensory and motor experiences in the preschool years enables the child to build a series of skills upon which he can call in response to the demands made by development and by society. The greater the variety of experience, the richer the resources for later use. It seems certain that long before going to school, children have many times made every movement of which their bodies are capable. Strength, speed, flexibility, and balance increase with growth as well as with exercise. Changing body proportions due to growth present ever-new problems of coordination. Physical abilities and motor coordinations develop by use.

It is probable that in a primitive environment experiences of daily life would provide adequate opportunity for exploration and development of all motor coordinations and the acquisition of special skills. Modern society imposes strict limitations on natural movements and because of this children may not develop efficient ways of using the body, good posture, and easy,

[5]Hebb, D. O. *A Textbook of Psychology.* Philadelphia: W. B. Saunders Co., 1958.

graceful carriage. Poor body mechanics are one cause of muscular strains and tensions which contribute to fatigue and irritability. In the physical education program, constant attention should be given throughout the early years to the prevention of defects or, if necessary, to the correction of those which occur. The latter requires specialists in the field and usually medical supervision or direction. Most bad movement habits are acquired during the elementary school years. These may lead eventually to structural changes in the body which affect health in adult years. It is unfortunate that so few communities provide the staff and facilities for proper care and prevention of defects in the elementary school.

Developing Game Skills

The years of early childhood have been referred to as the skill-learning years. In this period learning the game skills useful for participation with peers is considered an important developmental task. Many of these skills, such as ball throwing and catching, are taught to children by each other. The concentrated practice and devoted drill which these skills receive from highly motivated child participants is constantly astonishing to adults.

All children do not have opportunity to develop a wide variety of skills out of school, however, nor do all of them "catch on" readily without guidance. Systematic instruction should be provided in physical education classes. Most children have the ability to acquire sufficient skill in simple techniques to enable them to participate without handicap in group games. This amount of achievement and success is very important in social and emotional development. It should be possible for every child to find activities in which he can participate with satisfaction. This serves the dual purposes of a means of recreation and a way of maintaining physical fitness.

As children grow older, they are capable of more complex activities, both physically and intellectually. One study of children's interests attributed lack of interest in some games on the part of intellectually gifted children to boredom due to lack of challenge, rather than to dislike of activity. Widespread participation of elementary school boys in Little League baseball in the last ten years has demonstrated the fact that large numbers of nine-year-olds can and do master baseball skills and strategy to a degree that would not have been believed possible earlier. Although these participants may well be more mature or more gifted in physical abilities than the average, there are implications for the physical education program especially in grades five through eight.

Growing children enjoy using developing abilities. In these grades, however, individual differences in size and physique, as well as in motor ability, are more evident. In vigorous and in highly skilled activities, the class should be divided into homogeneous units, or teams should be equated for ability.

If body contact sports are included in the program for boys, the class should be divided according to sex. For most activities in the elementary program, individual differences will be greater than sex differences.

Research in the organization of motor abilities shows that these abilities tend to be fairly unique. Only narrow group factors appear. And there is no evident increase in interrelationships with age. Thus there is little prediction from one activity to another. The child must explore widely in order to know what he can do best and which activities appeal to him most. What does transfer, however, is attitude toward activity and possibly also methods of attacking the learning situations.

Effect of Cultural Influences

The need for activity is common to the young of every species and provides a built-in motivation for physical education and playground activities in the elementary schools. Cultural influences are strong, however, and subtly but insistently determine sex-appropriate behavior.

High prestige values are associated with physical activities for boys at all school ages. The role of girls, on the other hand, is not so clear cut. They are expected at times to be able to swim and play tennis, but this should not be a primary interest as they are expected to be available when boys are not occupied with their own pursuits. Studies show that these so-called typical adolescent behaviors occur in some parts of our country, at least, on the average two years earlier than they did a generation ago, and before the majority of girls have reached puberty. A seventh-grade girl stated recently at a Teen Town Meeting that she liked physical education because it was "all right" to play games there that she could no longer play after school. Since physical education is compulsory, no stigma could be attached to this participation. This places an additional responsibility on the physical education program since it apparently must provide a major part of the vigorous activity needed by pre-teen-age girls.

Personal Adjustment

In the preadolescent years, a new awareness of self is gradually developing. Physical development, especially anything that may appear atypical either to the individual himself or to his peers, may become a major source of anxiety. For example, the special problems of the early maturing girl, which have been so clearly pointed out in recent studies, occur during the elementary school years. The fat or awkward boy usually is a problem to himself, especially in physical activities where he finds himself expected to participate with the group. Guidance in these cases is certainly not the exclusive province of the teacher of physical education, should there be one, but recognition of the need for it may well take place in the physical education class.

Because of the natural interest which children have in play, it is an excellent medium for many types of learning. Physical activities provide a miniature world for the exploration of social relationships and for group interaction. Under expert guidance, children learn not only rules of the game but also codes of ethical behavior. They learn to cooperate with others, to work for the good of the whole, to submerge self in the team. They should learn also, in controlled situations, to handle stress, to endure frustration, to accept but not to overvalue success.

The emphasis in this article may appear to be placed most heavily upon implications from research in physical growth, development, and exercise. This has been done purposely because these findings emphasize the unique role of physical activity in development. Studies of interests, attitudes, and personal and social adjustments have implications for all aspects of the elementary school program, including physical education. These latter types of learnings are not inherent in physical activities themselves but are outcomes dependent upon good leadership and good planning. Some of them may be attained more readily for more children through physical education than other school subjects because of the strong motivation children bring to this class.

The Physiology of Motor Learning
F. A. HELLEBRANDT, M.D.[*]

Introductory Remarks:

The literature in the field of motor learning is surprisingly extensive. It provides the interested reader with a seemingly limitless reservoir of useful information that flows across many different areas of human knowledge. Among the latter may be listed the various branches of psychology, embryology, neurophysiology, clinical neurology, orthopaedic surgery, kinesiology, and physical education. As yet no one one has attempted to integrate the total evidence in a single definitive review. Whether the mind of one person can encompass the wealth of material available, and assess it critically, is a question yet to be answered.

My own interest in the subject of motor learning began in 1930 when I reviewed Coghill's classical work, *Anatomy and the Problem of Behavior,* at a seminar of the Department of Physiology at the University of Wisconsin. In the years that followed the recollection of Coghill's concepts remained undimmed, forming an ever-present frame of reference for a succession of

[*]Hellebrandt, F. A., "The Physiology of Motor Learning," *Cerebral Palsy Review.* July-August, 1958.

clinical and laboratory experiences. The publication of Coghill's London Lectures did, in effect, mark the beginning of a new multi-disciplinary area of investigative effort. Weiss has suggested that this be called *Genetic Neurology*. Almost 25 years elapsed before time and circumstance permitted the systematic accumulation of available source materials. That bibliography now contains approximately 1000 references. If all major leads were followed and important collateral paths pursued the literature would stand at about 2500 titles with at least one tenth of the whole classifiable as basic to a reasonably sound and comprehensive understanding of the subject.

The discussion to be presented is of necessity still incomplete. It is a progress report or a preview, a tentative summing up, strongly biased, as is inevitable, by the character of the research done in the disability evaluation laboratories of the Medical College of Virginia and the Research and Educational Hospitals of the University of Illinois. Although that research was designed to elucidate problems related to the rehabilitation of the disabled, much of the experimental work was done on normal subjects. The data throw light, therefore, on the mobilization of the physiological resources of normal men participating in sports and physical education activities. The selfsame mechanisms operate when the handicapped individual extends the performance of some prescribed rehabilitation task to the limits of his restricted capacity. Indeed, the biological responses evoked in the two situations may be virtually indistinguishable.

Movements not Muscles are Represented in the Cortex:

This aphorism, oft repeated, has lost meaning because of its familiarity. Its implications are increasingly challenging, however, as more is learned about the reflex and volitional control of movement.

If muscles participate in more than one movement, as most do, they must be represented diffusely in the cortex. Presumably different centers connect via internuncial neurons with groups of peripherally disposed motor units. The work of Seyffarth and of Denny-Brown has shown that motor units are activated in a definite sequence which varies with the movement elicited. As the severity of the effort increases, those involved primarily in one movement may be recruited to assist in the performance of others. During elbow flexion, for instance, certain motor units of the biceps brachii only appear at very high tension, whereas the same units go into action at the slightest provocation during supination. Reviewing this work Darcus suggests that the limited field of neurons excited at the onset of contraction widens concentrically as the effort augments. Eventually it overlaps neighboring fields, evoking a concurrent excitation of neurons primarily concerned in other movements by the same and by functionally related muscles.

Gellhorn and Hyde have shown that the size and configuration of the area of cortical representation of an extremity is influenced significantly by the proprioceptive inflow from the limb. Neurons destined to activate the motor units of a given muscle may be quite scattered. One might postulate that those concerned with the action of a particular muscle as a prime mover may be relatively concentrated and of low threshold. Others lie far removed from the primary focus, in association with low threshold neurons destined for other but related muscles. It would follow from such an hypothesis that the full complement of motor units present in any muscle can be activated volitionally only in association with other muscles attached to the same or contiguous anatomical segments. Perhaps, as we shall see, an all-out effort may even mobilize more remote parts of the same and/or opposite side in the resultant movement-complex.

The Prefiguration of Movement Responses:

Gellhorn has shown that supra-threshold cortical stimulation evokes patterned action in which several anatomical parts may participate. These responses are similar to the total synergies seen so commonly in the clinic. They are perfectly integrated. They range in complexity from agonist-antagonist contractions about a single joint to modifications in the functioning of muscles which are distributed so extensively as to change the total adjustmental design of the body and its appendages. We have had a particular interest in those associated with spontaneous variations in the positioning of the head and neck during heavy resistance exercise. Our own studies and innumerable clues in the literature suggest that the reflexes evoked under similar conditions are extraordinarily consistent. Indeed they are so repetitive as to warrant designating them patterned movements. If all the muscles in a synergy operate under a common governing force, as Seyffarth suggests, the fundamental unit of action may be thought of as a total response in which agonists and antagonists, synergists and fixators participate in balanced and harmonious activity. Partial patterns emerge secondarily, by virtue of special training, but remain forever yoked to the integrated primitive total response.

The concept being outlined is an important one of obvious utility in the rehabilitation of the disabled. If movements are represented in the cortex in their total complexity a muscle may be made to function as a synergist or fixator when it cannot be used as a prime mover. Partridge has shown that a muscle may be so strengthened through systematic participation in a patterned response that it can be emancipated eventually from the total synergy and made to act once again in its capacity as a prime mover.

The complexity of the picture being drawn increases many-fold when the concept of proprioceptive facilitation is added to it. Gellhorn and his associates have demonstrated that the sensory feed-back coming from muscles, tendons and joints greatly affects movement patterns. Central excitations have a tendency to flow always into stretched muscles. Thus, every change in body positioning alters the configuration of the next succeeding efferent response. It affects not only the muscle stretched, but all functionally related muscle groups as well. This means that a change in the responsiveness of one component of a movement-complex spreads autonomously to the other constituents.

Proprioceptive impulses not only increase the excitability of the motor cortex but affect the reflex activity of the cord as well. Electromyographic studies suggest that the myotatic reflex activates striated muscles in functional patterns similar to those elicited by cortical stimulation. The reflex arising in a single muscle excites not only this muscle and its synergists at the same joint, but also those synergists which act on neighboring parts and form with the stretched muscle, a functional association of ancient origin and obvious utility. The reflex linkage may be so strong that greater activity is evoked by impulses arising proprioceptively in other components of the synergy than by autogenous proprioceptive stimulation. This is of practical importance in muscle re-education and probably also affects the way in which skills are acquired by the normal individual.

Automation or the Emancipation of Voluntary Acts from Conscious Control:

Nielson believes that willed movements which are new and unfamiliar always demand cerebration. They are performed at first with more or less conscious attention to the details of their execution. Once mastered, they operate automatically. Conscious introspection at this stage may even disrupt the nicety of an established pattern. After an act has become automatic, says Nielsen, it is less well performed if it must first be considered and analyzed.

Nielsen's description of the learning of a planned act such as the tying of a square knot, is instructive. The first step calls for appreciation of the relative positions of each part of the rope. This requires inspection and analysis, to whit, cerebration. Vision then guides the moving parts. Kinesthesia is aroused by the act itself. A lasting trace or engram is left in the wake of repeated usage. Eventually a square knot can be tied with little or no thought. Feel is now sufficient. The learner can tie a square knot without looking or with the eyes shut. He can even tie a square knot without any memory of having done so. As Sherrington would say, consciousness is no longer adjunct to the act. This means that as an act becomes automatic the area of the cortex which initially serves in planning it, becomes unnecessary to its execution. If automaticity is lost, as a result of disease, the patient must re-plan the simplest acts and the results are as crude as his first attempts of initial learning.

A major component of the material from which a learned movement is built is the incessantly varying sensory input. To this must be added what Penfield calls "the guidance of memory and the conclusions of reason." No one knows for certain the seat of that integration which precedes willed movement. This is the so-called mind-brain problem which has puzzled biologists and philosophers for many decades.

Sperry argues that the primary business of the brain is the governing of overt behavior. Since overt behavior consists of no more nor less than patterns of muscular contraction, it follows that the principal function of the nervous system is the coordinated innervation of the musculature. The entire output of our thinking machine consists of nothing but patterns of motor coordination, says Sperry. It yields nothing but motor adjustment. This view will be recognized as the reverse of the one subscribed to by our British colleagues, who would have us believe that the motor cortex is not importantly involved in willed movements. The great pyramidal system has been dethroned by Walshe, Goody, and Bartlett, and reduced to a humbler status than that held formerly. To this Twitchell has added his voice. The pyramidal system initiates nothing of itself, they say. It is no more than a way-station in the stream of outgoing volitional impulses, an internuncial path interposed between the integrative system and the final common path over which effector impulses flow to selectively patterned constellations of motor units. The sensory input is the great initiator and moulder of muscular responses, for willed movements are activiated by controlling cortical afferent patterns of excitation. But none of this solves the mind-brain enigma. Interposed between the sensory input and the motor outflow is the integrative center. Nielsen localizes it in the posterior association area of Flechsig. But various ablation and sectioning experiments in animals and man suggest that integration does not reside in the cortex. Penfield therefore places it in a biencephalic brain-stem position, and calls this hypothetical seat of the mind-brain union the centrencephalic system.

Penfield conceives the outflow of the centrencephalic system as one arriving in already patterned form at the motor area of both hemispheres. If the cortex is damaged, the system can still operate on a limited but useful plan embracing the activation of primitive subcortical motor mechanisms. There is much of interest in this scheme which is deduced from a large series of human cortical ablations resorted to for the surgical treatment of focal epilepsy. It postulates a mechanism which insures integrated participation of the machine as a whole. Much of value may be learned by closer examination of the behavior pattern in toto, and less fixation of attention on the movement of the presenting part which is only a fraction of the neuro-muscular response evoked.

Spinal Cord Mechanisms and their Operation:

The outflow from the lower motor centers is a double one now known as the large and the small nerve systems because of the difference in the diameter of the fibers leaving the cord by the anterior roots. The large fibers innervate only the main muscle fibers responsible for the contractions which activate the bony levers for the production of movement. The muscle fibers are grouped into so-called motor units. All of the one hundred or more diffusely scattered muscle fibers of the motor unit shorten synchronously and to their maximal extent or not at all.

The small nerves, or gamma fibers, innervate the sparse intrafusal muscle fibers of the spindle. These are assembled in closely grouped clusters of six or eight fibers. They are considerably modified and bound together by a connective tissue capsule. The polar regions of the intrafusal fibers are muscular and contractile. Barker has shown that the equatorial zone is occupied by a nuclear bag which is packed with 40 or more nuclei. Around this the annulospiral ending winds itself. This is the primary stretch-afferent, or the nuclear bag afferent. When the small nerve fibers stimulate the intrafusal muscle fibers, they contract, stretch the spindle, and evoke a barrage of impulses from the annulospiral ending. These travel by way of large, rapidly transmitting afferent fibers, which form a monosynaptic loop, excitatory to the large motor fibers of the muscle concerned and also its associated synergists. This is a fast, facilitatory servo designed to adjust the level of muscular activity to the magnitude of the stress. Granit believes gamma impulses lead off at the onset of cortically induced movements. These then facilitate selected anterior horn cells which evoke the responses in the motor units which induce the movements willed. Excitation of the main motoneuron pool appears, therefore, to be dependent on the inflow from the spindle afferents, and the level of their activity is set by the gamma system, which according to Granit and Kaada is under cerebral control. Thus the small nerve innervation of skeletal muscles mediates the impulses which initiate and drive muscular contraction, especially that concerned with postural adjustments. Rapid movements are activated via the direct route utilizing the large anterior horn cells. Granit, Holmgren and Merton believe the adjustment of activity between the two modes of excitation is a function of the cerebellum. This acts as a neural switch which directs impulses originating in cortical or subcortical motor centers into the large or small nerve route.

Classified as a proprioceptor, the annulospiral feed-back operates preeminently on the cord level where it can in no way be introspected, and hence does not contribute to kinesthesia. Some proprioceptive circuits travel up the cord to the cerebellum, which also contributes to the reflex control of movement.

The muscle spindle also contains one or sometimes two flowerspray endings. These are located in the myotube region which is the transitional area of the intrafusal muscle fiber just before the fibril passes through the nuclear bag. This proprioceptive receptor has a higher threshold than the annulo-spiral ending. It takes stretch of higher intensity to elicit a response. The impulses evoked travel over smaller and hence slower circuits than those subserving the annulospiral flow. There is some evidence suggesting that they pass on to the somesthetic cortex and hence may reach consciousness. The richness of the alternate circuits discussed previously suggests that the motor moron, who cares nothing about his muscle sense or is incapable of bringing it to awareness, is still protected in the execution of physical skills by a compassionate Mother Nature.

Both the primary and secondary spindle afferents are facilitatory servo-mechanisms. They augment the functional capacity of the motor units from which they arise as well as those of synergically associated muscles. Inhibitory mechanisms also exist. They too are built-in devices, giving the muscle an extraordinarily rich autogenetic control. One is the system subserved by the Golgi end-organs. Their presence has long been recognized in at least one region, at the point where the main muscle fibers come together to form the tendons and aponeuroses by which muscles are attached to their bony levers. More recently Golgi end-organs also have been described at the point where the small modified intrafusal fibers of the muscle spindles attach, usually to extrafusal muscle fibers. Newer knowledge of some significance attaches to the function served by such an arrangement of Golgi receptors. The spindle is an excitatory afferent. The Golgi end-organs are inhibitory afferents. Thus the structural linkage of the two gives the muscle a perfect means of autonomous self-regulation. Facilitatory reflexes vie with inhibitory reflexes and the level of activity manifest is the resultant of the balanced activity of the two. It would appear that the small nerve fibers which activate the annulo-spiral and flower-spray endings of the muscle spindle do not have a completely free hand. Should they increase tension of the intrafusal muscle fibers to too high a level, and send too many facilitatory impulses tumbling over the servo loop, the Golgi end-organs can dampen the reactivity of the mechanisms involved.

Adequate as the Golgi system seems, still another autogenous cord level controlling device exists. The large nerve fibers innervating the motor units send a recurrent axon collateral back into the cord. These fibers synapse with Renshaw cells which are small internuncials closely associated with the motoneuron pool of the anterior horn. They fire at exceedingly high rates and are inhibitory in function. The backfire affects not only the given muscle but also its synergists. This means that outgoing impulses travelling in large nerve fibers inhibit, if not their own, adjacent ventral horn cells. Thus the small Renshaw internuncial cells serve as a kind of commutator which switches excitation to inhibition. Granit believes that the Renshaw negative feed-back stabilizes the output frequency of anterior horn cells to the values adapted for driving muscular tissue. It is a damping device which keeps the brakes on the anterior horn cells. They operate always with the inhibitory controls applied.

The post-war rapid development of electronics and the production of precision tools of extreme sensitivity are the two events which made possible the sudden significant enlargement of our information about muscle receptors and how they function. Proprioception is now considered to be one of the most highly developed senses, exceeded in complexity only by the receptors of the eye and the ear. Among the best recent reviews are the works of Barker, Tiegs, Granit and Eccles.

Less is known about the sensory inflow from the joints but this story is also unfolding due to the efforts of Boyd, Gardner, Andrew and others. Proximal sensitivity exceeds distal. The shoulder may be forty times as sensitive as a joint of the finger. Presumably two receptors are involved. The Pacinian corpuscles are rapidly adapting. They respond with a burst of action potentials during movement but cease to discharge when new positions are reached. The capsules of the joints are also supplied with spray-type endings called Ruffini corpuscles. These are slowly adapting and discharge indefinitely with a frequency characteristic for each position assumed.

I have dwelt thus exhaustively on the organization of the proprioceptive system because much has been added to our store of knowledge in recent years. Feed-back from the muscles, tendons and joints appears to be a cunningly devised and exceedingly complex mechanism, a large share of which operates at levels below consciousness. Not only has automation come to industry. We now know that the machinery of the living body is equipped with its own servo-mechanisms. Its operation proceeds to a large extent without placing the slightest demand on the cerebral cortex. Innumerable mechanisms exist which are beyond the reach of the most astute physical therapist or teacher of physical education. Perhaps what we need most are techniques of motor learning that free the subcortical motor mechanisms from an oppressive domination of a stressed cortex. Starting from scratch, decorticated as it were, primitively integrated, we might then explore the wonders of that inherent, ancestral movement repertoire and use it as Nature intended before encephalization produced its present degree of tension and inhibition.

Levels of Control:

Motor mechanisms operate normally under several categories of control. It is generally conceded that higher levels tend to exercise domination over lower levels. Yet many neuromuscular operations proceed in an orderly and integrated way without interference by the highest centers. They can, however, be modified at will. We also know that oft-repeated volitional acts sink to levels of operation which proceed with little or no awareness. They become submerged through the office of little understood mechanisms. They can be brought to the surface of the mind again and again and made to re-engage the attention. Similarly wholly involuntary or reflex movements may be brought under subjection to the will. Sherrington has said that when we know how the mind makes itself felt on the running of the reflex machinery we will have gone a long way toward understanding the basis of motor learning.

Our own work has been concerned primarily with the functional useful-ness of certain automatic reactions. These emerge sufficiently under stress to be studied. They are either frankly dynamogenic devices, that is, they ex-pedite work output when the machine begins to fail, or they contribute to the automatic training of symmetrical parts which takes place without direct practice and is known as the phenomenon of cross-education. They have one characteristic in common, an expanding pattern of operation which must greatly augment the sensory feed-back. The irradiation associated wtih ex-treme stress is so wide-spread that a willed movement limited to a single appendicular joint may evoke action potentials in muscles located in all four extremities, the head and neck, and the trunk. These seem to us to be orderly and wholly integrated total patterns of response. Observing them we get the impression that they are the obligatory concomitants of very severe stress, and the only way in which the highest threshold motor units of the muscle subjected to direct training can be activated. These are the motor units held in reserve and called upon when truly maximal effort is demanded — when you rush into a burning house and perform some phenomenal feat of strength, or when you break the 4-minute mile, or swing your paralyzed legs across a street in the time-span of the green light that gives you the right of way.

The evolution of the expanding patterns characteristic of the response to physical stress deserves attentive and meticulous study. Here we see primitive compensatory mechanisms of ancient origin coming to the surface in ways designed to reinforce functional capacity. If we understood these better, we might gain new insight into the mechanisms underlying coor-dination.

Theories of Motor Learning:

The theories of motor learning number at least three. No informed and understanding student can help but be impressed by the galaxy of built-in mechanisms with which we are endowed. These are the reflex responses which operate at spinal cord and sub-cortical levels. They are, as Sherrington taught, ancient, stable, certain, invariable, and stereotyped. Easily elicited, they run their course with a machine-like fatality once they have been evoked. Consciousness is not adjunct to their operation. They cannot be introspected. But they exist and must account for a substantial proportion of all of our daily neuromuscular activities.

Weiss proposes, on the basis of 30 years of experimental effort, that the fundamental patterns of coordination arise by self-differentiation within the nervous system, prior to, and irrespective of experience in their use. They form a repertoire of movement patterns which is pre-experiential in origin. The contemporary machine deserves no credit for these built-in skills. Weiss believes that every muscle has a distinctive constitutional specificity and that the nerves supplying the muscle acquire specific differentials of their own which match and centrally represent those of the muscles. Muscles transform nerves and modulate centers, thus elaborating patterns of coordination in what Weiss calls the myotypic code. There is a large and interesting literature on this subject. It is referred to also as the resonance phenomenon, and it explains in part why the "scores" of the movement repertoire are so repeatable in certain of their dimensions whether or not there has been an opportunity to practice them. Presumably they are full-blown when the maturation of the central nervous system is completed.

For more than 25 years controversy has centered about the primacy of the reflex vs. the primacy of an integrated total organization in embryological motor development. These concepts are associated with the names of Windle and of Coghill respectively. The literature on this subject runs into hundreds of papers. The heuristic concept presupposes that isolated reflexes, complete in themselves, are combined bit by bit into more and ever more complex chains and other circuits. Trial-and-error combinations of fragments leads to the development of serviceable constellations further modulated by practice and experience. Partial patterns may be disengaged at will, and re-engaged if desired, but each fragment is complete and autonomous in itself.

Much muscle training in physical therapy has been of this type. It begins with simple normal range movements, approached as though instigated by the isolated contraction of some prime mover. Purity of movement has been the ideal, and many a physical therapist has visualized this as the achievement of the particular muscle to which treatment was being directed. There has been much careful suppression of overflow, presumably because overflow is something indicative of decadence in coordination. Simple normal range movements have been added one to another like building blocks used to erect increasingly complex combinations of movement. There is much which is admirable in this approach. What is said about its rationale is perhaps more unacceptable than the technique itself, which has an obvious place in the clinic.

The opposite extreme is the holistic approach to motor learning. This contends that living protoplasm is endowed with a primordial dynamic ability to respond in toto in ways maximally advantageous to the organism as a whole. The whole is forever greater than its parts. It expands progressively, but always as a totally integrated mechanism. The boundless initial response of the developing organism becomes more circumscribed only with the emergence of inhibition. Lesser degrees of input are then required to trigger the same effector response and this too, is gradually narrowed as a result of experience and practice. Partial patterns are individuated within the total pattern and acquire varying degrees of discreteness. But they remain forever yoked to the primordial total response. The total system is thus an hierarchy of many smaller systems of various grades of autonomy and subordination, all of which are so related that their local and partial activities cooperate to maintain the integrity of the whole. Parts become integrated with each other because they are integral factors of a primarily integrated whole, and behavior is normal so long as this wholeness is maintained.

Anyone who has participated in sports or observed the muscle re-education of the disabled has seen precise partial patterns of movement revert to total patterning under the exigencies of fatigue or emotional stress. I have already suggested that such expansions of the response, secondary to strong affective states or other stimulation, are never haphazard movements. They are orderly and patterned. They greatly augment the sensory feed-back, and probably serve an automatic facilitatory function. Overflow patterns may be manifestations of a stress too great to be coped with by discretely individuated partial patterns, but they are in no sense grossly disrupted skills.

Some Unsolved Problems:

Recent studies of the performance of older workers in industry has turned up one surprising fact related to the thesis being developed. Motor goals are reached in many ways. The same task evokes a variety of responses. The same end-result may be achieved in an apparently infinite variety of ways. Rarely if ever are motor units of different muscles activated in exactly the same spatio-temporal pattern. When a task is learned a memory engram is supposedly laid down, but there is no constant use of the same combination of muscles. Rather, muscles are used in different ways to achieve the same result time and again. If the customary sequence of movements employed is impossible, another is used. Nature endows all organ systems with large margins of safety. The industrial studies of Welford and his associates suggest that as long as the goal has been particularized and as long as a sensory channel is available for estimating the extent to which the objective of the movement has been reached, the cerebrum will use any movements that it can command in an effort to reduce the gap between purpose and fulfillment. As the skill of older workers deteriorates, output may remain quite unchanged, because the experienced performer autonomously finds new ways of accomplishing the same task. Anyone who has worked with the disabled knows the fantastic facility with which trick movements are learned. Through their use we witness time and again, seemingly impossible motor achievement.

Welford and his associates have speculated extensively on the biological significance of this interesting behavior. They believe that such an operational plan automatically spreads the metabolic load over a greater mass of tissue. In this way fatigue is avoided, or its effects are mitigated to an appreciable degree. Denny-Brown has discussed the same point in his writings on electromyography. A normal man "eases the burden of fatigue by changing the nature of the contraction"; that is, he evokes a response in some new constellation of motor units capable of attaining the same objective when the first lot has fatigued. This appears to us to be exactly what occurs when stress becomes intolerable. The exercising subject is able to continue only if spontaneous irradiation patterns are permitted to run their course unhampered. If nicety of technique or purity of movement is the objective, functional capacity may be cut far short of the levels attainable through utilization of spontaneous, primitive, deep-seated facilitatory synergies.

Recently we had an opportunity to observe a severely disabled quarduplegic athetoid patient of reasonable intelligence perform certain sport skills. The extraordinary thing about these cinematographic and electromyographic studies was not how the normal subject differed from the pathological, or vice versa, but how easily the eye could catch the basic similarities in the underlying movement patterns. There are many ways in which the same goal can be reached, and man unconsciously picks and chooses among the gamut of those available, easing the burden of fatigue as Denny-Brown said, and thus extending the range and sensitivity of his movement vocabulary. The physical therapist, shop foreman, physical educator or coach may wish to impose upon the human subject some precise and specific technique of movement, but an infinitely wise living machine, drawing upon the experience of centuries, makes its own autonomous adjustments. Instead of suppressing these, we would do well to study them. Thus we might learn, perhaps, some of Nature's secrets.

Much has been written about methods of expediting motor learning, especially in the psychological literature. Psychical factors loom large as Bartlett and Gooddy have indicated. No one denies this. Bartlett believes it is more important to know *what* is to be done, than *how* to do it. Presumably he is willing to relegate the *how* to an experienced and well integrated neuromuscular machine, perfected through the ages. It is Bartlett who denies that it is practice which makes perfect. Only practice the results of which are known makes perfect.

The British school has placed great stress on the neglected sensory side of purposive motor behavior. Gooddy believes we learn patterns of sensation, not patterns of movement. Thus the sensory inflow in the initiator and molder of all movement. Feed-back mechanisms operate incessantly, without interruption. The degree to which visual and auditory cues modify movement has never been studied adequately. We have not begun to think in neurophysiological terms about the mechanisms underlying many of the things a good teacher does intuitively to achieve selected neuromuscular objectives. We might enhance the efficacy of our techniques of application if we understod them better.

Twitchell has shown that a limb deprived of sensation is more impaired than one suffering the residual effects of a rolandic cortical ablation. And yet, if the skin sensation of a portion of the palm of the hand is allowed to remain intact, the exteroceptive feed-back from that spared fragment of the whole is sufficient to integrate purposive movements of the total extremity. This may explain why hand positioning is the key to the whole intricate complex of a golf swing. Recent work by Hagbarth suggests that exteroceptive skin sensation alone is capable of evoking reflex movements similar to those elicited by cortical stimulation.

Sherrington more than anyone else has emphasized the importance of proprioception. Since movement begins and ends in posture, he postulates that the resident sensations emanating from the part in its resting state may be more important than those associated with movement per se. We have never given this proper attention in our analysis of muscular activities. Usually we think only of the moving part.

Much work was done during the war on many aspects of motor learning, especially those important to the operation of aircraft. This material, which is gradually being assimilated in the literature, is full of suggestive findings. Bartlett has discussed the fact that key cues only rise to awareness in the execution of certain skills, and that the bulk of what is happening proceeds at levels below consciousness. He even suggests that the less we know about this background of postural adjustment and associatel movement, the better. When it obtrudes in consciousness, performance deteriorates. These are new ideas, antithetic in a sense to those proposed by the neurophysiologist. Perhaps the kinesthetic acuity we should strive for is not enhanced general body awareness, but rather, a more sharply defined and specific sensitivity to what is happening in those key maneuvers upon which the success or failure of a complex movement pattern may depend.

The biomechanical approach to movement study is a vital step in any program of total understanding. It has been given more attention than the neurophysiological approach. What the normal human being does in the execution of a given skill must be disected and analyzed in biomechanical terms. I would only remind the biophysicists that behind the angles of projection measured so meticulously are patterns of innervation and servo-mechanisms of the greatest interest. Behind those variations in the velocity of moving part are living muscles. It is the contraction of muscles which develops the power to move the parts, and the functional capacity of muscles may be augmented by overload training. We must look behind the physical findings and ferret out the mechanisms which produce them. One side of the story without cognizance of the other gives a distorted picture, at least to the unwary and inexperienced observer.

Some of the references in the bibliography appended are easy reading. Others stretch the limits of the understanding of the trained and disciplined mind. In physical medicine we say a disabled man must rehabilitate himself. The student of motor learning must likewise seek out for himself those parts of the recorded history of this subject which are meaningful to him. I have stressed what seems important only to me, as of this moment, and that has been colored by a particular experience. Many topics remain yet to be studied.

BIBLIOGRAPHY

Andrew, B. L.: "The sensory innervation of the medial ligament of the knee joint," *J. Physiol.*, 123: 241-250, February, 1954.

Barker, D.: "The innervation of the muscle-spindle," *Quart. J. Microscopical Science*, 89: 143-186, June, 1948.

Bartlett, F. C.: "The measurement of human skill," *Brit. Med. J.*, 1: 835-838, June 14, 1947; 877-880, June 21, 1947.

Boyd, I. A.: "The histological structure of the receptors in the knee-joint of the cat correlated with their physiological response," *J. Physiol.*, 124: 476-488, June, 1954.

Boyd, I. A., and T. D. M. Roberts: "Proprioceptive discharges from stretch-receptors in the knee-joint of the cat," *J. Physiol.*, 122: 35-58, July, 1953.

Coghill, G. E.: *Anatomy and the Problem of Behaviour*, University Press, Cambridge, 1929.

Coghill, G. E.: "The early development of behavior in Amblystoma and in man," *Arch. Neurol. Psychiat.*, 21: 989-1009, May, 1929.

Coghill, G. E.: "The neuro-embryologic study of behavior: principles, perspective and aim," *Science*, 78: 131-138, Aug. 18, 1933.

Darcus, H. D.: "Discussion on an evaluation of the methods of increasing muscle strength," *Proc. Roy. Soc. Med.*, 49: 999-1008, December, 1956.

Denny-Brown, D.: "Interpretation of the electromyogram," *Arch. Neurol. Psychiat.*, 61: 99-128, February, 1949.

Eccles, John Carew: *The Neurophysiological Basis of Mind*, The Clarendon Press, Oxford, 1953.

Eccles, John Carew: *The Physiology of Nerve Cells*, The Johns Hopkins Press, Baltimore, 1957.

Eldred, E., R. Granit, and P. A. Merton: "Supraspinal control of the muscle spindles and its significance," *J. Physiol.*, 122: 498-523, December, 1953.

Gardner, Ernest: "Physiology of moveable joints," *Physiol. Rev.*, 30: 127-176, April, 1950.

Gellhorn, Ernst: "Patterns of muscular activity in man," *Arch. Phys. Med.*, 28: 568-574, September, 1947.

Gellhorn, Ernst: "The influence of alterations in posture of the limbs on cortically induced movements," *Brain*, 71: 26-33, March, 1948.

Gellhorn, E.: "Proprioception and the motor cortex," *Brain*, 72: 35-62, March, 1949.

Gellhorn, Ernst: *Physiological Foundations of Neurology and Psychiatry*, The University of Minnesota Press, Minneapolis, 1953.

Gellhorn, E., and J. Hyde: "Influence of proprioception on map of cortical responses," *J. Physiol.*, 122: 371-385, November, 1953.

Gooddy, William: "Sensation and volition," *Brain*, 72: 312-339, September, 1949.

Granit, R., and B. A. Kaada: "Influence of stimulation of central nervous structures on muscle spindles in cat," *Acta Physiol., Scand.*, 27: 130-160, 1952.

Granit, Ragnar: *Receptors and Sensory Perception*, Yale University Press, New Haven, 1955.

Granit, Ragnar, B. Holmgren, and P. A. Merton: "The two routes for excitation of muscle and their subservience to the cerebellum," *J. Physiol.*, 130: 213-224, October, 1955.

Hagbarth, K. E.: "Excitatory and inhibitory skin areas for flexor and extensor motoneurones," *Acta Physiol. Scand.*, 26: Suppl. 94, 1952.

Hellebrandt, F. A., Annie M. Parrish, and Sara Jane Houtz: "Cross education, the influence of unilateral exercise on the contralateral limb," *Arch. Physical Med.*, 28: 78-85, February, 1947.

Hellebrandt, F. A., Sara Jane Houtz, and A. Mary Krikorian: "Influence of bimanual exercise on unilateral work capacity," *J. Applied Physiol.*, 2: 446-452, February, 1950.

Hellebrandt, F. A.: "Cross education, ipsilateral and contralateral effects of unimanual training," *J. Applied Physiol.*, 4: 136-144, August, 1951.

Hellebrandt, F. A., Sara Jane Houtz, and Robert N. Eubank: "Influence of alternate and reciprocal exercise on work capacity," *Arch. Physical Med.*, 32: 766-776, December, 1951.

Hellebrandt, F. A., Sara Jane Houtz, Donald E. Hockman, and Miriam J. Partridge: "Physiological effects of simultaneous static and dynamic exercise," *Am. J. Physical Med.*, 35: 106-117, April, 1956.

Hellebrandt, F. A., Sara Jane Houtz, Miriam J. Partridge, and C. Etta Walters: "Tonic neck reflexes in exercises of stress in man," *Am. J. Physical Med.*, 35: 144-159, June, 1956.

Herrick, C. Judson: *George Ellett Coghill*, The University of Chicago Press, Chicago, 1949.

Nielsen, J. M.: "Ideational motor plan. Role of the parieto-occipital region in planned acts," *J. Nervous Mental Disease*, 108: 361-366, November, 1948.

Partridge, Miriam J.: "Electromyographic demonstration of facilitation," *Phys. Therapy Rev.*, 34: 227-223, May, 1954.

Penfield, Wilder: "Mechanisms of voluntary movement," *Brain*, 77; 1-17, March, 1954.

Seyffarth H., "The behavior of motor units in voluntary contraction," Skrifter Norske Videnskaps-Akademi, Oslo, Matematisk-Naturvid. Klasse, 5: 1-63, 1940.

Sherrington, Sir Charles: *The Integrative Action of the Nervous System*, Second edition, Yale University Press, New Haven, 1947.

Sperry, R. W.: "Neurology and the mind-brain problem," *Am. Scientist*, 40: 291-312, April, 1952.

Tiegs, O. W.: "Innervation of voluntary muscle," *Physiol. Rev.*, 33: 90-144, January, 1953.

Twitchell, Thomas Evans: "Sensory factors in purposive movement," *J. Neurophysiol.*, 17: 239-252, May, 1954.

Walshe, F. M. R.: *Critical Studies in Neurology*, The Williams and Wilkins Company, Baltimore, 1948.

Weiss, Paul: "Self-differentiation of the basic patterns of coordination," *Comp. Psychol. Monographs,* Vol. 17, Number 4, Serial Number 88, September, 1941.

Weiss, Paul: *Genetic Neurology,* The University of Chicago Press, Chicago, 1950.

Weiss, Paul: "Nervous System (Neurogenesis)," Chap. I, Sec. VII, Willier, Benjamin H., Paul A. Weiss, and Viktor Hamburger: *Analysis of Development,* W. B. Saunders Company, Philadelphia, 1955.

Welford, A. T.: *Skill and Age,* Oxford University Press, London, 1951.

Windle, William Frederick: *Physiology of the Fetus,* W. B. Saunders Company, Philadelphia, 1940.

Windle, William F.: "Genesis of somatic motor function in mammalian embryos: A synthesizing article," *Physiol. Zool.,* 17: 247-260, July, 1944.

Chapter

Physical Education
and the Culture

Sport and Culture
Rene Maheu[*]

If we consider sport and physical training as what they are in essence —
human disciplines with a social function and a role in the formation and full
development of personality — we at once begin to wonder what connections
and interactions there are between athletics and culture, seeing that both contribute to the enrichment of our human heritage, sport by the conscious and
rational development of our bodies and culture by a steady pursuit of perfection which appears to enlarge progressively the range of our intellects
and sensibilities.

What are the connections between sport and culture? This question is
one of the major problems of our age, and I have been thinking about it for
years. But in spite of this, I feel I have made hardly any progress toward
an understanding of it. This means that I shall not presume to offer any final
answer; all I shall do is put forward a few personal observations and if
my comments and speculations prompt any thoughts that may help to
elucidate this extremely difficult question I shall be happy.

I do not intend to examine the relations between culture and sport
from an historical angle. The problem of contemporary civilization is what
matters to us and though comparisons with the past may help throw light
on the subject, we must concentrate on the situation as it is today.

The first thing to be said is that if we take culture in the sense of any
of its forms of expression, present contacts between it and sport are ex-

*Rene Maheu, "Sport and Culture," *International Journal of Adult and Youth Edu-
cation.* Vol. 14, No. 4, 1962.

tremely slight, in fact practically nonexistent. In philosophy, literature, the theatre, even the cinema, in painting, sculpture, and music, works of merit based on sport either in form or substance are few indeed. It inspires only a very small number of works of the mind or of art of any aesthetic significance.

But this is not the worst. If we take France as our example (for what is true of this country appears to be broadly true of many others), we find that the few interesting works influenced by the highly idiosyncratic world of sport belong to a far distant and long since ended epoch when sport was still in the aggressive stage of seeking acceptance as a customary social activity. I need only name Giraudoux, Montherlant, Jean Prévost, André Obey, and Joseph Jolinon in literature and — if I may be permitted to annex Switzerland for argument's sake — Arthur Honegger in music. And nothing connected with sport by any of them is later than 1925.

Since that date sport has steadily continued not only to make its presence felt but to gain widespread social acceptance. Yet it is noticeable that in spite of this triumph as a social phenomenon there have been hardly any worthwhile cultural works with sport as their basis. Conversely, the world of sport is less and less informed with intellect and art. Where, in the stadiums, are there statues worthy of the beauty of the contestants' movements and the artistry of the games? At Helsinki, the bronze running figure of Nurmi moved me more by its fidelity to reality than by its aesthetic value as a statue. Where are the plays, the symphonies, the songs, and the ballets which should provide the counterpoint, the preludes, and the codas to the struggles and drama of athletics? Where are the meditations, the exordia, the musings which should reflect and deepen the concept of balanced mastery of body and soul? Who cannot fail to deplore the lamentable mediocrity of the literature and art in the contests which Pierre de Coubertin wanted to be an integral part of the Olympic Games, as in the days of antiquity, but which, since Melbourne, have come, understandably, to be treated as the merest sideshows? All this adds up to the astounding, dismaying, infuriating, and even, to be frank, scandalous situation in which sport, otherwise triumphant, is excluded from what I shall not call culture but culture's modes of expression.

It is from this that I want to start in an attempt to understand and, if possible, to find a solution to the problem of the mysterious relations between sport and culture. Of course, there is one explanation that immediately comes to mind which is accepted by many people. Sport, it is argued, is incompatible with culture or at most is still at its confines and only at a later stage in its evolution will it cross the threshold of acceptance into culture.

This opinion is still widespread in many quarters' considered intellectual and among many teachers and educators. Hence it is all the more urgent to show just how far from the truth it is. In my opinion sport is far from being incompatible with culture and inferior to it but is a variety of it, and as things stand it fulfills a cultural function for vast numbers. This is the idea I should like to develop by reviewing certain features which justify our regarding sport as a companion phenomenon to culture itself.

To begin with, sport and culture spring from the same source — that is, leisure. There can be neither culture nor sport without the luxury of leisure, without the spare time and the unspent energy left to a man after his work to use as he wishes. Now in today's civilization, leisure is constantly increasing. Over a very long period work was the essential occupation of civilization, but now with the great strides made in mechanization it is leisure that is the essential, if not the most important thing, in life. In the same way, in antiquity, the free man's life, except in time of war, was all leisure.

The pursuit of culture and the cultivation of certain values do in fact imply large surpluses of energy and time for man to use as he wishes — so much so that the Greeks used the same word for leisure, schooling, and education. Nowadays sport is perhaps the most widespread leisure activity. In many countries "sport" and "leisure activity" are practically synonymous, so if sport does not ally itself with culture, it is bound to contend with it. For, though both derive alike from leisure, we cannot but perceive that sport has a much stronger attraction for the masses than culture.

Sport, as we have seen, fulfills the same function as culture, for it too dignifies those hours and that energy not absorbed by our utilitarian work. That is why sport as a job is not really sport. The only true sport is amateur. The moment sport becomes a utilitarian activity practiced for profit it loses its connection with leisure from which it originally sprang and which gives it its essential dignity and its close affinity with culture.

Let us go a little farther. Among the various activities that fill our leisure, there is one, common to both sport and culture, that we call play. This introduces a new element, for play is indulged in for its own sake. It is a voluntary and unpaid activity of free men, valued for itself; it is its own reward and its own justification. But culture is the same; it is play, unrealistic comparison with the purposeful activities of life, and this is true even of the study of philosophy or the humanities. Sport, too, is essentially play. It is not by accident, for instance, that in English sports are "games" and are "played" not "practiced." Physical and intellectual play are both self-justifying, gratuitous activities.

The comparison could be carried much farther, to include even the details. Thus, the gratuitous nature of "play" is by no means exclusive of logical necessity — it may be said to generate such necessity. The less trammeled an activity is in itself, the greater its need for rules to give it the appearance of being bound by its own arbitrary laws; thus the fictional domain in which play takes place is given the same coherence and the same realism that the laws of nature confer on the real world. And so, in sport, progress always follows increased refinement of the rules. This means, not that sport is an activity born of necessity, but quite the contrary, that, as a gratuitous activity, it must look to the rules to provide it with standards and an anatomy.

If we carry the analysis further, yet another characteristic emerges. "Play" is divisible into two categories of game, games of chance and competitive games. On the one hand, there are the games in which man with his freedom to choose pits himself against chance (which is the absolute negation of rule and of fatality) and, on the other, there is what Roger Caillois calls the *agon*, the contest-game, the competitive game, where man (and this is true of all games of skill) pits himself against material objects and the forces of nature or against himself or, in competitive games, against other men. Of these two types of play, games of chance, e.g., dice and all their variants, and the contest-game, it is undoubtedly the second to which sport belongs. Now the distinctive feature of the contest-game essentially is to awaken in the spectator an understanding born of sympathy, which the game of chance in no way arouses. Take the case of a gamester, say, at roulette or dice. There is no current of sympathy (except fortuitous, born of personal links) between gamester and watcher, and the latter does not feel involved. If, on the other hand, we take a contest-game, we find a current of sympathetic participation linking watcher and player from the start.

Here we have an element common to sporting events and cultural spectacles. In the theatre, the audience involves itself in the drama being enacted before it (thus becoming, after a fashion, actor as well as spectator) and similarly in the stadium, an intense empathy develops between spectators and performer. I would even assert — and here we see how closely cultural spectacles (e.g., the theatre) and sports are parallel and comparable — I would even assert that spectator sports are the true theatre of our day. Think of the tens of thousands who fall silent as the athlete prepares to jump and shout with relief as he soars upward. In what theatre could one find an instance of comparable communion? This participation by the spectator as well as the performer, this close link generating a current of sympathy, understanding, and support from the nameless crowd of watchers or listeners to the individual taking the stage and expending himself, takes us back to the very start of the theatre of antiquity, the theatre of Greece. That is why sport, because it involves this particular facet of contest-play, is able to release and, in the Aristotelian sense, to "purge" the emotions of the spectator, just as effectively as any work of art in general and of the theatre in particular.

There is only one emotion that I know of which has absolutely no place in spectator sport and is death to it — laughter. Laughter is not for the sports ground, and if it occurs it means that sport has turned into something else. Sport is action which expresses the lyric or dramatic and sometimes even tragic emotions. It is play of extraordinary seriousness, with a place for the smile of satisfaction but none whatever for the destructive laughter which shatters the whole atmosphere and destroys the hold of the spectacle upon its audience; such laughter is the evil genius of sport and alone is barred from the stadium. All other human feelings, all other emotions, sport can express. Like culture and the arts in general, sport exteriorizes those feelings and emotions in the player and, by empathy, in the spectator, thereby assuming the function of "catharsis," of purification, which Aristotle had long ago remarked in the theatre.

It is therefore not astonishing that sport, like the theatre, like literature, and like the plastic arts, should be a creator of myths. There is indeed a mythology of sport, which may at times seem somewhat childish to intellectuals, but this mythology has its legends and its heroes and, however it is expressed, it evidences a power of creation which shows the close kinship of the "all-round" arts with sport.

I need hardly say that sport is a creator of beauty. In the action and rhythm which testify to mastery of space and time, sport becomes akin to the arts which create beauty. No athlete can accomplish a genuine feat without such perfect physical control, in time and space, that his movements and the rhythm of their timing are not to be differentiated from the finest ballet, the most splendid passage of prose or verse, the most glorious lines in architecture.

Lastly, in art as in sport, we find in the protagonist the same inimitable assertion of personality which we call style. Several runners may well achieve the same record time for the same distance, but no two of them will do it in the same way. Two athletes, or three, may clear the same height or reach the same distance with the javelin, but each will have his own style and stand out as a different personality. Thus individuality asserts itself even, seemingly, at that highest pitch of perfection which characterizes both art and sport.

In conclusion, to end this brief review of the analogies between culture and sport, we may note that they are both vehicles for ethical values, though not to be confused with them. Art and culture uphold a moral code but are not "identical" with it, in accord with Gide's celebrated dictum that there is more to writing true literature than having the right feelings. Both alike are the natural vehicles of moral values which they propagate and bring within the grasp of ever broader and deeper segments of the population.

Whether we consider the asceticism of training, the ideal of balanced personality, the sense of justice implicit in obedience to rules, or the brotherhood of classes, races, and people evinced on the field and in spectator sport, these major ethical values are sustained in our modern civilization by sport more than by anything else. I know of no social, ideological, or intellectual movement able to bring home the gamut of these basic values so directly to the young, to every class, and, overcoming political barriers and differences of race and language, to all peoples of the world.

Thus, not only do sport and culture have a common origin in leisure, but through the whole development and aesthetic refinement of their respective forms of expression, they express the same ethical values and serve parallel causes. Nevertheless, the initial fact remains true: in modern civilization, the artists and the intellectuals have not yet managed to master sport and incorporate it in their work. This, as I hope I have shown, is not because of any incompatibility between sport and culture; on the contrary, it would be hard to think of two phenomena which are such near neighbors, so closely related. That notwithstanding, sport has not yet crossed the threshold of the study. In other words, sport is a culture and corresponds in its content to all that a culture is, but it has not achieved the formal expression proper to culture.

It is precisely on this point that I should like to put forward certain reflections. Why should this be so? The causes of this astounding situation, I believe, are manifold and are such as to preclude any simplification of the problem. They can be divided into three distinct categories: sociological, ethical, and finally, strictly aesthetic. To my mind, they explain why a phenomenon as important socially, and even economically, as sport and so similar in other respects to the phenomenon of culture is still without the formal expression that we normally associate with cultural things.

Let us start with the sociological causes. Here we must have the courage to admit certain defects peculiar to contemporary society which are brought out at once by comparing with the society of antiquity or that of the Renaissance. In those earlier ages, it was the same society, the same social class, which pursued both culture and sport. We, however, have to recognize that in many contemporary societies cultural creation is the prerogative of a minority; culture is the property of a minority, be it a ruling class or a class of professional practitioners, and the bulk of sports supporters are not to be found in this minority. In class societies, culture can be found in a particular class (for instance, the bourgeoisie) which represents a relatively small proportion of the population. Let us once again take France as an example, and nobody, I think, will dispute the long standing either of its culture or of its democratic tradition. The plain fact is that nearly three-quarters of the French nation have no access directly to arts such as the theatre, painting, or sculpture. How many peasants or manual workers go to the theatre or visit art exhibitions? Fifty percent of the peasantry and 25 percent of the working class play no direct part in the cultural movement, even if we exclude for the moment those highly refined forms of culture such as philosophy, poetry, and others which have special language of their own. In many countries where there are class societies, it often seems as if culture were reserved for a favored élite, and this is also true of those societies where there is not the same stratification in classes but where the differentiations arise from the fact that culture is the prerogative of professionals. For it is one of the major aberrations of our culture that the forms of cultural expression lie beyond the reach of the worker or peasant to whom we have just referred. I say "forms of cultural expression" advisedly, for I recognize that, in fact, the same culture is shared by the theatregoers and by the peasants or workers who for obvious financial reasons do not go to the theatre. What they have not got is access to the artistic milieu in which that culture expresses itself.

Sport, on the other hand, has reached its heights in the classes which are often the least privileged. It thus represents, in class societies, a form of social advancement, just as elsewhere in the world it is a sign of a people's advance toward a status of equality or freedom. It is because the sports movement has been one of social, and sometimes even political, advance that it is a mass movement. But for this very reason its sociological roots are too often removed from those of culture. The sociologies of culture and of sport are not the same, even though, in certain circles and at certain periods, overlappings, which of course are extremely beneficial, are observable. Broadly speaking, we must recognize that if sport has not achieved cultural expression, it is to some extent because of the extreme conservatism of our culture, which remains far too much the preserve of minorities, instead of being open to all the vital influences of the country. So much for the sociological reasons or, at least, for the principal reasons in this category.

There are also causes which I shall describe as being of an ethical nature. Sport, like culture, is a vehicle of moral and ethical values, of which I quoted some examples. Unfortunately, what forms the basis of the ethical values of sport is not always recognized in the general culture of contemporary societies. The fact is that the ethics of sport are based on the body and, in our civilization, the body still ranks low in the scale of values. After having long been anathematized as sinful, by virtue of the teachings of certain religions, and after having long been the target for intellectual contempt, the body in our day is faced with a formidable competitor in the machine — which either makes it useless or to all intents and purposes turns it into another machine and develops in it the very mechanical reactions which it is the purpose of sport to put to service and transcend. The result is that the ethics of sport, even when they incorporate universally accepted values, start from a principle the dignity and validity of which are not universally recognized.

If sport is to cross the threshold to recognition through cultural expression, we need to establish that humanism of the body of which the first principles only have been outlined by Jean Prévost and which still remains to be worked out in full. What, however, is the body's place in our philosophies, arts, literature, and civilization as a whole? In many philosophies (and this is the result of obvious religious traditions) the body is considered as something unclean or inferior; it represents the animal part of man which must be kept under, mastered, sometimes forgotten and schooled. At no point is it admitted that the body may be of equal dignity with the mind, the heart, and the soul.

Things are no different in our literature, however far removed it may be from the philosophic or religious ideas I have just mentioned. For instance, how much does contemporary literature say about the body? The answer is quite simple — in contemporary novels, the body means sex, sexuality. For our young novelists in general, and female novelists in particular, nothing about the body appears to be of any interest except this single aspect, which I agree is extremely important but whose importance from the point of view of cultural expression may perhaps have been exaggerated. This of course is an intellectual prejudice, intelligence taking its vengeance on the body by only considering that aspect of physical being which is furthest from reason and intelligence, namely sexuality. But everything else about the body, particularly that marvelous coordination which in fact reaches its fullness in sport, where there is no sexual element, is left completely untouched by our poetry, our theatre, and our novels — in a word, by all our literature.

As far as the serious side of life is concerned, modern man could be almost glad to be able to do without his body. Machines are taking over more and more what the body used to do, and science, that essential and determining factor in modern civilization, is perhaps the most deadly enemy of any humanism of the body, for in the final count the whole teaching of science is that the body is merely a machine and can be improved by means which practically deny its humanity. I have in mind the fine physical specimens we are training for interplanetary journeys. I think of the photographs we have all seen of those splendid bodies, carefully selected and swathed in wrappings like those in which the ancient Egyptians bound the mummies of their Pharaohs for journeys into yet more endless space. Here, we imprison bodies made for movement and the joy of living; we make machines of them and all we ask of them is to remain perfectly still and, above all, to exert no weight in those realms of space where conditions are so completely incomparable to the concrete circumstances of our normal existence.

Thus, religious ethics, intellectual literature, the utilitarian ideology of mechanization, and absolute scientific positivism all have this disaparagement of the body in common. The body becomes a thing that one dare not discuss, that one strives to dispense with, that one would like to reduce to a minimum, because its manifestations are only to be seen in sin, passion, sickness, error, and weakness.

The ethics of sport, on the contrary, proclaim the dignity of the body and deny that there can be any possible comparison between the machine that is the human body and a machine fashioned by man, or even any comparison, as Jean Prévost has said, between the skill and strength of an animal and the skill and strength of man.

On the ethical plane, the battle is therefore not yet won, for the whole evolution of our moral concepts tends to drive us further and further away from that respect for the body which prevailed in antiquity and still prevailed at the time of the Renaissance.

Finally, we come to the third and last category of causes — those of a strictly aesthetic nature and deriving from the very nature of art, that is to say of cultural expression. For, while it is true that sport creates beauty, the beauty it begets is immanent in the very act which creates it. There is no difference, but an identity between the act which creates the beauty and that beauty itself, immanent in the act. The beauty of sport lies in movement, in the performance of an action that is unique; it is inseparable from the fleeting moment. I have spoken of mastery over time and space — but this is a mastery which is lost at the moment of its achievement.

Art, on the other hand, expresses itself quite differently, through signs, through the stylization, not of things, the body, or living creatures, but of signs. Thus it places a distance between the object and the creation of beauty. The substance of sport is the body and life itself. Sport belongs wholly to the present, the actor merging completely with his action. The substance of art, however, is the sign, a series of signs which are bound to the object or idea they are intended to evoke purely by a relationship of meaning, a relationship which is utterly arbitrary and removed from any natural context. The man of letters and the writer do not work with emotions or ideas or passions, but with words. It is these words which provide them with the raw material for their labors and which are ordered to form phrases of beauty; this is what we mean by literary beauty and beauty of language.

Similarly, the painter works with colors and light effects which represent, or can represent, other things or objects, but for him the sign is all important. Even in sculpture and the most concrete arts, even in music, it is the sign that counts. Between the creator and the object he creates is fixed that distance which liberates art and endows it with its quality of eternity. Sport consists wholly of action; art, on the contrary, by its employment of the sign which frees it from the object and from life, moves into eternity. Thus sport and art face in opposite directions.

The very success which sport has achieved in the sphere of a mass communication media offers us proof of this divergence. Not in literature or in music must we seek the image of sport, but in the press, in photography, and in television. All the mass communication media appear ready-made for sport and, between them and it, there exists that splendid harmony with which we are familiar.

The finest achievement in this field is clearly television, perhaps the most serious rival which the actual sporting event has ever known. At the Olympic Games in Rome, I saw many people for whom attendance at the Games meant sitting down in front of a television set. If the transmission is direct, as is often the case, the actual event and its appearance on the television screen are absolutely simultaneous. The distance between the event in which the athlete's performance takes place and the reporting, or more precisely, the projection of that event throughout the world, is completely eliminated. At the same time, television, like all projection, represents an analysis and thus splits up the athletic action into its different constituent elements. This may, however, be an advantage in certain respects, for what we lose in emotion by not participating, in the stadium itself, in that communion which invests the sporting event with its nobility, we gain in intellectual understanding, thanks to the remarkable analytical effects which can be achieved by variously focused and differently angled camera shots of specific details of the particular performance.

Mass communication and sport, which is action, fit in with each other quite naturally. Art and culture — cultural expression — on the other hand, because their substance is not the event but the sign, move in a diametrically opposite direction; they seek a representation which may remain fixed for all eternity. It must be admitted that this divergence is still further accentuated by our present-day culture. If we consider the most enterprising forms of expression of our contemporary culture, the *avant-garde* arts, which one might think would be highly receptive to such modern phenomena as sports, we realize that, on the contrary, they are moving far away from them. This is true of painting and sculpture and lyric poetry, which are undergoing a real revolution at the present time.

For this revolution consists not in bringing sign and object closer together, but rather in raising the sign to the status of an object in itself. I am thinking, for instance, of abstract painting in which the sign, that is to say the color, ceases even to be a sign since, by definition, all connection has been removed between this color and any object, idea, or sentiment.

This is the painting of color for the sake of color, the interplay of color and light, the interplay of form, color and light for their own sake, without any contextual significance whatever.

Sport is preeminently concrete action. It is bodily action, at a given moment, sufficient unto itself and never to be recaptured. How could this be expressed in the language of abstract painting? By definition there is a divorce between these two phenomena, which move in opposite directions. The sample applies, of course, to abstract sculpture and to what is called "concrete music" — which is one manner of saying that it is abstract in its own way — and likewise to lyric poetry, which is now engaged in the re-invention of language in isolation from the meaning of the words.

These, then, are the aesthetic reasons, some profound, others incidental, for considering that artistic expression and sport are, despite appearances, at opposite poles. Sport and art both create beauty, but in completely different ways. Sport is immanent beauty, identified with the act which creates it. Art, especially in its most recent forms, is an art of dissociation, whereby the sign creates a universe which, at one and the same time, competes with the real universe and withdraws from it. What is lacking in sport is precisely this distance which, in art or literature, lies between the event and the sign and is the dimension of conscious awareness, that is to say, of the whole area in which significance of universal appeal finds a place. It is there that this alchemy of reflection occurs and the final spiritual transformation takes place. What precisely, for instance, is the movement of the discus thrower which we have just admired in the stadium? No more than a single moment in time, a movement which had never been seen before and will never be seen again. Apart from the photographic image which has preserved it or the mass communication medium which has transmitted it instantaneously to the four corners of the world, nothing remains of it but a memory. If, on the other hand, I compare the movement of this athlete with Myron's *Discobolus*, I turn from momentary action to eternal movement. The spectacle confronting me now is not that of Oerter's victory which, in a few months' or a few years' time, we may well find difficult to visualize without certain effort. What I discover here, in its universal significance, is the beauty of the movement performed by all the champions who have ever thrown a discus. I have chosen a statue as my example, but I could as easily have chosen a poem, a musical score, or a painting. Sport cannot as yet give us what we are offered by artistic expression and culture, namely, a meaning which enables us to transcend the temporary, to transcend all that is ephemeral, and to discover something of eternal value.

One day, nonetheless, sport will have to cross this threshold and culture will have to emerge from this somewhat too narrow circle in which, at times, it appears to be the preserve of a small and select élite. One day sport must cease to be this pointless exhaustion of youth, as in the unending series of athletic feats in which the exhilaration of the "never before," which is the record, gives way to the sad anticlimax of the "never again," which is the act which will never be seen a second time. One day sport, too, must rise to those eternal heights which it can reach only through culture.

It may be that certain differences, such as the ethical and aesthetic differences to which I have referred, are inherent in the nature of things and that between sport and art there will always exist this parallelism and these resemblances, but never complete identity, never the profound harmony we desire. Yet it should be possible to bridge this gulf which we have observed, at any rate insofar as it is not due to the egoism of our culture or to a certain disdain for intellectuality and beauty on the part of some of our sportsmen. It is surely incumbent upon the specialists in general and physical education, and particularly upon all the organizations concerned with this field, to work for the establishment of a closer relationship between sport and culture, between the cultivation of the body and that of the mind, which constitute — or ought to do so — the two sides, the two facets of the same humanism.

For nothing in the world today is younger or has greater potentialities than sport, and nothing is older or richer than culture, and it is of vital importance to us that there should be interpenetration and mutual understanding between the two.

An Ethological Theory of Play

EVELYN BROWNE*

For a number of years I have been puzzling over what appears to me a curious dichotomy between the world of our profession, built on a complex of educational stilts, and the real-life, slam-bang, heart-stopping world of sports and athletics. It would seem that there are only two happenings in our culture today that can even begin to challenge our national obsession for sporting events. One is the awesome ritual and pageantry surrounding the death of a national hero; the other is war.

We of this profession know that the culture of sports is by no means unique to the United States in the twentieth century. With all the peoples of the world, communication through sports transcends language barriers. The sport may be soccer not baseball, rugby not football, field hockey for

*Browne, Evelyn "An Ethological Theory of Play," *Journal of Health, Physical Education, Recreation,* September 1968.

men not for women or dance not calisthenics, but the human need behind this variety of expression is not confined by territorial boundaries or geographical limitations. In our world today it is universal.

This universal need is also boundless in time. Pluck a first century Roman citizen out of his seat in the Colosseum and transport him in time, change his clothes, and pop him into a seat to watch a professional football game in any of our twentieth century American coliseums and my guess is that he would feel quite at home. He might miss the animals and the sand surface for absorbing blood of his home town sport center, but other than that, the violence and ritual would appeal to him and come close to his favorite sport at home, the gladiatorial combats.

My question is simple: What is it that links the Brazilian soccer fan to the Boston Red Sox fan? What links the wine drinking, wild-eyed spectator in Rome 2,000 years ago as he roars his disapproval and turns "thumbs down" on some unfortunate gladiator and the beer drinking, disheveled baseball fan leaping to his feet and, along with thousands who share his feelings, shouting at the top of his hoarse voice "Murder the bum!"?

I would like to suggest that the link both to the present and the past is genetic. I believe that its roots may be found in a study of the relatively new science of ethology, the precise study of animal behavior. I believe that man's ageless and universal passion for sports is based on instincts which we have inherited from our animal ancestry. Certainly the layers of civilized veneer, applied during the centuries, have failed to tame the sports fan. Whether he be a Christian martyr fan or a Cassius Clay fan, he remains a unique, violent, and primitive reminder of our ancient origins.

To this end, I am proposing an ethological theory of play. My reasons for this proposal are based on the premises outlined below.

In the controversial book, *African Genesis,* by Robert Ardrey, three major theories are presented which form the basis for this discussion.[1]

1. *TERRITORY.* Ardrey, through a series of well-documented "case studies" in the realms of animal, bird, and fish worlds, makes the point that the drive for territory comes first and the sex drive is of secondary importance and is aroused only when the male has secured his "territory." In his second book, *The Territorial Imperative,* Ardrey further expands his thesis that man is indeed a territorial animal. One of his most persuasive arguments is his brilliant analogy of the production *West Side Story,* in which the rumble between teenage gangs is compared to the law of the jungle ("One Tiger to a Hill"). One also thinks of Alexander the Great, the Peloponnesian wars, the Roman Empire,

---

[1]The author would like to acknowledge her indebtedness, primarily, to Robert Ardrey, whose book, *African Genesis,* started her thinking along ethological paths and whose latest book, *The Territorial Imperative,* served to increase the excitement of the quest for primary origins of human behavior.

and Adolph Hitler's fanatic scream for *Liebensraum.* Today one thinks of the conflict in the middle east, the war in Vietnam, and the civil rights issues in this country.

2. *THE PECKING ORDER.* Within each species, according to authorities, groups within the species establish a hierarchy of rank from the lowliest member of the group to the proud leader. This is a well-established ethological principle in regard to such bird colonies as ravens or chickens in a barnyard—hence the name "pecking order." But this ranking order is true of primates, such as a colony of gorillas in a natural state, and many other species of animals. In essence, it is nature's way of maintaining order and discipline and, as a result, the survival of the group as a whole. The pecking order is the competitive basis of survival in the animal world. There are many examples of this "social" process in our society today. Perhaps the best example is our military hierarchy from general down to the lowly buck private. But there are other less obvious examples; the jungle of the world of Madison Avenue, the Greek system in colleges and universities, Riesman's *Lonely Crowd,* Maslow's self-actualized man, India's caste system, and the presidential primaries in this election year.

3. *WEAPONRY.* This theory is based on the discoveries of Raymond Dart. In 1955 Dr. Dart submitted a report to the Smithsonian Institution regarding his discovery of the fossil of the skull of a human being which lived one million years ago near the present Kalahari Desert in South Africa. He named our earliest known ancestor, the Australopithecus (Southern Ape) man. This skull was that of a young male and his death had been caused by a blow to his face by a weapon which was probably the business end of an antelope's humerus bone. The implications of this discovery are tremendous. Ardrey has suggested on the basis of this evidence that man is not just a tool maker as so many scientific works insist, but primarily a *weapon maker.* He further makes the heretical suggestion that man's one million year old passion for making and manipulating weapons created man's renowned and revered "big brain," not the other way around, as our religions would have us believe. Further, the remains of the million year old Australopithecus boy indicate that he was killed deliberately, murdered by one of his own kind. Why? The paleontological evidence gives rise to the haunting thought that we are descendants of murderers and cannibals, Cain not Abel.

If one thinks *weapons* and takes a look into the past, scenes will jump to mind: David slinging his stone at Goliath; the horse-drawn chariots of the pharaohs of Egypt; the horse as a new dimension of hunting and warfare; Leonardo da Vinci's plans for battering rams; the glorious armor and finely chaced weapons of the age of chivalry; the long bows of England at Agincourt; and, of course, the eventual fruits of evolution, gunpowder, cannons, tanks, battleships, submarines, our airborne arsenal, and finally—the ultimate weapon—the nuclear bomb. Such a view of our past lends persuasive evidence in support of the theory that weapons played a major role in the evolution of Homo sapiens and the society in which he lives in the twentieth century today.

With this information serving as a brief and all too flimsy background, I would like to propose the following hypothesis:

- that all animals including man play.
- that play for any species at whatever age level involves the principles of territory and the pecking order.
- that play for primates and Homo sapiens also includes the use of weapons.
- that, through the process of evolution, man today gives expression to these genetic instincts through our social institutions of war, play, and pageantry.
- that, in the areas of play and pageantry (and in the absence of uninhibited warfare), these events are carried out strictly according to rules.
- that the rules of the game and the protocol of pageantry are the ethological counterparts of the inhibitory mechanisms that exist throughout the animal kingdom for the purpose of preventing intra-species murder.
- that play at all levels and for all participants consists of practice in an artificial but deadly serious arena, for entrance into an adult world which reflects its ancient origins through the quest for territory, status, and weaponry, all of which exist in many forms in our world today.
- that the closer every particular activity comes to clearly containing the elements of territory, the pecking order, and weaponry, the more successful that activity will be as a tool to teach our youth to know themselves and their relation to the real world they are about to enter.

Territory, Competition, Weaponry

To substantiate this theory I would like to point out that no form of play exists today that does not in some way include the concepts of territory, competition, and weaponry. There follows some examples from our own field.

TERRITORY. Children's games are a good place to begin. Without benefit of adult supervision and wisdom any number of games burst into being according to the season of the year. "I Am thè King of the Castle." (Young gorillas play this game.) Prisoner's Base. Hide-and-Go-Seek and its victory call: "Home Free." Hop Scotch. Red Light. The list of games could go on and on.

It is interesting that in the area of movement education, the concept of choosing and exploring an area of space is in essence a territorial concept. But perhaps the best example of the role of territory in sports in this country is football. In this game the object of territorial aggrandizement is spelled out in clear and unmistakable terms—yardage. The need to gain 10 yards of territory in four tries is what keeps the tribe alive. Implicit in the territorial theory is the principle that animals will fight hardest to defend their territory the closer the enemy comes to the heart of their territorial homeland. The aggressor, on the other hand, tends to lose his aggression the further he is from his own territory and the deeper he penetrates another's territory. Hence the fabled phenomenon of the "goal line stand" in football by the defensive team. To defend the team's heartland or goal is their raison d'etre. The odds are with them both in the animal world and on the playing fields. The odds also favor the team playing on its home ground.

THE PECKING ORDER. The pecking order in sports is almost as obvious as it is in a military hierarchy. Competition is the soul of all sporting contests. All over the country youth are competing for a place on a team and a renewed reason for living and being a person. Can you remember back to the days when you waited while two well-established leaders briskly took turns choosing individuals to play on their teams in the neighborhood softball contest about to commence? If you were small and skinny and the youngest you know what it's like to be at the bottom of the pecking-order. It's almost as bad as being cut from the pro roster and either dismissed or sent back to the farm system.

Once the team is chosen and the season under way, competition intensifies under the glaring light of publicity and the assiduous compiling of statistics. The goal now becomes winning the league championship and ultimately the national championship whether it is in Little League, the Santa Claus Bowl, the Rose Bowl, or the World Series in the professional world of sports. Today, as in ancient Greece, to become an Olympic champion is truly the epitome of standing at the top of the athletic hierarchy. Perhaps this is one reason for the aura and magic surrounding this greatest of all athletic events.

WEAPONRY. Many of our sports today consist of the use of weapons important in the warfare of our past: the javelin (spear), the discus, the shot-put, bows and arrows, fencing foils, and even rifles. Many sports use obvious weapons or weapon substitutes. Take a look at some sports: golf, baseball, hockey—clubs, bats, and sticks; cricket, hurley, and polo—bats, sticks, and mallets; badminton, tennis, and squash—rackets.

And let's not underestimate the power of the ball. The ball is the pitcher's weapon in baseball. If he can hurl it skillfully through the enemy's territory, he can eliminate his adversary and give his team a measure of security. The batter, defending his territory with his weapon, can knock the pitcher's weapon into the third row of the stands. Thus the pitcher and his team are rendered weaponless and helpless while the batter trots around the bases securing four outposts of the defending teams territory: first base, second base, third base, and home plate. Symbolically he has conquered the diamond.

The ball in football is equally important. No man can be stabbed without a weapon similar to a knife; no soldier can be shot without a bullet; in football no territory can be gained without the ball. The ball becomes the key to the combat whether passed, carried, or intercepted. The ball is football's weapon. The use of weapons is as true of women's sports as it is for the man's world. (The March, 1968 *Journal* cover is a reminder of this fact.)

In applying Ardrey's theories to the world of sports, it is difficult if not impossible to pick out one sport as an illustration of just one of these concepts. In one way or another, all three theories seem involved in all sports. Further, all sports have rules and a group of well-trained, although often much maligned, officials to enforce them. This point is imporant! It is analagous to the animal world. Evolution has equipped all species with a built-in inhibitory mechanism which prevents intra-species murder. On the human scale intra-species murder is what war is all about. With the exception of the one enormous and vital area of sports, man seems to have lost his animal inhibitory mechansims while retaining all his territorial avarice, obsession with weapons, and excessive preoccupation with world dominance on the ladder of the international pecking order.

I believe this ethological approach to our field may well give a new dimension and impetus to all of us involved in the profession. I have used some of these theories in teaching a principles course in physical education to major and minor students and athletes. They seem to like this approach; they become enthusiastic. They tell me that in pro-football circles the players are reading *African Genesis*. Students from other disciplines are also interested. Ardrey has greatly helped in closing a generation gap inside and outside the classroom. For almost the same reasons that Ardrey's theories interest professional athletes, experts in movement education at the elementary school level might wish to examine these concepts further. In any area throughout the world, a person who has actual contact with children and men and women playing, whether as coach, teacher, or Peace Corps volunteer, can gain a new insight as to what they are doing if they place the day's events against this ethological background.

This ethological approach could become a cross-disciplinary approach involving all the humanities. Our field, biologically oriented, might well get a new lease on life with some cross-fertilization from the fields of sociology, psychology, and the new generation of the behaviorial scientists. I can also envision a closer alignment of our physical education programs with the exciting, real-life competitive world of secondary school, college, and professional athletics.

I invite all disciplines to participate in a quest, but I would suggest that we travel light. Leave behind all cerebral baggage. Remember, theorists and researchers, how that "big brain" of yours evolved! I invite further inquiry into the animal origins of our wonderful, wide, and wild world of sports.

ADDITIONAL READING

Ardrey, Robert, *African Genesis*. New York: Atheneum, 1961.
———, *The Territorial Imperative*. New York: Atheneum, 1966.

Beisser, Arnold R., *The Madness in Sport*. New York: Appleton-Century-Crofts, 1967.

Berne, Eric, *Games People Play*. New York: Grove Press, Inc., 1964.

Daley, Robert, *Only a Game*. New York: New American Library, 1967.

Deetz, James, *Invitation to Archaeology*. New York: Natural History Press, 1967.

Frankl, Viktor E., *Man's Search for Meaning*. New York: Washington Square Press, Inc., 1967.

Hawkes, Jacquetta, *Prehistory*. New York: New American Library, 1965.

Howells, William W., *Back of History*. Garden City, New York: Natural History Library, 1963.

Kuhn, Herbert, *On the Track of Prehistoric Man*. New York: Random House, 1955.

Levi-Strauss, Claude, *The Savage Mind*. Chicago: University of Chicago Press, 1966.

Lorenz, Konrad, *King Solomon's Ring*. New York: Thomas J. Crowell, 1961.

————, *On Aggression*. New York: Harcourt, Brace and World, Inc., 1966.

Maslow, Abraham, *Motivation and Personality*. New York: Harper and Bros., 1954.

Morris, Desmond, *The Naked Ape*. New York: McGraw-Hill Book Co., 1968.

Riesman, David, *The Lonely Crowd*. New Haven: Yale University Press, 1964.

Schaller, George B., *The Year of the Gorilla*. Chicago: University of Chicago Press, 1964.

Storr, Anthony, *Human Aggression*. New York: Atheneum, 1968.

Tunis, John R., *The American Way in Sport*. New York: Duell, Sloan & Pearce, 1959.

PERIODICALS

George, Jean, "Why Do Animals Fight?" *Audubon Magazine*, January-February, 1966, pp. 18-20.

Howells, William W. "Homo Erectus." *Natural History*, March, 1967, pp. 46-53.

Johnsgaard, Paul A. "Dawn Rendezvous on the Lek." *Natural History*, March, 1967, pp. 16-21.

Payne, Melvin M. "Family in Search of Prehistoric Africa." *National Geographic*, February, 1965, pp. 194-231.

Schaller, George B. "The Tiger and Its Prey." *Natural History*, October, 1966, pp. 31-37.

Simons, Elwyn L. "The Earliest Apes." *Scientific American*, December, 1967, pp. 28-35.

Singer, Ronald. "Emerging Man in Africa." *Natural History*, November, 1962, pp. 10-21.

"War: The Anthropology of Armed Conflict." *Natural History*, December, 1967, pp. 39-70.

Weinper, Jeffrey. "The Battle Hymn of Jeffrey Weinper," *Avant Garde*, September, 1968, pp. 52-55.

The Tools of Physical Education
ROSALIND CASSIDY*

The Body, the Instrument for Expression

Responding, moving, behaving, feeling expressed in overt physical form, expression of the Self, are all terms meaning the same thing. They signify the dynamic of living. Movement, then, the stuff with which physical education is concerned, is the fundamental element of human life. Large patterns of movement have always been used by man as a means of saying to his fellow men or to his gods the things he has most urgently needed to communicate. Contrast the Navajo Rain Dance with our communal supplications,

---

*Statement made over thirty years ago, quoted from Cassidy, Rosalind: *New Directions in Physical Education for the Adolescent Girl—A Guide for Teachers in Cooperative Curriculum* Revision. New York: A. S. Barnes and Company, Inc., 1938, pp. 69-76.

or rather lack of them, and conclude that men no longer express what they feel in movement. It is true that the restraints, taboos, inhibitions, anxieties, and fatigues of our culture have blocked the fundamental channels of expression, but man today and in the future, as in the past, must express his needs in movement. There is ample proof for this previously emphasized fact that the human organism continually integrates all of its powers, emotions, mind or store of meanings, organic functioning, facial expressions, voice, muscular skills to respond appropriately. This integration is expressed by the body instrument in movement whether in a swan dive, acting in a play, responding to a lover, singing in a choir, kneeling at an altar, dancing to celebrate the advent of spring, nursing one's baby, testifying in court or clinging to a strap in the subway after a day of clerking in the "Five and Ten." The gaunt farmer in the stricken Mid-West dustbowl, kneeling with his family in a burnt-out grain field, is man expressing his urgent need to a God who withholds rains, as surely as is the Southwest Indian in his Rain Dance. It is significant that the solace of drum beat, color, ceremony, and the communal sharing of despair and supplication are denied the white man's rain prayer.

Expressions of Individual and Group Patterns of Leisure

It is also significant that every autumn over the face of America the people of our culture express communal group feelings by identifying with eleven men fighting over a pigskin ball. There is color, drum beat, song, serpentine dance, and gin to the tune of million dollar gate receipts in palatial stadiums built that thousands may sit to watch the few entertain. There is no denying that the pageantry of football is an expressive pattern. However, we must ask whether it brings to the individuals who participate the release and rebuilding of great dynamic forces in their lives. Does it reassure the individual, strengthen group values and ideals, re-create individual and group, or does it tend to disintegrate and destroy. Eduard Lindeman recently asked a group interested in summer camp education whether camping could meet the challenge of a creative period of history, into which he predicts America is moving, a period in which there will be a great flowering of the creative expressions of man such as appeared during the Renaissance, a period in which not the least of the arts will be the education of the Self for creative leisure.

The misdirection of the teachings of Jesus colored the Middle Ages with a philosophy of negation of full free expressive movement. Yet this very negation is an expression of need even though shown in a pattern of ascetic body-Self denial. It does not disprove but verifies the contention that the dance of life or the design of life in any age is made by the meanings and values of that age, either for release and growth or blocking and impoverishment of individual total powers, organic, intellectual, emotional, spiritual.

The perfect example of negation of the total design is Simeon Stylites on his pillar, while affirmation may be found in the Athens of 500 B. C.

Organismic Concept Fundamental

The dance of life is expressive movement. Our confusion in seeing this concept as fundamental for the area called Health and Physical Education is a result of our confusion about the full meaning of the organismic point of view. How can we accept that view and yet talk of physical health and mental health, how can we talk of physical education and mental education, and then talk about developing the personality as though that task were some sort of separate emotional education.

We have confused ourselves by thinking of what the individual inherits in structure, glandular tissue, and the like and what he builds in physical fitness and organic power, designated by Rogers as the ultimate imperatives, as separate from the inseparable other imperatives of emotional fitness, and mental and spiritual power. The psyche and the soma cannot be thought of or dealt with separately. The several thousand research studies reported by Dunbar support beyond denial this fact which man has always known, even if he did not apply it. Recent studies reported by Dershimer on childbearing among primitive and civilized women point to the delicate psychosomatic inter-relationship and show that the labor of civilized women is longer and more severe because of emotional conflicts and attitudes. The primitive women, most of whom were in very bad physical condition, did not find labor an ordeal.[1]

The physical education teacher must be extremely cautious in speaking of physical fitness, physical health, physical recreation as single objectives, since in truth they do not exist separately. The need to emphasize the word total in speaking of total-health, total-body education, total-organism-and-environment, seems regrettable but all teachers may find value in doing so until such time as attention is focused on the total unit. Williams in speaking of the "unity of man" which is basic to his philosophy of education and physical education, says:

> "Moreover this view should at once and for all times combat the pernicious and absurd contention that physical education is concerned with body-building, defect correcting, and health-producing results and with these alone. Indeed, it is argued by some that physical education is not concerned with moral and social qualities at all, but only with physical ones, and that any attempt to postulate moral education on a games-and-

---

[1]See Dershimer, F. W., The Influence of Mental Attitudes in Child Bearing, *American Journal of Obstetrics and Gynecology.* March, 1936, p. 444.

play level is not only ridiculous but indeed positively charlatanistic. Such
is a cause of error founded on incorrect physiology."[2]

We are educating a totality, a human personality; let us choose terms,
new ones if necessary, to aid us in emphasizing this fact.

The relationship of physical education and art — Movement is the expression of total-Self. Movement is the concern of physical education. But
also art is the expression of the total-Self and art is concerned with movement.
The expressive patterns of the Self in dance and play are creative, as are
those in dramatics, camping, outing, and the like. Creative behavior, the
expressive behavior of the individual, is that in which new patterns are created out of the store of past meanings as they are brought to bear in meeting
novel situations. It is an act of relating all the past meanings, in the purposes
of the present situation and evolving a new insight and a new response.

Physical education is concerned with rhythm, since the behaving organism has rhythmic laws as basic to its growth and development. There are
rhythms of metabolism and catabolism within the cell, rhythms of growth,
rhythm in the birth process. Infancy, childhood, puberty with its beginning
rhythms of menstruation and sex desire, maturity, age, and death, are
rhythmic cycles. Breathing, the heart beat, digestion and evacuation, sleeping
and walking, eating and fasting, effort and rest have their own timed pulse
beat. Life has the rhythm of the seasons, of night and day, of tides and noon.
Art, too, is concerned with rhythm.

The expressive patterns of the Self in play are developmental and social.
Shelly gives a skillful analysis of the relationships. She states:

> "The developmental contributions of art and play are identical in
> kind but strongly contrasted in degree."[3]

This variation in the degree of organic, neuromuscular, sensory, and intellectual development is easily observed in experiences centering in such expressions of the Self as the swan dive and in playing the violin, yet both are
developmental and rhythmic, and create new patterns in the use of the Self.

Play is done for its own sake, as is art, but in art the sharing with an audience is an important part of its social rôle. At present the audience in
play is a hampering influence. May it not come about, however, that when
the art of play is generally accepted and participated in, its appreciation by
an audience who have had creative experiences in play as a basis for enjoyment will be considered part of its social significance.

---

[2]Williams, Jesse F., Principles of Physical Education. Courtesy of W. B. Saunders
Company.
[3]Shelly, Mary Josephine, Art and Physical Education, an Educational Alliance. *Journal
of Health and Physical Education*, October, 1936, p. 477. (Permission to quote.)

Shelly compares art and play in the social sense thus:

> In their common origin. both were communal forms: both were instruments of socialization, of uniting people in a group and of inculcating attitudes and ideas of fundamental importance to the community. Play quite as much as art represents historically a form of profoundly serious group action and a vital mode of education. . . .
>
> "In a less generalized sense, art and play both incite to group action. Both are contagious, emotionally arousing, socially provocative. As social manifestations, play and art alike thrive in times of peace and leisure and are alike wielded as instruments of strife in times of disturbance. Deliberately put to the service of a cause, each reveals enormous power. The imprint of war or of conquest is to be found on the history of play as on the history of art. There has never been a revolt or a victory about which a song and a dance were not made. No country ever went to war without marching to it. The power of play and of art to unite people is as old as the race. In this deeply significant social sense they are akin.[4]

Experiences unique to physical education — Thus far a series of definitions has been discussed in order to understand the area of total-body education. Physical education has been accepted as a part of education, based in the sciences, but so closely related to the arts that the methods, materials, and techniques of art seem to be indicated in further development. Now, briefly, what are the experiences health and physical education teachers may select as patterns within which the adolescent girl may make her own designs of growth through meaningful response?

An analysis of the literature of progressive education gives the teacher of physical education an impression that progressive educators, who have used "the Play Way" from the outset, see patterns of dance as the only area offered by the physical education program for creative expression. In dance, the body structure, the laws of line, mass, color, and rhythm serve to restrict expression, yet it is true that dance, drama, and festival are freer, wider frames in which the child may experiment with and try out imaginings, fantasy, and his desire for new experiences.

The floor pattern of games and sports and the rules of play are a less flexible frame within which to make new designs, but new integrations of response must surely be created at each playing. No record of these designs can be retained to decorate school walls, yet these creations of the child often have more originality, color, movement, and evidence of growth of Self in relation to others.

There are countless patterns and sub-patterns in play that are neither games nor dance in which the individual tries out his ways of behaving. These offer in some lives more and in others less flexible frames than either games or dance. Such patterns range from the free uncharted designs in

---

[4]*Ibid.*, p. 529. (Permission to quote.)

camping, outing, picnics, and excursions to the closely framed skill of fencing. But even in the latter, success in the activity depends on achieving a creative pattern.

To guide selection there are the laws of maturation of body structure and interest and social sensitivity, and there are numerous elements unique to each situation which must determine the over-pattern of general experiences as well as the specific pattern for each girl. There are many ways of using these experiences in planning an over-pattern to guide the teachers within a given school.

Orientation in Problems of Living Toward Which Physical Education Contributes

If the body is the sole means of experience, and if experience is the sole means of learning, then what are the life situations faced by the adolescent girl in which experiences in physical education may help her to better orientation? As no one individual ever faces identical situations, it is obvious that in answering such a question areas of life needs only may be indicated, and within these only types of experiences. All these needs interact and are inter-related so that categories of persistent problems or basic relationships of living must be thought of only as focal points to direct attention since from each wide circles extend to include all others.

Living requires:

The use of the body as an integrated totality. This use indicates a need for experiences having to do with maintenance of total health balance and power; with locomotion and other aspects of bodily control, poise, and communication used in daily life.

In daily living, ease and enjoyment of body use, zest and self direction in enterprises, sense of values in life, give evidence of achievement in these patterns.

The use of the body in relation to others. This indicates a need for experiences allowing many opportunities for enjoyment of group enterprises.

Success is evidenced by willingness to share with others in many ways in order to arrive at individual and group goals which bring growth for all concerned.

The use of the body in relation to work. This indicates further integration and application of the meanings gained from experiences suggested in the first two areas.

Persons must have self-other integrations before success in work enterprises can be realized.

All these experiences, it is obvious, must be thought of as including interpretation in teacher-student thinking together as the activity proceeds.

This interpretation is essential so that the fact knowledge and the skill and the attitudes are integrated toward large related meanings which are here called "Understandings." These are the dynamics, the functional knowledge, the meanings accepted by the individual and therefore organically incorporated into his store of meanings to serve as the basis of next steps in experience.

Tools of the Physical Education Teacher

To outline briefly some of the patterns which physical education teachers actually use in the orienting of the individual toward his life needs:

Patterns of physical education

Play
    Natural activities of daily life.
    Free play and games.
    Athletics — intramural.
    Camping.
    Club activities and Excursions — socials — parties.
    Rhythmic activities in dance and dramatic activities — festivals — pageants.
    Self testing.

Validation or evaluation
    Health examination — diagnostic tests — records.

Interpretation
    Orientation courses — lecture courses — self survey.

Re-educative patterns
    Individual correction — relaxation and rest.

Environmental patterns
    Related
        To the gymnasium building, which include:
            Air, heat, color, smells, cleanliness, routines and regulations, office privacy for conferences.
        To the fields, which include:
            Distance, surface, surroundings.
        To the staff, janitors, matrons, which include:
            Attractiveness, skill, time for conferences.
        To the schedule, which include:
            Rigidity, richness of offering, time of day, conflicts.
        To the program, which include:
            Requirements, grades, penalties, tests, relationship to individual interests and needs, impartiality.
        To companions, which include:
            Hostile or friendly, "we group" or outsider, good or negative influences in standards of conduct.

To attitudes in the culture, which include:
Acceptance or disapproval of Play, advertising, propaganda, style, legal suppression of facts, religious taboos, and the like.

The Patterns of Play

Planning for play — points to consider:
Place and time — cost — costume — equipment.
Physical condition of participants — interest.
Leadership — officials.
Learning how.
Companions.
Outcomes.

To summarize, the question — what are the tools of Physical Education? — may be answered in this way:

In the main the physical education teacher may proceed on the assumption that she may contribute to the process of orienting the individual by means of these tools:

Her own skilled and affectional relation to each child.
The health examination, diagnostic testing, and guidance.
Wide play and dance experiences based on needs and desires.
Attention to remediable total health defects through whatever school agencies required.
Wide experiences in sharing in group enterprises.
Wide experiences in enjoying body expression alone and with others.
Wide experiences with valid information about the Use-of-the Self, related to values in a total life setting.

Physical Educational Experience in Relation to Cultural and Educational Values in a Dynamic Society
DAVID K. BRACE*

Because physical education has been an enduring experience, as ancient as man, it must be evident that there are enduring values which persist despite changes in civilization. The purposes change as the dominant forces change. Naturally, the leaders of each culture feel that the purposes for which they strive through physical education are the most worthwhile. Thus, they direct the experiences of physical education to produce the outcomes which they believe will engender the values desired.

*Reprinted from the *American Academy of Physical Education, Professional Contributions* No. 6, November, 1958.

The physical education experience is the sum of the things that have happened to or with the student or participant as he or she progresses through our schools and participates in the instructional or competitive phases of our programs. The experiences will depend upon the purposes of those in charge of the programs which are activated through the opportunities provided and the interests and abilities of the participants. Thus, the experiences and the outcomes will differ from time to time as purposes differ.

Purposes, of course, are merely reflections of the philosophy of the prevailing forces of the times. The values which accrue become values in the light of the philosophy of the times. Thus, the question presents itself: Is there any permanence as to the kinds of values received through the experience in physical education, or must we assume that the nature of physical education is destined to be continually in a state of uncertainty?

If time permitted, it would not be difficult to remind ourselves of the body control developed by the yogi of India; the grace of body and performance desired by the Athenians; the military skills and physical hardihood of the Roman legionnaire; the bravery and ethics of the feudal knight; the disciplined body of a Ling gymnast; the skill and will to win of the American athlete; or the drive of the Russian competitor for a dominance designed to contribute to the goal of self-justification and world supremacy.

Each nation at each epoch has endeavored to educate the body to perform acts conforming with, and furthering, the philosophy of the times. Similarly, in the United States, a physical education is emerging which is a direct result of the democratic philosophy, the religious concepts, and the social and economic forces of our culture.

Purposes of This Paper

The purpose of this paper is to consider this emerging physical education experience in relation to educational values in our dynamic society; also to try to indicate some directions in which the experiences should be guided if physical education is to produce the values needed by our people.

In a dynamic society, environmental conditions and ideals and social sanctions, singly or together, are in a state of change. New concepts are being encountered and evaluated. Often the new ideas appear unexpectedly and in unaccustomed form. The result often is to question old values and to release forces inimical to existing programs. Such situations confront physical education at the present time.

Today, education is under fire, often by people who are confused by new ideas suddenly encountered. Many suggestions involve physical education either by way of neglect, or by ignoring accepted values in an attempt to provide for new ideas or to correct supposed failure of existing concepts.

Values in Physical Education

Regardless of pressures or attacks on physical education, there are certain experiences which have enduring value. Let us examine some of the values, educational and cultural, that can result from our emerging physical education if we are smart enough to adjust our programs to meet the challenges of a dynamic society.

Values which should have been received by those who have gone through our school programs include the following:

1. Knowledge of one's health status.
2. Knowledge of one's physical abilities and limitations and how to adjust to them.
3. Confidence in the performance of motor skills and the body mechanics of life activities.
4. A personality adjusted to group endeavor and willing to accept assignments selected by the group.
5. Concepts of fair play, and respect and consideration for the shortcomings or achievements of opponents.
6. Respect for authority as embodied in the team captain, game official, coach, or school principal.
7. Skill, knowledge, and a real interest in several recreational sports that can be participated in as an adult.
8. Understanding of the purpose and educational and physical values of physical education.
9. An optimum condition of physical fitness in terms of strength, speed, agility, and endurance.
10. An appreciation of community resources and programs essential to preserve the health and fitness of our people.
11. Experience in coeducational recreation activities of an active or semi-active nature.
12. Knowledge and skill in forms of physical exercise, such as home calisthenics, which can be used to keep in condition when circumstances do not permit vigorous recreation participation.
13. Knowledge of the mechanics of sport skills, how to learn new skills, and how to improve performance.
14. An understanding of our heritage in sports and the place of sports in American culture.
15. Experience in leadership of fellow students in such capacities as team captain, scorekeeper, equipment manager, or official.

If we are to secure these values from physical education in the face of the challenges of a dynamic society, it appears obvious that we must make some changes in the nature of our purposes and programs.

Changes Which Should Be Made In Programs

We should cease thinking of physical education in terms of minutes, or periods, or semesters. Instead, we should direct our attention to achievements, competencies, and accomplishments of the children and youth served.

At each school level we should think in terms of graduation requirements or goals. These goals should be considered in terms of the needs of the individual pupil and the values to be gained from the program. We should ask ourselves: What are the experiences and the competencies which average youngsters should have gained upon completion of the sixth grades? What should have been gained by the completion of the junior high school, and upon graduation from high school; and what, upon graduation from college? Physical education as taught in public schools and colleges can no longer be justified as an exercise program only. It must be evaluated in terms of pupil achievement of standards or objectives carefully established. Thus, at each school level, certain experiences and resulting competencies must be provided. At present many, if not most, of our public school programs are teaching in high school many of the same skills and knowledges which were taught, and should have been mastered, in elementary schools. Many of our colleges are teaching the same activities taught in high schools.

It is true, of course, that some students have not mastered in a lower school level the skills and knowledge they should have. This merely indicates another need of modern programs. Curriculum experiences should be adjusted to individual needs. It is indefensible to require all students to repeat certain instruction merely because it has not been mastered by a few.

Under normal conditions, students graduating from high school should have achieved a physical education. Therefore, the college programs should be based entirely upon the status of incoming students. Examinations of both health and physical fitness, as well as knowledge and skills in body mechanics and in team and recreational sports, including swimming, should be the basis of a guidance service in physical education. These students who have met reasonable standards should then be excused from further instruction in physical education.

The reasonable standards should include the competencies previously mentioned. They should include at least a good degree of skill and knowledge in two team sports, in swimming, and in three other recreation sports suitable for adult life. An evaluation of status in these standards should be made during the first semester or year in college. Included in this year should be a sound orientation program. Those who meet the standards should be excused from further required class instruction in physical education. Students not able to meet the standard should continue in appropriate required courses as needed.

However, the college program should not stop at the end of the first year. It should continue to have an obligation for helping students to maintain fitness throughout the four years of college. Thus, students should be required to show by simple examinations each year that they are continuing to meet graduation requirements by maintaining optimum fitness. Such maintenance could be accomplished through the use of the college health service and by participation in intramural or intercollegiate athletics or other recreation activities. In addition, the modern college program would provide physical education credit courses for those who wish to enrich or improve their experience and ability in physical education.

The concept just indicated for college programs should apply also at the high school level. Requirements or standards for graduation from high school should include, for students not in adapted physical education, the same standards previously mentioned for college entrance. As a matter of fact, many high school students can and should meet these standards by the end of the tenth grade. Such students could be allowed to substitute other activities for physical education, provided they could show each year that they were maintaining physical fitness.

Summary

It is my opinion that physical education can meet the educational and cultural challenges of our dynamic society if we will do the following things:

Begin each year of class instruction at each grade level with appropriate and adequate orientation as to the nature and values of the year's experiences in physical education.

At the start of each year, begin with a unit of instruction on Appraisal of Health and Physical Fitness including medical and dental examinations and physical fitness tests. See that the meaning of the results is understood. Finish the year with a retest on the physical tests.

Provide guidance as to physical activity justified by health status and physical fitness and motor skills. Co-operate with school guidance programs by making physical education data available.

Provide a revitalized curriculum planned to meet needs of modern society, including:

Instruction in sound body mechanics of daily life activities.
Group experiences of participation in team sports.

Skill in three or four recreational sports suitable for adult life.

Skill in functional swimming.

Interest in continued participation in intramural sports and other physical recreation.

Fine attitudes toward sportsmanship, health, and safety.

Set up specific goals or achievement standards expected in each unit of instruction and insist on pupils exerting real effort to achieve them. At high school and college levels, establish reasonable graduation standards comparable to levels of physical fitness, and require physical education only until graduation standards are satisfied, provided the student gives evidence each year of maintaining his optimum level of physical fitness. Those pupils who have completed graduation requirements should be encouraged to participate in intramural or other recreation activities. Failure to maintain physical fitness would require the student to return to the basic conditioning program.

If the physical education experience is to make its contribution to youth in our dynamic society, certain basic changes must be made. Beginning with teacher education and extending to the teacher in elementary schools, a change in emphasis is needed. Basically, these changes relate to better individual guidance in an enriched curriculum in which pupils are encouraged and required to achieve specific standards, and, having achieved them, are released for additional experiences.

Sports Appreciation — A Neglected Frontier
C. O. Jackson*

In recent years, we have heard much about developing better and more functional curricula, improving our teaching methods, and especially doing everything possible to meet the needs of individual pupils. There have been a number of books and many articles dealing with these and related areas, and all have been directed toward improving and expanding our contributions to the boys and girls, the men and women of our country. To a greater or lesser degree, depending on our training, our philosophy, and our recognition of problems we have done a good, a fair, or a poor job of teaching.

Through most of the period of organized physical education, there has been one frontier that has been either overlooked, or neglected in most schools. It doesn't matter particularly whether the schools to which we refer are on the elementary, secondary, or college levels, sports appreciation has seldom received the attention and emphasis it deserves.

*C. O. Jackson, "Sports Appreciation—A Neglected Frontier," *American Academy of Physical Education, Professional Contribution* No. 4, 1955.

Definitions

Sports appreciation is a broad term, so we begin with a definition. The term "sports" refers to "a diversion of the field, as fowling, hunting, fishing, racing, games, especially athletic games, and the like; also, any of various similar games or diversions usually played under cover, as bowling, rackets, basketball, etc.; . . . that which diverts; . . . pastime; . . . diversion . . ." according to Webster.[1]

The word, "sports," includes anywhere from several hundred to a thousand or more different activities, depending upon how inclusive your definition becomes.

"Appreciation" according to the same word authority[2] is the "act of appreciating; appraisal; estimation; full recognition of worth; recognition through the senses; especially with delicacy of perception." It is an "expression of gratification and approval, of gratitude, or of aesthetic satisfaction" and should result in a "sensitive awareness of perception of worth or value, especially aesthetic." In education, it refers to "the study of aesthetic values (as distinguished from historical values), as in music, art, or literature."[2]

Sports appreciation, for the purpose of this discussion will be considered to mean understanding and recognizing the value or worth of the many sports activities we engage in, or observe, as well as a deeper awareness of the worth, especially aesthetically, of many others which we know and experience only vicariously.

The Place of Sport

Cozens and Stumpf[3] report that "few observers of life in America have failed to comment on the large place which sport fills in the public consciousness." Eight to fourteen per cent of the space in most newspapers is devoted to the field of sport. Three per cent of books published in the United States deal with sports. Everyone of the more than thirty thousand high schools and colleges offers opportunity for participation in this area, either as an active participant, or as an enthusiastic spectator. Sports tend to dominate school news in both the school and local papers.

In 1938, Staley[4] estimated that the "average individual spends more time observing sports, reading about sports, conversing about sports, in other

---

[1]By permission. From *Webster's New International Dictionary of the English Language,* Second Edition. Copyright, 1934, 1939, 1945, 1950, 1953, 1954, G. and C. Merriam Company.

[2]*Ibid.,* p. 132.

[3]Cozens, F. W. and Florence Stumpf, *Sports in American Life,* University of Chicago Press, Chicago, 1953, p. 1.

[4]Staley, S. C., "Sports Appreciation," *Journal of Health and Physical Education,* 9, 3:147, March, 1938.

words, appreciating sports, than in actually participating in them. . . ." This statement appears to be equally valid today.

In a recent publication, Duncan[5] stresses the need for acquiring an appreciation of sports common to our culture, because, as he points out "sports have tremendous social significance . . . and the physical education program should provide students an opportunity to develop an understanding and appreciation of this important aspect of American life. . . ."

With more than a hundred thousand persons actively engaged in teaching or coaching one or more of the many phases of sport commonly recognized in this country, with millions of participants, and many more spectators, the field of sport must be considered increasingly important. If we add to this, a consideration of the millions of dollars invested in facilities, the millions invested annually in equipment and the vast sums paid for admission to sports events, we must recognize the fact that "sport is big business."

The Challenge

What are we doing to help spectators and participants understand, appreciate, and recognize the many values in these activities, both in the sports they know something about, and those they have heard little or nothing about? Perhaps it is something like the problem of health. Every administrator, every school board member, every teacher and every parent agrees that it is the most important thing in life, and education in health is the number one function of the home, the community, and the school — working together cooperatively. But what happens is that everyone is often so busy teaching skills such as "reading, writing, and arithmetic" that health education becomes another neglected area in most schools.

Some Suggestions

What do some of our leaders say we should do in the area of sports? Oberteuffer[6] says

> . . . we should seek to produce people understanding and appreciative of the problems, the strategies, fine points, and nuances of the world of games. . . . The school population needs to be educated for a life-time of activity so that they will first of all become continuous participants, and second, appreciative and intelligent spectators. . . .

---

[5]Duncan, Ray O., *Suggestions for Improving the Curriculum in Physical Education for High School Boys*, Illinois Curriculum Program Bulletin No. 19, Circular Series A, No. 51, Springfield, January, 1954, p. 33.
[6]Oberteuffer, Delbert, *Physical Education*, Harper and Brothers, New York, 1951, p. 237.

Bovard,[7] in an article written almost twenty years ago, expresses a similar philosophy.

> We believe that physical education, properly interpreted, is not exclusively for making players or for developing highly skilled experts. Education lies not in the attainment of skills, not in the acquisition of tools, not in just language or other means of expression, but rather in the deeper significance, the finer distinctions, the powers of discrimination, the elements of appreciation and clearer understandings which such an education can bring about. . . .

While Scott[8] places his stress primarily on competition, his emphasis is similar when he states

> If competitive sports as an educational and social force is to be understood and appreciated, all students should be provided with opportunities for formal instruction in physical education appreciation as is universally practiced in art and music. . . .

The fact that an individual has participated in one sport or several at some time or other, and has been a spectator at many sports events is no assurance that he will understand and appreciate those activities. According to Cozens and Stumpf[9]

> The spectator-participant can get no more out of the experience than he brings to it in background perception or sensitivity. Yet the noblest qualities which can be perceived in human beings, rhythm and harmony are there. The very words with which human beings try to explain the effects of beauty are the same as used to denote elements of play, tension, poise, beauty, contrast, variation, solution, resolution. . . .

Other Areas

These thoughts suggested a search to see what was being done in other areas. The *Educational Index* listed appreciation of art, drama, literature, motion pictures, music, poetry, radio, and television.

A review of a recent university catalogue,[10] reveals some interesting facts concerning the matter of teaching appreciation. In floriculture, "Appreciation of Landscape Architecture" is a required course. In commerce, there are courses in literature and in the humanities. In education, such

---

[7]Bovard, John Freeman, "Some Underlying Motives in Physical Education," *Education Method* 15, 7:356, April, 1936.

[8]Scott, Harry A., *Competitive Sports in Schools and Colleges,* Harper and Brothers, New York, 1951, p. 372.

[9]Cozens, F. W. and F. Stumpf, *op. cit.,* p. 286.

[10]Undergraduate Study 1954-55, University of Illinois, Urbana, 52, 1:488, August, 1954.

courses as "Nature of Teaching," "Humanities," and "Foundations of American Education" are required of all students.

When we look at the fine arts courses, we find listed: "Music in Western Civilization" (a survey of the art of music), "Appreciation of Music," and "Introduction to the Art of Music." "History and Appreciation of Music" is required in all curricula in music education.

In art, we read of a course which is "an introduction to the factors inherent in architecture, sculpture, and other arts" primarily for non-art students. A course titled "Literature and Fine Arts" is explained as "an introduction to general principles by analysis of selected work of literature, music, painting, sculpture, and architecture."

Other courses which include some emphasis on appreciation are courses labelled Introduction to Poetry, Drama, Fiction, Literature. Still others are those listed as "Survey," "Orientation to," or "History." Even in the engineering field, a special lecture course without credit is required for two semesters which has as its goal, fundamentally, developing an understanding and appreciation of some of the many problems in the field of some branch of engineering.

The areas where appreciation is taught only incidentally, if at all, include mostly those in agriculture, home economics, and special areas such as vo-ag, dairy technology, food technology, and restaurant management, but even here we find introductory courses and inspection trips designed to help develop appreciation and understanding.

Instruction Needed

We must remember, however, that incidental instruction may often become accidental, and therefore of little value. As Scott[11] points out

> . . . Although aesthetic values may exist in all types of learning experiences, they do not automatically compel appreciation or expression. Aesthetic appreciation and expression should therefore be included among the educational objectives and consciously incorporated into the teaching and learning process.

While it is true that we sometimes include miscellaneous information such as a brief history of a sport, as part of learning it, along with rules and strategies, this does not appear to be common practice. In teacher training where we might be expected to do much more of this, it still appears to hinge so often on the whim or interest of the individual instructor. Most institutions, of course, do have courses in an introduction to or orientation in such matters as health education, physical education, recreation, and athletics.

---

[11]Scott, H. A., *Op. cit.*, p. 163.

It would seem, however, that we are not doing the detailed and intensive job that appears to be carried on in art, music, and literature.

According to Cozens and Stumpf[12]

> Sports and physical activities belong with the arts of humanity. Such activities have formed a basic part of all cultures, all racial groups, and all historical ages, because they are as fundamental as a form of human expression as music, poetry, painting. . . .

Values Differ

It must be admitted that in today's world, there appear to be different codes or sets of standards for different sports. For example, the conduct of participants and spectators at a prize fight, or a professional wrestling "exhibition," presents a picture of sportsmanship and appreciation which is not approved in educational circles, regardless of the grade level. Perhaps one of our contributions might be to help our students note these differences and understand and appreciate the all-around values of amateur sports in contrast with the two mentioned. Fortunately, many sports such as hunting, fishing, golf, and similar individual pastimes engaged in by millions seem to remain on a higher level from the standpoint of participation and appreciation.

Some Suggestions. We have now established a need for doing something about this matter of sports appreciation, and doing so in an organized, educational manner. What should be included, and how might such a program be developed? The balance of the paper will be developed to this topic.

Regardless of the level of education, whether elementary, secondary or college, we must surely first increase our offerings by broadening our curricula in physical education and by increasing the variety and opportunity for sports participation in intramurals and outside of school. The former, of course, is much easier to accomplish in the long run than the latter, but improvements can no doubt be made if leaders become concerned about the problem.

Early appreciations and attitudes are of course developed by parents, by brothers, sisters, relatives, and neighbors, and later by teachers so we must go beyond the walls of the school. Appreciation in the sports area can be taught in class, on the sports field, in the library through the newspapers, and by such media as radio, television, the motion pictures, and talks before community groups.

World-Wide Considerations

If we are to broaden and expand understanding, we should make use of the media just mentioned to present word or image pictures of sports over

---

[12]Cozens, F. W. and F. Stumpf, *op cit.,* p. 1.

and beyond those we are primarily interested in, or which are of concern only in the local community. We should go further and add ideas of sports in other countries. Other important areas might include an introduction to the history of sports and their social significance, the place of sport in the development of group thinking, the role of sports in culture, the deeper meaning of games, styles of play, evolution of the game, understanding of great athletic movements such as the Olympic games, why we have a physical education requirement, the hygiene of sport and such matters as sports in relation to climate and physical factors. The possibilities appear to be almost endless.

Other Considerations

Such a program, must, of course, be adapted to local conditions, and especially to the needs, interests, and background of the students. On the other hand, it must not be limited only to the interests, the background, and the local conditions. We surely are not making much progress if we merely add an extra film on how to play the various positions in football, and expose all students in school to one or more showings.

On the elementary level, the attitude of the instructor and what he says probably carries most weight. Instead of outside readings, assigned papers and so on, he can accomplish a good deal in the area of appreciation by presenting and discussing the matters during the period of participation. This technique should, of course, be continued to a degree in the other grade levels, but in the high school, we might either add a special period a week for this, or use some of the present activity periods throughout the year. Duncan[13] states that

> The prominent place which sports occupy on American culture seems to support the principle that sports appreciation should be part of the physical education curriculum. This may be developed in two ways. In addition to learning the skills, rules, and techniques of a sport, a student may learn about the history, cultural background, and world-wide status of the activity. . . .

Only a few schools appear to have a specific course intended on an elective basis to teach appreciation of the whole field of sports. It would appear that many more should do so. In colleges and universities, there appears to be even stronger educationally-sound reasons why such a course should be developed and made interesting and attractive enough to secure voluntary enrollment of large numbers of men and women.

---

[13]Duncan, R. O., *op. cit.*, p. 24.

An Example

At the University of Michigan,[14] there is a course for university men called "Sports Survey" which

> . . .is designed to acquaint students with the theories, techniques, practices, and appreciations of sports activities, and to orient students with respect to the sports suitable to their professional field. Deals with place of sports in our social, economic, and educational life. Strongly emphasizes the safety aspects of sports participation.

Outside of this, the investigator was unable to find a single instance where a specific course in sports appreciation is presently being offered, but is under the impression that such a plan is followed in several of the eastern schools. Perhaps some information will be forthcoming as a result of this presentation.

Expanding Libraries

One specific contribution that each instructor, each school, each educational agency can make is to provide a wide variety of reading material in sports for use by pupils, students, and participants. These should include books, magazines, outlines, in fact most any literature suitable for library use and relating to sports appreciation. If it is not possible to expand our present offerings within our classes, or to develop a special course to teach appreciation, the suggestion just made will be of much help, especially when coupled with specific assignments culminating in class discussions. Even "free reading" will be of interest to some and of value to many. Perhaps we may teach students to understand and appreciate the best in the sports pages. This in itself may eventually improve the offering here.

A Correlated Program

At the University of Illinois, a concerted effort is made in every course in the professional curriculum in health education, in physical education, and in recreation, to make a contribution in appreciation. The planed progrom of the School of Physical Education Lectures Committee each year is intended to supplement and complement such emphasis. Mention should also be made of the annual Inspection Trip, now in its fifteenth year, a required three-day trip of visitation, observation, and educational experience. Appreciation and understanding of various aspects of the profession is a fundamental objective.

---

[14]Personal letter from Howard C. Leibee, February 2, 1955.

In the service courses, those required with credit of the students in other areas in the university, i.e., not specializing in the fields mentioned in the preceding paragraph, the principal objectives of each course is two-fold;

> . . .participating in sports (and other physical activities) to the end that participation will contribute to the job of living, and, incidentally, contribute to the wholesome use of leisure, the creation of character, and the development of health. . . . Appreciating sports. . . to include appreciating technique, strategy, artistry, accomplishment, and similar qualities in the performance of sports . . . appreciating the history of sports . . . appreciating the social (cultural) significance of sports . . . appreciating the individual (personal) significance of sports and other physical education activities,[15]

In addition to discussions in the areas just listed, an occasional motion picture, or other visual aids, each student is expected to prepare a term paper as part of his course requirement. This is in line with the usual requirement in other areas as pointed out by Staley when he says "it is common practice . . . to require students to study textbooks, read magazines and books, write papers on assigned topics, and perform many other learning activities outside of class. . . ."[16]

The areas include such provocative titles as physical fitness, technique of outdoor sports, keeping fit, sporting literature classics, general history of sports, recreation, wildlife conservation, and leisure and recreation just to mention about half of them. As part of organized emphasis on appreciation, this extends the activity beyond the classroom or the playfield into other areas and into other sports "beyond the horizon." Individual guidance is intended to help in the wisest selection of a topic for the term paper. Since each student must complete four semesters of required or service physical education, he is not only exposed to four separate areas of activity, but also to four different avenues intended to bring growth and enjoyment through appreciation.

Expanding Appreciation

We are all aware of the contribution toward international understanding made by various international meetings and congresses, and the educational impact of such plans as the Fullbright and Smith-Mundt Acts for the exchange of educational personnel. These are all part of a broad plan to bring about better understanding and appreciation of each other by the peoples of

---

[15]Staley, S. C., H. E. Kenny, and J. O. Jones, *Sports Curriculum,* Stipes Publishing Company, Champaign, 1949, p. 6.
[16]Staley, S. C., "The Cultural Significance of Sports," *Journal of Health and Physical Education,* 7, 2:89, February, 1936.

the earth. The results have exceeded the fondest expectations of those supporting these movements, and indicate what can and should be done to promote better understanding, as well as the more complete appreciation. Perhaps on a smaller scale in our own schools, but reaching in the aggregate many individuals over a period of years, we can do much the same.

Summary and Conclusions

In summary, we might say that sports are an important part of the current social scene; the interest of a great portion of the population shows its impact, and its possible contribution on a scale of values; people, young and old, children and adults, need education in appreciation of sports as much as they need similar experiences in art, music, drama, and other media; and we must do more than accept sports as good . . . we must do something about raising the level of appreciation in this field.

Something is being done in an incidental way in many schools and in many course areas. We need, however, special emphasis beginning on the secondary level which can only come from an organized course, designed to teach appreciation of skill or condition and especially enjoyment and understanding of a wide variety of sports. Such a course should be as good as and probably better than many similar courses in the arts. Here, too often the objectives in music appreciation, for example, becomes merely the identification of titles, recognition of types of music, and association of musical moods with composers of certain typed music.

We need opportunity for all, especially those of school age, to come in contact with the best in sports literature seldom found on the sports page of the average newspaper.

The results of a good program designed to develop appreciation, knowledge and understanding of a wide variety of sports can only mean according to Staley[17] "better spectators, more discriminating readers, and more intelligent conversationalists in the field of sport, and an increase in participation. . . ." Sports will continue to be an increasingly important media of expression for participants and spectators. And with increased understanding and appreciation may come greater enjoyment, more relaxation, and more complete living for many!

Truly, sports appreciation has been a neglected frontier. Let us give leadership to movements and activities which will increase and improve appreciation of sport and we may make a greater contribution to many than we realize.

---

[17]Staley, S. C., "Sports Appreciation," *Journal of Health and Physical Education*, 9, 3:147, March, 1938.

BIBLIOGRAPHY

Bovard, John Freeman, "Some Underlying Motives in Physical Education," *Education Method* 15; 7:356, April, 1936.

Cozens, F. W. and Florence Stumpf, *Sports in American Life,* University of Chicago Press, Chicago, 1953, pp. 1, 286.

Duncan, Ray O., *Suggestions for Improving the Curriculum in Physical Education for High School Boys,* Illinois Curriculum Program Bulletin No. 19, Circular Series A, No. 51, State Department of Public Instruction, Springfield, January, 1954, pp. 24, 33.

Oberteuffer, Delbert, *Physical Education,* Harper and Brothers, Co., New York, 1951, p. 237.

Scott, Harry A., *Competitive Sports in Schools and Colleges,* Harper and Brothers Co., 1951, pp. 163, 372.

Staley, S. C., "Sports Appreciation," Editorial, *Journal of Health and Physical Education* 9; 3:147, March, 1938.

"The Cultural Significance of Sports," Editorial, *Journal of Health and Physical Education* 7; 2:89, February, 1936.

Staley, S. C., H. E. Kenny, and J. O. Jones, *Sports Curriculum,* Stipes Publishing Company, Champaign, Illinois, 1949, p. 6.

Undergraduate Study, 1954-55, University of Illinois, Urbana, 52:1, August, 1954, 448 pp.

On Learning Values Through Sport

DELBERT OBERTUEFFER*

Now, no fair peeking! And thus came to us the first admonition to assure our conformity to the standards of conduct with which games have been played in our land. We were not supposed to peek! Anyone should know that. The game—what was it?—ten steps or hide and go seek—presumed a code of honor mandatory upon us from the first instant we heard the rules. There were to be no exceptions. One simply did not entertain the idea of cheating. One went full-out for one's own honor and later for the honor of one's own school. After all, there were only two fates worse than death, and one was to be caught cheating at games!

With some reason, one might believe that this successful transmission of acceptable or traditional ethical values has been one of the reassuring and remarkable phenomena of our age. One comes to games, whether stickball in Manhattan or duck-on-the-rock in Grand Island with the understanding that there is a way of doing this and one would not, either as a matter of principle, or for self-preservative reasons be one to violate the code. "Play fair," "give him his turn," "I moved my ball in the rough," "I touched the channel marker with the tip of my boom," have become the confessions or

---

*Oberteuffer, Delbert, "On Learning Values Through Sport," *Quest* I, December, 1963.

commands heard by all and sundry as the standards of gentle folk have been transmitted through the games and sports of our people.

Games have thus been touched with a deserved halo of honor. They have become significant in life as experiences a bit different from the market place. When once the gladiator (or marbleshooter, or rope-skipper, or tennis player) sets foot on the field of play the count is assumed to be correct. The "call" will be without favor or advantage, the chips will fall where they will, and if he loses because of the inexorable forces at work he will withhold his tears and his alibi, acknowledge the superiority of his opponent, and, later, join him in a toast and song to the happy day of friendly contest!

Not yet has the cyncism of "nice guys finish last" penetrated *all* of sport and destroyed its virtue. Not yet has the sportsman who plays with honor and with respect in his heart for the traditions of the game and the rights of the opponent disappeared from the scene.

But almost. Games and sports are rapidly losing their simplicity of former days. They command now the attention of millions—of people and dollars. Fortunes are made from them. Reputations built or ruined. The sporting goods industry grosses within the top ten. Organized athletics in schools and communities have moved from the simple pleasures of a Yale-Harvard boat race to the spectacles of Canton-Massillon or the Cotton Bowl. Much is at stake—including the quality of morality which pervades the phenomenon.

And there is cause for alarm. No longer are all the games played on the high plane of respectability. There has crept into the program elements of immorality and greed which bid fair to spoil the fun. And it will take more effort on the part of many people to stem the tide of anti-morality and anti-intellectualism which is presently engulfing sport as it is engulfing many other aspects of our cultural, political and social existence.

Organized effort? Teach ethics—or morality—by organized effort? Well, let's examine the case for it.

How have any of us arrived at our present level of ethical behavior? How have we achieved the values we live by? Mainly by observing example and partly by responding to teaching and the force of law. We can remember being good boys and girls long enough in Sunday School to reflect upon the startling news that "blessed are the meek for they shall inherit the earth." So we were somewhat perplexed and shocked a little when the noted sports authority, Mr. Durocher was quoted as saying that "nice guys finish last."

Nor can we fail to be impressed with Norman Cozens when he points out how casually we regard violence whether it be in games, traffic or war and shows us how we completely repudiate the admonition to turn the other cheek or to love one's enemies in such situations.

It is going to take organized effort because of the great and powerful influences at work today which are bringing games and sports to their knees in a brutal assault to turn them into instruments not useful for perpetuating the gentle skills of friendly intercourse. They now can be powerful media for greed, bribery, and perhaps worst of all the dominating egocentrism of him who would use others not as Kant would have used them—as ends withal—but through the particularly immoral exploitation for ends which are *not* their own. In some quarters, if we hunger and thirst after righteousness it is becoming a little more difficult to be filled.

The case, as I see it, is alarming. Charlie, my neighboring twelve year old is ready with his alibi if he loses a bike race. He must save face. It does not dawn on him that Benny may have been faster. Parents in Little League and high school sport are becoming notoriously poor sports. The coaching from the bench (distinctly against the rules) in big-time football influences thousands in little-time football. A midwestern college athletic director and President *knew* of an All-American's scholastic ineligibility his sophomore year but by duplicity he continued to play until his eligibility was used up two years later! The cynicism of players, coaches, commissioners, and newsmen associated with tournaments, and championships invariably increases in volume as the gate swells and the audience enlarges. "Amateur" college athletics have all but disappeared leaving only the tears of a lamented Whitney Griswold or an irate Lewis Morrill. Bowl games multiply. To deny one leads to a display of bad temper on the part of the aggrieved press, alumni and students whose ethical standards are no higher than will allow them to throw bottles through the windows of the building where the faculty had voted to deny the darlings the chance to win—and thus gloat.

It is not a pretty picture.

But it ought not be surprising that it is not pretty. Because the decline in morality in sports, the abandonment of those sweet virtues of our polite childhood, are all related to the major transition taking place in the character of our culture.

Richard Hofstadter in that realistic tome "Anti-intellectualism in American Life" (1) traces this disease through our religious institutions, our politics, business, and education. He traces the beginning of the decline of the respect for the gentleman to the attacks on Thomas Jefferson, and he makes it clear that the learned man or woman, the nobleman and his principles of conduct, the gentility of the aristocrat has given way to standards of the mob and the slob. None of us has escaped, and some of us are bruised from this tidal wave of anti-intellectualism and anti-morality which holds our schools suspect of everything from the teaching of the doctrine of racial equality (of all things) to dealing realistically with the true nature of the democratic process!

To stem this tide is the greatest challenge confronting us all in education—and surely it confronts us in physical education. Where better than on the playing fields and in the gymnasiums of our schools and colleges can we demonstrate and evaluate the dynamics of ethical judgment? Our rules of the games *do not* and *can not* govern human conduct completely. Any more than can legislation guarantee equality of opportunity among men. As Martin Buber would put it the demands of authentic existence mean that man cannot blindly follow the prescripts of law but must accept "ethic of responsibility," in which moral action is a response to what the situation demands at a given time.

I wonder, for example, if we have not mis-read completely the "competitive spirit" as it flows so brightly in our culture. Competition has made us great—competition with nations, with nature, and with our fellow man. But we seem to have confused the uses of competition as between war and sport. To be sure of it we frequently compare the two by speaking of the invaluable training for sport one gets out of combat or, by claiming as one famous athletic figure did, that the best combat officers come from the ranks of letter winners in college! Maybe so, but there is a discrepancy. Competition in modern war holds no place of honor for the opponent. He is to be killed by the silent means of a missile or a bomber high overhead in a conspiracy of silence of which Nietzsche would have approved because it gave no hint of its actual aim or purpose.

Games are getting like that. We hold secret practice, we hold secret meetings. We learn to hit 'em hard and where they are weak and if we don't exploit the other's tender feelings we miss a bet. All this is, as Mencken would say, because we are fatally insecure, so uncertain of the outcome of the game, so fearful that we may lose that we have no honor to display because honor is predicated upon a feeling of absolute security.

But competition can have another quality. It is, after all, not an end in itself but merely a means. Being a means it must never become so useful as to over-shadow the need for developing mutual respect among men. If the very essence of the democratic way is not respect for personality—then what is it? And any device or practice that teaches the young to hate, to spit upon, or to paint his library needs examination to determine whether the means have grown more important than the ends. Competitive sport can be a fine tool for teaching of democratic morality, or it can, with equal facility, become destructive of it. To paraphrase Rousseau: those who would treat sport and morality apart will never understand the one or the other.

There are many violent critics of sports and of the vehicle which so often carries sport through the academic portals—the program of physical education. Why does Robert M. Hutchins so tartly oppose any effort to make a learning experience out of these activities? Why would Bestor, or Fadiman, or Mayer hold little respect for the attempt to claim educational virtue for modern physical education? Why does even a blue-chip educa-

tional statesman like James Bryant Conant find a place for physical education in the curriculum only because there is allegedly a body-building influence involved somewhere therein?

Could these phenomena possibly have resulted from the most effective
effort at self-destruction any group of well-meaning educators have engaged
in in this country? It seems actually that there has been a conspiracy *not*
to conduct sport programs upon an educational level, *not* to teach seriously
the ethical aspects of sports but to deny the educational implications of
physical education in face of a single concentration upon values in exercise
alone.

Perhaps it is, in the long run impossible for people in the field of physical
education to deal with more than one value at a time—and, if forced to
choose, the value of strength and sweat, being the easiest attainable will be
the most widely advertised.

With such a single value as the only one in view then the impresarios
of games are free to conduct them at any level they wish ethically and
educationally. As long as the illusory value of "physical fitness" is sought no
other standards need to be met. Neither personal satisfaction, nor social
competence nor continuous participation need to be sought. The anti-intellectual has taken over completely.

Perhaps games will never be returned, even in part, to those who play
them or to those who see them as instruments for educational development
but will remain forever in the hands of the one who gets the best price he
can out of the schedule. Perhaps there is no end to the wild distortion of
purpose. Consider, for example, the sorry plight of our modern interpretations
of "amateurism." If we had any respect for the English language (and for
our moral effect upon the young) we would understand clearly that probably only five percent of high school and college athletes of today are
"amateurs" in any decent interpretation of the word. The rank anti-ethic
involved constrains the ahletic administrator piously to claim amateur status
for the subsidized athlete and suggests that there still may be a social
or academic stigma to the professional!

In this day of subsidy? What nonsense! Let's face it morally, not in some
pseudo-legal "amateur code." A boy or girl who gets as much as a free
meal "on the house" is no longer an amateur but may and usually does
remain a splendid gentleman or lady. Let's abandon this immoral make-
believe of piety with which we color our concept of "amateur athletics."

Perhaps the academic eye-brow is raised at sport, and its badly named
family physical education, because of the internally generated confusion
relative to the discerned ends of its efforts. This confusion is patently self-
destructive. Right now the popular theme song is physical fitness. This is
the fourth time in this century programs of physical education have been

captured by this popular theme and bent to fit its illusions. A demigod comes out of the southwest with eloquent credentials in folk-lore but with knowledge of neither need nor know-how and asks us all to exercise and sweat and thus save the nation, or at least its youth, from devastation and desuetude. Bludgeoned by a Presidential plea for physical fitness we reluctantly test and exercise, push up, pull up and run-walk 600 yards thus chasing a biollogical end which not only has no relation to the educative process but which has a built-in rejection factor which dooms the program to failure in our kind of society.

For years physical education programs had been moving rather steadily towards accent on the noun. They had been exploring the ways experience in vigorous movement could be used for total development, to recapitulate the culture of our land, to bring the individual into possession of himself and his powers. The exploration was mainly in the area of social and psychological development because these were relatively unexplored fields and the biological virtue of exercise has been well known for years. Exercise is important to life and living. It is here to stay. Only academic fools are oblivious to that.

But what we needed in physical education was full blown research and clinical experience in the relation of movement to the teaching of ethics and morality, to the improvement of psychological states, and the cultivation of social gain between people and groups. These we need and these we are not getting because of the immoral stand we take of being glad to cultivate the sound body as the babysitter to the sound mind! We must follow the leader, sweat profusely, walk fifty miles, do our push-ups, patronize Vic Tanney and Bonnie Prudden, and thus will our population be made strong. Morally? Psychologically? Ethically? Socially? Or just muscularly? What are the great needs for successful life in our society? What kind of man-power does our society need for its preservation? This is the compelling question from the standpoint of national need and people in physical education had better have an answer or they will be lost in the oceans of sweat recommended by the muscle-building anti-intellectual.

But who was John Dewey? To refer to him is risky business in today's world of the Far Right, and the dynamometer! He once said that "The serious threat to our democracy is not the existence of foreign totalitarian states. It is the existence within our own personal attitudes and within our own institutions of conditions similar to those which have given a victory to external authority, discipline, uniformity, and dependence upon The Leader in foreign countries" (2:49).

It is within the repudiation of those idols that we will find the ultimate and eternal strength of free men in a free society. The individual to be educated is a social individual. He lives not alone as a recluse but in a society which is an organic unit of individuals. If we eliminate this social factor we are left with only a pulsating mass of protoplasm sans direction, sans purpose, sans reason for being.

No wonder Hutchins and his group snobbishly advise parents to avoid colleges where physical education is required. He knows that as likely as not the students may be asked to climb ropes ad nauseum or respond seriously to the pseudo-intellectual "fitness" expert who prepares the tables of "fitness" from dynamometers and rope climbs. No wonder. This sort of thing has about the same relation to the educational program as fertilizing the soil with worms does to raising flowers. It may have a part to play but it is a small one and a dubious one at that!

What we in phyiscal education must come soon to understand is that no one, but no one, will take us seriously until we begin to take ourselves seriously and become truly intelligent about exploring the contribution which the world of sports, games, and dance can have to the *education* of man.

Can this world have a bearing upon the Christian ethic? Or any other ethic? Is it to be taken seriously as a means by which the accepted moral standards of the group are to be passed on? Can it be an effective experience in the enrichment of judgment about relative values? Can it help in decision making?

Well, it always *has* had a bearing on these things since man first taught the young through the game and the dance. But right now—when we have organized a program we call physical education, brought into the school, used motor movement as it means and media, we need to get down to the business of teaching the behaviors this society of ours expects if it is to survive. We need to eliminate the casualness of the "Oh, I say Old Boy, that's not done" approach. We need to get serious about a search for our *total* potential, not merely our muscular.

This country is not going to be saved—or destroyed—by muscle. But by the quality of its moral fibre. What greater challenge can programs of physical education rise to meet?

REFERENCES

1. Hofstadter, Richard. *Anti-Intellectualism in American Life.* New York: Knopf, 1963.
2. Dewey, John. *Freedom and Culture.* New York: G. P. Putnam's Sons, 1939.

Chapter

Play, Dance and Sport

Must We Have a Rational Answer to the Question—Why Does Man Play?

R. SCOTT KRETCHMAR
WILLIAM A. HARPER*

Why do you play? Is it for health, fun, or social relationship? Are you satisfied with these answers? Are there other possibilities? Do these reasons accurately explain your presence in sport? Why *do* you play?

Health, fun, and social contact, among other factors, are utilized by many as short but sufficient solutions to the question of "why I play." It is difficult to find individuals who do not have logical explanations for an activity; it seems that nearly everybody knows why he plays.

Historically, play (the term, for the purpose of this paper includes the traditional activities within sport and dance while eliminating the nonactivity games such as chess or cards) precedes any formalized teaching. It precedes compilation of a body of knowledge which might constitute a discipline. Children play. Aboriginal tribesmen play. Animals play. And they all play without any sophisticated notions of *why* they should. Play is a more primary category than play *for* education, than play *for* health and fitness, than play *for* social acquaintances.

Individually, the physical education professional person generally encounters the intrigue of play prior to coming to any decision to pursue a

*Kretchmar, R. Scott and William A. Harper, "Why Does Man Play?" *Journal of Health, Physical Education and Recreation*, March, 1967.

career in the field. Much of the fervor which is at times apparent in the actions of the teacher usually stems from an exciting encounter, either past or present, with some form of play. The instructor knows this enjoyment to be a part of his own history, and he often continues to recreate the actual engagement of sport or dance throughout his active life.

Empirically, most of the research in physical education relates to play—how one can participate with greater skill or for a longer time; how one can train better and learn faster; or how one can play more safely. It seems then, that play is the cornerstone of the profession, of the professional man, and of the field's scientific research. Play precedes all of the superstructure which develops around it.

Given the significance of play for the field and the number of statements which purport to describe this relationship between man, play, and the profession, it is a curious fact that so little attention is *now* directed toward this issue. It is paradoxical that physical education, based on play should house several scientific and humanistic branches which at this time seem to consider themselves self-sufficient, intellectual disciplines apart from ties with actual activity. It seems that the end of research—an understanding of play in all of its parameters, both scientific and humanistic—has been forgotten and the means have become a new goal. Statistics are exciting; scientific research is a challenge; philosophical and historical study command a compelling interest. Yet the priority, play, remains forgotten in the background. Play, which initiated the profession, lies buried under mounds of research and academic discussion. It remains the victim of its own children. Is the issue of the relationship between man and play dead?

But perhaps the question of demise is premature. Many of the traditional answers or "solutions" appear inadequate. Many physical educators begin their theorizing with two assumptions, that one can logically deduce "ought" statements from "is" descriptions and that man is rational. The discipline's philosophers articulate the various benefits which accrue to man through participation. They argue for the goals of increased longevity, safety, greater vigor, and increased opportunity for social interaction, among countless others. Both on scientific and sociological grounds the arguments for these objectives carry some weight, though they certainly lack verification.

For the purpose of this paper, let us assume that they are, in toto, true. It may be said these idealisms do occur in play. But it is the subsequent utilization of these "facts" which lead the theoreticians astray. From the fact that various goals *are* realized, they progress to the proposition that goals *should* be achieved and, further, to the notion that man will work actively toward these objectives once he is convinced of the validity of the proposition. It is these latter two extensions of logic which place the rationale for play on tenuous ground.

These difficulties can be clarified by means of examples. An instructor may lecture on the dangers of sky diving in an effort to discourage participation by any of his pupils. He begins with several statements of fact: (1) sky diving has a relatively high mortality rate and (2) man does not search out situations in which he has a great chance of dying. Given the fact that every student is a man, the teacher believes he is justified in concluding that the student *should not* sky dive. However, the instructor, when he initiates his argument with descriptive statements (the "is" facts), can conclude only in that same mood. There are no grounds for his leap from an "is" *description* to an "ought" *prescription*. The theoretician cannot logically state:

       1. All men who do not want to die do not sky dive.
       2. John is a man who does not want to die.
Therefore: 3. John *should not* sky dive.

All he is justified in stating is:
       1. All men who do not want to die do not sky dive.
       2. John is a man who does not want to die.
Therefore: 3. John *does not* sky dive.

The physical educators, then, have many facts relative to the outcome or benefits of play. They incorrectly suggest that mere availability of the facts leads to valid conclusions concerning why man *should* play. Given the various facts of play, such as fitness, health, vigor, and community, the instructors suggest that the student *should* play for these ends. What these instructors assume with such argumentation is that these entities are, in themselves, universal values. Fitness is not only a *value* but equally a *necessity!* Man should become fit! But common sense rebels against this reasoning. An object can remain a "good" without any obligation to achieve it. Fitness can intellectually be recognized as a value without deciding it is necessary for oneself.

It is clear then, that one who attempts to describe man's contact with play on logical grounds has major difficulties. For his account to be valid he must assume that the values of health, fitness, and vigor carry with them their own command for action. But even if one could agree on the values of play, it would still not be clear why man *should* strive for these ends.

It might be objected, at this point, that man does and must make value judgments, whether they be logical or not. In this light, all of the foregoing discussion becomes a wasted intellectual exercise. Who cares if a value judgment lies behind much of the profession's theory? Physical education is willing to stand behind its claims of value!

It might be maintained, then, that the instructor has no difficulty convincing the student of a specific "good." For example, a teacher may argue for the value of fitness, and the student may accept his discussion. The student intellectually agrees to the proposition that fitness is a worthy value and that his subsequent actions should reflect that conviction. The student has complete knowledge of the connections between fitness and play and has no qualms in accepting the value of the former.

However, is it not paradoxical that man, with some consistency, acts contrary to knowledge and commitment? Many people acknowledge the value of fitness while maintaining a sedentary existence. Many people who value their lives and who know that smoking may shorten the expected life span continue to smoke. Evidence shows that man often acts irrationally. Even the most disciplined individuals do inexplicably act against reason or the knowledge suggesting a singular mode of behavior.

The rationalists want to make play the result of consciously accepted goals and understandings. Though play may be a result in isolated situations, though an individual may initiate activity on rationalist grounds (i.e., "it is good for me"), he may continue to play in ignorance of benefits and in spite of potential detrimental effects.

Perhaps man intuits that play is somehow an irrational activity. He often plays for no good reason, yet he cannot, it sems, let himself live with this fact. Play becomes acceptable when man can explain his activity on rational grounds. The rational is superimposed upon the irrational. The absurd is made to conform to the reasonable. Does one not hide behind the rational facade because he fears, as an academician, the indeterminate, the unpredictable? Is it not more comfortable to have the ready answer and finite reply for the interrogator? But does not this disposition restrict the search for answers to a predetermined arena, that of the rational? By limiting the range of the quest does one not presuppose the nature of the answer, that it must be logical? What if the truth were to fall outside of his realm?

Clearly, it has been suggested that the solution does supersede the rational cause-and-effect motif. Man's intrigue and persistent relationship with play cannot be sufficiently explained through a rationalist method. Health, fitness, strength, relaxation, and other objectives probably accrue from play, but to suggest that these *explain* man's presence in play seems unfounded. To propose that man is in sport because he should be, or that he participates as a result of knowledge of and commitment to a value, vastly oversimplifies the situation. Man is in sport or dance on grounds independent of the practical or rational.

It was once asked what would happen to play if it were shown to have absolutely no beneficial results. Would play terminate? Once its useful ends were negated would its captivating effect on man likewise end? It is contended that play would not cease. It would, in fact, continue as before, perhaps with even more success because of its less artificial place in man's life.

The riddle of "why I play" has no simple answer. Man plays before he asks the question. He plays while continually ignoring the question. He plays in spite of known detrimental effects. Play and man seem bound together with reason or without it.

To explain the relationship between the phenomena of man and play on rational, cause-and-effect grounds is to render both man and play lifeless. The problem of "why I play" is equal and related to the incredible complexity of man. Man plays for many reasons, yet he plays for no reason at all. Man cannot be given an input of reasons and be expected to produce consistent, mechanical behavior. Man will act with spontaneity, irrationality, and abandon. The lived reality of this union between man and play defies all attempts to reduce it to a rationally explicable understanding.

Dance Is Many Things
Lois Elizabeth Ellfeldt*

Dance is many things. It's the classical ballet with the breath-taking ballerina twirling on her toes, it's the polka at the ski lodge, the May festival folk dance, the high stepping performance of a chorus line, and it's you and your friends doing the latest fad dance. Dance is many things, but especially it is what you have known it to be.

If you have enjoyed the rhythmic beat of tap dancing or the exciting syncopation of jazz dance; if you remember a sentimental waltz or envision a swaying hula, then that is what you mean when you say "dance."

Sometimes it is the music that is called "dance," the music written long ago for a Louis XIV court minuet; then again it is the "dance of the planets and stars," the passage of the celestial bodies in the cosmos; or it is a "child dancing in the playground," the random movement of play; or even "the dancing raindrops" as they patter on a tin roof. Small wonder that we have difficulty in identifying the exact nature of this phenomonon, dance.

Few question the word "sport" which, as a general term, serves as a large umbrella to cover many kinds of competitive, recreational and socializing experiences. There is sport that tests the personal power, the ability to out-maneuver an opponent; some of sport is is a display of virtuosity, an exhibition of self; some is for the sheer fun of moving and in other there is the challenge of evading penalties set forth by the rules of the game. Whether the sport is for an individual or a group it serves as a situation in which human beings find a wide range of satisfactions, for many different reasons. People participate in the activity themselves and then sometimes watch others perform, each experience fulfilling a particular need.

And so it is with dance. There is dance which people do, with a partner or with others, that provides enjoyment or security in the doing. Then there

---

*Ellfeldt, Lois Elizabeth, "Dance Is Many Things." Written for this anthology.

is dance that is watched for its entertainment or display value, where the audience simply sits and is amazed. There is dance as a performance art which serves, in its medium, the same ends as other arts; an experience in which the sensitive audience interacts to the movement image created by the performer's action and projection of the choreographer's intent.

Among the ancient Greeks there were few differentiations made between dance and other movement forms. Indeed, a military parade, a circus juggling act, the action of an athlete or an actor were all called dance. Today we make more precise differentiations among movement forms, but the criteria for these differentiations are not always entirely clear. Basic to any attempted clarification of the term are the form-styles that our society has designated as "dance."

There is little doubt that dance is made up of movement, none of which is utilitarian in purpose. But neither are the movements of sport or play utilitarian in purpose! The most obvious difference between dance and sport-play is not in action, patterning or shape of movement but rather in the purpose for which the movement is formulated.

Why does man dance? Sometimes he dances for the social interaction and the fun of moving to popular or folk music, with a partner or others, in pre-formed patterns or in pure improvisation. Sometimes he dances because this is a part of his national or cultural heritage and he is perpetuating some movement sequence or motive. Man also dances to display his agility, grace and power, and others watch the dancers to be entertained or dazzled by the movement spectacle. Others dance to project the artist's illusion, the intensified awareness of some aspect of the human condition, as a performance art.

Even as these purposes differ from those of sport there are some which are remarkably similar. For example, social and recreational dance forms are very like play, but the art forms of dance are entirely different. And so it seems that the differences between certain dance forms are greater than the difference between some aspects of dance and sport-play.

Dance, like sport, is either for participation, that is for the sake of the one dancing, or it is for watching the performance of others. The participation dance forms include folk dance, recreational dance and social dance. The performance dance forms include spectacular dance, entertainment dance, ethnic dance and dance as a performing art. Each has a distinctly different purpose—but all are dance.

Participation Dance

Folk Dance. Folk dance is a traditional, nationalistic movement form which has gradually lost its original reason for being and remains today as a feeble reminder of the day when this form of dance was a vital part of a nation's behavior. Today it is little more than a rehearsal of nationalistic traditions or a means of celebrating some festive occasion. The action of folk dances around the world are all similar, as are the people, with some differences in their style and quality of performance. There are few nations which do not have at least one popular and fairly characteristic folk dance, though most of the dancers have lost contact with the original source.

Recreational Dance. Recreational dance forms are distinctly for the fun of participation, regardless of who is dancing, or what is being danced. Sometimes these are for couples, trios, or mixed groups; and performed in squares, lines, circles or unstructured formation. These fun dances range from old folk dances to improvised singing games; from the Virginia Reel to a revised Charleston. Different periods seem to develop or even rediscover their own versions of "fun dances," and the differences between these dances seem less apparent as each undergoes change. These are not nearly as interesting to watch as they are to do!

Social Dance. Social dance is a relatively simple, loosely structured movement form for both sexes. It is strictly a boy-girl couple dance, derived originally from primitive fertility rites. In our social order it is a most acceptable boy-girl activity, usually performed in a ballroom, club, restaurant, recreation center or home.

Social dance ranges from the traditional ballroom dance which includes the foxtrot, waltz, tango and cha cha—the man leading and the woman following—to the current fad dances where the closed dance position has been dropped and the couples dance opposite each other, seldom touching. There is a close relationship between current dance styles and current popular music. To a certain extent there is a reflection of the participant's point of view, for example, in terms of equal status of boy and girl, with a disregard for man's leadership role.

Performance Dance

The performance dance forms are choreographed and performed for an audience, and while the audience may generate great empathy, its members are *not* dancing, they are watching others dance.

The entertainment and spectacular forms are similar in that both are presented to an audience as a diversion, as a form to be watched and enjoyed with a minimum of involvement. Certainly little save the excitement of the event remains after the show is over.

Entertainment Dance. Entertainment dance is perhaps the most generally recognized as dance by most people. The stereotype is the clever combination of technically complicated movement routines or exotic movements, always "graceful" and usually performed by trim and glamorous females. Sometimes there is a blend of any conceivable style formed into a "catchy" action sequence, or maybe it is simply dancers shuffling or gyrating about "in time to the music." Whether the response sought is in terms of the dancer's charms, the excitement of the action-music combination, or the display of flexibility, costume or skin, it is all geared to attract the attention and to entertain a relatively unimaginative and undemanding audience.

Spectacular Dance. Spectacular dance is choreographed and performed in order to present a dazzling and exciting spectacle. Precise, though not necessarily complex movement patterns, performed by large numbers of dancers in brilliant costumes and settings, with captivating and loud music and all of the production fireworks possible to augment the impact on the audience are usually employed.

Ethnic Dance. Ethnic dance is the traditional and culturally identifiable dance form in which the choreography is developed out of the story and action of religious and ethnic figures and concepts, and most especially racial heroes both familiar and dear to the understanding audience. This is a highly sophisticated and symbolic performance spectacle closely allied to the racial-religious-cultural ties of a people. It goes far beyond national boundaries. The performers are usually highly skilled and of a family of dance performers. One of the most pervasive of the ethnic dance forms is the classical dance of India which has spread throughout all of Asia.

Dance as a Performing Art. Dance as a performing art, commonly called Modern Dance or Contemporary Ballet, strives to go beyond the spectacular display or the immediate entertainment, though it can be both spectacular and entertaining. As an art it exists because of two very important factors: first, the careful selection and organization of movement by the choreographer, and, second, the carefully rehearsed and sensitive performance of this choreography by able dance performers.

The dance is an illusive and immediate form—it exists only in its performance and then is gone. The content of the dance may be literally identifiable, relatively abstract or may exist as a non-representational dynamic image. But as an art form it exists as a product, created by a human being, as a vehicle for enriching the aesthetic taste of an audience.

Glossary. The following list gives brief definitions of some of the common differentiations made among dance forms:

Acrobatic Dance. With emphasis upon extremes of flexibility, wide range of movement and excellent control and balance. The intent of this kind of dance is to demonstrate the unusual skill and energy of the performer.

Ballet. Based upon strict positioning of feet, legs and arms in five basic "positions." Movement phrases, both in place and moving through space, are then developed out of this basic vocabulary. The classical ballet is a highly abstract movement form, depending upon music, setting, costume, libretto and pantomime for its ideational content.

Ballroom Dance. Refers almost entirely to the traditional social dance performed in dance position with the man leading and the lady following.

Children's Dance. Obviously concerned with dance for children, it encompasses a wide variety of experiences from the creative, exploratory approach to the imposed "fancy-dance" routines.

Classical Dance. Usually refers to the traditional ballet as the classical form of dance. Sometimes the term is used to describe the ceremonial or choral dance of classical Greece.

Contemporary Dance. The dance of today, usually refers to Modern Dance or to Modern or Contemporary Ballet.

Creative Dance. A designation given to a dance which is developed by discovering and building relevant movement, and manipulating it according to the intent of the creator. The alternative to this is using already formed movement sequences.

Interpretive Dance. A form which implies that movement is chosen according to its potential for interpreting either the music or some particular content.

Jazz Dance. (Sometimes called "Modern Jazz") A style of dance utilizing so called "primitive movement," essentially emphasizing pelvic and torso motion, often highly syncopated with alternating smooth and staccato qualities. Fundamentally Jazz is a music, not a dance style. The accompaniment for Jazz dance is seldom pure Jazz music but always has a persistent and obvious underlying duple beat. It might be more correctly called a source or a style for the use of the modern dancer.

Modern Dance. The dance form which depends primarily upon movement as its medium of expression, the other production elements being used to augment the movement statement. Dances are choreographed out of an exploration of any possible movement and a final selection and organization of the action which suits the intent of the choreographer. This is the art form of dance today.

Musical Comedy Dance. This is the dance which is developed in conjunction with the music and the content of the dramatic sequence. The dance serves only to forward the impact of the play.

Pantomime. Pantomime is not dance, but it may well be the "stuff" of a dance. It is stylized gesture, often exaggerated or refined to the very essence of its original. This necessarily has relationship to some identifiable aspect of human behavior. In its pure form it means "dumb action," that is, significant moving without speaking.

Pre-Classic Dance. During the Renaissance a wide variety of court dances developed throughout all of Europe. Many of these dances came from the folk dances of the peasants, were refined and adapted to the aristocratic courts, and had very special music written for them. This music later become the nucleus of the sonata, suite and symphony. It was Louis XIV himself who was responsible for the transition from the pre-classic court dance to the classic ballet.

Primitive Dance. Essentially this is the ritual dance of isolated peoples, with no written language, to whom the principles of magic are important. Dance serves as a major part of all important ceremonies. Just as there are few really primitive peoples left today, so there is little real primitive dance.

Religious Dance. Almost all religions of man have had, or continue to have some association with ceremonial movement, whether it is actually called dance or not. During the Middle Ages the Angel's Dance, or The Dance of the Angels was performed in many churches. It has been retained in the cathedral in Seville to this day. Contemporary religious dance usually refers to action interpreting psalms or hymns, to movement of reverence and solemnity sometimes performed as a part of religious services or on special religious holidays.

Rhythms. For a number of reasons, most of which are related to religious belief or social prejudice, the word "dance" has sometimes had a negative connotation. For this reason the word "Rhythms" or "Rhythmic Games" has often been substituted for dance, both in schools and in the community. To this day Dance in the Elementary School is almost always referred to as "Rhythms." Actually this is a complete misnomer for rhythm is an important part of *all* activities of children, not just their dance.

Square Dance. This is strictly an American version of the earlier quadrilles of England and France and is considered the characteristic folk dance of this country. It is a dance performed by four couples, starting and stopping in square formation, with a wide variety of changes and figures all directed by a prompter designated as the "caller."

Tap Dance. A dance form in which the foot strikes, beats and stamps the floor in a wide variety of rhythms but a fairly limited range of action. It serves as a vehicle for demonstrating the virtuosity and precision of the performer. For many years tap dancing has been a popular kind of theatrical dancing.

Therapy, Dance as. From earliest times movement has served as an adjunct to therapy for a variety of ills. Today Dance Therapy refers to movement experiences directed by a Dance Therapist, under the direction of a Psychiatrist or Psychologist, for emotionally disturbed or psychotic patients.

The Purposes of Competitive Athletics in American Education
HELEN M. STARR[*]

Definition of the Title

On the surface, the title of this discussion seems to be very clear and complete. However, in the process of reviewing the literature in the field, studying the policies which have been developed for competitive athletics, talking with those who are (a) administering general education programs, (b) coaching sports, (c) administering physical education programs, and (d) administering athletic programs, it was readily evidenced that there is much confusion as to just what the title of this paper, "The Purposes of Competitive Athletics in American Education," really means.

To some it means varsity athletics conducted on an interschool basis for gifted athletes. To others it means Little League competition in team sports beginning in the first and second grades and continuing as teams through high school and college. To others it means the promotion of a sports program for participation of the few in entertainment of the many. To others it means the provision of a sound program of physical education which in-

*Helen M. Starr, "The Purposes of Competitive Athletics in American Education," *American Academy of Physical Education, Professional Contributions* No. 7, 1961.

cludes a competition in sports as an outgrowth of class instruction and an opportunity for all to participate in intramural, extramural, and interscholastic or varsity competition according to needs, interests, and abilities. In short, the definition of the title takes on a meaning which best suits the interests of the persons in terms of the purposes which each person thinks competitive athletics should serve.

Therefore, in order to discuss the topic at all, I found it necessary to develop a definition which will be the framework in which the topic will be discussed. This definition is developed from the meaning of each word in the title as given in Webster's New Collegiate Dictionary.

The dictionary gives the meaning of *purpose* as "that which one sets before himself as an object to be attained;" an intention, an aim, or value. The second word, *competition,* according to the dictionary, means the act of competing, a contest where one is ambitious to equal another, a contest between rivals, a match. The third word in the title, *athletics,* according to the dictionary, means "athletic exercises; the games and sports of athletes; skill or activity in athletic exercises." *Education,* according to the dictionary, is "a science dealing with the principles and practice of teaching and learning." When we place the word "American" before education, we mean education which provides a program of teaching and learning for all according to their individual needs.

Therefore, the definition of the title for this discussion is as follows:

> The objectives of a sports program which includes an opportunity for all pupils (both boys and girls) in terms of individual needs and interests to participate in a wide range of games and sports which involve a rivalry, or match, with one's self or with others.

As stated earlier, the discussion of this paper will be limited to the meaning of the definition as just stated.

Analysis of the Definition

In addition to defining a topic, it is necessary to analyze its meaning and describe the definition clearly enough so that its meaning can be visualized. This is the only way that one can decide the extent to which such a program as described in the definition is in operation today. As stated earlier, each word in the definition had a very important role to play in giving clarification to the title of this paper. In an analysis, then, of this definition, it is necessary to study the meaning of each word or phrase.

A. The Objectives or Values to Be Realized

To find our values or objectives it is necessary to review the objectives of education in terms of the make-up of the individuals and of the society in which they live, particularly the objectives of health and physical education. Regardless of the size of the school system, the extent of professional leadership, or the interest in the field of health and physical education, all systems have objectives stating that each pupil should have the opportunity, insofar as he or she is able, (a) to develop and maintain good physical and mental health, (b) to develop avocational interests which are satisfying and provide for worthy use of leisure time, and (c) to learn to recognize ethical and esthetic values of experience and to act accordingly.

To sum up the objectives to be derived from a properly conducted program of "competitive athletics in American education," the following selected outcomes are indicated:

Competitive athletics

1. provide an opportunity for youth to achieve the goals of total "fitness;"
2. serve as a means of motivation to wholesome, vigorous, challenging activities which can be used throughout life;
3. allow each one to develop skills in sports suited to their individual choice, interest and ability;
4. serve as a channel for enjoyment and satisfaction in sports and for testing and matching one's self or one's team against an opponent;
5. provide a wholesome means for release of tension, hostility, and the like, which is basic to good mental health of individuals.

To summarize these statements, the Educational Policies Commission makes the following statement in *School Athletics* about the values of this program:

"Participation in sound athletic programs, we believe, contributes to health and happiness, physical skill and emotional maturity, social competence and moral values."

❈   ❈   ❈   ❈   ❈

"Playing hard and playing to win can help to build character. So also do learning to 'take it' in the rough and tumble of vigorous play, experiencing defeat without whimpering and victory without gloating, and disciplining one's self to comply with the rules of the games and of good sportsmanship."

In addition, the following statement is made in the report of the National Conference of 1958 on *Youth and Fitness*:

"One of the important aims of education is to provide opportunity and guidance which will enable youth to develop their potentialities and to receive experiences which will enable them to adjust in adult life. Toward this goal, athletics make a major contribution."

B. COMPETITION

The analysis of the second part of the definition deals with competition or competitive activities which include rivalry or matching skills as of utmost importance. Competition, naturally, can be competing by one's self against a standard or goal of achievement, competing against another individual in some type of dual or individual tests, or competing as a member of a team against another team such as in team sports.

To some people today, whether they are in general education, physical education, or lay members of the community, the word "competition" is one to be avoided in their professional or educational vocabulary. In fact, some educational programs have played down the meaning of competition so much that participants and others feel guilty if they have the desire to compete, to match, or to rival in any kind of activity.

To others, competition should be developed in all pupils to the extent that each one has an opportunity to match or rival others to their best possible level, and to receive the enjoyment and feel the success which comes from winning.

To others, competition means highly competitive organization, such as a varsity team of gifted athletes who see winning a match as the only important outcome of competition.

The importance of the word "competition" in this definition means the acceptance of competition as a valuable and worthwhile component of daily life activities and as a result a worthwhile purposes of athletics. In fact, the Educational Policies Commission makes the statement: "We believe that cooperation and competition are both important components of American life. Athletic participation can help teach the values of cooperation as well as the spirit of competition."

Again, quoting from the report of the National Conferenec on *Youth and Fitness*:

"Competitive sports provide living experiences in education. Such physical activity gives opportunity to make decisions, to work cooperatively, to assume responsibility, to be well disciplined, to function with a group, to be a leader, and to have a goal."

The report goes on to say that if pupils are to gain values of competition "various levels of competition are essential."

C. ATHLETICS

The meaning of the word "athletics" certainly needs no explanation to a group such as this. According to the report on *Youth and Fitness*, athletics means "competitive sports involving physical activity among two or more contesting individuals or teams." So often in current practice and in the literature or current articles, athletics seems to mean participation in a very narrow range of team sports such as basketball, baseball, and football, and participation in these at the varsity or interscholastic level. Athletics in this definition means a program including a wide range of sports such as the following:

Aquatics (Both speed and synchronized swimming)
Archery
Badminton
Baseball
Basketball
Bowling
Riflery
Sailing
Skating (Figure, Speed and Ice Hockey)
Skiing
Soccer
Cross Country
Curling
Fencing
Football
Golf
Gymnastics
Hockey
Softball
Tennis
Track and Field
Track (winter)
Volleyball
Wrestling

However, it seems today that the most participation in athletics and the most attention to athletics are in sports such as football, basketball, and baseball. In fact, a "Sports Participation Survey," made by the National Federation of State High School Athletic Associations from schools in this country, shows that approximately 28 percent of the boys participating in sports participated in football; 24 percent of the boys participated in basketball; and 14 percent participated in baseball. Participation in these three sports amounted to 66 percent of the total participation in all sports.

Sports such as archery, fencing, sailing, badminton, bowling, skiing, ice hockey, golf, volleyball, and swimming had less than 2 percent participation. In fact, many of them had one-tenth of one percent. This is certainly a very narrow program of sports participation. However, more schools in the United States are beginning to increase their offering of individual, dual, and seasonal sports.

To further explain the meaning of athletics in this definition it is necessary to discuss briefly the kinds of athletics which are included. It seems that in the literature and in observation of practice, participation in athletics is confined largely to the varsity player and to the gifted athlete. Very little attention is given to other types of athletics. This definition embraces the following kinds of athletics:

1. *Athletics Education* is part of a good physical education instructional program. Again, the Educational Policies Commission states:

   "We believe in athletics as an important part of the school physical education program. We believe that the experience of playing athletic games should be a part of the education of all children and youth who attend school in the United States."

In the physical education program the students can be taught the various sports skills needed, the values of cooperation and fair play, and the rules and regulations of the games. In fact, the positive values and skills claimed for varsity athletics should certainly be a basic part of education for every boy and girl if the purposes are to be gained. Through the after-school program pupils are given an opportunity to participate in competitive athletics on a voluntary level according to their needs and interests.

2. *Intramural Athletics* — organized competitive sports, outside the required physical education class, in which all participants are students in the same school.

3. *Extramural Athletics* — organized competitive sports between representatives of schools — such as play days, sports days, informal games — but not limited by interscholastic athletic regulations.

4. *Interscholastic Athletics* — organized competitive sports between representatives of two or more schools.

These four kinds of athletics stem out from the physical education instructional program and are an important part of health and physical education.

D. AMERICAN EDUCATION

The fourth part of the definition, "in American Education," means that a program of athletics should be available to all boys and girls. The report of the National Conference on *Youth and Fitness* states: "In view of the educational benefits that result from participation in athletics, such physical competitive activity should be provided for *all* boys in the secondary school. Athletics should be an integral part of the curriculum with a well-conducted and varied program of athletic experiences for *all* pupils." It should be added here, *all* girls as well.

Various programs should be offered so that all boys and girls can participate according to their needs and interests. In American education, participation in athletics then is the "right" of every boy and girl and not a "privilege." The Educational Policies Commission gives as a reason for this the following statement:

"Athletics may also exemplify the value of the democratic process and of fair play. Through team play the student athlete often learns how to work with others for the achievement of group goals. Athletic competition can be a wholesome equalizer. Individuals on the playing field are judged for what they are and for what they can do, not on the basis of the social, ethnic, or economic group to which their families belong."

Certainly, each boy and girl should have first-hand experience in a competitive sports program to achieve such worthy goals.

In getting into the heart of this discussion, the second phase, that of analyzing the definition, has been completed. From this analysis it is pointed out that competitive athletics serve a valuable purpose in the education of American youth.

If the preceding statements are accepted — that is, (a) the definition as developed in the first chapter of this paper and (b) the analysis of the definition as developed in the second chapter — the statement can be made without reserve that the competitive athletics program, if properly conducted, has a great potential in helping youth achieve the objectives of education and develop skills for living and contributing to the democratic way of life.

Guidelines for Program

Certainly, before we discuss any problems facing programs of competitive athletics, it is important to review some principles which have been set up to guide a sound program. Following are principles which are approved by all in theory, regardless of whether a person is an administrator, a teacher, a coach, an athletic director, or a parent:

1. The competitive athletics program is an outgrowth of a sound physical education program.
2. The health and physical characteristics of each pupil "should be considered in determining the extent and kind of athletic activities in which he participates."
3. The competitive athletics program, in the words of the Educational Policies Commission, "should be adapted to successive educational levels, that is, the program should be different in the lower elementary school than that of the varsity high school interscholastic program."

   Authorities agree that *in the elementary school* "athletic competition for young children should be limited." The Educational Policies Commission makes this further statement:

   "Athletics — that is, organized competitive physical sports — have less to contribute to growth and health in the early school years than is the case later on. For children in grades one through six, developmental needs will be met most adequately if physical activities are largely informal and non-competitive. Athletic competition should be introduced gradually, beginning with simple relays, tag games, and team games involving simple rules and relatively few players."

   The Commission also states that *in the junior high school* the program of athletics should be suited to boys and girls who are "undergoing rapid physical growth, who have special need for improving body coordination, who want to take part in an increasing number of activities, and who have strong desire for group acceptance." On the whole, competitive athletics for junior high school boys and girls should be limited to intramural and extramural sports on an invitational basis. It is recommended that body contact sports are not desirable in junior high school, and that varsity interscholastic sports as conducted in the senior high school have no place in the junior high school because of pressures and emphasis on a team keyed to win.

The program *at the senior high school* should be one which again provides all youth an opportunity to participate in competitive athletics, but in addition to the intramural and extramural, includes a program of varsity interschool athletics, with the exception of boxing, for the gifted in motor activities.

4. Sufficient resources are needed to provide staff and facilities for such a varied program.
5. Participation in competitive activities should be a source of fun, enjoyment, and satisfaction for participants.
6. A wide variety of sports should be offered so that each pupil can participate in a seasonal sport with a range of choice, as well as develop skill in the sports of his own choice which he can enjoy throughout his life.
7. The program should be properly administered so that unsound practices can be avoided.

The Gap Between Theory and Practice

So far in this discussion I have presented the meaning of the topic, analyzed it, and given some principles or guidelines of a desirable program in competitive athletics for all boys and girls. Certainly, the next question is in order: *Do we today accept this definition, do we believe in the analysis, and have the principles stated been implemented in our programs so that each boy and girl has the right (not the privilege) to participate in competitive athletics?*

Selected Problems, Practice, and Evidence

Following are two selected problems which need to be faced, studied, and solved by such a group as this if the objectives of competitive athletics are to be achieved by all boys and girls:

1. *Is the broad program as indicated by the definition of competitive athletics given in this paper accepted, and is it in operation today in school programs of this country?*

How would you answer this question? Following are opinions from leaders over the country about this question. Do you agree with them?

   a. The use of the phrase "competitive athletics" from the standpoint of the general educator means to a great extent interschool athletics of a highly competitive and selective nature. For some reason or other, whether from unsatisfying experience with the program or lack of information about the real meaning of competitive athletics, this phrase is not acceptable to many educators. In fact, many general educators, teachers — and even teachers of physical education — fear the phrase "competitive athletics." Therefore, it seems that they do not have an understanding of the real meaning of the phrase and are judging the program on a narrow definition and have limited the meaning of the term. They think of it as interscholastic athletics or professional athletics.

b. The word "athletics" has almost disappeared from the present vocabulary and thinking of many physical educators, and, also, the program has disappeared from the physical education curriculum. How often have you heard physical educators say, when they have seen competitive athletics in operation either on an intramural, extramural, or interscholastic level, "That is not physical education; that is athletics." It seems that we have taken so much away from the physical education program today that physical education is really an empty shell. Therefore, it seems that even physical educators do not accept or understand the real meaning of competitive athletics.

c. In a review of writings in the field of competitive athletics, many authors use the phrase in a very specific manner. For example, in an article in the *Journal of Health-Physical Education-Recreation*, December, 1959, the writer is talking about athletics for pre-high school age children. He states that, "Competitive athletics for pre-high school age children have been the most controversial issue of our Association during the decade 1950-1959." As one reads through the article, it becomes evident that he is talking about interscholastic, varsity-type athletics for elementary school children. This is an incorrect use of the term, "competitive athletics," because according to our broad definition competitive athletics for pre-high school age children is a very worthy and valuable part of the physical education, intramural, and extramural program. It seems, then, that there is evidence of a poorly selected vocabulary on the part of people in our own field as well as lay people in the use of the term "competitive athletics."

d. In meeting with lay people such as members of youth fitness councils of the community, the word "athletics" or the phrase "competitive athletics" means only one thing to most people in this group. It means to them that we should immediately embark upon a highly competitive athletic program which very quickly weeds out the weak and average-skilled player and glorifies the gifted or varsity player who is already having many opportunities for such participation. Programs of "competitive athletics" which put into operation the meaning of our definition are in existence, but in only such numbers that they do make headlines in our professional journals as something which is new and different. For example, a recent article featured a headline as follows: "*Extramurals for Boys — Something New.*" If we do accept the program and do have in operation a broad program of competitive athletics, would such articles be of headline interest?

2. Is participation in competitive athletics considered in all of the schools in this country today the right of every boy and girl in terms of his or her needs, interests, and abilities?

How would you answer this question? Following are opinions from leaders over the country about this question. Do you agree with them?

a. On the whole, boys and girls in the elementary school haven't had the opportunity to participate in a worthwhile competitive athletics program keyed to their needs, because the general educator and the physical educator haven't developed a program which is sound in keeping with the standards for such a program. Therefore, many boys and girls have never had the joy or satisfaction of competing in sports or games during this important period of growth. The program they have had is often one of unorganized play, and there is no semblance of organization for a competitive sports program. Also, teachers and others, because of the narrow concept of competitive athletics held by all concerned, have (and rightly so) resisted the development of a sound competitive athletics program. They do not seem to know what a good program is; they have only practice, past experiences, or observation to use as a measuring rod. This experience has often been of the varsity, interschool-type of competitive athletics which has moved down into the elementary school, which is, of course, not the program recommended.

b. From the standpoint of participation, young children are beginning to select, because of ability, one of two roles to play in competitive athletics. These are: the role of a spectator and the role of an athlete. Maybe one of the reasons for the selection of a role very early in life is the development of athletic programs which are based on the narrow meaning of athletics. In many communities, teams are selected, coached, and tournaments are played according to the high school, college, or professional pattern. Often, only the skilled and gifted athletes participate to a great extent, and those not chosen very soon learn that their participation is limited to the role of the spectator. How often have you heard an elementary school boy say that he will not be a basketball player because he is not going to be tall enough, or a football player because he is too light in weight, but that he might make a hockey player because he has speed? Because of the pressure of the community (and who knows in the community who these people are?) well-meaning leaders of athletics for boys and for girls are forced into working and devoting all their attention to the first or varsity teams in seasonal sports rather than a broad program for all levels of skills.

c. The pressure in some communities in this country upon school officials, coaches, and others for winning teams prevents them from thinking of or providing a program of competitive athletics for all boys and girls at elementary, junior high, and senior high school levels. For example, in a well-run interscholastic athletics program at the senior high school, many of the professionally qualified men teachers on the staff are involved in the conduct of "interschool athletics," and rightly so. They are fulfilling such roles as coaches and assistant coaches of from 3 to 13 sports, faculty managers, equipment managers, and members of boards of coaches. If an intramural or extramural program for boys and girls were offered according to the specifications in the definition, where would the professional leadership come from, as so many of the highly qualified persons are already tied up with varsity or interscholastic athletics.

In order for a school to operate a sound program of interschool athletics, facilities must be available for the varsity squad, for the "B" squad, and probably for "C," "D," and "E" squads. All of these squads need daily practice and coaching. For example, during the basketball season which begins before Christmas and ends in March, in certain areas of this country all of the facilities need to be used after school for varsity practice. Many junior high and elementary school gymnasiums are used as well for these activities. Where, then, can the intramural and the extramural programs for the remaining boys and girls be held?

Summary

So far in this discussion I have presented only two problems, stating a question and the opinions of leaders regarding an answer. No doubt many of you have other problems to raise. These will certainly come out in the discussion. Also, at no time have I talked about a girls program versus a boys program, or a high school program of athletics. Pitting one program against the other has been purposely avoided, because they are equally important and valuable to the school population. In the definition of competitive athletics given in this paper it is assumed that the program should be run for the boys and girls and that there is an acceptable program at each of the school levels — not a program for girls, a program for boys, or one program for all school levels.

If our country today is educating a group of young people who are unfit from the physical-mental-moral standpoint, who are overweight, who lack "get up and go," who fail to fight, to differ, who lack the courage to try, who fail to abide by ethical rules of competition in everyday living and in vocational pursuits, shouldn't we take a look at the conduct of the program of competitive athletics, which has a potential, if properly administered, for helping young people secure these benefits or objectives? The achievement of these goals through such a sound program is the "right" of every boy and girl and not a "privilege."

However, there are some issues to be faced before this can be accomplished. They are:

1. Should there be a new word or phrase for "competitive athletics" when referring to a program for all boys and girls? Practice seems to have limited the definition to interschool or varsity athletics.
2. Can we provide a program for all boys and girls and still maintain the high standards that have been set up for the interschool athletics program?

BIBLIOGRAPHY

1. American Academy of Pediatrics. *Competitive Athletics — A Statement of Policy.* Report of the Committee on School Health. Evanston, Illinois: the Academy, 1956.
2. American Association for Health, Physical Education, and Recreation. *Youth and Fitness — A Program for Secondary Schools.* Washington, D. C.: the Association, 1959.
3. *Meet the Press.* Transcript of the Proceedings of the National Broadcasting Company telecast on Sunday, January 24, 1960, on which Vice Admiral Hyman G. Rickover was a guest. Washington, D. C.: Merkle Press, Inc.

4. National Education Association and American Association of School Administrators, Educational Policies Commission. *School Athletics — Problems and Policies.* Washington, D. C.: the Commission, 1954.
5. *A Checklist on School Athletics.* (Based on *School Athletics — Problems and Policies.*) Washington, D. C.: the Commission, 1954.
6. Selected articles from the *Journal of Health-Physical Education-Recreation*, published by the American Association for Health, Physical Education, and Recreation, 1201 Sixteenth St., N.W., Washington 6, D. C.
    1. "Desirable Athletics for Children." 23; June, 1952.
    2. Duer, A. O. "Basic Issues of Intercollegiate Athletics." 31; January, 1960.
    3. Hale, Creighton J. "What Research Says About Athletics for Pre-High School Age Children." 30; December, 1959.
    4. Hamilton, T. J. "An Athletic Director Looks at Fitness." 28; September, 1957.
    5. Jaeger, Eloise M., and Bockstruck, Else H. "Effective Student Leadership." 30; December, 1959.

Athletics in Education*

Because athletics are of historical and social significance in our national culture. Because athletics provide a primary means through which may be developed and maintained the physical vigor and stamina required to defend successfully our concept of freedom; and to realize fully our potential as Americans. Because athletics provide a primary means through which may be developed the habits, attitudes, and ideals requisite to ethical competition and effective cooperation in a free society. Because athletics provide a primary means through which may be utilized in a healthful and wholesome fashion the leisure of our citizens and youth. Because athletics have a powerful appeal for young people during their formative years and can be utilized to further the harmonious development of youth. . .

We believe that participation in athletics should be included in the educational experiences offered to all students in the schools and the colleges of the United States.

We believe that these opportunities for all students to participate in athletics should be provided in the schools and the colleges through:

1. The basic physical education program for all students in which daily instruction and practice are provided in a variety of physical activities (in-

---

*This is reprinted from the pamphlet, *Athletics in Education.* This work is a platform statement by the Division of Men's Athletics, American Association for Health, Physical Education and Recreation. The Platform Statement Committee consisted of Ray O. Duncan (Chairman), Louis E. Alley, David Arnold, John Knight, Richard Larkins, John Lawther, James Long, Thomas McDonough, D. K. Stanley, Roswell Merrick. Consultants were as follows: Robert N. Brown, Arthur S. Daniels, Jack Daugherty, Creighton Hale, Paul Landis and Charles "Bud" Wilkinson.

cluding athletics) that are suited to the nature and needs of the students and that ensure the development of an adequate level of physical fitness.

2. The physical recreation program in which opportunities are provided for all students to participate informally in a variety of physical activities (including athletics).

3. The intramural athletic program in which opportunities are provided for all students to utilize, in organized competition with their schoolmates, the knowledge and skills acquired in the basic physical education program.

4. The interscholastic or intercollegiate athletic program in which opportunities are provided in secondary schools and colleges for students with superior athletic ability fully to develop and utilize this talent through organized competition with students of similar ability from other schools and colleges.

We believe that the opportunities for participation in athletics that are offered in the schools and the colleges should be complemented by well-organized and well-conducted athletic programs sponsored by appropriate community agencies.

Athletics, when utilized properly, serve as potential educational media through which the optimum growth — physical, mental, emotional, social, and moral — of the participants may be fostered. During the many arduous practice sessions and in the variety of situations that arise during the heat of the contests, the players must repeatedly react to their own capabilities and limitations and to the behavior of others. These repeated reactions, and the psychological conditioning that accompanies them, inevitably result in changes — mental, as well as physical — in the players. Because each contest is usually surrounded by an emotionally charged atmosphere and the players are vitally interested in the outcome of the game, the players are more pliable and, hence, more subject to change than in most educational endeavors. To ensure that these changes are educationally desirable, all phases of athletics should be expertly organized and conducted.

Physical Fitness

The desire to excel in athletics is one of the strongest forces available for motivating the American boy to expend voluntarily the vigorous efforts required to develop a high degree of fitness. Because of his desire to excel in athletic competition, he will willingly and eagerly participate in strenuous conditioning programs and practice sessions to develop the strength, the

---

Throughout this Platform Statement, the term athletics refers to competitive games and sports that require physical skill, agility, strength, and stamina of the participants (individual or teams) who compete in accordance with accepted rules of play and of scoring.

endurance, and the skill requisite to excellent performance. He will submit to regular physical examinations by a physician, abide by rigid training rules, and adhere to recommended diets. Because his performance is evaluated regularly and decisively during each athletic contest, the relationship between his efforts and his success is readily apparent to him. Thus, he learns how physical fitness is achieved and maintained. At the same time, he experiences the feeling of unbounded vigor and physical exuberance enjoyed only by those who are physically fit, and he may form favorable and lasting attitudes toward exercise and toward physical fitness.

Skill in Movement

To attain success in athletics, the participant must train his mind and body to respond instantly and effectively to the multitude of situations that arise during the course of play. The resultant development of skill in movement enables him to accomplish the everyday physical requirements of his work efficiently and with ease and to respond quickly and effectively in emergencies that demand unusual strength, endurance, speed, or coordination.

Social Development

Authorities on child growth and development agree that participation in competitive play provides the child with invaluable opportunities for expending effort that leads to success or failure, for judicious risks and thrills that build up his morale and his capacity to endure and to "stand the gaff," and from which he gains his early concepts of sportsmanship.

The competitive world — among children as well as adults — is neither gentle nor overly kind. In such a world, however, the youngster under wise direction begins to grow toward social maturity by learning to (1) suffer his mild hurts, mental or physical, in silence, (2) control his emotional outbursts, (3) disguise or hide his feelings of fear, (4) restrain the outward expression of sudden impulses, (5) understand and endure delays in getting what he wants, and (6) reject being "babied."

The intense and challenging situations in athletic competition provide the youth with socially acceptable channels through which he may express his aggressive tendencies and expend his excess energy. Opportunities in which he may control many of his antisocial tendencies through sublimation — and in which he may compensate for real or imagined inadequacies — are abundant. In athletics, he can express his emotions vigorously in a socially acceptable manner.

The growing boy earnestly desires recognition and prestige. He lacks self-confidence and needs some means of gaining it. Athletics provide him an opportunity to take his place on a team and thereby gain group acceptance and group approval. Through success in athletics, his feelings of inferiority may be assuaged. By trying himself out in highly competitive situations in which he is emotionally aroused and experiences deep-seated feelings, he may learn to perform acceptably despite the intense emotional upheaval. Gradually, he may attain a mental poise and an emotional stability that will serve him well in moments of stress.

In athletics, the boy may learn to work cooperatively as a member of a group that is striving for a common goal. He may learn to abide by the rules and to play fairly — not from fear of penalty, but because the success of his team and the enjoyment of all are thus enhanced. He may experience the humbling lessons of defeat and so learn to readjust his value concepts. He may learn that he must discipline himself to meet his responsibilities if the group of which he is a member is to achieve success in which he may share. He may learn that in all successful group enterprises, some must lead and others must follow. He may learn the meaning and the value of group loyalty and group morale and may experience the emotional responses associated with the esprit de corps that is developed as the members of the team practice together, suffer and endure together, and win and lose together.

In athletics, the boy may learn to tolerate the weaknesses and shortcomings of others and to understand that all men have common desires and aspirations. Prejudices toward others tend to melt away during the grueling practices and the "trial by ordeal" of the games. He may learn to judge his teammates by their behavior and their contribution to the success of the team and to disregard economic, racial, or religious differences.

Recreation

Athletics can provide the youth and the adult with abundant opportunities for utilizing their leisure in activities that are both healthful and wholesome. The highly mechanized nature of American society and the consequent degeneration in the physical fitness of citizens and youth make mandatory an increased emphasis on the utilization of athletics as a means of recreation.

Athletic games and contests are ideally suited to the leisure needs of youth. The normal boy is bursting with energy. He restlessly searches for excitement, adventure, and a cause for which to strive. Unless proper opportunities and proper direction are provided, he may find undesirable outlets for his boundless energy and his turbulent urges. Athletics — sponsored by schools, churches, clubs, industries, communities, and national organizations — offer him recreational pursuits that fulfill his immediate needs and provide a means through which he may develop qualities essential to living a useful and successful life.

Dual and individual sports, together with the team games that do not demand of participants high levels of physical fitness and skill, offer the adult opportunities for healthful exercise and a release from the tensions and the worries that beset him as he struggles with the problems of living in a complex world.

As spectators, both the youth and the adult can share vicariously in the spirit of the struggle, the despair of defeat, and the joy of victory experienced by teams and individual athletes performing in public contests. Such contests — between professionals as well as between amateurs — are common to the cultures of all modern nations and serve as a basis for world-wide communication and understanding between peoples of all nationalities and races.

Because all students can benefit from regular participation in appropriate athletic activities, opportunities for such participation should be provided at all grade levels in schools and colleges. The capacities, the needs, and the interests of the pupils differ markedly from grade level to grade level. Consequently, the nature of the athletic activities presented, the methods utilized in presenting them, and the emphasis given to each activity should differ in accordance with the characteristics of the students for whom the activities are intended.

Athletics in the Basic Physical Education Program

Under the guidance of a skillful teacher or coach, experiences in athletics provide unique opportunities in which the development of physical fitness and skill in movement, together with wholesome recreation and desirable social development, may be fostered. Hence, athletic activities should be a basic part of the physical education program for all students. In addition to instruction and practice in the fundamental skills of the athletics prominent in American culture, the students should receive instruction in the history, the rules, and the playing strategies associated with these sports. Provisions should be made for appropriate sequence and progression in both skill and knowledge from grade level to grade level. Particular attention should be given to developing in the students a lasting interest in athletics and an appreciation of the role of athletics in American culture.

In Elementary Schools: The basic physical education program should include rhythmical activities, creative play, gymnastic stunts, self-testing activities, and athletics that are suited to the nature, the needs, and the interest of elementary school youngsters. Basic instruction and practice should be provided in climbing, throwing, catching, kicking, running, jumping, dodging, tumbling, and similar skills, the mastery of which is requisite to skillful performance in athletics. In the primary grades (1-3), simple relays and games of low organization that have but few rules and that come quickly to a climax should be utilized to orient youngsters to informal competitive situations. In the intermediate grades (4-6), modified team games, together with relays that involve the fundamental skills of athletics, should be emphasized. The development of desirable habits of behavior in competitive situations should be stressed.

In Junior High Schools: The basic physical education program should provide opportunities for increased emphasis on instruction and practice in athletics, particularly in team games. The intense interest of adolescent boys in athletics, together with their urgent desire to gain status among their peers, causes team games to be especially effective vehicles through which the desirable social development of the participants may be fostered. Cooperation, loyalty, respect for others, conformity to the rules of play, and similar aspects of good sportsmanship should be stressed.

In Senior High Schools: From 30 to 50 percent of the basic physical education program for boys should be devoted to team sports. However, during the junior and senior years, individual and dual sports in which the students may continue to participate after they leave school should be given attention. Golf, tennis, archery, badminton, and bowling are examples of such activities.

In Colleges and Universities: The basic physical education program for men should provide opportunities for instruction and practice in all forms of athletics. Because the basic physical education programs in many high schools are inadequate, provisions should be made in college and university basic programs for all levels of instruction in athletics — beginning, intermediate, and advanced.

Athletics in Physical Recreation and Intramural Programs

Because the physical education classes are utilized primarily for physical conditioning and for instructional purposes, the physical recreation program and the intramural program should provide for all students opportunities to put voluntarily into practice the knowledge and skills acquired in the basic physical education program. In the physical recreation program, facilities and equipment (balls, bats, rackets, courts, playing fields, etc.) should be made readily available during specified hours to enable the students to participate informally during their free time in athletic activities of their own choosing. In the intramural program, organized competition in the athletics presented in the basic physical education program should be provided.

In Elementary Schools: Particular emphasis in the primary grades (1-3) should be placed on the physical recreation program. In the intermediate grades (4-6), organized intramural competition in athletics should be introduced. Suitable activities for intramural competition for boys in grades 4-6 include modified forms of soccer, softball, touch football, basketball, volleyball, and track and field athletics. Emphasis should be placed on participation rather than on the determination of championship teams. Under no circumstances should youngsters be denied the right to participate because of deficiencies in skill.

In Junior and Senior High Schools: Organized intramural competition should be offered in all athletics in which instruction and practice are given in the basic physical education classes. Every effort should be extended to make the intramural program as attractive to the students as the interscholastic athletic program. Definite procedures for the organization of teams and for conducting the intramural contests should be established and followed from year to year. Records of outstanding teams and of individual performances should be kept in an attempt to establish a tradition for participation in intramural competition.

In Colleges and Universities: Opportunities for organized intramural competition in many forms of athletics should be provided for all students. Because the academic class schedules vary markedly and students have free periods throughout the day, extensive opportunities in which facilities and equipment are made available for informal participation should be provided.

Interscholastic and Intercollegiate Athletic Programs

Interscholastic and intercollegiate athletic programs provide opportunities for students with superior talents to develop and utilize these talents fully in organized competition with students of similar ability from other schools and colleges. Rather than limiting interschool athletics to competion between varsity teams, competition between several levels of teams should be encouraged and fostered to provide opportunities for increased numbers of students to participate.

Because the extreme interest of the spectators and players in the outcome of the contests often creates highly emotional situations, interscholastic and intercollegiate athletics rank among the most effective means in the total educational program through which the values described in the first part of this document may be realized. However, the characteristics that cause well-organized and well-conducted programs of interscholastic and intercollegiate athletics to be usually potent tools for accomplishing educational objectives also cause poorly organized and poorly conducted programs to be equally potent in bringing about undesirable outcomes. Athletic programs in which the students are exploited to entertain the public, to advertise the school, to earn money for the school, or to enhance the professional reputation of the coach have no place in educational institutions and should not be tolerated.

To utilize fully the potential in athletics for educational experiences, interscholastic and intercollegiate athletic programs should be organized and conducted in accordance with these six basic principles.

1. Interscholastic and intercollegiate athletic programs should be regarded as integral parts of the total educational program and should be so conducted that they are worthy of such regard.

2. Interscholastic and intercollegiate athletic programs should supplement rather than serve as substitutes for basic physical education programs, physical recreation programs, and intramural athletic programs.

3. Interscholastic and intercollegiate athletic programs should be subject to the same administrative control as the total education program.

4. Interscholastic and intercollegiate athletic programs should be conducted by men with adequate training in physical education.

5. Interscholastic and intercollegiate athletic programs should be so conducted that the physical welfare and safety of the participants are protected and fostered.

6. Interscholastic and intercollegiate athletic programs should be conducted in accordance with the letter and the spirit of the rules and regulations of appropriate conference, state, and national athletic associations.

In Elementary Schools: Athletics between schools should be limited to informal games between teams from two or more schools and to occasional sports days when teams from several schools assemble for a day of friendly, informal competition. At such events, emphasis should be placed on participation by all students. The attendance of spectators (particularly students as spectators) should be discouraged. High-pressure programs of interscholastic athletics, in which varsity teams compete in regularly scheduled contests that are attended by partisan spectators, should not be allowed under any circumstances.

In Junior High Schools: Limited programs of interscholastic athletics that are adapted to the capacities and the needs of junior high school boys are desirable. The physical and emotional immaturity of the junior high youngster requires that such programs be controlled with extreme care to ensure that primary emphasis is placed on providing educational experiences for the participants rather than on producing winning teams and that the physical welfare of the participants is protected and fostered.

In Senior High Schools: Interscholastic athletic programs should include team and dual sports of a variety compatible with the enrollment, the equipment and facilities, and the professional personnel in the school. Every effort should be extended to provide opportunities for all interested boys to participate.

In Colleges and Universities: Intercollegiate athletic programs should include as many team, dual, and individual sports as finances will permit. Such programs should be conducted in strict adherence to the rules and regulations of the appropriate governing body.

Professional Personnel

Athletics at every level should be conducted by professionally prepared personnel of unquestionable integrity who are dedicated to the task of developing their charges to the highest degree possible — mentally, physically, and morally.

In addition to a knowledge of athletics, such personnel should have a knowledge of (1) the place and purpose of athletics in education, (2) the growth and development of children and youth, (3) the effects of exercise on the human organism, and (4) first aid. Certain basic competencies in physical education, specifically applicable to the welfare and success of participants in competitive sports, should be a minimum prerequisite for teaching or coaching athletics at any level.

A Philosophical Interpretation of the National Institute on Girls Sports

KATHERINE LEY*

I propose to discuss with you what would be more correctly titled a fundamental or operational point of view regarding sports programs and sports competition for girls and women. The term "operational" is used here to indicate action or functions. It is important to outline steps that I believe must be taken to improve and expand sports programs for girls and women and to increase the benefits to be derived by the participants.

Let us begin by setting the record straight. For many years many professional and nonprofessional sports personnel have believed that women have opposed competition for women. This belief is basically untrue. Women have opposed those competitive events in which harmful practices and exploitation have minimized the benefit to the competitor. And yet, as recently as the September 30, 1963 issue of *Sports Illustrated* this statement was made: "After a squabble over U. S. team leadership (in 1928), professional women physical education instructors were left off the U. S. team's staff. Scorned, the physical education teachers at most high schools and colleges immediately eliminated instruction in the techniques of running, jumping, and throwing. 'Ladies should not perspire.' This thinking still holds 35 years later, encouraging otherwise athletic young girls to retreat behind the pose of fraility when it comes to track and field." (1)

In 1922, the AAU sponsored a women's track and field team to the Olympic Games in Paris. In 1923, Mrs. Herbert Hoover called a national

*Reprinted from the *Proceedings of the First National Institute on Girls Sports*. Division For Girls and Women's Sport of the American Association for Health, Physical Education, and Recreation, 1965.

meeting of women interested in athletics. As a result, the Women's Division of the National Amateur Athletic Federation was organized. The platform statements of this group did a great deal to influence the attitude of women toward competition. Agnes Wayman, one of the members of the original group, wrote the following: "We have often heard it stated that the Women's Division does not believe in competition for women. As a matter of fact, the Women's Division was organized to promote participation in sports and games on a nation wide basis. . . .It is the intense, highly specialized type of competition of which the Women's Division disapproves." (2) The key words here are "participation in sports and games on a nationwide basis" versus "highly specialized type of competition." Briefed even more, one might conclude that the issue was "participation" versus "competition," but this would be a misinterpretation of the Division's intent. It was not a question of one or the other; the issue was to preserve sports for all girls and women as evidenced by this statement quoted from the Platform: "Resolved, that for any given group we approve and recommend such selection and administration of athletic activities as makes participation possible for all, and strongly condemn the sacrifice of this objective for the intensive training of the few. The misunderstanding and the misinterpretation of this philosophy has resulted in years of debate on the question, "Should we have competition for girls?" So far as the Women's Division was concerned, and so far as the Division for Girls and Women's Sports is concerned, the only issue is how can we best conduct competitive activities to benefit all girls. It is quite evident that these early women feared curtailment of participation in order to provide a few, highly specialized performers. Although these things happened 40 years ago, we could find ourselves engaged again in a needless battle of words that would be useless and wasteful of time, energy, and talent. We could find ourselves embroiled in such arguments because of questions such as: "Will United States women do their share in Tokyo in 1964?" There's urgency in that question, and unless we keep our perspective, we could panic and turn our girls' programs into a search for championship talent.

But let us pause a moment and take a closer look at the situation. In the 20's, when the issue of women in the Olympics was new, the only international competitions were the Olympic Games every four years. The world was still large and it took at least a week to get from New York to Europe. Now in the 60's, sport and sports competition have become a major factor in international prestige. The Federal government and the State Department regard excellence in sports as an essential weapon in the cold war. The world is smaller now, and in the interim between Olympics there are numerous international contests. With the United States and Russia playing a home-and-home series in track and field, the American public eye is kept trained on abilities of our athletes as compared with athletes of other countries — especially athletes from Iron Curtain countries. If we were to succumb to the pressures, we would concentrate all our efforts on the few talented prospects we could find. This is neither practical nor philosophically sound. We must do two things: train the best we have to perform to the best of their ability and at the same time promote all sports for all girls and women so that eventually we will have more prospects from which to choose the best.

I am really proposing that we have our cake and eat it too. As an educator living in a democracy, my major concern is that every girl in this country benefit from participation in sports, that every girl receive instruction and coaching in a wide variety of activities, that any girl who has the desire and the ability be provided with opportunities to excel in a sport and become a champion. The only sound philosophy that is operational in our world of today is one that promotes sport for the good of all who participate. A champion should benefit from participation; he or she should learn many things of great value. The champion learns the satisfaction of achievement, the discipline and self-sacrifice necessary in the pursuit of excellence, the thrill of winning and the disappointment of losing; the champion gains personal confidence and may come to know the advantages of teamwork and combined effort. There are many other benefits to be listed, but the point is that the little kid from Podunk Hollow who wins the 25-yard dash at the local Fireman's Picnic can derive many of the same benefits as the gold medal winner at the Olympics. There's a difference in degree and in the amount of prestige, but that's practically the only difference. We must be concerned that every participant benefit from participation in sports because, as we become better individuals, we become a stronger nation. This approach does not deny the development of champions, but it does emphasize the development of skill for many girls. Our great need is to raise the national average of performance by girls in all sports including gymnastics and track and field. I am not as concerned about our women champions as some people are, but if we had many, many more "near-champions," we would be a better nation, and it is very likely that we would have better national champions too.

Where shall we start? What steps shall we take? There are those who believe the best procedure is to increase the number of competitive events for girls and women — run more races, organize more meets, have more state, district, and national events. Others, including the Olympic Development Committee, believe we must first provide more instruction, more coaching and practice. Some of our national champions whose techniques were criticized by the Russians are self-taught. To provide more instruction, we must train more leaders. It was this philosophy that prompted the Olympic Development Committee to approve this Institute, and it was this philosophy that influenced the Division for Girls and Women's Sports and the American Association for Health, Physical Education, and Recreation to co-sponsor the

Institute. In an effort to extend the benefits of the Institute, each state team had to pledge itself to conduct one workshop on the state level for the folks at home.

There is little doubt that each of you has gained personally from the National Institute, but we are concerned that others gain, too. Do you care about improving and extending sports programs for girls? Are you convinced we should provide more opportunities for girls to participate, to improve, to excel? If you do care, may I suggest that you plan your state event so that the results of this Institute reverberate like ripples in a pool. For example, suppose your team arranged a state workshop for regional teams who would pledge themselves to at least one regional workshop for local teams. Or suppose you decide to do more than the one workshop to which you've pledged yourself. In any case, please do more than teach your local leaders how to teach gymnastics and track and field events—teach them the philosophy of more for everyone that goes with it. You have a unique opportunity to exert a positive influence for the betterment of sports programs for all participants at all levels of skill and in all degrees of competition. The quality of the job done will be directly proportional to the quality of leadership you demonstrate. I would like to list several steps that I believe must be taken to provide vital and constructive leadership for all girls and women who wish to participate in sports.

1. *We must keep the scope of our thinking and our influence as wide as possible to include all persons conducting all kinds of sport activities for girls and women.* All persons means men and women, professional and non-professional. If they are willing to help, let us see to it that they are taught how best to help. All kinds of sports activities means just that. The emphasis at this Institute has been track and gymnastics only because leadership is especially lacking in these two areas. We did not wish to imply that these two activities are more important than others.

2. *We must strive for balance in our programs.* Balance, as used here, has both a horizontal and a vertical connotation. The horizontal aspect implies a broad program that provides a variety of activities so that we provide an activity for every girl and have every girl active. The vertical aspect means depth of program — a program that provides for the girl who just wants to try as well as providing the extra training for the girl who wants to be a champion.

3. *We must coordinate our efforts and cooperate with each other for one purpose; to provide better programs and more of them.* Women physical education teachers have long been dedicated to providing activities for as many girls as possible. They now recognize the fact that too little has been done for the highly skilled girl. Few of our women are adequately trained to coach highly skilled performers so they need help preparing themselves

to do a better job for girls at the top of the scale. Women need the help of qualified men. They need their cooperation. It should be remembered, however, that women want to do the job themselves; they will accept help and cooperation but will resist having things taken out of their hands. Providing more opportunities for girls within the framework of the school program is extremely difficult because of the limitations of time, facilities, and money. Adding programs without curtailing already existing programs appears to be almost impossible. If we accept the fact that the schools are dedicated to education for all, school sports programs must serve the masses. But there is no good reason why we could not develop a cooperative plan whereby agencies and individuals outside the schools set up programs of extra opportunities for interested students and young adults, not in competition with school programs but coordinated with them, each with the purpose of complementing and supplementing school programs. Such programs should do more than provide competitive events; they should provide instruction and practice culminated by competitive events designed to stimulate more practice, more instruction, and to motivate participants to pursue excellence.

4. *We must protect the health and welfare of the participants, and must judge program results in terms of benefits to the participants.* This is obvious, you say and you are correct. A recent letter printed in *Sports Illustrated*, however, illustrates a lack of understanding of the welfare about which I am speaking. The letter writer suggests the reason for the low level of participation and performance by our women in track and field is due to rules that (1) limit the number of events a woman may enter in one day — men, he said, are limited by stamina; (2) require a woman traveling overnight to have a chaperone; and (3) until 1963 prohibited women from running a race of more than 880 yards. These rules were made to protect the social and/or physical welfare of the participants. There is very little research evidence on women in competition but we do know that what is done for and by men is not automatically the best design for women. It may be especially true if our best women competitors come from the 14 to 18 age bracket as they do in swimming. Our teachers, coaches, and leaders have a great responsibility for providing sound, constructive, and expert leadership. They must possess and be guided by a personal set of moral and ethical values and good, old-fashioned common sense. They must anticipate problems and be ready with sound solutions based on principles of integrity, dignity, justice, and self-sacrifice for the welfare of the participants.

5. *We must, above all, maintain our perspective.* If our leadership is strong enough, our programs will be balanced and every boy and girl who wants to run and jump and throw will be able to do so in any one of several different sports. At the same time, the boy or girl who has the desire, as well as the ability, can grow to be a champion. Our needs for better programs and

expanded programs are critical. The time is now! Never has the challenge been so great.

REFERENCES

1. "Why Can't We Beat This Girl?" *Sports Illustrated.* September 30, 1963.
2. Sefton, Anna. *The Women's Division National Amateur Athletic Federation.* Stanford University Press, 1941.

Is the Program of High School Athletics an Integral Part of Physical Education?
ELLIS H. CHAMPLIN*

I believe that the program of high school athletics is an integral part of physical education. In fact, athletics comprise a laboratory phase of physical education. Here, pupils are afforded an essential opportunity for the practice and perfection of personal and group skills which have been presented in the more formal physical education class instruction. It is during this laboratory experience that pupils become increasingly aware of the need for strength and stamina, so essential to full participation in many competitive sports. It is here that they perfect activity skills. It is here, also, that they develop qualities with themselves essential to successful democratic living. They cooperate with teammates, they observe the rules, they accept decisions, they are courteous toward opponents. In short, athletic participation motivates quality performance. It promotes in the performer some cultural appreciation of the genuine worth of these activities to his personal well-being and life satisfactions.

The athletic program is, in my opinion, not only an integral part of physical education, but also an intrinsic phase of the educational curriculum. It may be extra-class, but as an educational enterprise it is never extra-curricular. It involves a great variety of courses of instruction which contribute generously toward meeting the educational objectives of physical education.

Athletic activities comprise, for the most part, the games and sports phase of physical education. The element of competition is usually implied whenever we think of athletics. Such athletic competition is conducted with varying degrees of intensity and under a considerable variety of organizational patterns. Such terms as "pick up" team, informal game, scheduled game, league game, tournament game, invitation game, play day, sports day,

---

*Ellis H. Champlin, "Is the Program of High School Athletics an Integral Part of Physical Education?," *American Academy of Physical Education, Professional Contributions,* No. 5, November, 1956.

intramural, interschool, and others are used to indicate the kind of event, the intensity of play, the organizational plan as well as to imply to many people the "importance" of the contest.

If the emphasis is entirely on winning (and incidentally I would not give much for a player who did not do his best to win) league or tournament play becomes very "important" to the people involved. If, on the other hand, the emphasis is on the personal development of the boys or girls who play, the contest itself is but a vehicle which contributes worthwhile experiences toward their growth.

The skills attained in athletic play are potent motivators to continued participation. They contribute greatly toward giving the pupil a sense of satisfaction and success. They encourage a constructive cycle of practice and play which encompasses a multitude of worthwhile activity experiences. These, in turn contribute to progress toward worthy educational objectives. This is one of the situations which, while not confined to athletics alone, justifies athletics as a vital part of a program of education.

Movement, exercises and physical activity are not only adventures, which have great attraction for both children and adults, but are purposeful experiences in their education. The natural activities such as running, jumping, climbing, throwing, catching, hitting, in various combinations, are included in every phase of physical education. They are used as simple games, rhythmic activities, highly organized athletic sports, stunts and exercises for normal children, as well as for development and fun in programs adapted for the atypical and the handicapped. It is through participation in these activities that man has consistently gained competence and confidence and developed the initiative essential to survival. They are the media through which physical education becomes a fundamental and essential phase of any educational program designed to serve the growth and development needs of people.

As in the present program of physical education, the athletic phase of that program is composed also, in various combinations, of the natural, basic activities of running, jumping, throwing, catching, and the like. However, in athletics there is a natural interest and motivation to perfect the skills of the activity. Just as physical education activities must be modified and simplified for the slow learner or the handicapped so must they be accelerated and intensified to provide motivation and opportunity for the more mature and skillful, through the athletic phase of the program.

For many years we have talked about "meeting the needs of all the children" through physical education adapted to meet and satisfy those needs. Actually our programs have tended toward regimentation and conformity rather than adaptation to individual needs. Program pace needs to be slowed down for some and accelerated for others. In the high school athletic offerings of intramurals, sports days, invitational games and interscholastics we have a program with excellent variety in which most pupils can find a satisfying place and a pace suited to their needs.

In many high schools throughout the United States the athletic program serves only a few of the more mature and highly skilled. It is my candid opinion, after many years as a participant, teacher-coach and administrator of athletics from the elementary school to the college level, that athletic programs have fallen far short of their potential contribution. They tend to serve the few at the expense of the many and there are glaring inequities in the allotment of time, facilities and expert teaching personnel to the development of a select few. The development of the child tends to be less important than the game score. Frequently athletic programs are directed more at spectator interest and "the gate" than at the developmental and educational benefits of the players. Thus players may become the medium to secure a victory to satisfy a partisan mob rather than the reasons for a game designed to secure for them lasting educational benefits such as physical fitness, and the qualities of initiative, honesty, cooperation, loyalty, courtesy and other elements of social fitness so essential to the development of individual human personality. The very freedoms we enjoy in American Democracy are based upon the individual right of every person to achieve his highest potential in terms of human dignity and the ability to serve himself and his fellows. Athletic games and sports, properly used, are very effective media for developing social fitness. They are practical educational laboratories for inculcating the kind of attitudes and habits so necessary for effective living with others.

Yes, the athletic phase of physical education has great natural interest for both player and spectator. Perhaps, it is because of this interest that athletics has moved into the spotlight. This has tended to bring with it many problems. There is no phase of education with so many emotionally interested followers — followers with a deep sense of ownership and pseudo authority over the destinies of the team and especially the tenure of the teacher-coach. There is probably no area of education in which it is more difficult to develop a stable policy of administration. Athletics tend to be managed by incident rather than governed by policy. Loud emotional protests are often generated over the ineligibility by one player who has had his chance and little if any thought given the younger boy who takes his place and begins to have a chance at competitive athletic play. Again the question might be raised: "Is the boy being used as a medium for winning, regardless, or is the game to be a medium for developing the boy?

During the past two decades there have been a great many constructive efforts made to insure that high school athletics are being conducted as an integral phase of physical education. Nearly every state now has an association of high schools organized to conduct interscholastic athletics. Some states have regulated such programs under powers residing by law in their education departments. Local school officials and authorities have set up principles and policies for their own teams. Studies have been made concerning the effect of athletic activities on people of different ages and organized bodies of educators have published reports for the guidance of school officials. Notable among such reports are the following:

1. *Desirable Athletic Competition for Children,* a joint committe report published by the American Association for Health, Physical Education and Recreation. 1952 and 1953.
2. *The Bulletin of the National Association of Secondary School Principals,* Vol. 37, Number 195. May 1953. This issue constitutes a commendable cooperative enterprise by several departments of the National Education Association.
3. *School Athletics — Problems and Policies,* an Educational Policies Commission report published by the National Education Association in 1954.

The first of these reports deals with athletic programs suited to the needs of elementary and junior high school children. The second deals with problems in physical education. The emphasis is on high school competition and its valuable contribution as an important phase of physical education.

The report of the Educational Policies Commission constitutes recognition by this powerful group of educational representatives of the tremendous educational values inherent in athletics. The guiding purpose of the report is indicated by the Policies Commission in its introduction as follows: "(a) to increase understanding of athletic problems and potentialities; and (b) to stimulate the fuller achievement of educational objectives in school athletics." One of the paramount issues in this report is this: "Are we using athletics for educational purposes and for the growth and development of children?" The report faces squarely such issues as exploitation and the place of championships in an educational program. It discusses appropriate athletic activities of children of various developmental levels. Throughout the document athletics is considered as an integral part of physical education.

The more player domination and exploitation creeps in the more educational benefit seeps out. This is true whether such domination or exploitation is practiced by education officials including teacher-coaches or by individuals or groups having no official connection with the school. As Oberteuffer says in his book *Physical Education:*—"The more the adult control, the greater the depreciation of educational value to the students themselves." This is indeed a great loss to people when we sell the tremendous educational benefits to growing boys and girls which are inherent in the athletics phase of physical education for a few effervescent raucous cheers of a partisan mob which paid a money fee to watch the game.

Some will recall an important experiment in New York State which took place under the leadership of Dr. Frederick Rand Rogers over a quarter century ago. It was called "Player Control" and its objective was to "give the game back to the players." I had the great privilege of being closely associated, in over 6000 school athletics contests, with this great effort to make athletics more beneficial to players, thus more truly educational. The plan was to apply the principle of learning by doing. The coaches under this plan were required to do better teaching and the game itself became a demonstration of not only pupil learning and development but also the quality of teaching. During game time the coaches of the two teams sat in the stands where they had ample time to analyze the game in terms of both player improvement and their own teaching strengths and weaknesses. They were not permitted to give their students (players) the answers while the examination (game) was in process. They were permitted, in the interest of player protection, to withdraw a player from the game. Such withdrawn player could not, however, be returned to that contest. In other words, the plan set up a practical learning situation in which players chose their own plays and made their own substitutions. In short, they made their own decisions and accepted responsibility for those decisions. In this situation the coach could not direct each play and thus dominate and exploit each player for the purpose of satisfying his own ego or to cover up his own shortcomings as a teacher.

Player control was a noble effort, one that was and is, in my judgment, educationally sound and practical. It was not understood by most coaches and was violently opposed by them and by their allies, the local sports writers. They interpreted player control not as a worthy educational procedure but as a dangerous threat to their domination of school athletics which had become so popular with the general public.

Athletics can exert a wholesome and powerful educational influence. The selection of appropriate athletic activities for children of various ages and periods of development is a responsibility of great consequence. The manner in which they are conducted is even more important. The responsibilities should rest only on those whose prime interest is in the well-being of youngsters. It is a first responsibility of school authorities to provide facilities, staff and programs which will satisfy these needs. Frequently opportunities to participate in athletics are reserved for a few mature and highly skilled boys. Schools are responsible to provide athletics for all through physical education, including instructional classes, intramural and extramural athletic programs.

What happens in many American communities when a trained physical educator or school administrator sets out to "provide athletics for all" and to conduct them as an integral part of the community's over-all educational enterprise? He bumps head on into *special interest*. The ugly head of exploitation, with its many faces, shows itself clearly. Frequently the high school coach wants the elementary and junior high school programs delimited to providing more material for his teams. He must protect his reputation as a winning coach. He therefore attempts to adapt the professional athletic "Farm System" to his purpose with vicious results to children. Well-meaning but misguided adults in the community promote teams of children to provide athletic spectacles to satisfy their own vicarious interest in sports, through what they think is worthwhile community service. Commercial interests see advertising possibilities so they also cut rate their way into the act. To make the situation more completely phoney, in terms of the child's educational needs, these self-appointed do-gooders often wrap the whole package in the shining tinsel of sweet charity. To climax the sorry mess the local press sees many good stories ahead so it plays up individuals and all possible angles of controversy.

In view of these situations, which I assure you are not as unreal as they may sound to the naive, what does the teacher or school administrator do? He has at least two courses open: (1) He merely goes along and accepts exploitation of children as an inevitable evil about which he can do nothing; or (2) he acts on the principle that the well-being of children must come first in any school athletic program and sets out to provide a sound program in his school to satisfy their interests and needs. He also must act concurrently to get better understanding of these needs by his community leaders. Thus he may secure support for his program and insure its success.

Boards of Education are slowly coming to realize that athletics are a part of the physical education which is required by law in most states, and that this means that they are integral parts of the school curriculum. Let me re-emphasize a previous statement — athletics may be conducted either in class or after class, they may be intramural or extramural, but as far as the school is concerned athletic programs are never extracurricular.

It is the duty of a Board of Education to permit only qualified teachers to teach, coach or conduct school sponsored athletic activities. Coaching is teaching and teachers are licensed professionals who are trained to understand children and to conduct programs to meet their needs. The physical educator-coach has a potentially great opportunity to provide, in the athletic program, a realistic, interesting, purposeful and fruitful experience for boys and girls in democratic living, unmatched in all education — and which they will enjoy, profit from, remember, and support as citizens.

The well-being of boys and girls must receive first consideration by Boards of Education in determining both the breadth and the adequacy of their athletic programs. This should occupy the position of primary importance to each board member as he seeks to discharge his duty to all the children of all the people. Furthermore, such boards must accept, for the citizens of the community, full responsibility for providing adequate financial support from tax moneys for its athletic program.

In carrying on their duties to all children, state and local Boards of Education may properly formulate for the conduct of athletics, rules consistent with the best professional advice available to them. The most important of such rules deal with the protection and well-being of participants. Each child should receive a thorough health examination by a qualified physician before engaging in strenuous competitive sports and periodically throughout the season as indicated. There should also be a follow-through to inform parents and help them understand that they should secure indicated treatment of all remediable defects. This determination of health status is very important to insure the child's gaining the best results from his school experience. It is also important in planning the athletic program to best serve his needs. In fact it is basic to his eligibility to engage in athletics.

In my judgment, high school athletic officials have tended to promote eligibility rules on an expediency, "incident-management" basis rather than on a sound, continuing, policy-governed basis. Frequently, much time is spent trying to legislate the retention of a star athlete who has had his chance rather than to encourage giving more and more boys an opportunity to play.

Furthermore, the problem of equating competition on a scientific basis, so each team has a chance for success, has been all too frequently dodged by responsible school officials. We still seek, sometimes by questionable means, to secure advantage over our opponents before we enter the contest.

The widespread use of such scientific devices as McCloy's Classification Index or Rogers' Strength Index would do much to promote the acceptance and practice of the doctrine of equality between competitors in athletics. It is my view that athletics will never be fully effective as a worthy phase of education until responsible educators accept the principles and practice effectively the doctrines of both equality of competition and player control. To accomplish this there are two other principles which I believe must be accepted and practiced: (1) All school sponsored athletic activities should be conducted under the direct supervision of qualified school personnel; and (2) all costs of such activities should be paid by the school district from public funds.

How can we make progress in the use of athletics as an educational enterprise? We make progress pursuant to policies formulated from expert opinion. We must use the results of scientific study to help us make policy and test its practical results in terms of the common good. In the high school athletic programs we have a great opportunity to lead the way in making

athletic experiences wholesome and worthwhile parts of childhood education. We must insist on school officials governing the school athletic program. Boards of Education must accept full responsibility for adequate
financial support of this program. I venture to prophesy that if we provide
an equal chance for success in competition and permit athletes to take more
responsibility for playing their own games eligibility difficulties will tend
to disappear.

It is my view that the hope of athletics becoming truly an educational
enterprise rests in the high school program. At this time there is too much
special interest involved in college athletics. Intercollegiate sports have in
the main become commercial enterprises and public spectacles. The time
may come when this Frankenstein will destroy itself. But until that time we
professional physical educators must concentrate our energies on providing
the best possible educational experiences through athletics for elementary,
junior high school and senior high school pupils. In my opinion, this is the
surest way to establish the principle that athletic activity is an integral
part of physical education.

The athletic phase of physical education should, of course, be directed
to the same general educational objectives as the total program. The two
objectives we hear most about are physical fitness and social fitness. We
must keep in mind, however, that when we concentrate specifically on one
of these objectives we contribute at the same time to the other — at least in
general. Man is a total being and what affects one part of him affects all
of him. Man is mind and body together. In other words, mind is body and
body is mind.

Man, to live effectively and satisfactorily and fully must efficiently combine his mental and physical fitness. Man must have both intelligence and
physical fitness. Intelligence is somewhat static but physical fitness may be
improved. It is the prime responsibility of physical education to improve it.
How important to man is physical fitness? Is it as important as intelligence?
How may they combine to man's benefit? Do they, in right combination,
improve man's general potential to learn, to serve, to live? What is that right
combination? How may the athletic phase of physical education contribute
to man's capacity to learn, to serve, to live? Is this phase of physical education being used for purposes that are in man's best interest? Are athletics
legitimate parts of physical education? I believe that they are but the
answers to many of these random questions must be scientifically worked
out and put into a practice before athletics can take their rightful place
as an integral part of a program so fundamental to education as is physical
education.

Prevention of Sports Injury
Allan J. Ryan, M.D.*

Sports medicine is now undergoing a period of growth in interest which has begun a few decades later than the interest in other medical specialties but which will in the end show the same remarkable progress. This modern period can be traced back to the founding of the International Federation of Sports Medicine in 1928. In this country the two significant landmarks are the founding of the American College of Sports Medicine and the establishment in 1955 of the American Medical Association's Committee on Injuries in Sport.

Although European writers have been describing and classifying the injuries of sport and discussing their special treatment for many years, the impetus for the development of techniques and equipment for the prevention of sports injuries has developed largely in the United States. The advances which have been made in improving conditioning and equipment have resulted until recently almost entirely from the work of coaches, trainers and sporting good manufacturers rather than from that of physicians.

The beginning of the prevention of injury in sports comes with an understanding of what makes an injury in sports different from other injuries. The age and degree of physical fitness of the injured person are important factors in establishing this difference. The necessity for an early return to functional activity certainly makes a difference in the way in which the injury will be treated and in the individual's response to that injury. The serious consequences which may result from sustaining any residual, and particularly any permanent, disability again emphasize the difference in the entire management of sports injuries from other injuries.

The practical approach to the prevention of injuries requires an intimate knowledge of the techniques of all sports which are to be considered together with the particular hazards which are to be encountered by the competitors. Factors inherent in the performance of these techniques which may pose dangers to the body of the athlete either by acute or chronic trauma must be closely analyzed. External conditions including all those of the environment in which the sport is practiced must be taken into consideration. The rules and regulations of these sports must become thoroughly familiar to the person interested in injury prevention.

The investigator must further possess a detailed knowledge of the anatomy and physiology of the human body which will inform him of the

*Delivered at Northeastern Area Conference, American College of Sports Medicine at Springfield, Massachusetts, March 3, 1962. Reprinted from: *The Journal of Sports Medicine and Physical Fitness*. Vol. 2, No. 4, March, 1963.

physical and physiological limits which may not be exceeded without danger to the competitor. He must be aware of the effects which can be produced by the alteration of diet, climate, training schedules and even psychological factors, which may influence the injury potential.

The student of injury prevention must have sufficient knowledge and experience of methods and analysis of statistical studies in order to be able to determine where the greatest emphasis must be placed, and whether this emphasis must be along certain lines only, must take a broad approach, or whether, in fact, preventable factors are involved.

He will soon discover that certain types of injury are common to many sports. This is true with regard to certain commonly involved parts of the body such as the head, fingers, knees and ankles. It is also true with regard to certain typical tissues which are found commonly throughout the body such as ligaments and cartilages. It is true with regard to certain varieties of trauma which occur commonly in sports such as those caused by a small mass moving at a high velocity. It is true with regard to certain broad classifications of traumatic effects, such as lacerations and fractures. And finally he will find it is true with regard to conditions which are the effects of chronic trauma acting in a specific tissue, such as enthesitis.

All of this knowledge will eventually bring him to a focus on certain areas of the body where, in order to enable it to stand special stresses, he may wish to apply some sort of protective device. He must then learn what can be done with simple and readily available materials such as adhesive tape. He must become familiar with the properties of other materials which can be built into reusable protective equipment. He must find out how the applications of this equipment can be made effective without impairing the efficiency of the athlete. Not least important he must be assured that the fitting is correct and that the athlete will wear the equipment as it was designed to be worn.

The commencement of injury prevention in the actual sports situation is at the time of the pre-season physical examination. The physician who examines the athlete must realize by his careful evaluation of the whole individual from the standpoint of his structural and functional capabilities he may be preventing an injury by not allowing the occasion for it. Estimation of muscle strength, range of motion of joints, and appraisal of the skeletal structure must be considered an integral part of this examination. A search must be conducted for evidence of previous injuries. Potential hazards of the sport for which the examinee is a candidate must be kept in mind. Psychological factors, which might predispose to injury, may become apparent during the course of the examination.

The next steps in injury prevention fall in the planning and execution of the program of pre-season conditions and with the follow through during the season to maintain the peak of conditioning. Not only is the strengthening of muscles important, but also the balancing of strength in antagonistic muscle groups. Full ranges of motion in all joints essential to the sports action must be established without weakening the ligaments which protect these joints. Resistance to fatigue, which favors injury, is developed by endurance training.

When it comes to the consideration of protective equipment, there are many factors to be taken into account. Until very recently very little real research has gone into the development of this equipment. Custom, style and guesswork have played a big part in its design. How to make it efficient without being too cumbersome has been a big problem. The advent of new materials has begun to solve some of these questions. The proper wearing and fitting of equipment is now being stressed as it should be. The traditional reluctance of the athlete to be encumbered in any way is being overcome by practical demonstration of the value of the newer equipment.

In view of publicity given during the past few months to the 47 fatalities observed during the 1961 football season, a few remarks regarding the football headgear might be in order here. First, it should be noted that only 20 of these fatalities could be classified as "direct," that is they could be directly attributed to an injury sustained while playing or practicing football. Of these, 15 were apparently due to injuries to the brain, 3 to the neck, 1 to the spleen and 1 to the kidney. It has been alleged that the plastic helmet as presently designed can be forced back into the neck as it is hyperextended, causing a serious if not fatal compression of the spinal cord. In two of this year's fatalities due to cervical fracture, the mechanism is known to have been hyperflexion, and in the other the mechanism is unknown.

The rigid shell plastic helmet presently in use with various types of internal suspension is felt by most persons familiar with the problems of athletic headgear to provide the best protection so far available. That this protection is not perfect is evidenced by the fatalities which continue to occur. Other factors are operative, however, notably the increased height and weight of today's players which greatly increases the impact with which they meet in tackling or blocking. Changes in football tactics, such as the practice of using the helmet for "spearing" the opponent are bound to have an effect in producing injury. At least one fatality occurred in a boy who had already suffered a severe head injury earlier in the season.

The desire of many persons, including quite a few college football coaches, to return to the old leather helmet prompted me to undertake a historical consideration of the subject of helmets generally. The interesting conclusion is that there is a parallel between the development of the war helmet and the football helmet, and that the clock cannot be turned back for one any more than the other.

The face guard has come in for some criticism this year. It offers an inviting target to the opponent as currently designed. It has been inevitably grabbed and twisted, sometimes with unpleasant results to the neck. The number of facial and dental injuries has been greatly reduced, however. With modifications in design the face guard will continue. The use of a mouth or tooth protector has now also become mandatory in the National Football Alliance.

Injury prevention also implies control of the physical environment. Properly lighted, surfaced and sized playing fields and courts free of obstructions, defects and foreign objects are essential to safety in sports. Control and restraint of spectators is equally important. Where the climate cannot be controlled, its effect in favoring injuries or pathologic states must be acknowledged by cancelling practices or games when conditions are extremely unfavorable.

Good officiating, which means strict observance of the rules, is essential since many rules of sports are designed to minimize the possibility of injury. Good coaching aims at teaching these rules to the athletes until their observance becomes second nature. The development of facility in the techniques of sport is an added safeguard against injury which represents a contribution of coaching.

Finally the presence of the physician himself at the competition and of persons experienced in first-aid techniques at the practice is a form of prevention, in that minor injuries will not be converted into major ones by ill-advised emergency management of the injury or failure to do anything because the nature and extent of the injury is not appreciated. Correct and complete treatment for injury by the team approach to reconditioning plays a most important part in the prevention of re-injury.

It might be said today that for the athlete, coach, trainer or physician to think of any sport today without thinking of injury prevention in any one or all of the categories we have discussed, would be as unimaginable as an effort to organize a soccer game without a ball. Although our efforts so far may have met with a very variable degree of success, the great majority of those engaged in the supervision of athletes are at least thinking more and more in terms of accident prevention as well as treatment.

Chapter

The Discipline of Physical Education

Physical Education: An Academic Discipline
FRANKLIN M. HENRY*

College physical education in America owes much of its genesis to the concept that exercise and sports are therapeutic and prophylactic. In fact many directors of physical education of the preceding generation were medical doctors. The school program probably received its greatest impetus as an effort to reduce draft rejects and improve the fitness of youth for military service in World War I. This objective was of course re-emphasized in World War II. It is understandable that our professional concern has tended to center on what physical education can do for people rather than the development of a field of knowledge.

Since most of the present senior generation of physical educators received their doctorates in education, it is understandable that their orientation has been toward the profession of education rather than the development of a subject field of knowledge. In fact physical education has the doubtful distinction of being a school subject for which colleges prepare teachers but do not recognize as a subject field, since the typical physical education department is unique in being under the jurisdiction of or closely related to the school or department of education. Some schools or colleges of physical education do exist in large universities and are patterned after the schools or colleges of education.

*This article was adapted from a paper which first appeared in the 1964 proceedings of the National College Physical Education Association. The article has been reprinted from the *Journal of Health, Physical Education and Recreation*, Vol. 37, No. 7, September, 1964.

When a young person planning a high school teaching career begins his college or university degree work with a major in, for example, chemistry, he starts out with freshman chemistry, which has as a prerequisite a course in high school chemistry. He then takes other lower division chemistry courses, to which the first course is prerequisite. In his junior and senior years, he completes an upper division major in chemistry, in order to qualify for the bachelor's degree. This major consists entirely of course content far more advanced than anything he will teach in a high school. Similarly, the student who majors in mathematics must have an upper division major in advanced mathematics, and even his most elementary freshman course in mathematics will be at an advanced level in comparison with the usual high school mathematics courses. In marked contrast, the student who obtains a bachelor's degree in physical education typically has a major that is evaluated and oriented with respect to what he is to teach in the secondary schools, and how he is to do the teaching or how he is to administer the program. Many physical education major programs, for example, do not even require a course in exercise physiology.

Actually, it is both possible and practical to offer a degree with an academic major in the subject field of physical education, and several universities have such a degree. If the person obtaining this degree plans to teach in the schools, he supplements the academic major with the necessary courses in methods and other professional topics. Academic vs. professional is not an issue of having either the one or the other, since the two are not mutually exclusive. However, the present discussion is not concerned with the merits of one or the other or the nature of the best combination. Rather, it is concerned with defining, at least in a general way, the field of knowledge that constitutes the academic discipline of physical education in the college degree program.

An academic discipline is an organized body of knowledge collectively embraced in a formal course of learning. The acquisition of such knowledge is assumed to be an adequate and worthy objective as such, without any demonstration or requirement of practical application. The content is theoretical and scholarly as distinguished from technical and professional. (This statement is a synthesis of the appropriate definitions found in several lexicons and is probably acceptable to most college faculties.)

There is indeed a scholarly field of knowledge basic to physical education. It is constituted of certain portions of such diverse fields as anatomy, physics and physiology, cultural anthropology, history and sociology, as well as psychology. The focus of attention is on the study of man as an individual, engaging in the motor performances required by his daily life and in other motor performances yielding aesthetic values or serving as expressions of his physical and competitive nature, accepting challenges of his capability in pitting himself against a hostile environment and participating in the leisure time activities that have become of increasing importance in our culture. However, a person could be by ordinary standards well educated in the traditional fields listed above, and yet be quite ignorant with respect to comprehensive and integrated knowledge of the motor behavior and capabilities of man. The areas within these fields that are vital to physical education receive haphazard and peripheral treatment, rather than systematic development, since the focus of attention is directed elsewhere.

Thus, the academic discipline under consideration cannot be synthesized by a curriculum composed of carefully selected courses from departments listed under A, H, and P and S in a university catalog. True, the student who would master the field of knowledge must first be grounded in general courses in anatomy, physiology, physics and certain of the behavioral and social sciences. But upper division courses need to be specialized, or else the development of the subject field will be haphazard, incomplete, and ineffective. Twenty-four semester units, in fact, may well be insufficient to cover adequately the available body of knowledge. The areas to be covered include kinesiology and body mechanics; the physiology of exercise, training and environment; neuromotor coordination, the kinesthetic senses, motor learning and transfer; emotional and personality factors in physical performance; and the relation of all these to human development, the functional status of the individual, and his ability to engage in motor activity. They also include the role of athletics, dance, and other physical activities in the culture (both historic and contemporary) and in primitive as well as "advanced" societies. Consideration of the relation of these activities to the emotional and physical health and aesthetic development of the individual constitutes an application of the field of knowledge, but may well be presented and integrated with it, provided that priority is given to the basic knowledge rather than its application to health.

This field of study, considered as an academic discipline, does not consist of the application of the disciplines of anthropology, physiology, psychology and the like to the study of physical activity. On the contrary, it has to do with the study, as a discipline, of certain aspects of anatomy, anthropology, physiology, psychology, and other appropriate fields. The student who majors in this cross-disciplinary field of knowledge will not be a physiologist or a psychologist or an anthropologist, since there has necessarily been a restriction in breadth of study within each of the traditional fields. Moreover, the emphasis must frequently be placed on special areas within each of these fields — areas that receive little attention in the existing courses. Any one of these disciplines encompasses far more material than can be included in the usual course of study for a major in the subject.

This is comparable to the situation in a number of the disciplines. A biochemist, for example, is necessarily deficient in his breadth of training as a chemist, and he is also necessarily narrow as a biologist. Nevertheless, he is a more competent biochemist than is a chemist or a biologist.

Special hazards and special responsibilities attach to the introduction of any new field of study. In a major that is made up of courses in a cross-disciplinary department, there is a danger that normal academic standards of depth may be relaxed. For example, an upper division course in exercise physiology will not be respected, and in fact will not ordinarily be authorized in a college of exceptionally high standards, unless a thorough elementary course in human or mammalian physiology is required as a prerequisite. This reasoning holds for all upper division courses in any major that is accepted as a discipline in such a college.

Problems certainly occur in delimiting the field of knowledge outlined above. The development of personal skill in motor performance is without question a worthy objective in itself. But it should not be confused with the academic field of knowledge. Similarly, technical competence in measuring a chemical reaction, or computational skill in mathematics, are not components of the corresponding fields of knowledge. Learning the rules and strategy of sports may well be intellectual, but it is highly doubtful if a course on rules and strategy can be justified as a major component of an academic field of knowledge at the upper division college or university level.

One may well raise such a question as where is the borderline between a field such as physiology and the field of physical education? No simple definitive statement is possible, but it is not difficult to show examples that illustrate the region of demarcation. The existence of oxygen debt is physiology; the role of oxygen debt in various physical performances is physical education. We do not know why a muscle becomes stronger when it is exercised repeatedly. The ferreting out of the causal mechanism of this phenomenon can be considered a problem in physiology, although the explanation, when available, will be appropriate for inclusion in a physical education course. On the other hand, the derivation of laws governing the quantitative relation between an increase in strength and the amount, duration, and frequency of muscle forces exerted in training is surely more physical education than physiology. Determination of the intimate biochemical changes in a muscle during fatigue would seem to be a problem in physiology, although of direct interest to physical education. Here again, the quantification of relationships and the theoretical explanation of their pattern as observed in the intact human organism is more physical education than physiology. This is not mere application — it only becomes application when such laws are related to practical problems. The physiology of athletic training is not really application of physiology — rather it *is* physiology, of the sort that is part of the academic discipline of physical education, and only becomes applied when it is actually applied to practical problems. Unfortunately, in this particular area, what is called "physiology of training" consists to a large extent of over-generalized and speculative attempts to apply the incomplete and fragmentary fundamental knowledge currently available. It is to be hoped that this is but a temporary situation.

The study of the heart as an organ is physiology, whereas determining the quantitative role of heart action as a limiting factor in physical performance in normal individuals is perhaps more physical education than physiology. Thus the study of variables which cause individual differences in performance in the normal range of individuals is of particular concern to physical education but evidently of little interest to physiology. (All of these examples are of course borderline by intent.)

Textbooks on exercise physiology are written for physical education courses. Much of the research they describe was done by physiologists. On the other hand, a standard textbook on physiology written for physiologists may not even have a chapter on exercise, and if it does, the treatment is notably incomplete. Similar examples are to be found in the field of anatomy. Textbooks on psychology have at best a sparse treatment of such topics as reaction time, the kinesthetic sense, and motor performance. These are not matters of fundamental interest to present-day psychologists, although they did occupy a position of importance in the first two decades of the present century. Even though anthropologists have long been aware of the role of physical games and sports in all cultures, one cannot find any comprehensive treatment of the topic in anthropology textbooks.

It would be unfair to say that scholars in various fields such as those mentioned above feel that it is unimportant to study man as an individual engaging in physical activity. Rather, the neglect is because this aspect is of peripheral rather than central interest to the scholar in that field. To borrow a figure of speech (not to be taken too literally), anthropology and other fields mentioned approach the study of man longitudinally, whereas physical education proposes a cross-sectional look at man as he engages in physical activity.

I suggest that there is an increasing need for the organization and study of the academic discipline herein called physical education. As each of the traditional fields of knowledge concerning man becomes more specialized, complex, and detailed, it becomes more differentiated from physical education. Physiology of the first half of the century, for example, had a major interest in the total individual as a unit, whereas present-day physiology focuses attention on the biochemistry of cells and subcellular structures. While the importance of mitochondria in exercise cannot be denied, there is still need to study and understand the aspects and implications of exercise as a whole. Furthermore, the purely motor aspects of human behavior need far more attention than they currently receive in traditional fields of anthropology and psychology. If the academic discipline of physical education did not already exist, it would need to be invented.

The Domain of Physical Education as a Discipline
G. LAWRENCE RARICK*

Man's curiosity about the unknown is probably as old as man himself. Yet it is only in a relatively recent times that man has been able to offer plausible explanations of what he observed in nature. True, scholars in some ancient civilizations sought logical explanations of what they observed. They noted that there was order in the universe. They observed relationships and were concerned with causes and predictions. But it was not until well after the Dark Ages that science as we know it today began to flourish. Systematic observation provided data against which hypotheses could be tested. Theories were developed and scientific laws established. The scientific method was born.

With the advent of the scientific method, knowledge accumulated rapidly. From the very beginning, scientists classified like things together for systematic and detailed study. Thus separate fields of knowledge began to emerge on which scholars concentrated their attention. Some probed the mysteries of the universe, others examined the nature of matter, some studied living things. Each in his own field sought to extend the scope of knowledge. Knowledge thus gained has become part of our cultural heritage, passed from generation to generation in formal courses of study, each dealing with a closely related body of knowledge. Thus we have come to recognize segments of knowledge as disciplines.

As knowledge and technical skill advanced, new disciplines began to emerge. Today any first-class American university will offer an imposing list of courses in from seventy-five to a hundred fields of study. The last two decades have witnessed a marked increase in the number of fields of study, each with its own courses. What, then, does constitute the domain of a discipline? Fifty years ago the answer would have been relatively simple. Today it is highly complex except for the longstanding disciplines. We have come to realize that even though we live in an age of specialization, it is difficult to isolate one branch of knowledge from another. This is true even for such well-established disciplines as physics and chemistry. On the

---

*Rarick, G. Lawrence, "The Domain of Physical Eductaion as a Discipline," *Quest*, Monograph IX, December, 1967.

surface it would see that the lines here are neatly drawn. Yet there is some overlap, for the chemist must be informed about the intimate structure of matter, and the physicist must be informed about the transformations which matter undergoes. In fact today every self-respecting chemistry department offers at least one course in physical chemistry.

How have new disciplines emerged, and how have they been able to stake out their respective domains? Most often this has been done by developing a clearly defined segment of knowledge from an already existing discipline. Such, for example, occurred in microbiology, molecular biology, and, in the early days, botany and zoology. Each owed its origin to biology—the parent. Some disciplines of relatively long standing came into being without any apparent break from a parent discipline, such as astronomy, anthropology, psychology, and physiology.

Other fields have the dubious distinction of just now being on the threshold of becoming disciplines. For example, a brief commentary in a recent issue of *Science* points out that professors of computer science are sometimes asked whether there is a computer science, and if so, what it is. According to these professors, it is a science which studies computers, investigating them with the same intensity that others have studied natural phenomena, using the intellectual curiosity which is characteristic of all scientific inquiry. It is pointed out that while computers themselves belong to engineering and hence have a professional orientation, there is a difference between the study of computers and the application of the resulting knowledge.[1] In a sense this is the problem facing physical education today: the professional as against the disciplinary orientation.

In many quarters there has been a genuine concern about overspecialization and a recognition of the need for a synthesis of knowledge. Proponents of this viewpoint hold that students and scientists must view natural phenomena not in isolation, but in relation to other areas of inquiry and to the world at large. This has resulted not infrequently in a merger of disciplines, a breakdown of traditional disciplinary boundaries. We now see broad areas of study, such as geophysics, biochemistry, medical genetics, and medical physics. Similarly, the trend toward interdisciplinary research is gaining momentum rapidly. With this trend, the traditional concept of a discipline may have to be abandoned.

Physical education today is generally identified as a profession in much the same way as engineering, law, and medicine are. Just as Webster defines medicine as "the science or art concerned with the prevention, cure or alleviation of disease," physical education is defined as "education in its application to the development and care of the body, especially with reference to instruction in hygiene and systematic exercise." In both, the major emphasis is on application of knowledge rather than on scholarship. How the knowledge is used is of little concern to a discipline. As Henry points out, the content of a discipline is "theoretical and scholarly as distinguished from technical and professional."[2] Over the years this has not been our orientation in physical education. We have for the most part been doers, not thinkers.

It is nevertheless evident that physical education has within its scope a body of knowledge which is not the concern of any other academic discipline. It is equally clear that there is much that is borderline (handled in part by other disciplines). Most certainly human movement is a legitimate field of study and research. We have only just begun to explore it. There is need for a well-organized body of knowledge about how and why the human body moves, how simple and complex motor skills are acquired and executed, and how the effects (physical, psychological, and emotional) of physical activity may be immediate or lasting.

The question is sometimes raised: Is one justified in including the execution of a motor skill in and of itself as an integral part of a discipline? The mechanics of the skill can be observed and studied, the physiological responses monitored, the feeling states noted. These are areas of legitimate study and research. On the other hand, do we need to clarify for ourselves the level of cognition that is required in learning and executing semi-automatic motor skills? Perhaps we need to ask what level of insight and of understanding is required in a behavioral response in order for it to qualify as a part of an academic discipline. Can we justify as a part of our discipline behavioral responses which are for the most part automatically controlled even though there is conscious direction of certain aspects of the movement and interpretative and affective controls which give to the movement refinement, meaning, and beauty?

All would agree that physical education is concerned essentially with exercise, active games, sports, athletics, gymnastics, and dance. Yet one would be hard pressed to build a case to support this categorization as a logical framework within which to develop concepts, hypotheses, theories, and laws. Reference to the organizational framework of a long-established discipline might be useful here. The classical organizational pattern of physics is straightforward and logical. Its focus is on matter and energy. It is developed around core ideas, theories, and laws, neatly categorized into five distinct areas: namely, mechanics, heat, light, sound, and electricity. This provides a systematic approach in the search for orderliness in nature.

Physical education needs to come of age. As yet there is no agreement as to its focus. Nor does it have a clearly defined body of knowledge or scope of inquiry. Physical education does, however, have a focus: namely, human movement (i.e., bodily movements in sports, active games, gymnastics, and dance) and its correlates. This aspect of man's experience is our domain. No other discipline explores it. Thus we may state the following:

1. Physical education as a discipline is concerned with the mechanics of human movement, with the mode of acquisition and control of movement patterns, and with the psychological factors affecting movement responses.

2. Physical education is concerned with the physiology of man under the stresses of exercise, sports, and dance and with the immediate and lasting effects of physical activity.

3. The historical and cultural aspects of physical education and dance occupy a prominent place in our discipline. The roles of sports and dance in the cultures which have preceded ours and in our own culture need to be fully explored.

4. Lastly, in physical education we are aware that man does not function alone. Individual and group interactions in games, sports, and dance are an important area, one which needs our attention. As yet we have no rationale for explaining the diversified behavior patterns of individuals and groups as either participants or spectators.

We have a considerable body of knowledge to draw upon. However it is widely scattered and at the moment not well-structured. An immediate need is to bring order out of chaos. If, in fact, we are serious in our belief that there is an identifiable body of knowledge which belongs to what we call physical education, we need to begin at once to build the general framework for structuring this body of knowledge. With this accomplished, we can perhaps more clearly pinpoint the future direction of our research and other scholarly efforts.

REFERENCES

1. Newell, Allen, Alan J. Perlis, and Herbert A. Simon. "Computer Science," *Science,* CLVII (September, 1967), 1373-1374.
2. Henry, Franklin M. "Physical Education: An Academic Discipline," *Journal of Health, Physical Education and Recreation,* XXXV (1964), 32-33.

On the Conceptualization of Sub-Disciplines within an Academic Discipline Dealing with Human Movement*

GERALD S. KENYON**

I would like to begin with a quotation.

There seems to be a very general misapprehension, even among intelligent men, as to the nature of the work in which we are engaged. By

---

*I am indebted to Professors Frances Cumbee, Andreas Kazamias and G. Lawrence Rarick for comments based upon an earlier draft of this paper. A bibliography may be obtained from the author upon request.

**Kenyon, Gerald S. "On the Conceptualization of Sub-Disciplines within an Academic Discipline Dealing with Human Movement," *Proceedings* (National College Physical Education Association for Men, 1968).

many it is regarded simply as a specialty of medicine; others think it merely a department in athletics; others still, with more gross ideas, regard us as men who devote our time and energy to the building up of muscular tissue.[1]

Such sentiments are not unfamiliar to any of us. Those which I have just quoted, however, are not the feelings of a contemporary writer, rather, they are the words of Luther Gulick, expressed in 1890. Periodically since then, someone has raised the same persistent issue, namely that of our uncertain identity. The last restatement of what has become our "locus problem"[2] was made in 1964, when Franklin Henry, in a paper given before this body, and in this state, reopened Pandora's box by raising and answering the question, "Is physical education an academic discipline?"[3] As you all know, this was the precursor to considerable discussion and informal debate, special convention sessions, a number of articles, and even special conferences, each concerned with one or more facets of the subject. Of course, such continued interest derives from many different motives, whether they be a desire for greater individual or professional status, a desire to improve upon preparation of teachers, a wish to make it easier for editors of encyclopedias, information retrieval specialists or writers of textbooks, a desire for a new physical education curriculum, or perhaps for fulfilling a need for professional self-abasement.

In view of the uncertainty of my own motivations, together with the thousands of words spoken or printed on this issue already, I was somewhat reluctant to accept the invitation to speak today. I concluded, however, that someone needs to play the role of "sitting duck" for the philosophers' "blood sport"—namely, *critical analysis.* So far be it for me to be a "spoil sport."

I accepted on other grounds, however. For some time I have appreciated the utility, if not the necessity of a sound conceptual system as a prerequisite to thought and research. [4,5] On the other hand, there is, I believe, a danger in devoting too much of our efforts to self-analysis, for in the end, the field will be judged not by the elegance of its super structure but by the quantity and quality of that which it supports. Its form will arise more from a kind of intellectual "natural selection" than from all the efforts we can produce from afar. Thus, the first point I would like to make is that we should worry less about how to describe ourselves, and more about producing something

[1]Luther Gulick, "Physical Education: A New Profession," *Proceedings,* American Association for the Advancement of Physical Education, 1890, p. 59.

[2]A. Kaplan, *The Conduct of Inquiry.* San Francisco: Chandler, 1964, p. 78.

[3]F. Henry, "Physical Education: An Academic Discipline," *Proceedings,* National College Physical Education Association for Men, 67th Annual Meeting, Dallas, Texas, 1964.

[4]J. S. Bruner, *The Process of Education.* Cambridge: Harvard University Press, 1960.

[5]P. H. Phenix, "The Architectonics of Knowledge," (in S. Elam), *Education and the Structure of Knowledge.* Chicago: Rand McNally, 1964.

worth describing.[6] While I believe our efforts from the armchair can make some contribution, they will never substitute for actual efforts to create new knowledge.

Although I cannot expect to have much impact upon the ultimate form of a field of study devoted to understanding human movement, even if what I propose meets with any kind of favor, I intend to pursue the topic largely as it was given to me, but with certain differences. I will devote greater attention to what for me are the logical prerequisites of a particular discipline, than to some arbitrary classification of the existing or hypothetical components of a *movement* discipline. I have taken this approach partly out of cowardice— to avoid commitment is chacteristic of the times—and partly out of what I believe has been the shortcoming of attempts to date.

By way of a preview, my argument goes something like this: If one wishes to ascertain the nature of a discipline devoted to the study of human movement, he first raises the question, "What is a discipline?" Upon identifying some criteria that seem to characterize most disciplines, the question is then asked, "Can the study of human movement meet these criteria?" Up until now, the answer has usually been, "Yes." Having thus established the study of human movement as *disciplinary,* a given writer will then proceed to structure the discipline. While I believe there have been some excellent efforts in this regard, I question whether sufficient attention has been paid to the implications for structuring a discipline of the assumptions upon which the discipline rests. More specifically, although we generally agree that a discipline is a field of inquiry providing man with knowledge, it has been my observation that too little attention has been given to the rather basic questions, "What is knowledge?" and "How do we 'know'?" For it is the way we answer these questions that determines to a large extent the nature of the discipline.

With this in mind, I will follow the traditional pattern of identifying the characteristics of a discipline, consider whether a discipline for human movement is plausible, make a commitment to a particular theory of knowledge, explore the nature of a field of study concerned with human movement when so committed, and finally, consider briefly the implications of such a commitment. In so doing, I must stress that in the main, I am treating only *one* aspect of the "Who are we—what are we doing?" issue. For example, what is presented in this paper is not meant to have a *direct* bearing upon school curriculum in physical education or the preparation of researchers or physical education teachers. I will make no attempt to be particularly global. I will

---

[6]Nevertheless, a conceptualization job needs to be done, if for no other reason than if we don't do the job ourselves, others will, apparently. For example, efforts to develop a taxonomy for educational objectives in the psychomotor domain have already been made by industrial psychologists and home economists.

be talking about only a part of what we, as physical educators, are concerned with every day.

What Is a Discipline?

By now, most of us have discovered that little agreement exists over the definition of a discipline. Unfortunately, there is no credentials committee armed with some absolute criteria for determining the qualifications of fields which aspire to be a discipline. In its simplest sense, "discipline" is an abstract noun representing both a cultural process and cultural product. Its dictionary definition ranges from "a branch of learning, a field of study"[7] to "training obtained by misfortune, trouble, etc."[8] Despite such diversity, some concensus can be found if we go beyond the dictionary and examine the characteristics of disciplines and what is written about these.

Certainly disciplines provide us with structured knowledge. However, I would like to make some important distinctions here. A given structure of knowledge is not necessarily the structure of a curriculum, nor does the structure of knowledge always correspond with departmental structure, found in colleges and universities, nor need it correspond to the structure of professional organizations or learned societies.

Pursuing further what a discipline is not, I would like to suggest that a discipline is not synonymous with a profession. Nor do disciplines evolve from professions as is implied by those who suggest that physical education is *becoming* a discipline.[9] Since I believe failure to make the distinction has

---

[7]Webster's Third International, 1961, p. 644.

[8]Funk and Wagnalls, 1963, p. 721.

[9]It is interesting to note that another field of inquiry, namely Comparative Education appears to be misunderstood even by workers in the area, in much the same way. For example, Kazamias and Massialas distinguish between the "meliorist" and the "scholar." "While it may be true to say that the scholarly and the melioristic aims would remain undistinguished and unseparated in the mind of the social investigator their blending would render any objective analysis quite difficult. If *ab initio,* we assume what education *ought* to be, then it would be quite difficult to examine with any degree of objectivity what education *is.* The two can logically be distinguished and the methods by which we arrive at the *ought* and the *is* are different. The researcher and the reformer may, indeed, be one and the same person; however, unless the reformer's preconceptions are somehow held as constant as possible, the researcher's findings will suffer." Kazamias and Massialas, 1965, p. 10.

For those who like to think of a discipline as "academic," the dictionary (Webster's Seventh New Collegiate, 1963, p. 4), provides the following definitions of this term:
Academic—
1. of, relating to, or associated with an academy or school especially of higher learning
2. of or relating to literary or art rather than technical or professional studies
3. conforming to the traditions or rules of a school (as of literature or art) or an official academy; convential
4. a. theoretical without having an immediate or practical bearing abstract
   b. having no practical or useful significance.
   It is interesting to note that none suggests a professional orientation of the work.
Moreover, the second and fourth definitions are precisely the opposite of a professional connotation.

hampered communication among us, I would like to expand upon what I feel to be a logical necessity, that is to distinguish between a discipline and a profession.

> To be a discipline implies among other things, having as an objective the *understanding at some portion of reality*—that is, *its description, its explanation,* and *sometimes its prediction.* A profession, on the other hand, has as its fundamental goal the *altering of some aspects of reality* with a view to *improving the lot of mankind.* If a discipline has curiosity as its motivation, a profession has as its motive service, i.e., the welfare of humanity. It is simply a matter of "what is" vs "what ought to be." It follows, therefore, that arguing that a given field can be simultaneously a profession and a discipline is little else save a logically invalid contradiction of terms. The only solution to this dilemma, as I see it, is to recognize that, while it is possible for the same phenomenon to serve as the focal point of both a profession and a discipline (subject matter for one, a medium for the other), it is there that the similarity ends. Thus, the expression "physical education" with its obvious professional connotations, is not a suitable label for both the professional *and* disciplinary aspects of human physical activity. However, because of its widespread currency, and despite the semantic difficulties long alluded to, the term might be retained, but in a restricted sense. Those who would use physical activity to change behavior—whether it be cognitive, affective or psychomotor—I would call *physical educators.* On the other hand, those whose objective it is to understand the phenomenon, I would consider members of a discipline, the name of which is still a topic of much debate.[10]

Taking a positive turn, I would like to look at some criteria that I believe permit fields of study to be classified as disciplines, while at the same time permit us to distinguish one discipline from another. Although it appears at times that a discipline is almost what we make it, it seems to me that there are three major criteria about which agreement could be obtained: *a particular focus of attention, unique body of knowledge* and *particular mode of inquiry.*

Focus of Attention. It can be readily observed that the boundaries of disciplines are indeterminant and usually in flux. It might be expected that the resulting grey areas[11] would lead to many jurisdictional disputes. That these seldom occur suggests that in defining a particular discipline, its boundaries are of little importance. Rather, a particular discipline is better characterized by its *focus of attention,* its more or less unique "topics" or "commonplaces."[12] Although sometimes broad in scope, disciplines are usually

---

[10]G. S. Kenyon, "A Sociology of Sport: On Becoming a Sub-Discipline," (in R. C. Brown and B. J. Cratty), *New Perspectives of Man in Action.* Englewood Cliffs: Prentice-Hall, 1968.

[11]G. Bergmann, *Philosophy of Science.* Madison: The University of Wisconsin Press, 1957, pp. 163-164.

[12]J. J. Schwab, "Problems, Topics and Issues," (in S. Elam), *Education and the Structure of Knowledge.* Chicago: Rand McNally, 1964.

concerned with more or less a singular set of non-trivial phenomena. For example, the physical sciences are concerned with physical reality,[13] or the behavior of inanimate material or matter. Biological sciences are concerned with understanding the nature of living things, or animate material, while the social sciences are interested in relationships among animate things. Despite inevitable overlap, each concentrates upon a particular piece of reality. It is possible that two or more disciplines have a common focus, e.g., social psychology, anthropology and sociology, all are concerned with man as a social being. Thus, focus of inquiry is not in itself enough to distinguish one discipline from another.

A Unique Body of Knowledge. Although a focus of attention is a necessary condition for achieving discipline status, it is not a sufficient condition. A set of phenomena must have attracted the attention of a substantial number of investigators who in turn must have generated knowledge unique in substance and of a particular form. The substantiveness of the knowledge stems largely from the focus of inquiry. The form depends somewhat upon the epistemology or theory of knowledge a particular discipline has adopted. To be rather liberal at this point, the form knowledge takes is often said to be of two types: *discursive*—that is, in the form of systematically arranged linguistic statements such as found in mathematics and the sciences, and *non-discursive,* or non-linguistic experiences, such as feeling states, visual or auditory experiences, intuitions, emotions and lyric visions such as those associated with arts.[14] A given discipline will consider its subject matter as being either discursive or non-discursive, that is, capable of expression in linguistic symbols or not.

In the final analysis, however, the uniqueness of a body of knowledge comes about through the presence of at least some concepts not found in another body of knowledge. Although ultimately it may be possible to deduce the concepts of one field from those of another—the so-called "reduction argument"—little progress has been made to date with respect to concepts and propositions of existing fields of inquiry.[15] If indeed a field has formulated unique concepts, it follows that their linking together in some logical way will provide unique explanations.

A Particular Mode of Inquiry. The knowledge generated by a given discipline is, in general, derived from the use of a particular mode of inquiry

---

[13]The term "reality" obviously is a relative one, the meaning of which can be expected to differ somewhat among the disciplines. For example, the scientist has committed himself to a metaphysics of naturalism, and as such perceives physical or social reality in naturalistic terms (see Margenau, 1950).

[14]S. K. Langer, *Philosophy in a New Key.* New York: Mentor Books, 1951.

[15]For example, see Nagel (1961), particularly Chapters 11 and 12 for a discussion of the logical requirements of reduction, and an analysis of efforts to date in the sciences.

or methodology.[16] For example, it is unlikely that we would encounter an explanation in the sciences based upon the methodology of the arts. Nor does the artist employ the methods of science to establish the "truth" of his particular form of expression.

Although somewhat oversimplified, there are basically three "ways of knowing": through *empirical* operations or the experience of physical or social reality through actual observation employing the senses; through *formal* operations or the ordering of symbols without recourse to observation of reality, as in mathematics or logic; and through *intuitive* or *mystical* operations wherein knowledge is alleged to accrue from some inner spontaneous experience, as in revelation or the experience of the poet. The established disciplines, at least when seen in their ideal form, have adopted a mode of inquiry corresponding to either empirical, formal or intuitive operations. Thus, for the most part, the sciences employ empirical operations, mathematics formal, and the arts intuitive. Although methods and technique may come and go, a discipline persists in its adherence to its methodology.

Returning to the question, "What is discipline?" we are now in a position to provide a more definitive answer. A discipline is a branch of inquiry characterized by having (1) a particular focus of attention, (2) a unique body of knowledge, and (3) a particular mode of inquiry.

Can There Be a Discipline Dealing with Human Movement?

This question has been answered in the affirmative on many occasions. Nevertheless, I would like to examine it once more, in terms of the three major characteristics of a discipline just outlined; a particular focus, a unique body of knowledge and a particular mode of inquiry.

A Particular Focus. One of the major outcomes of the debates over the "discipline" issue has been a remarkable unanimity concerning the focus of inquiry for a discipline concerned with human movement. Few have disputed that *man in motion* is the central phenomenon about which knowledge is sought. The scope varies sometimes, but nevertheless, for most writers human movement is taken to include the full range of organized gross physical activities, whether manifested in active games, dance, aquatics, gymnastics, or developmental exercise. As already argued, any attempt to establish more precise limits is to be preoccupied with the *boundaries* of a discipline, and as such is a futile pursuit. Despite the variety and complexity of the phenomena, none of the established disciplines have claimed human movement as their central concern. It follows, therefore, that if we wish to entertain the

---

[16]"Methodology" refers to a "logic of discovery," not the instruments and techniques employed in the laboratory or field. ". . . The study—the description, the explanation, and the justification—of methods, not the methods themselves." Kaplan, 1964, p. 18.

concept of a discipline for the study of human movement, it meets the first criterion without much difficulty.

A Unique Body of Knowledge. On the one hand, we have shown that a distinguishing characteristic of an established discipline is that it has generated a body of knowledge containing at least some elements not contained in any other discipline. On the other hand, investigations of various aspects of human movement have been undertaken for many decades. The critical question is whether there is anything unique in the conceptual systems used or the knowledge generated. If this condition is not met, then existing fields, such as exercise physiology and sport sociology, are merely subfields of physiology and sociology.[17]

Upon analysis of existing knowledge, it must be acknowledged that the majority of concepts used in the propositions associated with inquiry into human movement are borrowed. This is likewise the case when it comes to laws, theories, paradigms and models. Nevertheless, we are more concerned with whether there are logical barriers preventing the attainment of a substantial degree of uniqueness. Although no subfield has as yet developed an elaborate conceptual system, insofar as some manifestation of movement is the dependent variable about which understanding is sought, there is no reason to believe that special concepts and constructs will not be created to facilitate description and explanation.[18] Already we have conceptual terms that are of first concern to the investigator of human movement. For example, we talk about "steady state," "oxygen debt," "second wind," "accuracy," "athlete," "coach," "sport," "interval training," "repetitions maximum," and many others. However, we may have to accept the use of such terms to differ among the various subfields. For example, the concepts used in sport sociology need to have meanings commensurate with sport as a *social* phenomenon. Thus, the concept "athlete" refers not to a trained physiological organism, but rather to a social role.[19] Whether there now exists a unique body of knowledge extensive enough to warrant meeting the second criterion is a moot point. Nevertheless, there seems to be no logical barrier preventing a substantial expansion of knowledge, given an increase in the number of research efforts and an improvement in the level of conceptual sophistication underlying these.

---

[17]It may be that much of the research into understanding human movement will not be providing new and powerful laws of an original nature, but rather will consist more of "filling the hollow frontier." Homans, 1967.

[18]M. Brodbeck, "Logic and Scientific Method in Research on Teaching," (in N. Gage), *Handbook of Research on Teaching.* Chicago: Rand McNally, 1963.

[19]G. S. Kenyon, G. Luschen, and H. Webb, "The Sociology of Sport As an Area of Specialization," Report of Subcommittee for the Sociology of Sport, Big Ten Body of Knowledge Project. Chicago, December, 1966, mimeographed.

A Particular Mode of Inquiry. As indicated earlier, disciplines tend to adopt a single mode of inquiry or methodology, upon which they rely for the creation of knowledge in their domain. Now, if we examine those efforts to date attempting to further our understanding of human movement, we find empirical, formal and intuitive methodologies employed. Work has been underway ranging from the biomechanics of swimming to sport as an existential experience; from sport and social stratification, to the phenomenology of dance. It is frequently suggested that all such efforts may lay claim to being a part of the same discipline. Yet how many other disciplines are there which have developed a body of knowledge based upon three different methodologies? Insofar as we can have a single discipline devoted to the study of human movement employing three different modes of inquiry is to fail to meet the third criterion.

Summarizing at this point, efforts to conceive of an integrated discipline devoted to human movement are likely to encounter little difficulty, at least potentially, in meeting the criteria of particular focus and unique body of knowledge. The difficulty arises when we consider the third criterion, namely, the use of a particular mode of inquiry. In this regard, I would like to examine very briefly the degree to which recent attempts to partition a human movement discipline have met the methodology criterion.

Recent Efforts—How Successful?

Since the body of knowledge question has been rekindled a few years ago, a number of well conceived attempts have been made to structure a hypothetical body of knowledge into a series of subfields. In each case, the formulator assumed, at least implicitly, that knowledge of human movement was indeed worth pursuing and that the results of so doing could be ordered into a single body of knowledge (criterion one and two). However, little attention has been paid to the methodology criterion.

For example, representatives of the Big Ten universities have been meeting annually for several years in an attempt to identify and structure a body of knowledge for human movement phenomena.[20] The latest structure consists of six areas:

1. Sociology of Sport and Physical Education
2. Administrative Theory
3. History, Philosophy and Comparative Physical Education
4. Exercise Physiology
5. Biomechanics
6. Motor Learning and Sport Psychology

---

[20]E. F. Zeigler and K. J. McCristal, "The Big Ten Body of Knowledge Project," *Quest*, Monograph IX, Winter Issue, 1967.

As with any committee formulation, consensus can outweigh consistency. Insofar as these subfields are to represent a single discipline, there is an obvious methodology conflict. Moreover, the structure carries with it elements of a *professional* orientation, which I have already argued, may not be "cricket."

Fraleigh,[21] in a carefully thought out paper presented to this body one year ago, provided probably the most elaborate and thorough framework developed to date. His typology included everything from science to religion. Moreover, he did draw attention to the methodological question, but unfortunately, in my opinion, called for the necessity of a partnership between methods of inquiry associated with the humanities and arts, and those associated with the sciences.[22]

Another sophisticated approach has been one contributed by Paddick.[23] He has endeavored to show that there can be an extensive scholarly subject matter concerning "performance" ("the interaction of man and his movements") which arises from the study of the subject matter of physical education. In his analysis, he has structured his subject matter into five subfields:

1. The mechanical process
2. The energy process
3. The organizational process
4. The growth process
5. The learning process

The striking feature of Paddick's framework is its methodological consistency. Implicit in each subfield is an empirical methodology.

A most recent example of structuring is that of Rarick.[24] After pointing out the many difficulties of formulating a lasting framework, he suggests the field (in this case, what he terms physical education) could be broken down into four subfields.

1. Physical Education as a discipline is concerned with the mechanics of human movement, with the mode of acquisition and control of movement patterns and with the psychological factors affecting movement responses.

---

[21]W. P. Fraleigh, "Toward a Conceptual Model of the Academic Subject Matter of Physical Education as a Discipline." Paper presented to the Annual Meeting of the National College Physical Education Association for Men, San Diego, California, December, 1966, mimeographed.

[22]*Ibid.*, p. 14.

[23]R. J. Paddick, "The Nature and Place of a Field of Knowledge in Physical Education," (unpublished M.A. Thesis, University of Alberta, 1967).

[24]G. L. Rarick, "The Domain of a Discipline," *Quest*, Monograph IX, Winter Issue, 1967.

2. Physical Education is concerned with the physiology of man under stresses of exercise, sports and dance, and with the immediate and more lasting effects of physical activity.

3. The historical and cultural aspects of physical education.

4. Knowledge about individual and group interactions in games, sports and dance.

Although not as methodologically clean as Paddick's work, he would appear to be accepting less methodological diversity than many writers.

Thus, on the basis of recent efforts to structure a human movement discipline, it would seem that the methodology employed to develop a body of knowledge has not, for most writers, been a major concern. Such a state of affairs probably bothers very few people. Yet it behooves us to consider carefully the consequences of such an approach. True, tradition among physical educators has called for the whole man concept, brief excursions into the primacy of physical fitness notwithstanding. However appropriate it may be to retain this approach for *physical education,* it is at best a romantic one when faced with the goal of developing an integrated body of knowledge. Moreover, with the great increase in complexity and diversity of approaches taken toward expanding knowledge about moving man, it is simply unrealistic. I submit that to persist in pursuing the single integrated discipline goal is to invite intellectual anarchy.

Where to from Here?

At this point, I seem to be bogged down in the depths of some logical, or illogical labyrinth, which has fallen far short of structuring a discipline. The question is, how do I get out in ten words or less? May I propose the following: I propose that we stop talking about a single discipline concerned with generating a body of knowledge "dealing with human movement." In its place, I suggest we begin referring to the field as *human movement studies* and that these consist of a consortium of discipline-like subfields, each focusing attention upon one or more aspects of human movement, each working within the frame of reference of a unique conceptual system, and each adopting an *empiricist* epistemology. Thus, the knowledge generated by the subfields of the human movement studies will be restricted to those propositions about which some degree of public consensus or "universal agreement"[25] is attainable. Moreover, I propose that the admissible means for acquiring such knowledge be via "controlled empirical inquiry"[26]

---

[25]N. Campbell, *What Is Science?* New York: Dover, 1921, Dover reprint, 1952.

[26]Nagel considers "controlled empirical inquiry" as being either "controlled experimentation" or "controlled investigation." With regard to the latter, he argues that this procedure does not require ". . . either the reproduction at will of the phenomena under study or the overt manipulation of variables; . . ." Nagel, 1961, pp. 452-453.

consisting of *formal* or *empirical* operations, and that the form of any knowledge generated be *discursive* propositions about both *generalities* and *particulars*. Obviously, the consequence of imposing such limitations upon inquiry is to exclude knowledge based upon intuitive operations and non-discursive forms of experience. ("Whereof one cannot speak, thereof one must be silent.")[27] I hasten to add here that this in no way denies the existence of the several cultural products thus excluded. Howard Slusher's book, *Man, Sport and Existence*,[28] makes an important contribution to the literature on human movement, but for the most part does not make a contribution to knowledge as defined here. Nor does my framework deny the existence of the *art* of human movement. The use of human movement as a *medium* for expression clearly adds much to the quality of our lives. However, the artist in this case does not produce knowledge, he produces art. The existential act of dance is purely an experience for either the dancer or the audience, and cannot be reduced to commonly agreed upon discursive propositions. However, there is much about dance that we *can* "know." When we consider movement as a *phenomenon*, we can and do have a history of dance, and even a science of dance.

Human Movement Studies

By adopting a "controlled empirical inquiry" epistemology, we are permitted to conceive of several discipline-like subfields, each with the potentiality for becoming a discipline in its own right, that is, each capable of satisfying the three criteria for establishing a discipline. These subfelds may be grouped into two main classes: the *human movement sciences* and *human movement history*. Despite Bergmann's observation that "The traditional names of the sciences are chapter heading words. . . . Like fillers they are expendable."[29] I suggest that at least for the time being, we employ some efficacious combination of the labels used for the existing sciences, together with those used for the traditional movement subfields. By so doing, we recognize and indeed take advantage of the fact that most of our conceptual and observational tools are borrowed. The dependence upon other disciplines would no doubt lessen in time, but probably never disappear.

Human Movement Sciences. It seems appropriate then to encourage the structure of the human movement sciences around (1) the *physical science* of human movement which accounts for much of what we refer to as bio-

[27]G. Ferree, "Philosophy and the Body of Knowledge Unique to the Profession of Education," (in J. M. Hill, editor, *The Body of Knowledge Unique to the Profession of Education*). Washington, D.C.: Pi Lambda Theta, 1966.

[28]H. Slusher, *Man, Sport and Existence*. Philadelphia: Lea and Febiger, 1967.

[29]Bergmann, *op. cit.*, p. 163.

mechanics[30] and kinesiology in its traditional sense and based upon the concepts of classical mechanics for the most part; (2) the *biology* of human movement which includes the traditional physiology of exercise, the physiological and experimental psychology of human movement; and (3) the *social science* of human movement, which includes the social psychology, sociology, anthropology, economics and political science of human physical activity. Any attempt to further delineate the subject matter would be highly presumptuous of me. Such a task calls for extensive knowledge of several subfields, thus it must come from specialists within each field.

Human Movement History. Although the philosophy of history is a very active field today, with historians finding themselves as much in a dilemma as we, it would seem that historical inquiry can meet a "controlled empirical inquiry" criterion[31] and therefore be considered as a legitimate class of subfields which have as their goal the description and explanation of past events in the realm of human movement. The distinction between historical inquiry and scientific inquiry is much debated. Yet on one point considerable agreement exists, namely, the difference in their respective goals. The scientist endeavors to establish *generalizations* in the form of verified laws and theories having maximum explanatory power. The historian, on the other hand, is primarily concerned with *particulars.* Although he seeks their explanation through the acquisition of empirical data, much of which is "second hand" and incomplete, he seldom formulates his findings into general laws, even though the phenomena may be lawfully related. Nor does he attempt to predict, Toynbee and Spengler notwithstanding. However, many contemporary historians use the laws and concepts of the sciences, particularly the social sciences, to augment their explanations.[32]

For those who choose to investigate the history of human movement, it is conceivable that they could make a more than substantial contribution to our knowledge in view of its great diversity of use and form throughout the history of man. As more scholars are attracted to this subfield, specialization would likely occur, not only temporally, but also around various manifestations of movement, such as sport, dance and physical education.

Summary

In summary, I have tried to identify some of the logical problems confronting us when we set out to structure a highly complex and imperfectly conceptualized field of study. I have looked just at what characterizes a discipline;

---

[30]L. Alley, J. Cooper, and J. Councilman, "Report of Subcommittee on Biomechanics," Big Ten Body of Knowledge Project, Chicago, December, 1966, mimeographed.

[31]Nagel, *op. cit.*

[32]H. Stuart Hughes, "The Historian and the Social Scientists," *The American Historical Review 66.* October, 1960, pp. 20-46.

concluding that there are three major criteria that need to be met by a field of study before it can be considered a discipline: a particular focus of attention, a unique body of knowledge, and a particular mode of inquiry or methodology. Given these criteria, I tried to show that the fusion of the widespread diversity in contemporary approaches to the study of human movement is difficult to defend. Moreover, I suggest that we not think in terms of a single integrated discipline at all, but rather encourage the development of semi-autonomous discipline-like subfields, which, because of their common interest in human movement might be loosely affiliated in a consortium of movement studies. On the premise that the primary purpose of each of these subfields is to contribute to and organize knowledge, it behooves us to consider what we mean by knowledge and as such adopt a particular epistemology. I proposed an empiricist frame of reference on the grounds that such an approach has been the most successful to date in generating knowledge capable of public verification, i.e., the criterion of potential universal agreement, or the "principal of verification," as Ayer would have it. Despite the alleged naturalistic heritage of physical education, I expect many would disagree with my choice and be more eclectic, allowing for perhaps intuitional or even mystical bases for new knowledge. If we *do* adopt an empiricist theory of knowledge, I suggest that we are restricted to human movement sciences, and human movement history, although even the latter may not be on the firmest of ground.

Some Implications

I would be remiss if I did not touch upon some of the many implications of my stand. I shall do so briely with reference to the influence of subfield autonomy, preparation of the movement studies specialist, and future organization of professionals and movement studies specialists.

Subfield Autonomy. I suggest that in the long run, the quality and quantity of knowledge about man moving will be enhanced rather than inhibited by the specialization within the movement sciences. The concept of a discipline is a dynamic one—from natural philosophy came natural science, from natural science came the natural sciences, etc.[33] This is not to suggest that the subfields can be placed into mutually exclusive categories, but rather to acknowledge differences in basic units of analysis and conceptual frames of references. If we are honest, it is apparent that the subfields concerned with human movement have more in common, conceptually and technologically,

---

[33]The failure of the Unified Science movement does not sem to have inhibited discovery in the particular sciences. Just as the attempt by physical educators to be all things to all men has become unrealistic (although we are sometimes reluctant to admit it), to expect some general competence on the part of today's researcher is to spread himself too thin.

with disciplines not at all concerned with movement, than with each other. It is already easier for the exercise physiologist to talk to the biochemist than to the sport sociologist; in turn, the latter feels more at home with the literature of sociology or social psychology.[34]

Communication among subfields would not stop, however. Rather, it would occur on a higher level. For example, true interdisciplinary research may (though not always) help to further explain particular human movement phenomena. Instead of two generalists working together, each with a rudimentary grasp of several subfields, we have two or more specialists cooperating, each of whom brings more sophistication and depth than can reasonably be expected today from a generalist.

Preparation of Disciplinarians. Implied in what I have said thus far is preparation in depth of researchers in the movement sciences. Greater depth can only come by concentration in a particular subfield, i.e., course work, seminars and research experience in the subfield itself and in related disciplines. This implies some specialization to occur in the undergraduate years. At the University of Wisconsin, we have just instituted a program based upon this approach. At the moment, we permit graduate students to select one of the six discipline-like subfields or a professionally-oriented subfield, (namely, Curriculum, Supervision, and Administration in physical education). We anticipate that the program will enhance considerably the quality of inquiry. For example, given better conceptual tools, we can expect research to become less method or technique oriented, and more content oriented.

The Organization of the Disciplinarians and the Professionals. Given a greater division of labor, it can be expected that the character of existing professional organizations will change. First, we can expect an increase in the movement toward organizations whose primary concern is the promotion of various subfields. In the past four years, there have appeared the International Committee on the Sociology of Sport, and the International Society for the Psychology of Sport, with several regional societies having formed also, including the North American Society for the Psychology of Sport and Physical Activity. Before these groups existed, the Sports Medicine movement, which primarily supported studies in exercise physiology, had already become firmly established.[35] In my opinion, the time is ripe for a unification of all these groups into a Society for Sport Science, or perhaps a Federation of Societies for Sport Science. Whether this will occur, and if so, in what form, is yet to be seen, of course.

---

[34]However, by adopting a uniform methodology, a basic aspect of communication *is* assured. ". . . all sciences, whatever their subject matter, are methodologically of one species: they can interbreed." Kaplan, 1964, p. 31.

[35]As interest increases, I would not be surprised to find an organization of sport historians.

The already strong professional organizations are bound to be influenced by these new developments—influenced, I believe, in a positive way. Groups such as the AAHPER would be able to check the dissipation of interests and concentrate upon a great and profound challenge—finding the best ways to produce the educated and the physically educated child and adult. In a word, AAHPER would be returned to its rightful owners.

Despite the proliferation of organizations, there is no reason to believe that cooperation among the various groups would diminish. Many would no doubt choose to hold membership in both professional and disciplinary organizations. Moreover, joint meetings would be inevitable.

In closing, may I suggest that whether we like it or not, a deep change is just around the corner, easily as profound as the outcome of the battle of the systems in the latter part of the last century, or the call for a "new" physical education early in this century. None of us can be sure what the study of human movement will be like a few years from now, whether we perceive it as a profession, a discipline, or both. In any case, I, for one, find the prospects and possibilities most exciting.

Toward a Discipline: First Steps First

RUTH ABERNATHY
MARYANN WALTZ*

One of the exciting challenges of any field lies in the continuing struggle to sharpen definitions, to extend horizons, or to envision a more coherent or provocative theoretical framework. The purpose of this paper is to present some views and to propose some elements for examination, rather than to indicate ultimate parameters or a sequential arrangement of concepts. A major concern was to illustrate an approach to the conceptualization of the art and science of human movement. In other words, rather than defining or tentatively framing a "discipline" it has appeared more provocative to suggest a way *of looking at* or *for* the substantive base of the area of concern. Primary emphasis, therefore, is given to an elaboration of some of the assumptions and basic issues as well as the presentation of some areas for investigation which should lead toward a more comprehensive formulation.

Basic Considerations

Common usage provides ample evidence that the words *physical education* lack clarity in denoting the nature of a field of inquiry or a discipline.

---

*Abernathy, Ruth and Maryann Waltz, "Toward a Discipline: First Steps First," *Quest*, Monograph II, April, 1964.

For example, physical education is described as a program or series of programs and, at the same time, as an activity or group of activities. In addition, there are variant definitions couched in terms of purposes, process, organization, procedures and outcomes. Physical education apepars to be at once a means and an end but by common connotation at least, not a domain of knowledge (1:65).

In spite of this ambiguity in definition, it is possible to identify a recurrent theme that transcends differences in interpretation. The words *human movement* are used to describe the field of inquiry for two reasons. First, to avoid the major obstacle presented by lack of clear parameters for what has been called *physical education*. And, second, the term human movement is appropriate because it most accurately identifies the major concern of inquiry.

It is important to emphasize the distinction between terms, for physical education and human movement are not synonymous. Physical education is viewed as the school or college program utilizing movement experiences in developing concepts, enriching percepts, and otherwise modifying the organism in keeping with broad educational goals. Physical eductaion is, in this sense, an applied field. It is concerned with facts and beliefs derived from the meaning of movement in human life and with the foundations for and the conditions of significant application of such facts and beliefs in the process of education. Inquiry into the phenomenon of human movement, on the other hand, obviously encompasses a search for knowledge beyond the scope of immediate or even subsequent application in physical education.

Since no aspect or special orientation dealing with the larger complex of man and his universe can be understood out of context, investigation in the art and science of human movement must be related to findings in allied fields. In light of this, the field of inquiry must be undergirded by both general and specific understandings from the natural, physical, and behavioral sciences, as well as the humanities (not to mention the skills and abilities requisite to achieving such understandings). If the body of knowledge in human movement grows into an inherently coherent conceptual system, it will reflect the results of inquiry in its own as well as in related fields. The separate identity of the field, in the family of intellectual specializations lealing with man, will be established only if it plays a critical role through its primary or even unique concern with the phenomenon of man *moving* in his environment.

The preceding treatment of the meanings of physical education and human movement, and of relationships with cognate disciplines, was undertaken as a result of the need to be free from *what has been,* to be free to think inventively about *what is* and *what might be,* and clear the air of semantic "tension" which might restrict the development of a tentative framework and of a structure for inquiry.

An Approach to Inquiry

The disciplinary level of understanding about a phenomenon is achieved only after concerted inquiry into the specifics, abstractions, theories, and structures comprising that domain of knowledge. It follows, that while the expanding body of knowledge relating to human movement ultimately may be so organized as to constitute a discipline, a *first step* in this direction must be the delineation of the field of inquiry.

While it may be hazardous to deal briefly with framework and structure for the field of inquiry, it does seem essential that there be *a way of looking* at the phenomenon. Various perspectives and limitations on the study of human movement have been proposed. One effort toward a frame of reference for looking at the field was diagrammed by Waltz for use with freshmen students. (See diagram.) In this model, major variables are depicted as horizontal planes or dimensions across the page, e.g., "purpose," "physical limits," "movement experiences." The nature of the basic concepts necessary to the understanding of the variable represented by each of these dimensions is suggested by sub-set labels appearing under each plane. The "physical limits" dimension is drawn in a distinctive manner to suggest the restrictive characteristics of the "two halves" of the construct it represents.

The diagonal lines running through dimensions typify the many interaction possibilities and emphasize the importance of the structure of interaction in understanding the variables. Each connected sequence of diagonals is a hypothetical profile of intra and inter dimensional interaction. Each of the points at which a plane is interesected represents a different theoretical composite of the interaction of all the sub-sets in that coordinate.

Reading from the top, the initial concern of the chart is with internal and external determinants of movement or the interacting factors effecting the initiation, limitation, and modification of movement. The "process of moving" follows and the focus of the chart changes from the determinants to the nature of movement. The act of moving, set apart graphically in this section of the model, is viewed from the perspectives of both mover and observer. Major descriptive constructs are identified including an implicit operational definition of human movement in terms of time, space, and force.

The final dimension deals with effects of the movement process. From here, and reading upward, the circular and reciprocal relationships of man, movement and environment become apparent in that the movement experience in turn modifies the factors which have previously effected variability in the process of moving. Sequentially then, this diagrammatic "Approach to the Study of Observable Movement" portrays three basic areas of concern: determinants of movement variance; the nature of human movement; and effects of movement experiences.

Human Movement is initiated by

P U R P O S E

to achieve — to communicate — to express — to relate

is restricted by

P H Y S I C A L   L I M I T S

the limits of body potential (structure . . . function)	the limits of environmental laws (gravity . . . motion . . . force)

and modified by

M O V E M E N T   E X P E R I E N C E S

condition — habits — skills — style — knowledges

P E R S O N A L I T Y   S T R U C T U R E

attitudes — traits — emotions — constructs — goals

P E R S O N A L   P E R C E P T I O N

of self — of others — of universe

S O C I A L - C U L T U R A L   E N V I R O N M E N T

customs — expectancies — roles — models — patterns

P H Y S I C A L   E N V I R O N M E N T

sounds — space — equipment — weather — time

The Process of Moving

Occurs through space, in time, with quality (level-tempo-force . . .) Can be described in terms of its components: dimensions, basic movements, fundamental skills; its design: patterns and style. Can be used to control equilibrium—to give and receive impetus. May or may not be efficient in terms of mechanics and purpose. Is perceived variantly with occurrence, the mover, and observers.

and

IS A MODIFIER OF ITS OWN DETERMINANTS

The model was designed to emphasize the interrelationships of what were assumed to be the major descriptive and theoretical constructs, and to promote a "situations" or "relations" approach wherein movement would be studied in the context of occurrence. Variables were represented as continuums interacting in, and in relation to, a physical-social-internal environment to avoid any suggestion of additive segments or of one-to-one causal connections and, to imply the necessary reference to duration in time. Other considerations in the selection of design and content included efforts to show the relatedness of the movement phenomenon to concerns derived from other fields of inquiry, and to establish some operational boundaries by which the breadth of study might be limited. Numerous assumptions, including an obvious idiomatic and emergent approach to the nature of man, are implicit in the model as well as in the proposed areas of inquiry which follow.

A Structure for Inquiry

If a discipline is viewed as a sequential arrangement of a body of knowledge, and if a body of knowledge is derived from a field of inquiry which, in turn is defined by the problems it seeks to resolve, a structure for inquiry may be approached through an identification of general areas of concern within which questions can be asked. With this in mind, problem areas have been selected with sights lifted beyond the circumferences to which many of us have become habituated, toward a domain of knowledge aspired rather than funded. This by no means negates the importance nor precludes the acceptance of existing knowledge, it simply suggests room both for accumulated facts and for untested theories.

The latitude of this approach in developing a problem-question framework was anchored by attention to three specific considerations. First, the importance of devising a framework that would give emphasis to the three major variables of concern, *man—movement—environment*. Second, the need for a structuring that would allow freedom for the generation of testable hypotheses and foster synthesis of expanding knowledge. And, third, the establishing of a perspective that would provide for a coherent view of a complex phenomenon. In light of these criteria the following questions are offered as a first step toward the first step of establishing parameters for inquiry.

I What is the nature of human movement?
II What are the determinants of human movement—the bases of inter and intra individual differences in movement?
   A. What are the effects of the physical environment on movement?
   B. What are the effects of the socio-cultural environment on movement?
   C. What are the effects of the internal environment on movement?

III What is the role of movement in the growth-development-learning complex?
   A. What is the relationship of movement development to total development?
   B. What are the effects of movement on conceptual and other aspects of development?

Extended treatment of the implications for inquiry in these basic problem areas is beyond the scope of this paper. However, selected exemplary concerns suggestive of the possible scope of inquiry might include study of factors, concepts, relationships, and patterns as:
   — characteristics and dimensions of movement
   — classifications of movement
   — perception of the moving experience
   — the mechanics of movement or movement efficiency
   — dissonance and congruence in movement expectations and roles
   — the purposes of human movement
   — cultural derivation of movement patterns
   — the desirability of directed change of movement behavior
   — media and movement
   — models and variability of movement style
   — idealized self-image and acceptance of moving images
   — growth gradients and developmental direction of movement components
   — motivation and mastery of movement skills
   — movement experience and movement capacity
   — movement experience and concept formation
   — movement and communication-expression
   —perceptual development and movement behavior
   — the need for achievement and movement skill

Many of the concepts implicit in both the structure and the exemplary concerns are from the "left hand." That is, they are derived from hunches and intuition or, as Bruner says, are the "combinatorial products of . . . metamorphic activities" (2:4). Much information, some of it contradictory, is available about some of the exemplary items, and little or none is available about others. As the body of knowledge of human movement is enriched by research findings, emergent theory should suggest many refinements in analysis and synthesis. Both the structure and the parameters of inquiry should, in turn, reflect this greater clarification.

In the last analysis, the ideal framework will be the one that best serves the goal of inquiry in the art and science of human movement: the one that best serves to further understandings about the nature of human movement, the principles of movement development, and the interrelationships of affective variables as well as the effects of varying movement experience. The building of knowledge toward this goal is the second step in forging a discipline.

Implications and Prospect

In this day of exploding knowledge and emphasis on rational man, the concepts underlying physical education must be elaborated if it is to remain a part of the school program. There has been some re-examination of function and of relative values as can be seen in program modification as well as in the added attention to "what ought to be." However, justification in the long run, will rest upon the utilization of principles drawn from scholarly inquiry into the phenomenon of human movement.

It is evident that this approach, in which subject matter in physical education is seen as an application of knowledge, is not synonymous with that in which the descriptive emphasis is upon a program of movement exploration, exercise, or activities. It should not be concluded however, that the differences are necessarily antithetical. Apparent disparity in conceptions of meaning can be viewed in the Hegelian sense of opposites; that is, as compatible "others" in a continuum of ideas which compliment rather than exclude one another. Attention to the structure of physical education as an application of disciplined knowledge in an educational situation, does not negate the functional role of traditional activities in the conduct of the program. Organized experience in sports, dance, gymnastics . . . is not incompatible with a program based upon movement inquiry. However, in such a program, activities can not be perceived as ends in themselves since they do not define the nature or purpose of the experience.

As gaps in the existing body of knowledge are filled, some of that which has formerly been affirmed by insight may be confirmed by facts and some that has been assumed may be denied. A physical education program built upon a sound foundation of knowledge about human movement could have much greater potential for the realization of the goals of education.

> "Instead of lamenting, as a threat, the disintegration of many traditional values and the lack of clear definition with which our historical period presents us, we may attempt to understand and use the very conflicts and ambiguities of the time to open the way for realization of new possibilities." (3:219).

REFERENCES

1. *Report of the National Conference on Interpretation of Physical Education.* Chicago: The Athletic Institute, 1961.
2. Bruner, Jerome S. *On Knowing—essays for the left hand.* Cambridge: Harvard University Press, 1962.
3. Lynd, Helen Merrell. *On Shame and the Search for Identity.* New York: Science Editions, 1961.

Chapter

The Profession of
Physical Education

The Confessions of a Once Strict Formalist
ETHEL PERRIN[*]

I know it is dangerous to reminisce, give me credit for that much, but I'm not going to begin with an apology, for that is even worse—that is poor psychology. I am giving you some personal experiences, which is almost as boring as telling one's dreams at the breakfast table, but it is with the hope that you of my generation who read this will at least find some amusement in hearing experiences laid bare which resemble your own, and that the youth of the Association will see a bit more clearly how to meet some of their difficulties, and will also decide it is wiser in the long run not to take yourself too seriously.

In 1892—yes, do your own figuring—I graduated from the Boston Normal School of Gymnastics, and have held some sort of a professional job without a break till 1936. The pathetic part is the downward trend in the mental caliber of my pupils. I began with the highest, the students of the Boston Normal School of Gymnastics, where I taught as soon as I graduated, for fifteen years. From there I descended to the college level, thence to high school, from there to elementary, and now I am in full charge of the day-old chicks on my farm.

Going back to the beginning of things when I was a student forty-six years ago, we find the graduates of the Boston Normal School of Gymnastics

*Perrin, Ethel, "The Confessions of a Once Strict Formalist," *Journal of Health and Physical Education,* IX, November, 1938.
A paper presented before the Central District Association Convention, April 1938, Minneapolis.

firmly believing this school to be the best school of physical education in the world. It was founded and grounded in the Swedish system of gymnastics and no other system or mixture of systems could be mentioned in the same breath. I remember speaking in disparaging terms, after I had attended this school for a few months, of a fine teacher in a nearby high school because she ran in a few dumbbells and clubs with her Swedish work. I claimed that her Swedish gymnastics were not pure—a terrible thing—and got myself great-ly disliked by the lady, and no wonder—but I stuck to it. It seems impossible now that we could have been so narrow-minded, but on the other hand it was wonderful to be cocksure that we alone were on the right track. It gave us a great sense of responsibility and we felt it was our mission to spread pure Swedish gymnastics from Maine to California. I suppose many of you never heard of the Swedish Days Order, but I assure you, after going through one under the skilled leadership of Dr. Enebuske or Dr. Collin, for sixty minutes, there was a satisfied feeling of exhilaration and well-being. Just so much time for waking-up exercises: right race, one step forward, side step to the right and about—*march.* Then just so much exercise for head and chest; for arms, legs, trunk. Then the great climax, the jump and run, fol-lowed by the quieting down exercises and the deep, deep breathing to be heard all over the room. It was the perfect example of the "I yell, you jump" method and this I taught for fifteen years and never dreamed I could do anything else.

We all gave our commands as nearly like Dr. Collin as we could. He would stand at one end of the gymnasium and say, "With right hip and left neck firm and trunk twisting to the right, left outward fall—out," while we would stand in line at the other end of the room and in concert imitate his inflection over and over again. We were taught that in order to make our pupils put the right amount of energy into their exercises, we should exaggerate in all of our demonstrations when teaching—work much harder than we expected them to work. We practiced being a split second ahead in response to our own commands in order to get them there on time. When we said "At-tention!" every pair of heels had to click and every head come up at least two inches.

Professional formality surrounded me and this included not only formal and stereotyped teaching but all matters of behavior and of dress. After seventeen years of this I was sent as a substitute for a year as Director of the Women's Gymnasium at the University of Michigan. It was a far cry from Boston and I shall never forget my astonishment when a freshman looked me over and said "What a pretty dress you have on." A personal remark from a student to a member of the faculty was a new one to me, but I liked the friendliness of it. Then a wild idea came into my head. Why not take these girls out for hikes instead of staying in the gymnasium on nice autumn days—my first really original act in my teaching. I had always before done just what I had been taught to do, and there was no place for a walk in the woods in the Swedish Days Order.

A Middle West college group was a wonderful one to try my wings on, and while they were perfectly willing to conform to some of my Boston idiosyncracies, such as no gum chewing in the gymnasium and keeping both feet on the floor in my office, still I learned more from them than they from me. Anyway, we had a happy year even if the Senior Basketball Team and I did have some rough sledding. Their methods and manners were terrible and I was wickedly glad when my freshmen beat them. The colored janitress and I retired to my dressing room and shook hands on it.

Then came the next step in my downward path when I was asked to interview the Superintendent of Schools and the Principal of Central High School regarding the directorship of the work in the first girls' gymnasium in the Detroit public schools. I had never been interviewed in my life and had never even seen, much less spoken to a Superintendent of Schools. I brushed up my physiology, anatomy, and kinesiology, read over seventeen-year-old notebooks—anyone knows how discouraging and futile that is—bought a new pair of gloves, the only point I could remember from my training in regard to interviews, and took the train to Detroit in fear and trembling. I had no knowledge of public high schools, having been to a private school only, and no particular interest in them, I went as I had done everything else professionally, because my school asked me to go.

The Superintendent, the Principal, and I sat solemnly looking at each other, my mind a blank, when the Superintendent burst out with "Can you swim?" Aghast, for I had never even heard of a high school with a pool, I said "Yes, I can swim" and thereupon they hired me. If they had asked me to describe my method of teaching swimming, I might not have been hired.

Here was my first opportunity to build something of my own, for my experience had all been in carrying out work planned by others. I had no educational philosophy—had never heard of one, and doubt if many of us in physical education had heard of one in 1908. I had many strong convictions and prejudices but no methodology. One conviction was that friction and success did not go hand in hand and that I must have the respect and willing cooperation of those high school girls and of the faculty, whether I got my way in all matters or not. This was very daring of me because in the Boston Normal School of Gymnastics there was but one way of doing things and we did as we were told, whether we liked it or not, because someone else knew what was best for us. I had always followed this regime willingly because I believed that the one in authority always was right, but somehow where I had a chance to be the dictator, I wanted to try out other methods. I was not quite so sure that I was always right.

My first problem was in basketball, which game I thoroughly enjoyed and had taught ever since it was originated by Mr. Naismith. I had a very strong prejudice against interscholastic basketball competition, although I had had no experience with it in the past. I found this to be well organized beween the three high schools of Detroit in 1908. It had been started and gratuitously coached and run by enthusiastic graduates of the University of Michigan. Some were teachers of other subjects and some were entirely outside the school system. Each school had its coach. The schedule for the school year was made at the close of the preceding season and the referees engaged. My principal was against it but public opinion and the newspapers had forced him into it. When he found that I too was against it, he jumped at the chance of saying there should be no Central High Girls' Team, but I would not agree. We cancelled out-of-town games, but played the schedule between Detroit high schools as already planned for that year. I know I was right. The games were well played and the sportsmanship of the players was pretty good, except for the spirit of "getting by" which would crop up. But the audiences were terrible—just a screaming mass of maniacs. I shall never forget my astonishment when I first saw it. We managed to improve the behavior of the audiences at the games held in Central's gymnasium by inviting the boys in. Previously they had only been allowed to see by climbing and peeking from the outside—more fun for them perhaps but not so good for us to contend with. I visited one of their games and saw a well-behaved mixed audience of boys and girls. I corralled a few of the leaders among the boys and got them interested in helping us out of our difficulties. At our next game they scattered through the audience and we had no more screaming girls; a girl intuitively knows that she does not look her best when screaming.

I have told you that I had no educational principles or practical guides to follow but we might draw a few out of these experiences. After all, I suppose experiences did come before principles. From the success which these boys had with my school girl audiences, we might say *coeducation has its place in physical education*—a long way from what we now mean by this, but it was a start. With basketball came my old enemy, gum chewing. My team all indulged in it during our first practice. I had a talk with the captain— a real leader, not only of her team but in the whole school. I simply told her how I felt about gum chewing and left it up to her without making any suggestion. I can see her leading the team down the winding stairs from the dressing rooms to the gymnasium, every girl chewing her hardest. She halted at an open window at the foot of the stairs and, saying "One of the new rules girls—out goes your gum," she threw hers out of the window. Every girl followed suit and never a shot missed. That was that, and think of the time and words I would have spent had I attempted to force them into it myself.

Shall we say as a principle, *never do yourself what a pupil may be able to do better.*

At the end of an unsuccessful season as far as winning goes, Central decided to give up its girls' team, and this ended the league. There were so many activities going on, there was not much time for the team to practice, and I guess I wasn't a particularly good coach. It seemed to die a natural death. Nobody cared much, not even the team. But I am sure there would have been a rumpus if we had killed it before they had learned through experience that a gymnasium was good for other things than basketball games. So, shall we say as another guide that it is well to *build up before you break down.*

I still clung to much of my formal work that year and I filled the gymnasium with Swedish booms and window ladders and horses and bucks and boxes and all sorts of truck. I did know enough to get plenty of balls and everybody had a chance to play. I gave every girl an examination and wrote to all mothers of narrow chests, round shoulders, and crooked backs for permission to give their children special exercises. Please note the following very important item. In this group fell the favorite daughter of the Superintendent of Schools and as luck would have it, this procedure both astonished and pleased the Superintendent for he thought only the strong received special training in physical education, and instead of being peeved at my saying his daughter was crooked, he was gratified with the attention. The girl liked to take her exercises and she and I got on together famously. I tell you this because I have always felt I never would have been a supervisor in the Detroit public schools if her back had been straight. The Superintendent did not pay me a visit the whole year through but on the day schools opened the next fall he suddenly appeared before me with the following, "The Board of Education will vote tonight for a Supervisor of Physical Culture. We have had two and they were both dead failures. Somebody is going to present the name of another candidate whom I do not want. May I propose your name?" I had never thought of being a supervisor, but that Superintendent had a forceful personality and a steely blue eye. I seemed to feel him saying to himself "Has she got the nerve?" and I said "Yes" but felt terrified. He always had his way with his Board, so of course I was elected. One member said he would have liked to see me, as he voted for my predecessor because of her fine "fizzykew."

I had no knowledge of elementary schools in general or in Detroit. I had never supervised anything nor anybody, nor had I taken a course or read a book on supervision. School principals, teachers, and school children were unknown quantities. I have always felt that it was the confidence of the Superintendent's daughter and his steely blue eye that drove me to it. So I say to you young people, *never be afraid to take a chance even if the opportunity comes by chance.*

All that the Superintendent asked of me for the first year was to make teachers and children like it, for in 1908 one and all hated it. I made a few trial visits to discover what was left by my predecessor with the fine "fizzy-kew." I found black looks from teachers and disgust from children when they stood up and clapped their hands eight times on the right and eight times on the left—all they could remember.

There must have been about eighty schools in Detroit at that time and I knew that my success or failure depended upon the principals and the teachers, and I shall add the janitors, for if they reported me "downtown"— as our headquarters were familiarly called—as a nuisance in their building, there was the devil to pay. And so, I laid my plans for friendliness first and foremost. Shall we say then, *gain friendliness before you ask for cooperation.*

The first thing I did was to open the Central High pool for free use of principals and teachers every evening. The comradeship we established lasted me during my fourteen years of service in Detroit, and these few teachers formed a nucleus of friendliness. Next I held those bugbears called teachers' meetings to put across my "subject" as this seemed the way of all supervisors, *but* I never asked a teacher to take an exercise. They sat after a hard day's work, while I, in a gymnasium suit, stood on a table, gave myself commands and did the exercises, much like a monkey on a string. It seems that my predecessor had stood them up in rows and kept them till six o'clock clapping their hands and what not. Anyway, I scored a hit, and shall we say, *if you cannot make your co-workers happy, make them as happy as you can.*

I advised them not to demonstrate to the children but to follow the simple directions I was sending them in mimeographed form and to let the children help them work it out and to use children as demonstrators.

Next I selected simple exercises that brought big muscles into play but took little skill and could not easily go wrong. I threw away complicated demands and made short cuts, all of which probably made the founders of Swedish gymnastics turn in their graves. I showed the teachers what I wanted the children to do and said that they, the teachers, could use any method they found worked best to get results. Another guide then might be, *be willing to throw past practices to the winds if they do not fit the situation,* or shall we put it, *separate essentials from nonessentials.*

I soon yielded my place on the demonstration platform to children who were delighted to be selected and become part of a lesson to teachers. As I visited classrooms I was astonished at the excellent results of untrained people, I mean untrained in physical education. They violated all hard and fast rules I had always thought essential to success. They followed with joy my request that they never demonstrate and that eliminated one great chance for error. I remember one very lame teacher who sat at her desk during the lesson and she had the peppiest sort of response from her huge eighth-grade class and exactly the sort of work I wanted. Of course there were funny mistakes. I was still a believer in deep breathing, and we called it West Point Breathing—rolling our hands and arms backwards and puffing out our chests like soldiers. In one room I saw the children in perfect unison and with great pride turn and point to the west, but the breaths were very deep and the teacher had no sense of humor so I praised them highly and let it go—a case of relative importance—of essentials versus nonessentials.

When I waxed enthusiastic over a room to a principal, she would say "Why not, she is the best teacher I have." I learned from hundreds of best teachers that perfect rapport between teacher and pupils, which only comes with character, intelligence, and a sense of humor, counts more than methods of teaching.

You remember that the Superintendent required me to make them like it the first year, and I never shall forget my joy the first day the children rubbed their stomachs when I entered the door. That was the Detroit method of expressing perfect satisfaction. It seemed, however, that there was a limit to enthusiasm in the mind of the Superintendent for one day with fire in his eye he told me that staying after school to dance had got to stop— the doors must close at four o'clock and the children should go home. I found out that a complaint had come over the dance idea so for a while we did "rhythms" instead, without changing the activities, and all was well. What's in a name anyway?

As for games, we had a terrible enemy in the Supervisor of Buildings. We probably did make some of those old school houses rock, for we played hard, so we made compromises and in some of the worst places the children used a sort of shuffling run that didn't shake the floor. That supervisor one day saw the children sitting on their desks to do some exercises and after that every scratch was laid to me. He said it was their buttons, and my assertion that they didn't have buttons where they sat was of no avail. One of the nicest uses for desks came as a surprise in a third-grade room when on command every boy slowly uncurled in his seat and stood on his head on top of his desk and slowly curled up again and sat down. We had chinning bars in the doorways and when children got restless they would work it off on those bars. I have seen boys turning cart wheels on their way up to the teacher's desk, rather than walk. I remember taking visitors to one room where games were a great success and on leaving I foolishly said "We would like to stay and play with you all day but we must go." Up jumped a little girl and leaning toward me hopefully with both hands on her desk, she said "Oh hey—come on." I want you to get the idea that out of my formal gymnastic background came a program enriched by a corps of the finest teachers and children a greenhorn ever met.

The contrast between our rather haphazard methods and what I saw in another city not long ago will show you into what I might have grown. There was a supervisor who knew what he wanted and got it. He could go into any school, jump up onto the teacher's platform, and say "Monday— *Begin*, 1, 2, 3, 4" and away they went. He could do that for any day of the week and not a mistake or a variation in the whole city. That was truly wonderful organization and both he and the city were proud of it.

By the end of the first year I had not satisfactorily covered every school and I asked for four assistants. No other supervisor had any, and the Superintendent said I was crazy and extravagant, but he would ask the Board for two. Another principle might be, *it is sometimes wise to ask for more than you expect*. But this demands caution and careful study of your superiors. It was quite an issue because it set a policy and I had to interview Board members. The last one came the day the Board met and I was pretty nervous. He shot the question "How many minutes do you plan that each assistant supervisor will spend in each room?" I had been so busy trying to get them that I had made no plans like that—besides it seemed like a waste of time till I got them. But something told me that with this business man I must be quick and definite so I looked him in the eye and said "Thirteen minutes." I don't know why thirteen unless I thought it would bring me luck. He took out a notebook and began to figure. My knees shook, but the mahogany board table hid them. I didn't know if he would discover that we three would reach each school once a month or once in ten years. He finally closed his book with a snap and said "I can see that you have worked this out very carefully and I shall vote for your two assistants." His bluff was as good as mine for I don't believe he knew how many rooms there were either. I'm afraid I can drag out no educational principle from this, unless we say *it sometimes is better to be quick on the trigger than cautious*.

Next morning the *Free Press* announced in big front page letters "Miss Perrin Gets Her Two Assistants," and the department began to grow. When I left in 1923 there were over three hundred of us. Now that has doubled and it is still growing. For several years my elementary supervisors were women, but there came a lucky year when I appointed Mr. Pearl and Mr. Post in charge of athletics for boys. About this time my old school sent out a scout to discover if I had gone crazy. I was appointing graduates from physical education schools and college departments of physical education from all over the country. That was bad enough, but these two men had never attended a physical education school in their lives. They were just plain elementary school principals from Butte, Montana—of all places! The men members of the department who taught in our high schools protested, but things were going my way in those days. *Select your assistants for what they can do, not only for their training.* These two men knew schools far better than I did and they knew and loved children. They had a philosophy of real education, what we now call Progressive Education; they had lived in the big open spaces and were athletes of the finest type. The enthusiasm, the new ideas, and the hard work of these two were never ending. The happiness of the children and the good of the department were always uppermost with them and they put new life into our work. The Decathlon for boys and Pentathlon for girls, old-time stunts for all, and the Belle Isle Field Day with its huge clock by which events were run, are outstanding results of those days.

Our program grew more and more informal because we seemed able to accomplish more that way and the more we tried informality the more we liked it. Then came a period of great growth when the platoon schools were started, each with one and many with two gymnasiums, and children in them and on the playground every period, necessitating from three to six special teachers in a building. At the same time came the intermediate or junior high schools, each with two gymnasiums and two swimming pools and special teachers to man them. Everywhere the classes were large and we found that the informal small squad work with much pupil responsibility produced the best results.

We of course had failures, but we were always ready to acknowledge them and give them up. One was our Health Clubs. We tried pupil leadership where it did not belong. One day I took visitors to a room where I had seen a Health Club running on greased wheels. Every personal health habit of every pupil for the past twenty-four hours was tabulated on the blackboard in three minutes under Johnnie's leadership. When I arrived with guests the Principal's face fell. Johnnie was at home sick-a-bed. No Health Club possible! But she was equal to the emergency; a telephone call, a car, Johnnie was dragged out of bed, he appeared, performed, and we had our show.

Another illuminating experience came to me when I saw a small boy sitting while the other children in his row stood up in answer to the question "How many slept with their windows open last night?" Public opinion was clearly against him for the standing ones pouted and stamped their feet because their row could not score, but the child still sat. When attention was away from him, I stood by him and asked why he didn't open his window. His answer? "I haven't any window in my room." We settled it easily by means of his door and the window in the next room, so all were satisfied but—something was wrong and we had a change of heart about Health Clubs. Shall we add to our principles by saying, *don't ask young shoulders to carry adult burdens.*

We went through the button stage, a button for this and a button for that. The children loved being squires and knights and kings and queens or whatever chance offered. We also had Cho Cho, the health clown all the way from New York. A crop of little Cho Chos sprang up in the schools. We talked about Susie Spinach and Bobby Beet and we played the health game. But we came to our senses in time and found that health instruction could be just as straightforward and just as interesting as any other subject. The trouble was the buttons and the camouflages outshone the health habits so we gave up the buttons.

It was through the American Child Health Association that I became interested in the field of health education, and one summer I was invited to attend a Health Education Conference called by Miss Sally Lucas Jean at Lake Mohunk. Once again my old game of chance led me on, for I had always wanted to see Lake Mohunk and so I accepted. I was the only physical educator to accept, though many were invited, and when I pointed out that physical education was not included in their health education program, they said, "Very well then, will you join our force in New York and put it in?" There were so many fine people in Detroit that I was not needed there any more. We might add as a final principle, *if you do not wish to leave a job don't organize yourself out,* and again I took the chance. For twelve years I worked in a national organization trying to help physical education make its great contribution to the field of health education. At the same time I tried to bring to health workers the importance of physical education. And so I hope to have made some small contributions to the American Association for Health, Physical Education, and Recreation.

Professional Preparation for the Activity Sciences
LEONARD A. LARSON*

Human activity consists of many facets. An attempt, thru the years, has been made to study each systematically. The part has become the central focus and has developed specifically and independently. The result is fragmentation of highly related fields of activity.

The product of man's professional efforts in the USA, is professionally extensive and intensive. The components of human activity have been developed and progressively advanced as physical education, athletics, health education, recreation, physical therapy, safety, dance, corrective physical education, et al. Although these activities have much in common philosoph-

---

*Leonard A. Larson, "Professional Preparation for the Activity Sciences," *The Journal of Sports Medicine.* March, 1965.

ically, educationally and scientifically, the common cores have not been identified.

The work and developments of the early years, as well as present efforts, have and are taking the direction of separation. This is causing confusion and concern. The institutions preparing leaders deal with each program as highly specific and unrelated activities. Several limitations, both educationally and economically, are being placed on the institution and students. And, the institutions using activity as a way of achieving educational goals, are confused by the many programs that apparently have much in common.

The bases for integration are two — the goals to be achieved and the medium for achievement. Physical education, athletics, recreation, health education, et al. meet both. With the exception of commercial enterprise, these activities are included in institutional programs to meet one set of educational goals. The objectives then are identical.

The medium of achievement is human activity, movement, action, etc. for the accomplishment of those phases of educational goals that can be gained thru activity. All of the now fragmented programs have a central focus in activity as the base for achievement. And, most importantly, for qualitative and quantitative results, the participant must regard and include all conditions, factors, circumstances and elements needed to give fullness to development. This not only includes the physical body but also the individual as an intellectual, emotional and social being.

Thus, the need to bring common fields of activity together is quite apparent. The first effort must be philosophical; the second, scientific. To accomplish the philosophic requirement, common purposes and goals will determine the degree of specificity. Some, of course, does exist. Each part has a unique contribution. For the second, the common procedures and media will indicate likenesses and differences. In both instances, likenesses, no doubt, constitute the largest relationships. The bases for integration, if this is established, is then determined.

Modern Society and Specialization

Specialization has always been a part of civilizations. It has served as the foundations for the social structures and cultures throughout the world. The great Roman Empire with its art, music, military skill, and government represented special skills of a high order to cite one example. Progress came to a large degree through these skills.

Specialization is accountable for the 20th century developments in science and technology. It has progressed so rapidly that hardly a job exists that does not use some technical device or implement.

The intense concentration on specialization tends to break with uniformity in society, and this is both good and bad. A specialist is often considered competent and expert in the over-all problems of society. This is a major danger. Generalization must go along with specialization.

De-emphasis in specialization is not going to occur during the modern age. The trend toward technology is advancing. Higher levels of specialization are needed.

Specialization for technological advances is no different than specialization for the solution of social, educational, and political issues. Society is highly complex. One must understand the part in order to understand the whole — much like in technology.

Specialization occurs in all fields. Technical knowledge and skills are needed. This is especially true in the philosophies and sciences dealing with the human personality and organism. Understanding structure and functions and their growth and development is specialization of the first order. The bases for knowledge and understanding come from and are developed by the sciences and philosophies.

The Science Foundations

The sciences which deal with human values, qualities, abilities, and characteristics must start with philosophy. Science should have direction and purpose. Philosophy serves these ends.

Given direction and purpose for the individual and group, procedures then start on how the goals might be achieved. This is the beginning of science and scientific inquiry. It is the examination of a phenomenon to gain ideas, judgment or fact which can be constantly tested and verified. And, when the phenomenon is found valid and sound, it may become a part of knowledge. Knowledge can then be put into practice.

Science and scientific inquiry does not need to be practical to be useful. In an age of technology it might be judged only on this basis. However, science might not have anything to do with the practical life and affairs. It may deal with pure intellectual curiosity. Only then are the needs of the mind satisfied.

The classification and definition of the various sciences today is the result, to a large degree, of historical accident. One investigation leads to another with the result of many lines of inquiry. The process of classifying types of scientific investigations has led to differentiation of the various sciences. An example is the distinction within the area of sociology — the social sciences and the political sciences.

Science is the study of judgements or phenomena on which universal agreements can be obtained. If agreement cannot be secured, the most fundamental criterion is not satisfied. The subject matter cannot then be classified as a true science. The application of this criterion has made science truly scientific.

A complexed phenomenon needs to be analyzed in parts and by separate factors. The human organism is not only physical but is characterized by social, emotional, and intellectual qualities and abilities. These components have unique characteristics but are all highly interrelated. For detailed study, it is necessary to sub-divide the whole. As knowledge increases, further sub-division may be necessary. As these divisions occur, new fields of knowledge are established. The most rapid development is in applied sciences. New concentrations are now being developed — biophysics, for example.

Everything that exists supposedly falls into one of the sciences. This is based on an assumption that all sciences are known. Apparently the assumption is false because many problems do not fall into a science classification. These problems do not have the benefit of the scientific discipline and method.

Knowledge about the human organism and how it develops, adjusts, and is modified by environmental forces represents complex phenomena. Only the most disciplined study and analysis could yield facts that meet the highest tests of validity. Anything less than a scientific analysis by procedure and method would be inadequate. The content represents a field of science of some classification. The question — what is the nature of this science as it is applied to the human organism in **action?**

The Activity Sciences

The components of "The Activity Sciences" are all structured and directed toward the achievement of health and human efficiency (Table 1). Each has sufficient uniqueness to be recognized as a component but each is interdependent. In achievement all most be closely correlated and unified to gain full results.

The common cores for "The Activity Sciences" are instruction, laboratory, environment, and research. These cores run through the five components with the content in each contributing toward the broad objectives of health and efficiency for the individual and the group.

TABLE 1.—*The Activity Sciences*
(*The Components*)

The knowledge, understanding and skill functions, potentials and requirements of human activity	The Science Classifications
The human organism and environmental influences	The Health Sciences
Neuromuscular movement	The Bio-Kinetic Sciences
Development-adjustment of the human personality	The Socio-Cultural Sciences
Maintenance and restoration of organic powers	The Therapeutic Sciences
Protection from environmental forces	The Safety Sciences

THE INSTRUCTIONAL CORE:

The development, integration, and adjustment of the organism toward optimal health, efficiency, and well-being is founded upon philosophic and scientific facts. These must be learned and practiced. The content is knowledge, understanding, and appreciation of the nature and requirements for health (the health sciences); it is the development of the organic powers of the body through the proper use in activity (the bio-kinetic sciences); it is instruction in development of the social qualities closely integrated with other outcomes from activity (socio-cultural sciences); it is instruction in the care of the organism, the injuries, the defects in order to maintain and advance organic health (the therapeuptic sciences); and it is instruction in participation which is vigorous and potentially dangerous for favorable results (the safety sciences). All components are essential, all are interdependent. The results of closely related instruction is a better understanding and achievement of health and efficiency.

THE LABORATORY CORE:

The achievement of optimal health is much more than an academic affair. The knowledges, understandings, and skills gained through instruction must be practiced daily. Daily living requires an environment which favorably contributes to health, the proper care of the body in daily living, and the avoidance of the dangers to health from some environmental conditions (the health sciences); it requires opportunities for participation sufficiently frequent and intense to cause changes in the organism for power and its proper use (the bio-kinetic sciences); it is the activity providing opportunities for development of the total personality for social integration and adjustment essential in health (the socio-cultural sciences); it includes provisions for restoration of organic losses to maintain an optimal level of health (the therapeutic sciences); and it also is the opportunity for activities without danger or the loss of health (the safety sciences). These experiences complement each other. The omission of any reduces the quality of another, and the loss of an important experience for the development and maintenance of health and efficiency.

THE ENVIRONMENTAL CORE:

The individual must be protected from the loss of health and must live daily with knowledge of practices which will prevent reduction or losses. All five components of "The Activity Sciences" need to be applied directly and in coordination for the achievement of this goal. These include knowledge, understanding, and appreciation of dangers (the health sciences), the hazards in vigorous participation (the bio-kinetic sciences), the balanced life which uses leisure to restore energy and vitality (the socio-cultural sciences), the correction of malfunctions resulting from injury (the therapeutic sciences), and the development of knowledge and skill for full living in an environment and under conditions which are safe. Prevention in the loss of health and protection of the gains in health need all these disciplines of knowledge and skills.

THE RESEARCH CORE:

Philosophic and scientific facts are needed about the individual as a total personality and the group as an inter-personal developing and integrating medium. All the component parts of "The Activity Sciences" react and interact as a whole. Facts include the relationship of knowledge and action, the nature and scope of human development in part and as a whole, the strength of activity in the development and maintenance of health and well-being, the losses in health through injury and malfunction and how much loss can be avoided or reduced, and facts on how to gain optimal health without danger or losses. For full understanding and practices, all components of the activity sciences must be closely correlated in research and in interpretation.

Professional Preparation

The preparation of professional personnel for the activity sciences must take into account at least two major functions — the practitioner and the specialist. Each requires significantly different preparation.

TABLE 2.—*Curriculum Requirements—The Practitioner*

Degree	Liberal Arts and Science	Professional Education	Specialization	Total
Bachelor's	60 (basic and applied)°	42 (all phases of operations)°°°	18 (all teachers)°°	120
Master's°°°°	10 (basic and/or applied)	20 (specialization thru applied sciences and philosophies)		30
Doctorate°°°°	17 (applied)	25 (an interpretation and application of research)		42
Total	87	87	18	192

°   Same for all five components of "The Activity Sciences."
°°   For teachers with special adjustments for others.
°°° Special requirements for each of the five components.
°°°° Special requirements for each component with a large common core in the liberal arts — science and a small core in specialization.

    The practitioner must be prepared in the specifics and in the differences. The uniquenesses and specificities among the components does make a difference; and, the practitioners must gain the skills, techniques, and procedures. Preparation should then recognize each component (Table 2) in addition to other requirements in leadership roles with the general population. Basically, preparation is in breadth of knowledge and understanding and depth in skills.

    For the specialist, preparation is in depth and the differences are in the sciences, not the professional components as in the case of the practitioner. The specialist should have knowledge and understanding of the scientific and philosophic natures of human activity not particularly in skills, techniques and procedures.

    The basic differences (many in the details) then in the preparation of the practitioner and the specialist is in breadth and in the special components for the former and in the various sciences and philosophies and depth in the latter. Curriculum patterns are suggested on these principles.

CURRICULA — THE PRACTITIONER

    For practical operations of the activity sciences in schools, colleges and organizations, each component requires special preparation. Of course, a large common core exists but a degree of uniqueness and specificity does also. These are the five components presented (Table 1) as the health sciences, the bio-kinetic sciences, the socio-cultural sciences, the therapeutic sciences and the safety sciences.

In addition to the special components, the practitioner's preparation should be in breadth with each component. This should include knowledge, understanding and skills of the school and community conditions, the people and the pupils, the worth of the activity sciences in achieving goals set for the pupils, and the teaching and leadership methods skills and procedures for optimal achievement. And, preparation should qualify the student to teach or lead children, adults, normal and the atypical, within various institutions. The emphasis is, however, on breadth of understanding with the skills for operations.

In order to yield a more tangible presentation on the preparation of the practitioner, credit illustrations are applied (Table 2). This is the general framework for each of the five components (Table 1). For the B. S. degree, 78 credits (liberal arts and science and professional educations) are identical with one exception. Those not wishing to qualify for the public schools could have some choice within the professional education requirement, although this phase of preparation is most desirable for all. Within the area of specialization (42 credits) the differences in the five components are quite significant.

Beyond the B. S. level, differences among the five components will require more than a majority of the requirements within each component. A common core does exist, but on the graduate level, it tends to be less than on the undergraduate.

The results of preparation will qualify the student for work in many agencies-schools, colleges, organizations, clubs, private health-fitness enterprises, coaching, among many other opportunities. Positions will include administration, teaching, informal leadership, supervision, technical specialists in activity adaptation, and others.

The individual is equipped to practice all facets of a component with some special emphasis within this context.

Curricula — The Specialist

The specialists concentrate on the sciences and philosophies within the context of human activity. The scope is limited to one science or philosophy. The specialist is qualified professionally for work in all five components within the limits of the selected science or philosophy. The selection opportunities are: Biology, psychology, sociology, physical sciences, philosophy, history or education.

Preparation should emphasize depth, in the selected science or philosophy, to yield knowledge and understanding of "The Activity Sciences" as a medium for human development. Knowledge and understanding of the science or philosophy of and from participation is transmitted to the practitioners by the professional specialist. The specialist serves as a resource of knowledge and understanding. The practitioner, with resources from the several sciences and philosophies, is prepared to apply the activity sciences more effectively as a medium for human development.

The curricula for the specialist have one basic framework with applications to the several sciences and philosophies (Table 3). The basic pattern thru all degree stages is the co-major. For the B. S. degree the major is in the activity sciences and one of the seven sciences or philosophies. The co-major is continued into the graduate program providing an academic preparation for the activity sciences. The emphasis is on depth in the basic science and breadth on application to "The Activity Sciences."

TABLE 3.—*Curriculum Requirements—The Specialist.*

Degree	Liberal Arts and Science	Science or Philosophy Major	Activity Science Major	Total
B. S. or B. A.	50 (all basic sciences and philosophy)	35 (one science or philosophy)	35 (all components of the Activity Sciences)	120
M. S. or M. A.	6 (the correlated sciences or philosophies)	12 (one science or philosophy)	12 (all components of the Activity Sciences)	30
Ph. D.	8 (one science or philosophy)	17 (one science or philosophy)	17 (all components of the Activity Sciences)	42
Total Credits	64	64	64	192

An equal emphasis is placed on the three phases of preparation (liberal arts, science or philosophy and the Activity Sciences). This requires some adjustment in the basic science and in the Activity Sciences. In the Activity Sciences preparation includes the applied sciences of all components (Table 1). The requirements for professional education and the laboratory experiences in activity will need to be reduced or modified in credit allowances. The emphasis in specialization is a science or philosophy, not activity.

To implement the curriculum for the specialist, some modifications are necessary from the current institutional practices. This is largely in the Activity Sciences with little modification needed in the basic science or philosophy. For example: Zoology. It is possible to achieve a graduate major in physiology with a Ph.D. degree in the Activity Sciences within a period of seven years (Table 4). Similar patterns are possible in the other six areas of sciences and philosophy in a co-major with the Activity Sciences.

The specialist qualification prepares one to teach and research in colleges and universities. For a balanced staff, the college or university will

TABLE 4.—*Co-Major: Physiology and the Activity Sciences.*

Degree	Liberal Arts and Science	Biological Science	Activity Sciences	Total
B. S. or B. A.	English literature language chemistry physics mathematics anthropology history Total: 65	biology comparative anatomy comparative physiology vertebrate embryology vertebrate biology endocrinology genetics Total: 30	anatomy physiology applied anatomy applied physiology measurement correctives adaptives activity Total: 32	127
M. A. or M. S. in Physiology and Ph.D. in The Activity Sciences		human physiology neuro-anatomy physiological chemistry medical physiology cellular physiology research Total: 32	experimental physiology experimental anatomy measurement designs experimental designs statistical designs problems seminars research Total: 32	64
Total	65	62	64	191

*Similar patterns are possible for psychology, sociology, physical sciences, philosophy, history and education.

need a minimum of seven individuals to be properly equipped to deal with the scientific and philosophic aspects of the activity sciences. In addition, individuals prepared as practitioners are needed.

Summary

The rapid advances in science and technology require a critical evaluation of all educational programs. Preparation for work and living in the modern world is considerably different than a mere twenty-five years ago. Transportation, communications, industry, health are all directed and advanced by science and technology.

In physical education, et al. the emphasis during the past years has been largely toward preparing the individual as practitioners. It has been skills to teach activities, knowledge, administer and supervise. The curriculum content has been on methods and procedures with a minimum content in science and philosophy.

Major changes are needed. The first step is redirection and the integration of all correlated fragments. The proposal is "The Activity Sciences." The discipline becomes "science" and the integration "human activity" broadly conceived.

The order for reorganization is large indeed. But reorganization is possible and desirable. In order to provide strength to all phases of the activity sciences, a division of preparation is recommended. Special emphasis then becomes possible. Currently, the emphasis is on process and not content. A reverse is desirable.

It is suggested that the decision for professional preparation be determined at the junior year in the undergraduate school. The individual will then decide whether to prepare for work as a practitioner or to prepare as a specialist. The former will apply to students interested and qualified for the operations of the profession, the latter for leadership in the preparation of the practitioner. The division will improve both phases of the profession. It is not desirable to attempt a middle road.

The practitioner should be prepared in breadth of knowledge, understanding and skills. High specialization as one phase is not desirable, except in the activity science component. The specialist, however, can only prepare in one science or philosophy in order to gain knowledge and understanding of the science or philosophy as it applies to the activity sciences. In the former the five components of the activity sciences required special concentration while in the latter such specialization is unnecessary.

The professional opportunities for the practitioners are on all educational levels and institutions applying the activity sciences to achieve institutional goals. For the specialist, only research and professional teaching positions are open. These would include research agencies, colleges and universities.

Principles of Learning
with Implications for Teaching Tennis
CHET MURPHY*

It has been said that if you know something, you can teach it. But a tennis instructor who has tried the "Watch me, do as I do" approach (and which one of us hasn't?) knows that there is much more to teaching than merely knowing the subject, important as that is. A perfect demonstration of a serve or a backhand by a tennis instructor does not always result in a perfect imitation by the pupil. He often does not do it the way the instructor does or the way the instructor tells him to. Why not? Is the pupil stupid? Maybe, but probably not. Is the instructor stupid? Of course not! What, then, is the reason for the pupil's not being able to make the stroke as the instructor would like it to be made?

Probably the instructor did not do or say the right thing to call forth the desired response from the pupil. The instructor is not likely to succeed

---

*Chet Murphy, "Principles of Learning with Implications for Teaching Tennis," *Journal of Health, Physical Education and Recreation*, February, 1962.

in teaching unless he learns to bridge the gap that exists between his own knowledge and skill in the game and his pupils' lack of knowledge and skill in it. To transmit his knowledge to his pupils, he must know his subject, he must know his pupils, and he must know how learning takes place.

Experiments have led researchers to conclude that motor learning takes place more rapidly and most effectively when it is directed by the teacher under a certain set of conditions in accordance with certain principles. Several such principles will be presented here with their implications for tennis teachers. Through awareness of these principles and their application to the teaching situation, tennis teachers can best convey their knowledge of the game to their pupils.

Motivating the Learner

"Telling," we are told, "is not teaching; the learner learns by doing if he is interested in what he is doing." Experienced teachers recognize this as the ever-present problem of creating readiness or motivating pupils to want to learn. To the young, inexperienced tennis teacher, this is often his most difficult problem.

An individual is likely to respond favorably to suggestions for improvement only if he has been made "ready" to learn, either by a personal liking for the game or by artificial or extrinsic motives. He is not likely to profit much from any teaching if he is forced to play the game against his will.

Every teacher wants his pupils to learn. For this reason, he attempts to select as materials to be learned only those which are within the capabilities of his pupils, and he attempts to present the material in such a way as to make it interesting and meaningful to all of his pupils.

What complicates the process of selection and presentation of skills is the fact that no two pupils are alike. They differ in interest, in temperament, in physique, and in skill performance. Each pupil grows and develops at his own rate, and he brings to class his own pattern of readiness. The teacher's task, then, is to adapt his methods to as many of the different patterns of readiness as is possible.

The problems associated with readiness, however, are not as difficult as they at first appear to be. For even though children in the same class are in different stages of development and have different needs and interests, there are, at the same time, some basic needs or desires which every pupil strives to satisfy and which the teacher can utilize in his classwork.

One such desire is the eagerness to achieve mastery over things. Why not, then, conduct tennis class instruction in such a manner that at least some early success by at least some members of the class is assured. By selecting early learning tasks which are certain to be performed well by the more skillful pupils, the teacher can subtly provide the remaining pupils with proof that "it can be done." Less skilled pupils will be encouraged to attempt to do as well as their classmates.

The question one so often hears from tennis teachers is, "How easy can we make it? If a boy or girl cannot make a bounce-and-hit accurately over the net to his partner so that the partner gets a play on the ball, what can be done?"

The answer is provided by experienced professional tennis instructors, who, even in private lessons, have their beginning students and intermediate students spend a great deal of time hitting at accurately tossed balls. Only when pupils have learned to hit these tossed balls with a reasonable degree of form and skill are they permitted to advance to the rallying stage. Gradual progression from simple tossing drills to more difficult rallying drills is the procedure.

Why not, then, use tossed ball procedures in classwork until pupils are able to hit accurately enough to avoid having to chase wildly-hit balls. Time is better spent in practicing tossing drills than in chasing wild, uncontrolled shots on the court. And what better way to assure early success for the learner than to give him the easiest of all balls to hit, namely, an accurately tossed ball.

Tests and Awards as Incentives

The teacher should be aware that children need to know the purpose of each drill and the rate at which they are progressing on the skill at which they are working. When a pupil knows this, he is working under one of the most powerful of all incentives to learning. It would be wise, then, for tennis teachers to devise simple tests of skill and form on which pupils can be scored periodically. Counting the number of balls stroked into a certain court area, or the successful hits made against the wall, or times a ball is made to cross the net in a rally (even if the rally is begun by stroking a tossed ball) are examples of such tests. Charts and graphs showing the improved scores on these tests can create a desire in pupils to better their scores. The pupils must understand, however, that such tests are being used as a device to help them reach *their* goals.

Various kinds of awards and point systems can be worked out. The pupils who perform well may be permitted to move from one court or one section of the gymnasium to another where a more advanced skill is being taught. They may be permitted to wear a breast patch or an arm band with some suitable inscription such as "Best Forehand" or "Backboard Rally Champ." Or, they may be awarded points, at intervals, for accomplishment on each drill, with the points being totaled at longer intervals in order to determine standings and placement. If, while the ultimate goal of being a skillful tennis player is still far away, learners can be made to feel satisfied with small steps in this manner, the whole process of learning will be made easier.

Diversity in Learning Abilities

Teachers know that individuals differ in the manner in which they learn. Because of this, the most effective methods of learning and of presenting material will differ, depending on the pupil. Some learn most quickly from verbal cues and guides; hints and suggestions from the teacher are quickly acted upon and successfully applied. Others may depend more on visual guidance as a method of learning; they profit more from demonstrations or photographs from which they can "get a picture" of the movement or skill desired. Others may rely more on mechanical guidance, or what may be called the manual methods; they want the teacher to guide their hands or arms through the desired movement so that they may remember and duplicate the feel of it. (This is usually the least valuable of the three types of learning and should be used only after the pupils have a definite idea of the complete movement they are trying to learn.)

The most effective method of presenting material to large groups is that which satisfies or "reaches" all individuals regardless of the type presentation on which they rely. Each teaching situation should begin with a brief explanation, offer a brief demonstration, and then provide much opportunity for practice so that learners may get the feel of an act or movement.

The demonstration should be conducted both at slow speed and at regular speed, because different pupils see things differently. It should be slow enough for all to see the important elements of the skill (and these should be indicated clearly to the class), and yet fast enough for the class to understand how the parts, or elements, combine to make the whole, or fit into larger parts of the pattern. Any peculiar mannerisms of the demonstrator, or unnecessary items of the skill should be omitted from the demonstration because some pupils will adopt them (either inadvertently or consciously), considering them to be important items in the skill. The demonstration should, whenever possible, be conducted in the actual setting, in the proper position and direction in which the skill is to be practiced, and the class should be oriented in that direction. The site of the demonstration should be a pleasant one in which the pupils can be comfortable, not facing sun or wind (when outdoors) and not bothered by distracting noises or movements.

Transfer of Training

Another method by which the teacher can promote early success in tennis is by making use of the principles of transfer of training. Transfer is the name applied to the process of utilizing past experiences in meeting new situations. It refers to the fact that an individual acquires habits and skills in one activity which can prove useful and helpful in another activity. Certain knowledge and skills carried over from some sports and games can be useful to pupils in their efforts to learn to play tennis. If a pupil has played baseball, for example, he can be shown the similarity between the hitting stances in each sport and that between the service swing in tennis and the overhand throwing motion in baseball. He should then be encouraged to apply those already learned baseball skills to tennis. By relating one set of facts to another, in this manner, the teacher is expressing one of the essentials of good teaching.

An extremely important point for teachers to remember is that it is possible for negative transfer to occur. Negative transfer implies that habits or skills learned in one activity may interfere with or retard learning in another activity if there are mutually interfering habits between the two activities. For example, a pupil may find it difficult to learn to block or punch his forehand volley if he has just finished practicing his forehand ground stroke, which he has been taught to hit with a long, smooth follow-through. The habit of following through may have a retarding effect on his ability to learn the shorter stroke required for volleys.

Negative transfer gives rise to the question, "What is the best method of progression in teaching, from ground stroke to ground stroke, or from ground stroke to volley?" Each teacher, analyzing his methods and theories of stroking, decides the answer for himself. If analysis of a teaching system indicates that there are more similarities and fewer conflicting habits between ground strokes (that is, the forehand ground stroke as compared with the backhand ground stroke) than between the ground strokes and the volley, then the order of progression should be from one ground stroke to the other. However, it must be remembered that individuals vary in their ability to carry-over or to exclude movements between activities.

Whole and Part Methods of Teaching

In the teaching of tennis skills one of the major problems the teacher must face is whether to use the whole method or the drill-on-parts method of teaching, both for the entire game and for particular strokes.

Some advocate beginning instruction with the whole method, by having the learner start "playing the game" immediately. They claim that this method will be the best way to acquire the necessary automatic habit patterns. Experiments indicate, however, that the efficiency of learning by wholes, as compared with learning by parts, appears to depend on the meaningfulness of the material to be learned, which, in turn, depends on the intelligence of the learner in each particular learning experience. Learning by the whole method is more efficient only when the material to be learned is easy, unified, and of a definite pattern that unites many single items into a significant whole. One can hardly say this is a description of a tennis game with its various strokes, its subtleties in pace and depth, and the necessity for good court position. Because of the complexity of the pattern of tennis play, the whole method does not seem to be well adapted to early tennis instruction.

A reasonable amount of proficiency in the basic strokes is a prerequisite to tennis play, and the drill-on-parts method is the most effective method of acquiring these and other necessary skills. Some tennis teachers advocate as many as eight or ten lessons in drill-on-parts (the strokes) before letting the pupil begin the total game.

However, it appears that an early, brief introduction to the total pattern of a game of tennis (serving and rallying to win the point) will make a more meaningful activity out of the drill-on-parts methods which follow, provided that the learner can perform to some degree at least, the movements necessary to serve and rally. The whole method should be used only after the pupil has achieved a reasonable degree of success in the basic strokes. Then alternate practice and emphasis on the total game and on specific strokes becomes even *more* meaningful and is likely to be more rewarding.

For the complete stroke, with its components as the parts, however, it is generally conceded that the whole method is superior to parts training. The tennis swing is a coordinated movement in which the force is applied at the start and carried through chiefly by momentum. To strip the unity of a stroke by segregating it into parts would defeat its purpose.

However, there are check points in each of the various strokes. These are the features upon which a teacher can ascertain the degree to which an individual's stroke conforms to the desired pattern. The start of the backswing and the point at which it ends, the start of the forward swing, the point of contact, the follow-through, and the finish position are generally regarded as ordinary check points in a single stroke. For the best results, check points should be employed merely as a means to an end, the end being the entire coordinated swing.

Trial and Error Learning

One of the most often repeated statements in the area of skill acquisition is "practice makes perfect." The experienced teacher, however, knows that this is not true, that motor learning is not merely a process of repetition until a habit is formed. Instead, it is more of a process of constant change and variation. Tries are made, errors noticed, and other tries made. This is often called "trial-and-error" learning, but perhaps this is an inaccurate description of the process, for the learner in succeeding trials does not purposely repeat errors of earlier trials. If he did there would be no improvement. Instead, he makes variations in later trials so that they are more nearly correct than earlier ones.

In tennis, for example, the learner may note that the racket was held too loosely or that the racket face was tilted back too much. When he repeats the action he corrects the mistake; he changes a part here or there, noting whether or not the change makes any difference in the end result. A series of such modified repetitions made under the watchful eye of the instructor constitutes effective practice. For this reason, the process of skill acquisition might more accurately be termed "progressive approximation," wherein the learner progressively approximates the correct form or action, after each trial that did not produce the desired result.

How can the learner best be guided in this practice in which he attempts to modify every unsuccessful execution? In the initial stages of such practice, the properly motivated learner responds to verbal cues made by the teacher. The cues, of course, must be carefully selected and must be in keeping with the general method of stroking recommended by the teacher. "Elbow down at the finish," for example, could be a valuable guide to a beginner who tends to turn the racket over in contradiction to the teacher's instructions to "finish with the racket face perpendicular to the ground."

If the learner does manage to finish with the elbow down as the teacher suggests, and if his hitting and his placement begins to improve, then the learner will be encouraged to continue to practice keeping the elbow down. What seems to follow, then, is a process in which the student takes over the guidance of his performance by learning to feel that his elbow is in the right or wrong position. Usually, the ability to feel the stroke comes only after many repetitions of verbal cues by the teacher.

But "keeping the elbow down" may not mean the same thing to every pupil, nor may it be equally effective in developing proper form with every pupil. To some pupils there may be a better way of saying what there is to say about the kind of finish required. Perhaps "stand the racket on edge" will serve the purpose, or "don't roll the wrist" may do it.

The teacher must say the same thing in as many different ways as he can in order to reach as many of his pupils as possible. He must also define his terms so that they mean exactly what he wants them to mean to his pupils. In the final analysis, what a learner does depends on how he interprets the instructions. Since the essence of the learning process is pupil activity, it follows that seeing or hearing will not teach a youngster to play tennis. This may help, but in order to learn he must go through the motions; he must feel the act, the movement, or the stroke. By demonstration and verbal description, the teacher may provide the starting point from which the learner is to proceed. Then, by doing, by practicing the act under the watchful eye of the instructor, the learner begins to acquire skill.

Overlearning

Tennis teachers must remember that a skill can be considered to be learned only when it can be called out without a great deal of conscious attention being directed toward it. One or two successful performances do not mean an act has been learned. Constant practice and repetition, even after a pupil has acquired a fair degree of skill, will lead to *overlearning*. Overlearning means an act is so definitely established as a habit that it is repeated "subconsciously" when the proper stimulus is present even under conditions of violent emotion or extreme fatigue. Teachers, then, should continue to drill pupils on a performance until they act subconsciously in the desired manner. When pupils have over-learned in this manner they will be able to execute the stroke under the stress and strain of competition.

Summary

Skill demands repetition and practice, but learning is subject to certain principles which indicate that practice and repetition are not enough to account for skill. The effectiveness of practice is dependent upon the mental condition of the learner, who must be ready and willing to learn and should experience feelings of satisfaction.

Learning is hastened by making use of habits and skills carried over from other activities. Teachers can help increase the rate of learning by helping the learner recognize progress and success. They must always remember that individuals differ in their ability to learn, in the methods by which they learn, and in their emotional reactions to various learning situations. The many principles of learning, then, are of value only when they are applied with an awareness and understanding of individual differences.

How You Can Become a Master Teacher
KEITH PITCHFORD*

It is not unusual for the physical education instructor to find himself confronted with the task of teaching an activity in which he is not highly skilled. Although he may have taken a major in physical education, it is almost impossible for him to obtain the necessary experiences in the fundamentals of all physical education activities, to the extent that he could demonstrate them well, because of the number of activities alone. Second, age may be a factor which affects the skills of the instructor. An activity which

---

*Keith Pitchford, "How You Can Become A Master Teacher," *Journal of Health Physical Education and Recreation.* Vol. 31, No. 2, February, 1960.

may have been easy and a pleasure to perform when the teacher was younger may become difficult and even dangerous in later years. Third, due to the teacher shortage, teachers with little physical education and sports background are being called upon to instruct in these areas. And fourth, especially on the elementary level, women classroom teachers quite often must instruct their pupils in fundamental movements, such as running, jumping, climbing, and throwing, when they themselves are not able to perform these activities well enough to set a good example.

Therefore, whether we like it or not, we must be truthful and say that at times we find ourselves teaching some phase of physical education in which we are unskilled, for one reason or another. We might as well be realistic and make an effort to solve this problem when we face it.

Can we teach well those physical education activities which we cannot demonstrate well? Although no defense of a lack of skills is being made, the answer to the question is "Yes." Many excellent teachers seldom perform before their students but use other teaching methods and procedures to produce desired results.

Although skills in sports and physical education activities acquired by the teacher are valuable and should be prized by the individual, their greatest value in teaching lies in the understanding and insight into the activity which they give. The values of being able to demonstrate are not questioned or discounted; we are dealing here only with those who have not or cannot become highly skilled, so that a topnotch demonstration is not possible. It is also true to say that a poor demonstration by the teacher may be much less valuable than no demonstration at all.

How do instructors obtain desired results without the ability to demonstrate to their students? Successful physical education teachers who are unable to perform well use a variety of methods of instruction to secure their objectives.

Know and Understand the Skill

First, teachers should learn everything possible about the activity through reading, watching others perform, studying movements necessary in performing the skills involved, movies, sequence pictures, slide films, and other available means. This arms them with an understanding and knowledge of the activities which they cannot demonstrate.

Enlist the Aid of Star Performers

A simple diagnostic test of skills in the sport may point out a student who can perform on a high plane — one who can demonstrate for the class. If such a student is not available, a varsity player may be willing to assist. Often a person in the neighborhood, such as a golf or tennis professional, is glad to give a demonstration of his skills.

Visual aids may be the answer to the teaching problem. These are many and varied and instruction should not be limited to one type. Particularly useful are slow motion movies, if they are available, and especially slow motion loop film. Loops are excellent in teaching of skills such as the golf or tennis swing, punting a football, basketball goal shooting, or hitting a baseball.

Some teachers like to use sequence pictures of highly skilled athletes in action, for these pictures show the progression of action from the beginning of the particular act, with each individual picture stopped or "frozen" in the natural position or pose at that phase of the action's natural progression. The action can be seen and learned simply by reading it from left to right.

Slide films are used frequently by teachers as a visual aid in instruction in the skills of archery, bowling, badminton, tennis, and many other sports. Still pictures of athletes as they pose, at bat, in the correct golf stance, the position of readiness when receiving the tennis serve, free throw stances on the basketball court, etc., are used advantageously.

Television, in effect a moving picture, is not to be overlooked as a teaching aid. The televised all-star games, tournaments of the masters, or top professional games in many sports offer an opportunity for the class to view highly skilled performances. More and more sports events are being televised for the public, and many schools are able to own television sets which can and should be used by the physical education teacher in the teaching of sports.

Visual aids must be used as teaching devices not as recreation periods. Their use must be planned, just as a demonstration must be, if much learning is to result.

Some very good instructors are able to explain how an activity should be accomplished. Even though unskilled, these teachers know very well how the skills are performed, and they are masters in the ability to draw word pictures of the procedure they have in mind. They can make contact with the student so vividly that he is able to reproduce his thought image of the action. Teachers who use this method of developing skills must be able to talk the student into the correct action.

When asked "Do you demonstrate for your students?" a leading college swimming teacher and coach gave this answer: "I quit demonstrating years ago when I decided that my swimmers probably learned more bad habits from me than they did good points." This master teacher, in his classes, posted action pictures of great swimmers on his bulletin board; he placed students in correct positions and explained what he wanted them to do; he used varsity swimmers for demonstration purposes; he placed a mirror

in a position that permitted students to observe themselves while performing certain strokes; and he walked along the edge of the pool correcting
mistakes as the swimmers attempted to develop good swimming form.

Correction is another technique which all teachers need to master. When
the golf shot or tennis stroke goes sour, and the student asks, "Coach, what
am I doing wrong?" then the time is ripe for corrections to be made. The
teacher must be able to help the student make adjustments when his performance is incorrect.

Most physical education teachers are unskilled in some activities which
they may have to instruct. They can still do a good job of teaching if they
apply themselves to the methods and techniques outlined here.

The Tomorrow Mind
Implications of Research for Teaching
Junior-Senior High School Girls and College Women
CELESTE ULRICH*

There are times when I feel as if we in physical education talk about
research as if it was akin in complexity to the theory of relativity. It has always puzzled me that educators should be afraid of a fact-oriented field and
that because of our fear and our timidity in understanding the complex, we
have ignored the meaning of the educational noun in our discipline. Do we
realize that in this way we may have curtailed the obvious frontier of our
knowledge, we may have dulled our own educational cutting edge? I find
it tremendously heartening to find a group of enthusiastic and alert educators excited about the meaning of recent research in our field.

If teaching is the reiteration of past truths and the sowing of yester-
day's facts in the fertile fields of a new generation, then we do *not* need to
pay attention to research, but if teaching is the search for new truths and
the use of known ideas to fertilize the growth of newer and more meaningful concepts, then we *do* need to pay attention to research and we need to
become a part of the great research venture. Only thus can we hope to improve our teaching.

Education, more than any other field, must place its faith in the "tomorrow mind," and it is research which is the bedrock of such a plan of action.
All of us must continually apply ourselves to the concept of the acquisition
of knowledge and that means that you and I are obliged to read periodicals

---

*Celeste Ulrich, "The Tomorrow Mind," *Journal of Health, Physical Education
and Recreation.* Vol. 35, No. 8, October, 1964.

such as the *Research Quarterly, Journal of Motor Behavior, The Journal of Applied Physiology* and *Perceptual and Motor Skills;* to suggest a few. It means that we must attend research sections at conventions and hear research papers read and critiqued. It means that we must read the news and current events with a critical mind, ever cognizant of the concept that something may present itself which will have meaning for our teaching tomorrow. It means that we must be alert to professional meanings in articles and stories and most of all, it means that we must assume the obligation of making a contribution toward research—for only thus will the tomorrow mind be operant.

So today let us quickly scan some of the most recent knowledge extracted from research to see how such knowledge can be applied to the practicality of "on the job" action.

Recently some very interesting work has been revealed with regard to the student whom we teach. There is such a tremendous difference between Susie age 13 and Sue aged 22 that it is difficult to generalize about pubescent and post-pubescent girls. We do know that girls are maturing more rapidly today than they used to mature. The average age of the onset of menarchy has advanced in our culture almost a year and a half in the last hundred years. This may be due to the high protein diet that we stress in this country, or it may be due to endocrine changes that are brought about through psychological stressors. In light of this physiological fact and with the strong influence of behavioral patterns fostered by a social structure which prizes maturity as a desired goal, it is easy to see why our junior high school girls are insisting that certain activities are too childish and are demanding that they be allowed to participate in more adult activities. A society that encourages a dating pattern to begin at 10 is going to have a difficult time insisting that dodgeball and hop scotch are appropriate activities for the same 10-year-old girl.

We also need to know that the research knowledge with reference to cardio-respiratory endurance tells us that it is practically impossible to damage the normal heart through exercise and we can "take heart" from this statement and stop babying our girls as though they were made of Dresden china. You just can't hurt a person through activity and the time has come when we should push our girls harder than teaching them how to recognize the primary onset of fatigue. As an illustration of this point, just this past winter I was observing a high school teacher in our community teach a tenth grade class basketball. The teaching facilities were horrible and this young woman had forty girls in one-half of a "too small" gymnasium using two baskets to practice the lay-up from a dribble. I watched those forty girls stand and wait their turn for six minutes each, only to have the ball in their hands for all of 20 seconds. They did this three times around so each girl had one minute of exercise and had waited for 17 minutes. After that tasking cardio-respiratory feat, this young teacher suggested that the class come over to the sidelines and sit down and *rest* while she talked with them. And worst of all, the situation was not atypical. Let's start to push our girls hard, knowing that the only cardio-respiratory response will be one of amelioration instead of degeneration. And for those of us who teach in colleges and universities, I would stress this even more. I would almost welcome the smell of sweat in a women's gymnasium, not for its odoriferous quality but for its physiological worth.

There has also been a great deal of attention drawn with regard to the development of strength through isometric contractions. This concept has been long acknowledged in therapy and was utilized by Charles Atlas long before the term isometrics ever reared its magical head. But the enchantment occurred when *The Reader's Digest* suggested in an article that it would be possible to "get one's exercise" by exercising for six seconds a day. Just "tense up" and give it your all and you've completed the daily routine. That even has the ten minutes per day advocated by national councils put to shame. To many young women the six-second exercise had great appeal because it didn't take much effort, but that's all right because the results are limited too. I do not mean to be disillusioning about isometric contractions, because they do produce muscular strength, but that is all that they do, and there is nothing magic about the system. If you want girls to play tennis better, isometric exercises do not help with flexibility, timing, coordination, and general skill patterning. You have to hit a tennis ball with a tennis racket to get at that. But you can increase grip strength and if this is important to the student's tennis game, then isometrics may be indicated.

Another fairly recent research concept has come to light regarding warm-up activities. A number of researches have indicated that physiologically there is no need to warm up the muscle before exercise and further evidence has indicated that warm-up is much more related to psychological expectations than to physiological changes induced by activity. I must hasten to add that I know of no research that indicates that warm-up activities are harmful and there is some conflicting research which is weighted toward the concept that related warm-ups are by far the best of all activities used. In other words, don't be afraid to put a group of girls in a game situation without warm-up drills but understand that although this will not be functionally harmful, it may foster poorer performance, especially if the team is conditioned to the concept that warm-up is helpful in preparing for play. But for goodness sake, don't put girls through a gymnastic drill before their basketball or hockey game — if you insist that they must warm up, make sure that they do so by practicing basketball or hockey skills.

We also have information regarding the effect of the neural system on exercises involving strength. There is a current theory, being subjected to concerted investigation, that a shout or scream will actually aid muscular contraction at the moment of maximum strength need. Thus, it may be logical to have girls grunt or shout when they are taking a field shot or driving the hockey ball from the edge of the circle. It is possible that such noises actually assist in contraction and should be encouraged rather than discouraged. We also know that strength utilizes the muscular contraction of muscles other than those employed for the activity itself. Consequently, it is normal for facial grimaces and contorted movements to accompany any all-out strength effort on the part of students. And in this connection, it is wise to remember than an all-out effort for a beginner is considerably less in terms of the task at hand than that of the experienced player.

Another interesting facet of recent research reveals the fact that exercise does control weight to a much greater degree than we have acknowledged in the past decade. A very interesting study done on Boston school girls who were weighed periodically indicated that although the entire group ate identical teen age diets (hamburgers, cokes, pizza, and what complete home meals you can get into them) the ones that gained weight during post-pubescence were those who had no regular activity schedule, while those who maintained their weight did so because of systematic activity regardless of diet. Dr. Jean Mayer of Harvard has also indicated that lack of activity may be the primary cause of "creeping overweight" in college women and housewives rather than inattention to proper diet.

Of particular interest to many of us is the research which has indicated that movement in and of itself may be the best ataraxic or tranquilizer available to man. There is convincing evidence that movement dissipates the stress products and consequently generalizes reactions to psychic stressors rather than permitting such products to bring about a local reaction which might augment pathological conditions of systematic function and behavior. Such knowledge should be brought to the attention of the college woman so that she can utilize movement for herself and her family in assisting them to resolve the natural stressful situations with which life is filled.

However, it is to be remembered that the student's reactions are not always measured in terms of physiological response and research has provided us with some interesting psychological data which can enhance our teaching. Some of the most interesting work lately has been done with regard to the self-image, movement image, and body image concepts of the individual. The young child does not think of herself as a player because play is a natural response to the stimuli which she meets. However, for the older girl, there are many implications of the concept of self with regard to play. We know that young women are very conscious of their

bodies, of their movement patterns and of their selves when they are participating in a physical education class. There are some indications to suggest that those women who consider themselves as unacceptable with regard
to what their body form appears to be have a very difficult time in moving
with any fluidity. I think that many of us see this day by day when we note
how often the fat girls dislike physical education classes and how often
these same girls are poorly skilled individuals. We may intensify this situation when we insist that all girls wear gymnasium uniforms that are unattractive for the atypical. Thus to put all girls in short shorts or bermudas
may actually affect the performance of those who do not think that they
look well in such an outfit. Surely many of us have felt this way ourselves
with regard to donning a leotard. Putting on the skin tight dance costume
can actually change your movement. There also seems to be some indication that those girls who think that they move poorly seek to compensate
for that lack of ability by ignoring all movement activities and concentrate on those activities which are verbal and manual in nature.

We also know that performance is significantly affected by motivation
and by individual level of aspiration. It appears that students should have
some goal for which to aim if they are to expect to achieve realistic gains in
performance. The level of aspiration may be a standard set by the teacher
or it may be a student-oriented goal — but it should exist if the best performance is to be expected. This would indicate that a clear outline of
the expected goals should be set before the student early in the course so
that her level of aspiration may be affected by knowledge of goals. In other
words, don't come up with unexpected skill tests at the end of the course
if you expect good results. Instead let the class know what is expected of
them early in the course and indicate when and how often they are to be
tested.

In many ways level of aspiration is a motivational device and as such is
subject to the generalizations that we can make with regard to motivation.
Positive motivation seems to enhance performance to the same degree that
negative motivation enhances performance, but the physiological cost is
different. You can spur people to greater performance by encouraging or
deriding them, but the encouragement is preferable since it elicits less
physiological cost. We also know that motivation in terms of appraisal (such
as grades) will cause a change in performance patterns and this change
may augment or deter performance. It would appear that the direction of
the change depends upon the experience of the student. Thus, it is not
especially wise to pull out your little black book and grade students openly
— such a device may seriously impair the performance of the beginner or
stimulate her to give a performance not indicative of her actual skill level.
If you want a change in performance while testing, the "black book" method

is a good one to use, but if you want a pattern which is typical of the student's actual work, then leave your grade book in your office and use some less conspicuous method of grading.

With regard to the student's social desires, research indicates that those individuals who move with freedom and security tend to be adjusted individuals in other aspects of their being. In adolescent and post-adolescent girls there does not seem to be any indication that peer status is related to sport but peer status and ability to handle one's body *may* have a significant correlation.

Research tells us not only about the nature of the learner but also about the nature of the learning process. This research offers hints on how best to teach. For example, we have recently learned that students have the ability to retain skill patterns for a long time after the initial learning process. You can learn much faster a second time than you can the first. Such research certainly indicates that there is the distinct possibility that we all spend too much time on review of skills. The research might also indicate that the teaching of the correct skill patterns to the elementary and nursery school child might accelerate the learning time and movement pattern later on in life. Thus, letting little girls play tennis, swim, arch, and bowl can be of help if those same girls are taught the skills for a second time later on. Better still, such early training might eliminate the need for the second time teaching at all.

Several studies have also suggested that motor learning occurs fastest when there is little verbalization. All of us talk too much in class when what we should be doing is giving the students the opportunity of learning by doing rather than learning by listening.

There also appears to be a good deal of evidence to support the concept that there is really no such thing as general motor ability. Motor ability appears to be specific to the activity and while the motor ability tests should not be thrown out on the strength of this statement, there would be the very serious admonition to insist that grades should *never* be determined by general motor ability tests. These tests are good for diagnosis of gross differences between individuals but they are not adequate for more critical assessments.

As a matter of fact, research tells us so many things about how to teach the junior-senior high school girls that we hardly know what matters to emphasize. Did you know that it is better to teach for speed first and then accuracy rather than the reverse way? Thus teach your students to roll a bowling ball as hard as they can and then work on accuracy. Did you know that there is no way that exercise can be harmful during the menstrual period to the normal young woman? Let's stop excusing girls from physical education during their menstrual periods. There is no sound reason to continue this practice at all. Did you know an understanding of mechanical principles can augment skill learning for the older girl? So dig out your old kinesiology texts and review your work on forces, torques, and levers and then explain skills in terms of these principles of physics and note the improvement that your classes make. Did you know that older girls desire to specialize in activity rather than generalize? So maybe it would be a good idea to eliminate programs in high school and especially in college which insist that all girls have a team sport, an individual sport, aquatics, and dance. Instead maybe four semesters of tennis might be the best approach for the mature girl. Did you know that endurance can be increased through mental practice and that it is possible to learn a skill pattern through mental practice? So let's not be hesitant about attempting to have our students practice their skills even when they do not have the equipment available — a great deal can be accomplished by just thinking through the skill process.

Research is not the frightening and awesome word that we have made it to be. It is just the best and most rewarding way to solve problems with regard to tomorrow. You don't have to be a Doctor of Philosophy or a statistical expert to contribute toward the research endeavor. All you need is an inquiring, inquisitive attitude toward your work and your students and you can structure problems and seek their resolution in such a way that the results will have meaning to both you and your colleagues. Why not "team up" with the home economics teacher or the biology teacher or the chemistry teacher and attempt to look at a joint problem which will help each of you if it is solved? Team research can be fun and professionally stimulating as as well as educational.

And while we are talking about research participation, let me make a plea to those of you who are college and public school administrators to allow some time for your staff to participate in research projects. Insist upon reports, make the presentation of papers and seminars a requirement if you wish, but allow the time for these things to be done and remember that research cannot be accomplished in one's spare time. Administrators have to foster the tomorrow mind by allowing time for it to develop and I am convinced that time to participate in research is just as important as advising a cheerleaders club. If we can make time for the one, then surely we should be able to make time for the other.

For those who profess to be teachers of girls and women in movement, the clarion call is clear. We must utilize, augment, and contribute to the knowledge of our field and thus enhance the intellectual responsibility that is ours in developing the tomorrow mind.

The Future of Physical Education
ERNST JOKL, M.D.*

The distinguished German Physicist, Max Planck — one of the chief architects of the nuclear age, peer of Galileo, Newton, and Einstein — told me a few months before his death in 1947 at an age of 90 that if he had his life over again, he would not take up the study of the natural sciences. Instead, he would concern himself with ethics. "Scientific discoveries," so he explained, "even if they are of exceptional originality are ephemeral; bound to be superseded within a short time. By contrast, ethical truths, once they are formulated, have eternal validity. Like time and space, they remain with us forever."

Up to the present, physical education has been an empirical subject. It is only recently that its uniqueness is being understood, a uniqueness which it shares with only one other branch of science, namely neuro-physiology. Both, physical education and neuro-physiology are concerned with the mechanisms by which mind obtains leverage upon matter. This leverage is mediated through the remarkable capacity of the human brain to "materialize" mental events through movements. Nowhere else throughout the macrocosmos or microcosmos of the world as far as we know it do we encounter similar phenomena. In the physical movements of man, mind — "going more ghostly than a ghost," as Sir Charles Sherrington wrote in a memorable passage — establishes intimate as well as demonstrable contact with a kinetic system that forms part of ourselves.

This is how Sherrington's mastermind has encompassed the issue:

"In the energy-pattern which is the brain, two sets of events happen such as, to human knowledge, happen nowhere else the perceptible universe over. In that universe, sampling it on our planet's side, ourselves compact of energy, nowhere does our glimpse detect in all the immensity of energy any relation of energy except to energy save in this one instance, the brain."

On such a lofty conceptual level, physical education will eventually have to establish its place among the sciences. It is only through movements that human mind can communicate with other minds. For the appreciation of terrestial existence this fact is so important that muscle has been referred to as "the cradle of recognizable mind." With the arts, physical education shares an interest in and special knowledge of the processes by which movements can be shaped and changed and perfected. Thus our subject, even

---

*Ernst Jokl, "The Future of Physical Education," *Physical Education Today.* Vol. 10, Nos. 1 and 2, March-June, 1963.

though it is only on the threshold of understanding its scientific background, is destined to play a significant role in the universitas literarum.

The great 16th century French physician, Jean Fernel wrote:

"What geography is to history such is anatomy to medicine. Both define theatres of events."

The same relationship pertains to scientific research on exercise on the one side, and to motor acts on the other. Quantitative evidence such as is adduced in many books on "Tests and Measurements" that are currently being written, is concerned exclusively with "the theatre of the event." This statement applies in particular to statistics, important as it is as tool of research. But statistics is today looked upon by all too many investigators as a golden calf around which they dance with reckless abandon. By contrast, motor acts at their best are "events themselves," events played on a theatre whose careful construction is but a prerequisite for their execution. The theatre as such, even if it were perfectly designed, is devoid of "values." Structures and measurements do not possess a soul. But it is values alone that determine the status of any human event, its dignity, its beauty and its introspective content.

The time has arrived for physical education to take at long last cognizance of the fact that quantitative evidence as such means nothing. For the evaluation of exercise, of training, of physical education, of dancing, of sports, and of athletics, mechanical analyses of movements alone cannot provide relevant criteria. This point has been emphasized by recent researches with crippled individuals who exceled in athletics and in the arts. It has been one of the most fateful errors in the conceptual treatment of our subject that hitherto research in physical education has taken so little notice of this axiom. Those who have chosen the "scientific" approach have almost without exception abstained from an "existential" interpretation of their labors; while the philosophers of physical education have often treated the material side of their problem with inappropriate disdain. We must in the future utilize the rich tradition of the arts which though very much aware of the decisive part played by technique, have always acknowledged the primacy of content.

In a model study on "The Upright posture" the great psychiatrist Erwin Straus has pointed out that the term under reference has a double connotation, refering to the verticality which characterizes man's position in space as well as to his capacity to display attitudes of nobility. The two, kinetic pattern, and ethical content, are but different manifestations of one and the same situation. No "objective" research conducted along traditional lines can encompass both in their entirety.

In as far as movements can be defined in engineering terms, such definitions pertain to the "theatre of the events" only. The "events themselves" transcend the kinetic sector. The poetic genius of Robert Browning has provided a magnificent glimpse into the unlimited scope lying beyond the measurable when he spoke of:

"Fancies that broke through language and escaped."